Competition Law and Collusion in Public Procurement

This book examines infringements of competition law in public procurement settings, evaluating the latest European Procurement Directive 2014/24/EU to examine to what extent its provisions facilitate or deter collusion during specific award procedures.

Public contracts account for a significant proportion of EU expenditure. In sectors such as energy, transport, social protection and the provision of health or education services, public authorities are the main purchasers. It is important to ensure that public contracts are awarded in an open, fair and transparent manner that enables domestic and non-domestic firms to compete on an equal basis, with the aim of improving the quality and lowering the price of purchases made by public authorities. This book assesses the competition law enforcement mechanisms that competition regulators bring to the area of public procurement in the attempt to deter bid rigging. It analyzes key tools for the public and private enforcement of competition law in the domain of public contracts, such as the leniency programme, damages claims for bid rigging and the whistle blower programme. The book uses auction theory as benchmark to assess the risk of collusion in the context of procurement procedures and techniques. Offering a holistic analysis informed by research, it makes recommendations for better design, set up and management of public tenders without distorting competition. Highlighting the need to make use of competition law enforcement mechanisms in the battle against collusion in public procurement, it identifies ways in which the procurement process can be improved, to reduce and prevent bid rigging.

The book will be of interest to researchers in the field of competition law, public procurement and EU law.

Penelope Giosa is a Lecturer in Law at the University of Reading and an Associate Fellow of the Higher Education Academy. She is also a qualified lawyer (not currently practising law) in two countries, Greece and Cyprus and the Convenor of the SLS Comparative Law section. Her research interests extend to the fields of Competition Law, Public Contracts and Economic Crime. She also takes a particular interest in State Aid and the role of Food Law in sustainable development and addressing climate change.

Routledge Research in Competition Law

Merger Control in Europe
The Gap in the ECMR and National Merger Legislations
Ioannis Kokkoris

Harmonising Regulatory and Antitrust Regimes for International Air Transport
Jan Walulik

Collective Redress and EU Competition Law
Eda Sahin

Competition Policy and Network Industries
Structural Separation in the Telecommunications Sector
Pierluigi Congedo

Competition Laws, National Interests and International Relations
Ko Unoki

Private Law and Competition Regulation
A Comparative Study
Alberto Brown

Competition Law in China and the EU
Institutional Dynamics and Theories of Harm
Xingyu Yan

Antitrust Law and Mergers
David Hansen

Agriculture, Sustainability and Competition Law
Policy Paradigms and Their Legal Implications
Martin Milán Csirszki

Competition Law and Collusion in Public Procurement
Penelope Giosa

Competition Law and Collusion in Public Procurement

Penelope Giosa

Routledge
Taylor & Francis Group
LONDON AND NEW YORK

First published 2026
by Routledge
4 Park Square, Milton Park, Abingdon, Oxon OX14 4RN

and by Routledge
605 Third Avenue, New York, NY 10158

Routledge is an imprint of the Taylor & Francis Group, an informa business

British Library Cataloguing-in-Publication Data
A catalogue record for this book is available from the British Library

ISBN: 978-1-032-41839-1 (hbk)
ISBN: 978-1-032-41840-7 (pbk)
ISBN: 978-1-003-35999-9 (ebk)

DOI: 10.4324/9781003359999

Typeset in Times New Roman
by Deanta Global Publishing Services, Chennai, India

To my son Andreas

Contents

List of Figures

List of Tables

Foreword

Public procurement is a fundamental pillar of the EU's economic strategy, a key instrument in fostering innovation, promoting clean and strategic technologies, and ensuring the Union's global competitiveness. Efficient public procurement procedures are essential for creating fair and open markets, encouraging robust competition and achieving value-for-money for the taxpayer. However, despite the 2014 reforms, competition for public procurement contracts has been in decline over the past decade, as highlighted in the European Court of Auditors' 2023 report.

The Commission's announced revision of the Public Procurement Directives in its Political Guidelines 2024–2029 demonstrates that the need for changes to strengthen competition and thus harness the full potential of the EU's procurement market remains urgent.

Against this backdrop, this book makes a highly relevant contribution to the ongoing discussions regarding the reform of the legal framework by providing an in-depth analysis of the EU procurement rules through the lens of auction theory. It assesses the risk of collusion within procurement procedures and techniques, shedding light on how specific provisions may either facilitate or deter anti-competitive practices.

By offering a structured assessment of the procurement process and practical recommendations, this study provides a valuable foundation for legal and regulatory advancements in the field. Each chapter examines the stages of the procurement process meticulously, from planning and preparation to the application of various procedures and techniques, offering practical insights into mitigating collusion risks.

One of the book's most compelling aspects is its pragmatic approach to bid rigging prevention. The author highlights that collusion prevention is not solely connected with the promotion of competition in procurement markets but is also a crucial element in ensuring the integrity and fairness of public purchasing. The book underscores that competition enforcement and broader policy objectives – such as sustainability, innovation and strategic autonomy – are not necessarily at odds, but rather can be balanced effectively through well-designed procurement regulations. This nuanced perspective enriches the discussion and provides a constructive framework for understanding procurement regulation.

Having had the pleasure to engage with the research at an earlier stage, I am delighted to see it now developed into a monograph which will undoubtedly contribute to future debates on procurement policy and competition enforcement in the EU and beyond. It is a must-read for anyone interested in ensuring that public procurement remains a powerful tool for economic growth, innovation and fair market competition.

Aris Georgopoulos,
Nottingham, March 27, 2025

Acknowledgements

I would like to dedicate this book to my son, Andreas, who came into our lives and filled them with light and inspiration. I would also like to thank my husband Constantinos, my parents Eleni and Yannis, my sister Efthymia, my aunt Filio and my grandmother Niki for their unwavering support and love.

I also gratefully acknowledge the funding I received from the American Bar Association, Section of Antitrust Law. Thanks to their research grant, I had the opportunity to be a Visiting Researcher at the Georgetown University Law Centre in Washington DC and write Chapters 7 and 9 of this book. I am especially thankful to Professor Andrew Gavil, who initiated the relevant International Scholar-in-Residence programme.

Additionally, I would like to express my deepest gratitude to Professor Malin Arve from NHH Norwegian School of Economics and Dr Ricardo Gonçalves from Católica Porto Business School for reading Chapter 2 of my book and providing me with their feedback. Last but not least, I want to thank the academic mentors who supported me throughout the years. In particular, I am grateful to my PhD supervisors, Professor Andreas Stephan, Dr Sebastian Peyer and the formerly Emeritus Professor Peter Kunzlik for their patience and insightful comments during my PhD journey. I also want to extend my sincere thanks to Professor Belen Olmos-Giupponi, whose selfless support for younger colleagues is truly inspiring.

1 Introductory Chapter

1.1 Defining Bid Rigging

Public procurement accounts for a significant proportion of EU expenditure. Each year, over 250,000 public authorities in the EU spend approximately 14% of the gross domestic product ("GDP") of the EU on public procurement, totalling around €2 trillion.[1] In many sectors, such as energy, transport, social protection and the provision of health or education services, public authorities are the main purchasers.[2] Therefore, it is crucial to ensure that public contracts are awarded in an open, fair and transparent manner that allows both domestic and non-domestic firms to compete on an equal basis. This aims to improve the quality and lower the price of purchases made by public authorities. Effective public procurement leads to effective public spending, which can result in significant budget savings. Even a 1% efficiency gain can save €20 billion per year.[3] On the contrary, without effective public procurement, money is wasted on a large scale, causing delays in hospitals receiving drugs, teachers getting textbooks and cities constructing roads.[4]

Effective procurement may be distorted by collusive tendering, where tenders submitted by bidders are not based on individual economic calculations but on the knowledge of the submissions of other participants.[5] This can lead to distortions in large-scale projects, as seen in England when 103 construction companies were found to engage in bid rigging.[6] The investigated contracts included public sector construction projects for schools, hospitals and social housing. Bid rigging is a "particular form of co-ordination between firms which can adversely affect

1 European Commission "Internal Market, Industry, Entrepreneurship and SMEs" <https://single-market-economy.ec.europa.eu/single-market/public-procurement_en> accessed January 25, 2025.

2 Ibid.

3 Ibid.

4 Philipp Krause and Lina Tutunji-World Bank "Three Reasons Procurement Is Essential for Development" <https://blogs.worldbank.org/governance/three-reasons-procurement-essential-development> accessed January 25, 2025.

5 See the European Commission's decision in IV/26 918 – European Sugar Industry (1973) OJ L140/17.

6 Case C-1114/1/09 Kier Group PLC and others v Office of Fair Trading (2011) CAT 3. See also Aris Georgopoulos "Office of FairTrading Report: The Impact of Public Procurement on Competition" (2005), 14(2), *PPLR*.

DOI: 10.4324/9781003359999-1

the outcome of any sale or purchasing process in which bids are submitted".[7] It is an anticompetitive activity that is significantly widespread in public procurement markets. It is not surprising that bid rigging is viewed as a hard-core infringement which restricts competition by object, like price-fixing and market allocation agreements, according to article 101 of the Treaty on the Functioning of the European Union ("TFEU"). Similarly, the United States of America views bid rigging as a *per se* violation of the Sherman Act that cannot be legally justified in any way, even by arguing that the agreed-upon prices were reasonable or that the colluders simply tried to secure their fair share in the market.[8]

Bid rigging schemes can take various forms such as bid suppression, bid rotation, market allocation, cover pricing and sub-contracting. *Bid suppression* involves an agreement where competitors who would normally bid, or have bid in the past agree to abstain from bidding or withdraw a previously submitted bid to support the bid of a chosen winner.[9] By eliminating competition among the conspiring vendors, members of a bidding ring ensure that outside companies are prevented from bidding, manipulating the competitive process so that the predetermined bidder of their collusive agreement wins the bid.[10] Bid suppression is achieved not only by an agreement[11] but also by paying off an interloper or by using threats and violence towards outside companies in order to coerce them to refrain or withdraw from bidding.[12] The bid riggers can also "submit fabricated bid protests or urge suppliers and subcontractors not to do business with the outside companies" in order to protect their collusive scheme.[13]

7 European Commission – Directorate General for Competition "Glossary of Terms Used in EU Competition Policy – Antitrust and Control of Concentrations, 2002" <http://ec.europa.eu/translation/spanish/documents/glossary_competition_archived_en.pdf> accessed January 25, 2025.

8 The United States Department of Justice "Preventing and Detecting Bid Rigging, Price Fixing and Market Allocation in Post-Disaster Rebuilding Projects" <www.justice.gov/atr/preventing-and-detecting-bid-rigging-price-fixing-and-market-allocation-post-disaster-rebuilding> accessed January 25, 2025.

9 The United States Department of Justice "Price Fixing, Bid Rigging and Market Allocation Schemes: What They Are and What to Look For" <www.justice.gov/atr/price-fixing-bid-rigging-and-market-allocation-schemes> accessed January 25, 2025.

10 The United States Department of Justice "Price Fixing, Bid Rigging and Market Allocation Schemes" (fn 9).

11 An illustrative example is the US case United States of America v Daniel Rosenbledt where investors agreed not to bid against their fellow conspirators on properties that were in foreclosure auctions in specific counties of the United States, in order to enable the designated winning bidder to obtain these properties at a price favourable to all members of the ring. See more about the case at <www.justice.gov/atr/case-document/file/509036/download> accessed January 25, 2025.

12 International Anti-corruption Resource Center "Guide to Combating Corruption & Fraud in Development Projects-Collusive Bidding Schemes" <https://guide.iacrc.org/potential-scheme-collusive-bidding/> accessed January 25, 2025.

13 International Anti-corruption Resource Center "Guide to Combating Corruption & Fraud in Development Projects-Collusive Bidding Schemes" <https://guide.iacrc.org/potential-scheme-collusive-bidding/> accessed January 25, 2025.

A *bid rotation scheme* occurs when competitors agree to submit the lowest bid on a rotating basis. The terms of the rotation may vary, with competitors taking turns based on the contract size, allocating equal amounts to each bid rigger or volumes corresponding to the size of each rigging firm.[14] In addition to allocating the project, bid rotation schemes often involve side payments to divide spoils and establishment of geographic territories as parts of the bid rigging arrangements.[15] They can also be used in combination with other forms of bid rigging, such as bid suppression or cover bidding.[16] Bid rotation predetermines the winning bidder and reduces competition by excluding successful lower bids from the procurement process.[17] As a consequence, bid rotation deprives the public buyer of the benefits of competitive bidding and leads to higher costs for the procured products, services or works.

Market allocation is another form of bid rigging that involves an agreement to divide the market or product lines among bidders, prohibiting competition in certain geographic areas[18] or for certain customers.[19] This ensures that the winning bid is determined based on this allocation.[20] While the illusion of a competitive process may still exist, the firm allocated to a particular geographic region will always be the lowest bidder. By sharing markets, competitors protect themselves from competition pressures and can exert market power within their exclusive territory.[21] In the EU market, allocation schemes hinder the goal of achieving national market integration and establishing a single market.[22] It is also remarkable that price fixing allows for residual competition on aspects such as quality of service, while market

14 The United States Department of Justice (fn 9).

15 Patrick Bajari and Lixin Ye "Deciding between Competition and Collusion", 85(4), *The Review of Economics and Statistics*, 973.

16 Kei Kawai, Jun Nakabayashi, Juan Ortner and Sylvain Chassang "Using Bid Rotation and Incumbency to Detect Collusion: A Regression Discontinuity Approach" (2023), 90(1), *The Review of Economic Studies*, 376–403.

17 The United States Department of Justice (fn 9).

18 IV/30.907-Peroxygen Products, OJ L 35/1 1985; Case COMP/E-2/27.978 Methylglucamine [2004] OJ L38/18; Addyston Pipe and Steel Co. v United States [175 U.S. 211(1899)] where the defendants colluded by allocating territories and rigging bids.

19 Case No IV/35.691/E-4 Pre-Insulated Pipe Cartel OJ [1999] L24/1, [1999], 4, CMLR 402, para. 147.

20 International Anti-Corruption Resource Center "Guide to Combating Corruption and Fraud in Development Projects" <http://guide.iacrc.org/potential-scheme-collusive-bidding/> accessed January 25, 2025.

21 Ariel Ezrachi *EU Competition Law: An Analytical Guide to the Leading Cases* (Hart Publishing, 2018, 6th edition), 150.

22 Cases 96/82 to 102/82, 104/82, 105/82, 108/82 and 110/82 IAZ International Belgium and Others v Commission [1983] ECR 3369, paras 23 to 27; Case C-306/96 Javico [1998] ECR I1983, paras 13 and 14; Case C-551/03 P General Motors v Commission [2006] ECR I3173, paras 67–69; Cases C-468/06 to C-478/06 Sot Lélos kai Sia EE and Others v GlaxoSmithKline AEVE [2008] ECR I-7139, para. 65.

sharing eliminates competition, leading to authorities paying more for poorer quality services or goods.[23]

Cover pricing occurs when a firm wants to appear to bid for specific products, services or works but either does not want to win the tender or lacks the resources to prepare a competitive bid.[24] For this reason, the firm submits a bid at a deliberately high price or with terms it knows will be rejected by the relevant contracting authorities. This creates the false impression of genuine competition in the procurement process.[25] While submitting a higher bid is not illegal, communicating cover prices with competitors to manipulate tender outcomes is an unlawful practice and an infringement of competition law "by object".[26] Where a firm, which does not wish to win the tender, chooses to submit a cover bid instead of declining to bid, it prevents a genuine bidder from replacing the colluding firm and submitting a competitive bid.[27] Moreover, cover pricing is deceptive and fraudulent, misleading public buyers about the level of competition and potentially having anticompetitive effects on the tendering process and future exercises.[28]

Subcontracting arrangements are often a part of bid rigging schemes when they are used as a payback ("*quid pro quo*") given from the successful low bidder to one or more of the losers. This payback can be for not bidding at all, submitting a deliberately losing bid in favour of the winning bidder or withdrawing their bids.[29] Also in some cases, the subcontractor's customer may actually be its competitor, rather than the true end-customer.[30] In these situations, the subcontracting arrangement can be seen as the implementation of a customer allocation cartel under which only the incumbent supplier has direct contractual relations with the customer, as a payoff for their participation in the collusive scheme.[31] The result of these subcontracting arrangements is that rigging firms are able to share in the spoils of the artificially high profit margin created by the absence of an accurately low-priced bid.

23 Ezrachi (fn 21), 150.

24 Nick McHugh and Claire Forster "Cover Pricing and Bid Rigging: Illegal and on the ACCC's Radar" <www.lexology.com/library/detail.aspx?g=49947859-e19b-4a44-b651-c7dc13502743> accessed January 25, 2025.

25 Case COMP/39.125 Car Glass OJ [2009] C173/08; Case COMP/38.543 *I*nternational Removal Services OJ [2009] C188/07.

26 Infringement of competition law "by object" means that it is a form of collusion which is regarded by its very nature as being injurious to the proper functioning of normal competition. See case C-209/07 Competition Authority v Beef Industry Development Society Ltd [2009], 4, CMLR 6, [2008]ECR I-8637, para. 17. Case 1114/1/09 Kier Group PLC and others v Office of Fair Trading [2011] CAT 3.

27 Case 1061/1//1/06 Makers UK Ltd v Office of FairTrading Competition Appeal Tribunal [2007] CAT 11, para. 15.

28 Case 1114/1/09 Kier Group PLC and others v Office of Fair Trading [2011] CAT 3, para. 99.

29 The United States Department of Justice (fn 9), para. 147.

30 Christopher Thomas "Two Bids Or Not to Bid? An Exploration of the Legality of Joint Bidding and Subcontracting under EU Competition Law", 6(9), *Journal of European Competition Law and Practice*, 636.

31 ibid.

1.2 Why Does Bid Rigging Matter? Significance of the Topic

The magnitude of the problem in Europe is demonstrated by the frequency and scope of bid-rigging cases. For example, in 2009 the Office of Fair Trading ("OFT") in the United Kingdom imposed fines totalling £129.2 million on 103 construction firms in England for engaging in anticompetitive bid rigging activities on 199 tenders from 2000 to 2006.[32] The value of the building projects affected across England exceeded £200 million including schools, universities, hospitals and various private projects ranging from the construction of apartment blocks to housing refurbishments.[33] In France, 21 construction companies were fined for colluding in the procurement process for the building of a highway.[34] In Sweden, some of the largest construction companies in the country, such as NCC, Skanska and PEAB were found guilty of forming a cartel that enriched itself at the expense of customers, taxpayers and consumers.[35] Similarly, between February and May 2004 almost 150 Dutch construction companies reported themselves at the Netherlands Competition Authority for bid rigging activities, while in October 2004 almost 500 construction companies received a report by the Netherlands Competition Authority in which they were accused of violating the Competition Act.[36] The media suggested that these malpractices cost the taxpayer about €0.5 billion each year.[37] Apart from the construction industry, bidding rings were detected in various other markets, such as the market for installation and maintenance of elevators and escalators[38] as well as the market for heating pipes.[39] These are just illustrative examples of some of the cases, but they give an indication of the scale of bid-rigging practices.[40]

32 OFT "Bid Rigging in the Construction Industry in England" <http://webarchive.nationalarchives.gov.uk/20140402142426/http:/www.oft.gov.uk/OFTwork/competition-act-and-cartels/ca98/decisions/bid_rigging_construction> accessed January 25, 2025. See also Georgopoulos (fn 6).

33 Ibid.

34 Gian Luigi Albano, Paolo Buccirossi, Giancarlo Spagnolo and Matteo Zanza "Preventing Collusion in Procurement" in Nicola Dimitri, Gustavo Piga and Giancarlo Spagnolo (eds), *Handbook of Procurement* (Cambridge University Press 2006), 348.

35 Anders Gerde and Anne Vadasz-Nilsson "The Swedish Asphalt Cartel and Methods to Detect Cartel Activity The Asphalt Case" <www.piarc.org/ressources/documents/553,2.4-Gerde-Vadasz-Nilsson-1005C13.pdf> accessed January 25, 2025.

36 Authority for Consumers and Markets "NMa Fines 22 Construction Companies for Cartel Agreements" <www.acm.nl/en/publications/publication/6024/NMa-Fines-22-Construction-Companies-for-Cartel-Agreements> accessed January 25, 2025.

37 André Dorée "Collusion in the Dutch Construction Industry: An Industrial Organisation Perspective" (2004), 32(2), *Building Research and Information*, 146–156.

38 Elevators and Escalators OJ C75/19 (2008).

39 Pre-Insulated Pipe Cartel OJ L24/1 (1999).

40 Indicatively see Belgian Competition Authority "The Belgian Competition Authority Fines Several Companies for Bid-Rigging (Siemens)", May 3, 2017, e-Competitions Bulletin May 2017, Art. No 84204; Croatian Competition Authority "The Croatian High Administrative Court Fines Several Personal Protection Firms for Cartel (Sokol Marić)", May 30, 2016, e-Competitions Bulletin, May 2016, Art. No 79884; Cypriot Competition Authority "The Cypriot Competition Authority Fines Several Companies for Bid-Rigging in the Supply and Transportation of Ready-Mix Con-

It is difficult to change problematic practices such as these, as they are deeply rooted and systematic. This is particularly true in public procurement markets where the stability of bidding rings makes it hard to prove their existence and the relevant undertakings cooperate regularly with each other either by bidding or by subcontracting. This close relationship established among competitors in procurement markets significantly reduces any incentive to cheat and deviate from their anticompetitive tactics that generate many profits otherwise unachievable. Moreover, even the European leniency programme,[41] which is supposed to be the most important tool for detecting cartels, has done little to deter future infringements from occurring, as many of the cartels which were revealed through leniency applications had already ceased to operate at the time or were very likely to be caught.[42] Therefore, greater emphasis should be given on the design of the procurement system to minimize any opportunities for bid rigging. The necessity to prevent bid rigging in Europe is also understood if one considers the fact that public procurement is a highly significant area of law and policy for the European Union

crete Market (Mattheos Ioannou Ready Mix Concrete/C. Kythreotis Skyrodema/ Skyramix…), May 15, 2019, e-Competitions Bulletin May 2019, Art. No 90627; Danish Competition Authority "The City Court of Hillerød Fines Two Members of the Management of a Now Dissolved Demolition Company for Bid Rigging", January 11, 2019, e-Competitions Bulletin January 2019, Art. No 89002; Katri Havu "The Finnish Market Court Imposes Fines for Price Fixing and Bid Rigging (Asunto-Vayla, CSC Consulting, Hansatalot, Kiinteisto, Rovakartano, Sata-Vayla", February 28, 2013, Bulletin e-Competitions February 2013, Art. No 51787; French Competition Authority "The French Competition Authority Fines Three Companies for Bid-Rigging in the Public Lighting Sector (Lapize de Sallée)", September 24, 2018, e-Competitions Bulletin September 2018, Art. No 87999; German Competition Authority "The German Competition Authority Imposes Fines on Five Providers of Underground Mining Services for Having Implemented a Price-Fixing Agreement and Bid-Rigging (BeMo Tunnelling, Deilmann-Haniel)", August 28, 2014, e-Competitions Bullettin, August 2014, Art. No 68925; Hellenic Competition Authority "The Hellenic Competition Authority Fines Several Construction Companies for Bid-Rigging in the Public Works of Infrastructure (Alpine Bau)", March 5, 2019, e-Competitions Bulletin, March 2019, Art. No 89894; Hungarian Competition Authority "The Hungarian Competition Authority Fines Providers of Medical Products and Medical Devices for Bid Rigging (Chirmax)", August 5, 2016, e-Competitions Bulletin, August 2016, Art. No 80988; Latvian Competition Authority "The Latvian Competition Authority Fines Nine Distributors of Professional Stage Equipment for Bid-Rigging (SGS Sistemas)", May 30, 2017, e-Competitions Bulletin, May 2017, Art. No 84326; Lithuanian Competition Authority "The Vilnius Regional Administrative Court Upholds the Decision of the Lithuanian Competition Authority Fining Two Undertakings for Bid Rigging in the Market of Radioactive Scrap Metal (Norvesta/Sypra)", September 10, 2018, e-Competitions Bulletin, September 2018, Art. No 88003.

41 The European Commission operates a leniency policy whereby companies that provide information about a cartel in which they participate might receive full or partial immunity from fines. See European Commission "Leniency" <http://ec.europa.eu/competition/cartels/leniency/leniency.html> accessed January 25, 2025.

42 Andreas Stephan and Ali Nikpay "Leniency Decision-Making from a Corporate Perspective: Complex Realities" in C. Beaton-Wells and C. Tran (eds), *Anti-Cartel Enforcement in a Contemporary Age: The Leniency Religion* (Hart Publishing, 2015); Andreas Stephan "An Empirical Assessment of the European Leniency Notice" (2009), 593, *Journal of Competition Law and Economics*, 537–561.

("EU"), accounting for approximately 14% of the EU Member States' combined gross domestic product.[43]

The delinquency of bid rigging has also been underlined by the Court of Justice of the European Union ("CJEU"), which highlights its huge impact on the tax paying citizens who are deprived of the advantages of competition, as most of the rigged projects are public tenders financed by the State.[44] In this way, prices are inflated without reflecting the accurate costs and so society's resources are not allocated efficiently.[45] As a result, there is not only a loss to the economy of each Member State, but also to consumers and taxpayers, who are harmed by having to pay more for products and services of potentially low quality and low-level innovation, without any choice of other by-products of true competition.[46] Indicatively, it has been estimated that such collusive practices in the domain of public procurements "can raise the price of a product or service by more than 10 percent, sometimes much more".[47] The importance of tackling this problem has been heightened in the last decade by the era of austerity that followed the 2007 financial crisis.

For these reasons, it is completely understandable why in some jurisdictions, such as the UK, Germany and the United States, certain aspects of bid rigging might be considered akin to fraud and theft of taxpayers' money, which is a criminal offence.[48] The deceptive and criminal nature of bid rigging is primarily based on the dishonest agreement made among bid riggers not to compete but to deliberately subvert the competitive process by lying and "continuing to hold themselves out as competitors" against the standards of reasonable people.[49] What is

43 Commission Staff Working Paper Evaluation Report, Impact and Effectiveness of EU Public Procurement Legislation, SEC (2011), 853 final.

44 Case T-151/07 Kone Oyj and Others v European Commission [2011] ECR II-5313; [2011], 5, CMLR 29.

45 US Department of Justice "Price Fixing, Bid Rigging, and Market Allocation Schemes: What They Are and What to Look for: An Antitrust Primer" <www.justice.gov/d9/pages/attachments/2016/01/05/211578.pdf> accessed January 25, 2025.

46 Ibid.

47 Ibid.

48 Ibid; The United States Department of Justice (fn 9); In the UK, the White Paper that precedes the Enterprise Act, that is, the "World Class Competition Regime/ Department of Trade and Industry" states in para. 7.35 that hard-core cartels, such as bid rigging are serious conspiracies that defraud business customers and consumers and have wide economic impacts. In addition to this, the House of Lords in Regina v Goldshield Group plc and others [2008] UKHL 17; [2009] 1 W.L.R. 458; [2009] 2 All E.R. 738; [2009] 1 Cr. App. R. 33; [2009] Crim. L.R. 433 put bid riggers on notice that they are potentially in the front line for prosecution for fraud, if they keep on providing "non-collusion" certificates. The judgment was primarily about price fixing and the misrepresentation as an aggravating element that elevates price fixing into an indictable conspiracy to defraud. This case is parallel to the case Norris v Government of the United States of America, [2008] UKHL 16; [2008] 1 A.C. 920; [2008] 2 W.L.R. 673; [2008] 2 All E.R. 1103; [2008] UKCLR, 69, where it was held that mere price fixing without any aggravating features, such as fraud and misrepresentation had never been a criminal offence at common law and only became a criminal offence with the commencement of the Enterprise Act 2002, Section 188.

49 The United States Department of Justice "Preventing and Detecting Bid Rigging, Price Fixing and Market Allocation in Post-Disaster Rebuilding Projects" <www.justice.gov/atr/preventing-and

more, bid rigging would amount to the offence of fraud if the warranty given by the bid riggers before the initiation of the procurement process, that they had not entered into any kind of agreement distorting competition, turned out to be a false representation.

1.3 The Existing Literature

Most of the literature on public procurement has until recently been based on an internal market approach. This approach sees the focus of regulation as being on discrimination and transparency to ensure equal opportunities to bid.[50] Nevertheless, competition law practitioners and academics have recently taken an interest in the field. Some of them tend to approach the subject from a different perspective, arguing that the European public procurement regime seeks value for taxpayers' money. For this reason it has a duty to replicate the competitive process of the private market by awarding contracts to the best tenderer when public goods, works or services are procured.[51] Hence, there has been a significant amount of discussion

---

-detecting-bid-rigging-price-fixing-and-market-allocation-post-disaster-rebuilding> accessed January 25, 2025; The United States Department of Justice (fn 9); Richard Whish and David Bailey *Competition Law* (Oxford University Press 2012), 426; R v Ghosh [1982]QB 1053, [1982] 2 All ER 689; R v George & Ors [2010] EWCA Crim 1148, [2010] UKCLR, 1383, para. 6.

50 Friedl Weiss *Public Procurement in European Community Law* (Athlone Press, London 1993); Jose Fernandez Martin *The EC Procurement Rules: A Critical Analysis* (Clarendon Press, 1996); Sue Arrowsmith *The Law of Public and Utilities Procurement Volume 1: Regulation in the EU and UK* (Sweet & Maxwell 2014); Christopher Bovis *EU Public Procurement Law* (Elgar European Law, 2007); Peter Trepte *Public Procurement in the EU-A Practitioner's Guide* (Oxford University Press, 2007); Peter Kunzlik "Neoliberalism and the European Public Procurement Regime" in *Cambridge Yearbook of European Legal Studies* (Cambridge University Press, 2013), 321; Sue Arrowsmith "The TFEU Rules" in Sue Arrowsmith (ed) *EU Public Procurement Law: An Introduction* (2011) <www.nottingham.ac.uk/pprg/documentsarchive/asialinkmaterials/eupublicprocurementlawintroduction.pdf> accessed January 25, 2025; Sue Arrowsmith "The Purpose of the EU Procurement Directives: Ends, Means and the Implications for National Regulatory Space for Commercial and Horizontal Procurement Policies" in M. W. Gehring et al. (eds) *Cambridge Yearbook of European Legal Studies, Volume 14* (Bloomsbury Publishing 2012); Sue Arrowsmith "The Application of the E.C. Treaty Rules to Public and Utilities Procurement" (1995), 6, *PPLR*, 261; Sue Arrowsmith and Peter Kunzlik, "EC Regulation of Public Procurement" in Sue Arrowsmith and Peter Kunzlik (eds) *Social and Environmental Policies in EC Procurement Law* (Cambridge University Publishing 2009); Berend Jan Drijber and Hélène Stergiou "Public Procurement Law and Internal Market Law" (2009), 46(3), *Common Market Law Review*.

51 Albert Sanchez Graells "Truly Competitive Public Procurement as a Europe 2020 Lever: What Role for the Principle of Competition in Moderating Horizontal Policies?" (2016), 22(2), *European Public Law*, 377–394; A. Sanchez Graells "More Competition-Oriented Public Procurement to Foster Social Welfare" in KV Thai (ed) *Towards New Horizons in Public Procurement* (Florida, PRAcademics Press, 2010), 81, 84–89, 105; A. Sanchez Graells *Public Procurement and the EU Competition Rules* (Oxford: Bloomsbury, 2015, 2nd edn).

on the interface between procurement and competition law in both academic[52] and policymaking circles.[53]

The existing literature highlights the need for a pro-competitive design of public procurement procedures and emphasizes the importance of preventing bid rigging among suppliers to promote effective competition in public procurement markets.[54] Without addressing bid rigging, efforts to ensure free and fair competition in the public procurement market are undermined, regardless of the quality of the public procurement regime. Therefore, competition law must prevent bid rigging, while the public procurement regime must ensure the effectiveness of competition law

52 Sue Arrowsmith "The Purpose of the EU Procurement Directives (fn 50); Sue Arrowsmith and Steen Treumer (eds) *Competitive Dialogue in EU Procurement* (Cambridge University Press, 2012); Sue Arrowsmith "The Revised Agreement on Government Procurement: Changes to the Procedural Rules and Other Transparency Provisions" in S. Arrowsmith and R.D. Anderson (eds) *The WTO Regime on Government Procurement: Challenge and Reform* (Cambridge University Press, 2011); Paul Klemperer "Competition Policy in Auctions and Bidding Markets" in P. Buccirossi (ed) *Handbook of Antitrust Economics* (Cambridge MA: MIT Press, 2008), 583; Mario Comba "Variations in the Scope of the New EU Public Procurement Directives of 2014: Efficiency in Public Spending and a Major Role of the Approximation of Laws" in François Lichère, Roberto Caranta and Steen Treumer (eds) *Modernising Public Procurement Law: The New Directive* (Elgar, 2014); Carmen Estevan de Quesada "Competition and Transparency in Public Procurement Markets"(2014), 5, *Public Procurement Law Review*, 229–244; Robert D Anderson, William E Kovacic and Anna Caroline Muller "Ensuring integrity and competition in public procurement markets: a dual challenge for good governance" in Sue Arrowsmith and Robert D. Anderson (eds) *The WTO Regime on Government Procurement: Challenge and Reform* (CUP, 2011), 681–718; Grith Skovgaard Olykke "How Does the Court of Justice of the European Union Pursue Competition Concerns in a Public Procurement Context" (2011), 6, *Public Procurement Law Review*, 179–192; Grith Skovgaard Olykke "Abnormally Low Tenders, with an Emphasis on Public Tenderers" (Scandinavia: DØJF, 2010); Devika Malhotra "Study on Government Procurement. Study for Evidence Based Competition Advocacy" (CUTS Institute for Regulation and Competition, January 2012) <http://www.circ.in/pdf/Government_Procurement.pdf> accessed January 25, 2025; Albert Sanchez Graells *Public Procurement and the EU Competition Rules* (fn 51); Omer Dekel "The Legal Theory of Competitive Bidding for Government Contracts" (2008), 37(2), *Public Contract Law Journal*, 237–268; Pal Szilagyi "Bidding Markets and Competition Law in the European Union and the United Kingdom: Part 1 and 2" (2008), 29(1), *European Competition Law Review*, 16, 89; Catriona Munro "Competition Law and Public Procurement: Two Sides of the Same Coin?" (2006), 15(6), *Public Procurement Law Review* 352–361; Maria Ath. Alexopoulou and Albert Sanchez Graells "Competition and Public Procurement – An Overview" (2009), *CCLP(S)*, 3; Arkadiusz Borowiec "The Impact of Public Procurement System on the Development of Competition in the Economy in the Light of Empirical Research" (2017), 8(1), *Oeconomia Copernicana*, 37–50.

53 Office of Fair Trading "Assessing the Impact of Public Sector Procurement on Competition" (September 2004) <https://webarchive.nationalarchives.gov.uk/20140402182823/http://www.oft.gov.uk/shared_oft/reports/comp_policy/oft742a.pdf> accessed January 25, 2025; International Competition Network "Anti-Cartel Enforcement Manual – Relationships between Competition Agencies and Public Procurement Bodies" (April 2015) <www.internationalcompetitionnetwork.org/portfolio/public-procurement-relationships/> accessed January 25, 2025.

54 Robert D. Anderson, William E. Kovacic and Anna Caroline Müller "Promoting Competition and Deterring Corruption in Public Procurement Markets: Synergies with Trade Liberalisation" (2017), 2, *Public Procurement Law Review*, 77.

sanctions.[55] In view of the interdependence and complementarity of these two areas of law, the rules on public procurement should be coherent with those on competition to achieve this goal. The European Commission, in its Green Paper on the modernization of EU public procurement policy, stressed the importance of strong competition in public contracts to avoid competition distortion and ensure best value for money.[56] The Europe 2020 strategy for smart, sustainable and inclusive growth also emphasized the great role of public procurement policy in maximizing the efficient use of public funds and promoting open procurement markets across Europe.[57] Additionally, in 2020 the European Commission was committed to provide guidance on fighting collusion in public procurement.[58]

In an attempt to address collusion before public contracts are awarded, various policy papers have explored the relationship between public procurement with market competition, focusing on factors that increase the likelihood of collusion in public procurement. In 2021, the European Commission issued the Notice on tools to fight collusion in public procurement to effectively assist Member States and their Contracting Authorities in countering the problem of collusion in public procurement.[59] In this Notice, the Commission stressed the importance of strong competition in public contracts to avoid bid rigging.[60] They emphasized that bid rigging is a "recurring phenomenon" that leads to excess payments, ultimately harming efficient and accountable public spending.[61] Also, most EU Member States' National Competition Authorities ("CAs") have issued specific guidance on combatting collusion. Likewise, many CAs around the world have identified common trends in spotting cartels in public procurement.[62] The most illustrative example is

55 Ciara Kennedy-Loest and Christopher Thomas "EU Public Procurement and Competition Law: The Yin and Yang of the Legal World?" (2011), 7, *Competition Law International*, 77.

56 European Commission "Green Paper on the Modernisation of EU Public Procurement Policy towards a More Efficient European Procurement Market Synthesis of Replies" <https://op.europa.eu/en/publication-detail/-/publication/04a30c4a-e533-41ec-a039-231f1aa39645/language-en> accessed January 25, 2025; Europa "Public Contracts: EU Rules & Procedures" <http://europa.eu/youreurope/business/public-tenders/rules-procedures/index_en.htm> accessed January 25, 2025.

57 European Commission "Europe 2020-A Strategy for Smart, Sustainable and Inclusive Growth" <http://eur-lex.europa.eu/legal-content/EN/TXT/PDF/?uri=CELEX:52010DC2020&from=EN> accessed January 25, 2025.

58 European Commission "Long Term Action Plan for Better Implementation and Enforcement of Single Market Rules" COM (2020), 94 final, Brussels 10.3.2020 <https://eur-lex.europa.eu/legal-content/EN/TXT/?uri=COM%3A2020%3A94%3AFIN> accessed January 22, 2025.

59 European Commission "Notice on tools to fight collusion in public procurement and on guidance on how to apply the related exclusion ground" C (2021), 1631 final, Brussels 15.3.2021.

60 Ibid.

61 Ibid.

62 Australian Competition and Consumer Commission "Cartels Deterrence and Detection: A Guide for Government Procurement Officers" <www.jcu.edu.au/__data/assets/pdf_file/0007/101779/jcu_148836.pdf> accessed January 25, 2025; Commission on Protection of Competition Bulgaria "Guidelines for Fighting Bid-Rigging in Public Procurement" <https://unctad.org/meetings/en/Contribution/ccpb_SCF_Bid-rigging%20Guidelines_en.pdf> accessed January 25, 2025; Canadian Competition Bureau "Bid-Rigging: Detecting, Preventing and Reporting" <www.competitionbureau.gc.ca/eic/site/cb-bc.nsf/eng/02646.html> accessed January 25, 2025; The Competition

the Competition and Markets Authority ("CMA") in the United Kingdom, which produced a free tool to help procurers screen their tender data for bid rigging activity, based on indicators associated with bid rigging.[63]

Guidance on the collaboration between procurement and competition authorities has also been developed within the International Competition Network, which the European Commission is a part of.[64] Additionally, in November 2017, the European Anti-fraud Office (OLAF) published a handbook titled "Fraud in Public Procurement: A Collection of Red Flags and Best Practices", which was developed with input from Member States' experts in the Advisory Committee for the Coordination of Fraud Prevention (COCOLAF).[65] The handbook includes a section on collusion, offering a comprehensive list of red flags and tips for detecting collusion in the pre-tendering and tendering phases.

Other organizations, such as the Organisation for Economic Cooperation and Development ("OECD") and the World Bank, have also conducted significant research on the issue of collusion in public procurement. The OECD has organized a number of policy roundtables and has issued several guidelines and recommendations about competition in bidding markets and how any anticompetitive activities, such as bid rigging, could be reduced in public procurement.[66] In this context, the

---

Authority Ireland "The Detection and Prevention of Collusive Tendering" <www.ccpc.ie/business/wp-content/uploads/sites/3/2017/02/Booklet-The-Detection-and-Prevention-of-Collusive-Tendering.pdf> accessed January 25, 2025; Competition Commission South Africa "How to Prevent, Detect and Report Collusive Tendering" <www.compcom.co.za/wp-content/uploads/2014/09/Bid-rigging2-2.pdf> accessed January 25, 2025; Swedish Competition Authority "Twelve Ways to Detect Did-Rigging Cartels" <www.scribd.com/document/108855148/Checklist> accessed July 2, 2019; see also Francesco Anglani "Antitrust and Public Tenders: Is This a New Challenge?" (2017), 4(2), *Italian Antitrust Review*, 112–127.

63 Competition & Markets Authority "Public Sector Procurers: Bid-Rigging Advice" <www.gov.uk/government/collections/bid-rigging-advice-and-tools-for-public-sector-procurers> accessed January 25, 2025.

64 International Competition Network "Anti-Cartel Enforcement Manual – Chapter on Relationships Between Competition Agencies and Public Procurement Bodies" <www.internationalcompetitionnetwork.org/wp-content/uploads/2018/05/CWG_ACEMPublicProcurement.pdf> accessed January 22, 2025.

65 OLAF "Fraud in Public Procurement – A collection of Red Flags and Best Practices" <https://sfc.ec.europa.eu/system/files/documents/sfc-files/fraud-public-procurement-final-20122017-ares20176254403.pdf> accessed January 22, 2025.

66 OECD "Recommendation of the Council on Fighting Bid Rigging in Public Procurement", OECD/LEGAL/0396 <https://legalinstruments.oecd.org/en/instruments/OECD-LEGAL-0396> accessed January 22, 2025; OECD "Revised Recommendation of the Council on Fighting Bid Rigging in Public Procurement" <https://one.oecd.org/document/C/MIN(2023)15/FINAL/en/pdf> accessed January 22, 2025; OECD Competition Committee "Competition and Procurement – Key Findings 2011" <www.oecd.org/en/publications/competition-and-procurement-key-findings_c6e6d5ae-en.html> accessed January 25, 2025; OECD Competition Committee "Public Procurement: The Role of Competition Authorities in Promoting Competition" <www.oecd.org/en/publications/public-procurement-the-role-of-competition-authorities-in-promoting-competition_8ed0c7ba-en.html> accessed January 25, 2025; OECD "Policy Roundtables: Collusion and Corruption in Public Procurement 2010" <www.oecd.org/en/publications/collusion-and-corruption-in-public-procurement_ef957f70-en.html> accessed January 25, 2025; OECD "Guidelines for Fighting Bid Rigging in

OECD has also suggested a great variety of practices that could install a culture of integrity throughout the public procurement cycle, so that integrity violations such as collusion and corruption may be limited.[67] In 2013, the World Bank issued a handbook for government employees involved in public procurement, which includes a dedicated section on collusion.[68]

In addition to the research on bidding rings conducted by policy makers, legal and economic academics have provided comprehensive insights into the conditions that favour collusive behaviour among participants in competitive tendering. They have recommended various strategies to minimize the risk of collusion, based on the "red flags" of collusion that they have identified.[69] Many of them have also studied auctions, which share common structures with procurements, to better understand bidder behaviour and the mechanisms that bidding rings use to stifle competition and increase profits.[70] Thus, auction theory has offered valuable

Public Procurement" (fn 62); OECD "Policy Roundtables: Competition in Bidding Markets 2006" <www.oecd.org/en/publications/competition-in-bidding-markets_af4c1b4b-en.html> accessed January 25, 2025.

67 OECD Recommendation of the Council on Enhancing Integrity in Public Procurement, OECD/LEGAL/0369 < https://legalinstruments.oecd.org/public/doc/131/131.en.pdf> accessed January 25, 2025; OECD "Principles for Integrity in Public Procurement" <http://oecd.org/gov/ethics/48994520.pdf> accessed January 25, 2025.

68 World Bank (2013) "Fraud and Corruption Awareness Handbook: A Handbook for Civil Servants Involved in Public Procurement" <https://openknowledge.worldbank.org/entities/publication/72e9570c-d49a-5c96-8aad-f4a918140bf0> accessed January 22, 2025.

69 Robert C. Marshall and Leslie M. Marx, *The Economics of Collusion: Cartels and Bidding Rings* (The MIT Press, 2012); Stefan Weishaar, *Cartels, Competition and Public Procurement: Law and Economic Approaches to Bid Rigging* (Edward Elgar, 2013); Nicola Dimitri, Gustavo Piga and Giancarlo Spagnolo, *Handbook of Procurement* (Cambridge University Press 2006); Caroline Nicholas and Gian Luigi Albano, *The Law and Economics of Framework Agreements* (Cambridge University Press 2016); Bence Tóth, Mihály Fazekas, Agnes Czibik and István János Tóth "Toolkit for Detecting Collusive Bidding in Public Procurement: With Examples from Hungary" (April 2015) <www.crcb.eu/wp-content/uploads/2015/04/Toth-et-al_CRCB_WP_v2_150413.pdf> accessed January 25, 2025; Robert D Anderson and William E Kovacic "Competition Policy and International Trade Liberalisation: Essential Complements to Ensure Good Performance in Public Procurement Markets" (2009), 2, *Public Procurement Law Review*; Alberto Heimler "Cartels in Public Procurement"(2012), 8(4), *Journal of Competition Law and Economics*; Antonio Lopez Mino and Patricia Valcarcel Fernandez "Contracting Authorities Inability to Fight Bid Rigging in Public Procurement: Reasons and Remedies" in Gabriella M. Racca and Christopher R. Yukins (eds), *Integrity and Efficiency in Sustainable Public Contracts. Balancing Corruption Concerns in Public Procurement Internationally* (Bruylant, Brussels, 2014); Gian Luigi Albano "Demand Aggregation and Collusion Prevention in Public Procurement" in Gabriella M. Racca and Christopher R. Yukins (eds), *Integrity and Efficiency in Sustainable Public Contracts. Balancing Corruption Concerns in Public Procurement Internationally* (Bruylant, Brussels, 2014); Albert Sanchez Graells "Prevention and Deterrence of Bid Rigging: A Look from the New EU Directive on Public Procurement" in Gabriella M. Racca and Christopher R. Yukins (eds), *Integrity and Efficiency in Sustainable Public Contracts. Balancing Corruption Concerns in Public Procurement Internationally* (Bruylant, Brussels, 2014); Robert D. Anderson, William E. Kovacic and Anna Caroline Müller "Promoting Competition and Deterring Corruption in Public Procurement Markets" (fn 54).

70 See indicatively Ralph Jr. Cassady *Auctions and Auctioneering* (University of California Press, 1967); Levitan J.R. Griesmer and Martin Shubik "Toward a Study of Bidding Processes, Part IV:

advice on preventing bid rigging conspiracies and addressing the "breakdown" of such anticompetitive schemes if they are formed. Policy makers can borrow and apply these insights in the realm of public procurement. However, the literature connecting auction theory and public procurement rules, does not address the latest European Directive 2014/24/EU on the public sector, nor does it thoroughly and systematically evaluate the risks of collusion in current procurement procedures and techniques.

For example, in his book "Cartels, Competition and Public Procurement: Law and Economic Approaches to Bid Rigging", Stefan Weishaar explores the relationship between public procurement law and competition law in bid rigging conspiracies from a law and economics perspective.[71] He assesses the effectiveness of the legal regime governing bid rigging in Europe and whether the earlier European Directive 2004/18/EC on the public sector aligned with auction theoretic insights. Weishaar does not delve into the current European Directive 2014/24/EU on the public sector and his analysis of the earlier European Directive 2004/18/EC is brief and confined to specific topics. It occupies only one chapter of his book and the issues reviewed encompass only winner determination and the distribution of auction proceeds, new entrants and the auctioneer's response.

Contrary to Weishaar, the book by Gian Luigi Albano and Caroline Nicholas, "The Law and Economics of Framework Agreements: Designing Flexible Solutions for Public Procurement", examines the current European Directive 2014/24/EU on the public sector from an economic perspective. However, it only focuses on framework agreements, which are a procurement technique, as will be explained in Chapter 6.[72] The book does not address the risks of bid rigging that may arise in current procurement procedures and other techniques apart from framework agreements.

Games with Unknown Costs" (1967), 14, *Naval Research Logistics Quarterly*, 415–433; Robert M. Stark and Michael H. Rothkopf "Competitive Bidding: A Comprehensive Bibliography" (1979), 27, *Operations Research*, 364–390; Richard Engelbrecht-Wiggans "Auctions and Bidding Models: A Survey" (1980)26 *Management Science*, 119–142; Paul R. Milgrom "The Economics of Competitive Bidding: A Selective Survey" in L. Hurwicz, D. Schmeidler and H. Sonnenschein (eds) *Social Goals and Social Organization* (Cambridge University Press, 1985); Robert Wilson "Game-Theoretic Analyses of Trading Processes" in T. Bewley (ed) *Advances in Economic Theory: Fifth World Congress* (Cambridge University Press, 1987); Leo K. Smith "Games with Discontinuous Payoffs" (1987), 54, *Review of Economic Studies*, 569–598; Preston R. McAfee and John McMillan "Auctions and Bidding" (1987), 25, *Journal of Economic Literature*, 699–738; Paul R. Milgrom "Auctions and Bidding: A Primer" (1989), 3, *Journal of Economic Perspectives*, 3–22; Robert Wilson "Strategic Analysis of Auctions" in R. Aumann and S. Hart (eds) *Handbook of Game Theory with Economic Applications* (Elsevier, 1992); Michael H. Rothkopf and Ronald M. Harstad "Modelling Competitive Bidding: A Critical Survey" (1994), 40(3), *Management Science*, 364–384; John Kagel "Auctions: A survey of experimental research" in: J.H. Kagel, A. Roth (eds) *The Handbook of Experimental Economics* (Princeton University Press, 1995), 501–586.

71 Stefan Weishaar (fn 69).

72 Caroline Nicholas and Gian Luigi Albano *The Law and Economics of Framework Agreements* (Cambridge University Press 2016).

Similarly, the most insightful studies of the current European Directive 2014/24/EU on public sector do not draw insights from auction theory for the assessment of the risk of collusion in the procurement process. Indicatively, the second edition of Albert Sanchez-Graells' book, *Public Procurement and the EU Competition Rules* analyzes the current Directive and its interpretative case law from a competition perspective, putting special emphasis on identifying instances of potential distortions of competition derived from the current public procurement rules and/or their interpretation.[73] His analysis is primarily legal and only where required does he rely on economic considerations, as a complement to the legal analysis. Moreover, in Chapter 6 of his book, Sanchez-Graells reviews different types of competition distortions arising from the current procurement rules and practices, without focusing on bid rigging. On the other hand, Marsela Maci, in her PhD thesis examines exclusively bid rigging cartels in Europe.[74] Yet, what interests her is only the competition enforcement against bid rigging, first by addressing the issue of the cooperation between CAs and public procurement authorities in the EU in tackling bid rigging and second by ending the fragmentation of competition enforcement among EU Member States. The prevention of collusion in the public procurement process is out of her study scope.

Katarzyna Kuźma and Wojciech Hartung's book titled "Combating Collusion in Public Procurement: Legal Limitations on Joint Bidding" examines how joint bidding structures comply with competition rules in Europe and explains how joint bids could be perceived as bid rigging schemes.[75] The book also demonstrates how the formation of joint bid agreements could lead to exclusion from public procurement proceedings under Article 57(4)(d) of Directive 2014/24/EU. Another insightful study of the European Directive 2014/24/EU on public sector is the Master dissertation of a student at Lund University in Sweden, which aims to determine how the Directive and the changes introduced therein are capable of affecting competition on the public market, both in general but also through the fighting of competition violation amongst the tenderers.[76] However, this Master dissertation is also based on traditional legal method and not on the economic theory. Finally, Robert D Anderson et al.'s book titled "Combatting Corruption and Collusion in Public Procurement: A Challenge for Governments Worldwide" explores the persistent issue of corruption and collusion in public procurement processes, despite ongoing national and international efforts to address them.[77] However, it does not

73 Albert Sanchez Graells *Public Procurement and the EU Competition Rules* (fn 51).

74 Marsela Maci "Bid Rigging in the EU Public Procurement Markets" (PhD Thesis, Queen Mary, University of London, 2010).

75 Katarzyna Kuźma and Wojciech Hartung *Combating Collusion in Public Procurement: Legal Limitations on Joint Bidding* (Edward Elgar, 2020).

76 See Amanda Claeson "Modernisation of Public Procurement – Making the Public Market More Competitive and Collusion Proof?" (2014) <https://lup.lub.lu.se/student-papers/search/publication/4459522> accessed January 25, 2025.

77 Robert D. Anderson, Alison Jones and William E Kovacic *Combatting Corruption and Collusion in Public Procurement: A Challenge for Governments Worldwide* (Oxford University Press, 2024).

focus on the EU. Instead, it makes proposals for reform in the United Kingdom, the United States, Brazil, Hungary, Poland, Ukraine and Canada. Likewise, Carlotta Carbone, Francesco Calderoni and Maria Jofre's paper "Bid-rigging in public procurement: cartel strategies and bidding patterns", analyzes bid-rigging behaviours, focusing on how cartels operate within public procurement, but it does not examine the current European Directive 2014/24/EU on the public sector.[78]

In addition to the above gap in the existing body of literature, there are only few legal papers regarding the use of leniency to uncover bid rigging arrangements, and the legal reparation of contracting authorities as private litigants in case they are victims of bid rigging. What is more, there is lack of insightful studies examining how these two tools from cartel enforcement interplay with the procurement remedies, in particular the debarment mechanism and the self-cleaning defence under the current European Directive 2014/24/EU on the public sector. For example, Claudia Cerrone, Yoan Hermstrüwer and Pedro Robalo in their paper "Debarment and collusion in procurement auctions" found that deterrent impact of debarments grows as the length of the punishment increases, while shorter debarments encourage tacit collusion among remaining bidders in the market.[79] Alberto Heimler in his paper "Cartels in Public Procurement: A Reassessment" argued that leniency programmes are not very effective in bid rigging cases because bid rigging is often a criminal offence, making immunity from an administrative fine insufficient.[80] In his earlier paper "Cartels in Public Procurement", Heimler also considers the reasons why the use of leniency is quite uncommon in bid-rigging cartels, but without discussing how the leniency mechanism interacts with procurement remedies such as the debarment mechanism and self-cleaning defence, and to what extent they oppose each other.[81] Anderson, Jones and Kovacic in one of their recent papers underline the significance of leniency programme in public procurement, but their emphasis is on the interaction between anti-corruption and pro-competition measures.[82] Similarly, Wouter Wils analyzes the impact of the EU Competition Damages Directive on leniency programmes, without addressing public procurement markets.[83] He examines a proposal by the German Monopolies Commission to grant

78 Carlotta Carbone, Francesco Calderoni and Maria Jofre "Bid-Rigging in Public Procurement: Cartel Strategies and Bidding Patterns" (2024), 82, *Crime, Law and Social Change*, 249–281.

79 Claudia Cerrone, Yoan Hermstrüwer and Pedro Robalo "Debarment and Collusion in Procurement Auctions" (2021), 129 *Games and Economic Behaviour*, 114–143.

80 Alberto Heimler "Cartels in Public Procurement: A Reassessment" CPI Antitrust Chronicle October 2023 <https://www.pymnts.com/wp-content/uploads/2023/10/1-CARTELS-IN-PUBLIC-PROCUREMENT-A-REASSESSMENT-Alberto-Heimler.pdf> accessed January 22, 2025.

81 Alberto Heimler (fn 69).

82 Robert D. Anderson, Alison Jones and William E. Kovacic "Preventing Corruption, Supplier Collusion and the Corrosion of Civic Trust: A Procompetitive Program to Improve the Effectiveness and Legitimacy of Public Procurement" (2019), 5, *George Mason Law Review* <https://papers.ssrn.com/sol3/papers.cfm?abstract_id=3289170> accessed January 25, 2025.

83 Wouter Wils "Should the EU Competition Damages Directive be revised to grant companies that have received immunity from fines under the competition authorities' leniency programmes also immunity from damages?", September 2023, Concurrences N° 3-2023, Art. N° 112968, 52–71.

full immunity from damages to companies receiving immunity from fines under leniency programmes. Wils argues against this proposal, citing concerns about fairness, potential harm to public enforcement and increased market concentration. A broad overview of how public and private enforcement interact within competition law is also provided by Pedro Caro de Sousa in his book "The Private Enforcement of Competition Law", focusing on the inherent tensions and challenges in balancing these two enforcement mechanisms and discussing the proposal to amend the EU Competition Damages Directive 2014/104/EU to grant immunity recipients full protection from damage claims.[84] However, the book does not examine the interplay between competition enforcement mechanisms and public procurement.

On the other hand, Emmanuelle Auriol, Erling Hjelmeng and Tina Søreide address the interaction between leniency and the debarment mechanism, but they take into account other parameters as well.[85] They consider how leniency and cartel settlements in competition law, criminal sanctions and debarment of suppliers from participation in public tenders for bribery work all together. Moreover, they merely pinpoint some challenges in the function of these policy tools vis-à-vis the others, without focusing on the complexity of challenges associated with the interaction between these different policy tools. In the same vein, Sarah Schoenmaekers discusses leniency and self-cleaning policies, but she restricts herself to the comparison of their underlying rationale.[86]Furthermore, her focus is mainly on explaining the level of success of leniency programmes vis-à-vis incentive-based self-cleaning policies and on establishing whether the self-cleaning policy under the European Directive 2014/24/EU is effective to increase integrity in public procurement.

Regarding the legal reparation of contracting authorities as private litigants in case of bid rigging, Marsela Maci considers the challenges around an attempt to utilize private enforcement against bid rigging cartels, but her analysis is rather obsolete, as it was made prior to the adoption of the Damages Directive 2014/104/EU.[87] Moreover, her paper looks at one element of private litigation only, that is, the quantum of damages, without dealing with other elements, such as litigation costs. Giancarlo Spagnolo also addresses damages for bid rigging, which are available to contracting authorities in case they eventually fall victim to tenderers engaged in bid rigging and other collusive practices. He made a presentation on this topic in the 7th LEAR conference, attempting to explain why the public sector

84 Pedro Caro de Sousa *The Private Enforcement of Competition Law* (1st Edition, Oxford University Press, 2024).

85 Emmanuelle Auriol, Erling Hjelmeng and Tina Søreide "Deterring Corruption and Cartels: In Search of a Coherent Approach", November 2016 <https://www.tse-fr.eu/sites/default/files/TSE/documents/doc/wp/2016/wp_tse_728.pdf> accessed January 25, 2025. See also Emmanuelle Auriol and Tina Søreide "An Economic Analysis of Debarment" (2017), 50, *International Review of Law and Economics*.

86 Sarah Schoenmaekers "Self-Cleaning and Leniency: Comparable Objectives but Different Levels of Success?" (2018), 1(13), *European Procurement and Public Private Partnership Law Review*.

87 Marsela Maci "Private Enforcement in Bid Rigging Cases in the European Union" (2012), 8(I), *ECJ*.

is reluctant to bring damages for bid rigging and what are the possible solutions to this matter.[88] Also, in 2023 the Catalan Competition Authority issued a practical guide for public administrations seeking to pursue damages claims for bid-rigging and other competition law infringements. The guide outlines the legal framework, evidentiary requirements and practical strategies for initiating and managing such claims while highlighting the importance of collaboration and information sharing. The fact that there are only a few studies published on this topic leaves this area of law largely unexplored.

Based on this brief literature review, my monograph steps in and makes a significant contribution by filling important gaps in the literature. The book utilizes auction theory as a benchmark to evaluate the risk of collusion in the procurement procedures and techniques under the latest European Directive 2014/24/EU on the public sector. It also explores the relationship between procurement remedies and competition regulators' policies to deter bid rigging in public procurement. The next section will delve deeper into the innovation presented in this monograph.

1.4 Contribution of This Book to the Academic and Policy Debate

Public procurement directives and efficient public procurement procedures are crucial for ensuring the EU's global competitiveness. They serve as one of the main tools for the EU to develop innovative goods and services and to create leading markets in clean and strategic technologies. Nonetheless, the 2023 special report from the European Court of Auditors[89] regarding public procurement within the EU, along with the subsequent Council Conclusions (C/2024/3521),[90] concluded that competition decreased in the EU Single Market over the last decade (2011–2021). The Report also revealed that while the reforms of 2014 established a strong foundation, additional measures are necessary to fully tackle the issue of reduced competition in public procurement and leverage the potential of the EU's public procurement market. Likewise, in the Political Guidelines 2024–2029 for the next European Commission, President Ursula von der Leyen announced a revision of the public procurement directives and the Commission is now launching an evaluation of Directive 2014/24/EU on public sector. This assessment includes whether the directive has been effective in contributing to a high level of competition in the single market.

88 Giancarlo Spagnolo "Public Procurement, Bid Rigging and (the Lack of) Actions for Damages", Lear Conference on Public Procurement and Competition Policy, Rome, July 3–5 2017 <www.learconference.com/wp-content/uploads/2017/07/SPAGNOLO_Damages_Lear_2017.pdf> accessed January 25, 2025.

89 European Court of Auditors "Special Report 28: Public procurement in the EU – Less competition for contracts awarded for works, goods and services in the 10 years up to 2021" <www.eca.europa.eu/en/publications?ref=sr-2023-28> accessed January 25, 2025.

90 Council Conclusions on the European Court of Auditors' Special Report No. 28/2023: Improve a fair and effective competition for EU public procurement contracts awarded for works, goods, and services; OJ C, C/2024/3521, 3.6.2024.

In view of the recent developments and the on-going concerns at the academic, policy and regulatory levels regarding the need for a pro-competitive design of public procurement procedures, this monograph is topical, interesting and original in various ways. It is the first comprehensive study of the latest European Directive 2014/24/EU on public sector, using auction theory as a benchmark to assess the risk of collusion in the context of procurement procedures and techniques. It examines the extent to which the provisions under the latest European procurement Directive facilitate or deter collusion during specific award procedures.

Previous literature on the European Directive 2014/24/EU has mainly aimed to place the legal framework in a theoretical context and criticize it either from a strictly public procurement perspective or from a neoliberal point of view that promotes the concept of "efficiency" in competition similar to that in private markets. As explained in the section above, no research has been conducted on the current Directive, using auction theory as benchmark to assess the risk of collusion in the procurement process. Hence, this book adds to the existing body of literature by studying the provisions of the European Directive 2014/24/EU, using economic literature as a benchmark for assessing the risk of collusion in the procurement process. The assessment of the European procurement Directive is structured around the stages of a public procurement process from planning and preparation to the relevant procurement procedures and techniques. Each chapter of the book delves deeply into specific topics and highlights potential pitfalls of collusion to avoid during specific procurement procedures and techniques, based on the findings of auction theory, which has provided a valuable set of collusion countermeasures. The insights drawn from the book's analysis will not only apply to the upcoming revised public procurement directives, but also to procurement rules worldwide.

Moreover, the main focus drive of this monograph is practical,[91] without adopting the neoliberal ideology[92] that prioritizes profit-seeking over social values. As will be highlighted in Section 1.6 below, the framing of procurement regulation in a way that encourages public purchasers to mimic private buyers, is not the book's focus. What is within the scope of this book is the prevention of bid rigging. Just

91 This means that the book heads out beyond black-letterism and neoliberalism, as its primary aim is to draw out general lessons for public procurement policy makers and officers in Europe and across the world.

92 For a full review of the neoliberal point of view and arguments see Albert Sanchez Graells "Truly Competitive Public Procurement as a Europe 2020 Lever (fn 51), 377–394; Albert Sanchez Graells "More Competition-Oriented Public Procurement to Foster Social Welfare" (fn 51), 81, 84–89, 105; Albert Sanchez Graells "Public Procurement and the EU Competition Rules" (fn 51). The replication of the competitive process of private markets is not an actual function of the procurement rules and if it were, this would remove commercial decision-making from the national level to the EU level, as an element of the operation of a competitive market. For a full review of this conception of the directives see Sue Arrowsmith "The Purpose of the EU Procurement Directives" (fn 50), 1–47; Peter Kunzlik "Neoliberalism and the European Public Procurement Regime" (fn 50), 283–356; Peter Kunzlik "The 2014 Public Procurement Package: One-step Forward and Two Back for Green and Social Procurement?" in K. Wauters and Y. Marique (eds) EU Directive 2014/24 on Public Procurement: A New Turn for Competition in Public Markets? (Brussels, Larcier 2016), XXXX–XXX.

because preventing bid rigging is seen as part of the effort to promote competition in public procurement markets, does not necessarily mean that a neoliberal approach to public procurement markets must be taken. After all, competition does not necessarily conflict with a social market economy. In order to understand this paradox, it is necessary to remember that the historical but also the current interpretation of the "social market" concept is not the same as the traditional leftist "welfare state" ideology, and so it is not hostile to the vigorous enforcement of competition law.[93] The social market economy is built on two clearly distinct but complementary pillars: Competition enforcement and social policy measures to ensure social justice and provide social protection.[94] Moreover, the concept of the "social market economy" emphasizes reliance on the market mechanism and advocates for maximum free market and competition wherever possible.[95]

After assessing the relevant provisions of the latest procurement Directive, the book delves into the policies that competition regulators implement in the realm of public procurement to combat bid rigging. The design of procurement rules is just one piece of the puzzle, as we know from the study of cartels that determined individuals and firms will deliberately collude and hide their behaviour to maximize profits. Therefore, in addition to examining the design of procurement rules, this book also explores the use of leniency programmes to uncover bid rigging schemes. Leniency is crucial for exposing secretive collusive behaviour that is difficult to detect. Therefore, it is important to examine in the book how leniency programmes interact with procurement remedies – such as debarring bidders and the self-cleaning defence under the latest European procurement Directive 2014/24/EU. Unique recommendations are proposed to better align cartel enforcement policy objectives with procurement remedies. Equally, when a bid rigging arrangement is uncovered, it is important that government authorities who overpaid for rigged contracts have a means of recourse, to recover damages. Therefore, private enforcement in the context of procurement is considered as well. Specifically, the book addresses challenges related to legal redress for contracting authorities as private litigants under the latest European Damages Directive 2014/104/EU. Suggestions are put forth to encourage contracting authorities to pursue private enforcement in case they fall victim to collusion.

With the completion of the second research matter, the book provides a holistic dimension and perspective to the underlying research, aiming to offer recommendations for law and policy makers as well as procurement officers, on how to better

93 Václav Šmejkal "Competition Law and the Social Market Economy Goal of the EU" (2015), 1, *International Comparative Jurisprudence*, 35.

94 Lázló Andor, former European Commissioner responsible for Employment, Social Affairs and Inclusion "Building a Social Market Economy in the European Union", Speech 11/695, Manchester, October 20, 2011 <https://europa.eu/rapid/press-release_SPEECH-11-695_en.htm> accessed January 25, 2025.

95 Mario Monti, former European Commissioner "Competition in a Social Market Economy", Speech 2000/022, Freiburg, 9–10 November 2000 <https://ec.europa.eu/competition/speeches/text/sp2000_022_en.pdf> accessed January 25, 2025.

design, set up and manage public tenders without distorting competition. It also emphasizes the importance of utilizing competition law enforcement mechanisms to combat collusion in public procurement. For this reason, the book makes several recommendations to help achieve this goal and strike a fair balance among different policy objectives. Its appeal lies in its contribution to both procurement law and competition law literatures. The main contribution is its identification of ways to improve the procurement process to reduce and prevent bid rigging. Additionally, it aids competition lawyers and economists in understanding the procurement process and the specific incentives it creates for collusive practices.

1.5 Research Questions

In view of the book's purpose and further to the brief review of the existing literature above, a number of research questions arise.

1. How can anticompetitive conduct undermine the procurement process?
2. What is the scope of bid rigging during the procurement planning phase?
3. What legislative and soft law tools are necessary to restrict or prevent bid rigging among economic operators during the procurement planning phase of a public tender?
4. What aspects of procurement procedure and techniques increase the chances of bid rigging and could be exploited by (potential) suppliers?
5. What legislative and soft law tools are required to deter collusion[96] when using relevant procurement procedures and techniques?
6. Can collusive schemes in public procurement be prevented through competition law enforcement mechanisms? If so, what steps should be taken to strengthen the role of public and private enforcement as deterrents to collusion in public procurement?
7. What recommendations can be identified based on private enforcement to address bid rigging outcomes in EU procurement law?

1.6 Limitations and Methodology

The book considers the issue of collusion in the European public procurement regime. The EU was chosen because it is an illustrative example of a supranational jurisdiction, the rules of which have a direct impact on all 28 Member States. The European public procurement regime is the one that regulates the purchasing activities of contracting authorities in each Member State. Therefore, the systematic and close examination of its provisions has a very high research value. This book only covers the Public Sector Directive 2014/24/EU, though the latest public procurement regime consists of two additional Directives, Directive 2014/23/EU, which regulates the award of concession contracts and Directive 2014/25/EU,

96 The term "collusion" which is used throughout the book refers to explicit collusion.

which regulates procurement in the water, energy, transport and postal services. The focus of the book is on explicit collusion on the part of suppliers in public procurement. Other aspects of competition in the procurement context – notably monopsony and the framing of procurement regulation in a way that makes public purchasers behave as closely as possible such as private buyers – are outside that focus. Yet, as the book progresses, some aspects of those wider themes are indirectly addressed, in so far as they are relevant to the core focus. Moreover, the book does not cover the topic of corruption or "vertical bid rigging", which involves a vertical agreement between one or more bidders and a public official to illegally allocate a public contract.[97] However, frequent reference is made to corruption throughout the book, because collusion and corruption often occur together and have a mutually reinforcing effect.[98]

The method of the book is a doctrinal and economic analysis of the latest European procurement Directive. Auction theory is applied to the current procurement rules in order to examine their effectiveness in preventing and deterring collusion in the context of public tenders. Therefore, this book does not address the deterrence of collusion in the marketplace, as this form of collusion is addressed by competition law and industrial economics. Other methodological tools, such as legal history and policy analysis assist the doctrinal method in the book.

After identifying the original contribution of this book and the research are, it is time outline EU public procurement rules and provide a brief introduction to EU competition rules. This will ensure that the book is valuable and understandable to both disciplines.

1.7 Explaining the Public Procurement – Setting the Scene

In this section the basic procurement rules that are relevant to the core focus of the book will be explained.

Public procurement defines the ways that the public sector, through contracting authorities, chooses a contractor to provide works (e.g. building of roads, bridges and government buildings), goods (products or supplies, such as office furniture for government buildings) or services (manual services, such as maintenance of government buildings, or professional services, such as architectural and engineering services). Contracting authorities may be the State itself, regional or local authorities, bodies governed by public law or associations formed by one or more such authorities or one or more such bodies governed by public law.[99] Other systems, such as the World Trade Organization or the US system, use different terminology

97 OECD "Policy Roundtables: Collusion and Corruption in Public Procurement 2010" (fn 66).

98 Ibid; Michael Kramer and International Anti-Corruption Resource Center "The Most Common Procurement Fraud Schemes and Their Primary Red Flags" <http://iacrc.org/procurement-fraud/the-most-common-procurement-fraud-schemes-and-their-primary-red-flags/> accessed January 25, 2025.

99 Article 2, para. 1(1) of the Directive 2014/24/EU.

to cover the same concept, such as "government procurement" and "government/public contracts".[100]

The European public procurement is regulated by the European Directive 2014/24/EU, the effectiveness of which is examined in the book in terms of collusion deterrence. However, not all public contracts fall within the scope of the European Directive, but only those whose value exceeds specified thresholds.[101] The public contracts which are below the *de minimis* rule are governed by the TFEU and its principles, such as equal treatment, proportionality and transparency.[102] The TFEU provisions also apply on a supplementary basis in the case of public contracts above the relevant thresholds. This means that in any case contracting authorities must respect and comply with the "Treaty Principles".

The public procurement process is divided into three stages:[103]

a) The procurement planning, when the contracting authorities decide which goods, works or services they need and when they will acquire them.
b) The process of placing a contract in order to purchase the goods, works, services they need, which involves the selection of the contractor and the choice of terms on which the goods, works or services are to be supplied.
c) The process of administering the contract to secure its effective performance.

The concept of public procurement refers to all three stages, but the focus of this book will be only on the first two stages of this cohesive public procurement cycle, as it is in these phases that collusion arises and so it is in these stages that the procurement rules become important tools of policy.[104]

1.7.1 Procurement Planning

Before launching a procurement procedure, contracting authorities devise a procurement plan that helps them to identify their need(s) and decide accordingly what to buy, when and from what source. For this purpose and in order to be sure that their expectations are realistic, contracting authorities may seek or accept advice from independent experts or authorities or from market participants.[105] This

100 Sue Arrowsmith "Public Procurement: Basic Concepts and the Coverage of Procurement Rules" in S. Arrowsmith (ed) *Public Procurement Regulation: An Introduction* <www.nottingham.ac.uk/pprg/documentsarchive/asialinkmaterials/publicprocurementregulationintroduction.pdf> accessed January 25, 2025.

101 For public works contracts, the threshold is €5,186,000, for public supply and service contracts awarded by central government authorities is €134,000 and for public supply and service contracts awarded by sub-central contracting authorities is €207,000. See also Article 4 of the Directive 2014/24/EU.

102 Case C-324/98 *Telaustria and Telefonadress* (2000) ECR I-10745, para. 60; Vestergaard [2001] ECR I-9505, paras. 20 and 21; Case C-264/03 Commission v France (2005) ECR I-8831, para. 32 and Case C-6/05 *Medipac-Kazantzidis* (2007) ECR I-4557, para. 33.

103 Sue Arrowsmith "Public Procurement: Basic Concepts and the Coverage of Procurement Rules" (fn 100)

104 Ibid.

105 Please see Appendix 1 for further details regarding the Articles of Directive 2014/24/EU that apply here.

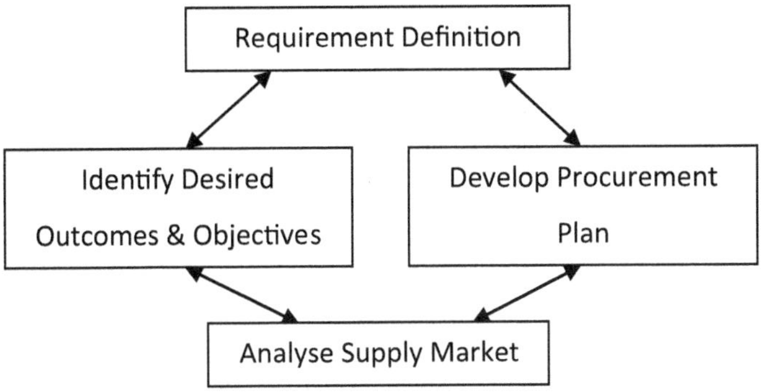

Figure 1.1 Information gathering

permits a strong understanding of the market dynamics of the relevant industry, a spend analysis and an accurate needs analysis, which make the "work plan" of contracting authorities run successfully.[106] Figure 1.1 shows the stages of a procurement planning process:[107]

1.7.2 Procurement/Tendering Procedures

The different basic methods of procurement for goods, works and services are the following ones:

1) Open tender
2) Restricted tender
3) Competitive dialogue
4) Competitive procedure with negotiation
5) Innovation partnership

Open tender is the procedure that the State, through contracting authorities, uses in case of low value purchases as well as where the requirement is straightforward and the procurer is looking for the least expensive supplier.[108] In the open tender, contracting authorities and entities call for competition by publishing in the Official Journal of the EU a "contract notice", in response to which any interested economic operator may submit a tender. Amongst the tenderers that meet the selection criteria set out at the stage of the procurement planning, the contracting

106 Achilles "3 Factors Affecting Procurement Planning" (2016) <www.achilles.com/industry-insights/3-factors-affecting-procurement-planning/> accessed January 25, 2025.

107 The diagram was inspired by the website of the United Nations "UN Procurement Practitioner's Handbook" <www.ungm.org/Shared/KnowledgeCenter/Pages/PPH2> accessed January 25, 2025.

108 PwC, London Economics and Ecorys for the European Commission "Public Procurement in Europe-Cost and Effectiveness" (2011) <https://op.europa.eu/en/publication-detail/-/publication/0cfa3445-7724-4af5-8c2b-d657cd690c03> accessed December 3, 2024, 5.

authorities choose the tender which is either the lowest in terms of price or the most economically advantageous on the basis of qualitative and cost[109] criteria.[110] Open procedures have the lion's share of public procurement (i.e. 73% of all tender announcements in the Official Journal of the EU).[111]

Restricted tender is the procedure that contracting authorities use if they have set as a priority the shorter timeframes, the reduction of the wasted transaction costs,[112] or the reduction of bid and evaluation costs when the procurement is complex, and so by reason of its highly complex or specialized nature the spread of tenders is limited.[113] In the restricted procedure, all economic operators can respond to the call for competition which is published in the Official Journal of the EU, expressing in this way their interest to participate, but only certain candidates that meet specific selection criteria[114] are invited to submit tenders. These "qualified" suppliers are chosen on the basis of objective criteria indicated in the contract notice.[115] Restricted procedures account for about 9% of total procurements.[116] Public procurers are absolutely free to choose between the open and the restricted procedure.[117]

Competitive dialogue is the procedure that contracting authorities use in case of complex contracts and high value purchases, such as large infrastructure projects. Where the public authority cannot define the technical specifications of the products, works or services procured and the use of the open procedure as well as of the restricted procedure will be rather costly and time consuming, without necessarily allowing the award of the contract to the tender offering the best value for money, competitive dialogue is the best choice.[118] Like in restricted procedures, all economic operators can respond to the contract notice of the contracting authority and request participation in the process, within 30 days from the publication in the Official Journal of the EU. Then, the contracting authority must invite at least three economic operators to an open dialogue in which the final technical, legal and economic aspects of the public contract are defined.[119] In this way, more intense

109 The cost criterion may be, at the choice of the contracting authority, either the price or a cost-effectiveness approach, such as life-cycling costing.

110 These are the award criteria which are indicated in the contract notice. See European Commission "Green Paper on the Modernisation of EU Public Procurement Policy Towards A More Efficient European Procurement Market, Brussels, 27.1.2011" (fn 56), 13, fn 27.

111 PwC, London Economics and Ecorys for the European Commission (fn 108), 4–5.

112 Transaction costs occur when economic operators submit expression of interest for public contracts which are not relevant or attractive to them.

113 Abby Semple *A Practical Guide to Public Procurement* (Oxford University Press, 2015), 73–75; Sue Arrowsmith *The Law of Public and Utilities Procurement: Regulation in the EU and UK* (3rd edition, Sweet & Maxwell, 2014), 608–609.

114 This is a "pre-qualification stage" that takes place before the contracting authorities invite tenders.

115 European Commission "Green Paper on the Modernisation of EU Public Procurement Policy towards a More Efficient European Procurement Market, Brussels (fn 56), 13, (fn 28).

116 PwC, London Economics and Ecorys for the European Commission "Public Procurement in Europe-Cost and Effectiveness" (fn 108), 4–5.

117 See article 26, para. 2 of the 2014/24/EU Directive.

118 European Commission "Guide for Tenderers-Submitting Bids in Response to a Call for Tenders Published by the Office for Infrastructure and Logistics-Brussels" <http://ec.europa.eu/oib/doc/tenders-submission-guide_en.pdf> accessed January 25, 2025.

119 Article 65, para. 2 of Directive 2014/24/EU.

competition is achieved between economic operators with regard to price and quality elements in the tender.[120] The competitive dialogue is used in about 0.4% of award notices annually across the European Economic Area",[121] but "it is the fastest growing procedure from about 1,5–2 million in contract value".[122]

Competitive procedure with negotiation is a procedural type that receives only a few offers.[123] Therefore, this procedure is used only in specific cases. For instance, competitive negotiated procedure may take place where other procedures will not work because competition is not viable or appropriate or where the other procedures have not produced an acceptable tender.[124] What should be clarified at this point is that the competitive procedures with negotiation have the same conditions for use as the competitive dialogue. Article 26, paragraph 4 of the 2014/24/EU Directive contemplates in which situations contracting authorities may apply either a competitive procedure with negotiation or a competitive dialogue. Hence, this provision implies that there is no hierarchy between the two procurement procedures. The primary difference between them is that the competitive procedure with negotiation starts with an initial tender as a basis for subsequent negotiations, while the competitive dialogue does not. There are cases that the competitive procedure with negotiation is used without call for competition, meaning without a prior publication of a contract notice. This may happen in cases of natural catastrophes that require immediate action.[125] Where contracting authorities rely on this exception, they always have to provide reasons why there are no reasonable alternatives, substitutes or functionally comparable works, supplies and services to the ones they decided to procure.[126] The negotiated procedure without prior publication accounts for about seven percent of procurements where the authority is allowed to consult the contractor(s) of its own choice and negotiate with them. It is frequently used for service procurements, that is, education and training services (30%); and services related to the oil and gas industry (18.6%), as for this procedure type the utilities sector comprises most.[127] It amounts to about 5% in value and most purchases using this procedure type are in the low end of the value range.[128]

Innovation partnership is a new procurement procedure introduced by the 2014/24/EU Directive in order to be used where there is a need for "an innovative product, service or work that cannot be met by those… already available on the

120 OECD "Implementing the EU Directives on the Selection of Economic Operators in Public Procurement Procedures-SIGMA Paper No. 56" <www.sigmaweb.org/publications/Selection-of-economic-operators-in-public-procurement-procedures-SIGMA-Paper-56-September-2018.pdf> accessed January 25, 2025.

121 PwC, London Economics and Ecorys for the European Commission (fn 108), 12.

122 Ibid, 21.

123 Ibid, 94.

124 Office of Government Commerce "An Introduction to Public Procurement" <www.scribd.com/document/72138907/Introduction-to-Public-Procurement> accessed January 25, 2025.

125 Recital 80 of the 2014/24/EU Directive.

126 Recital 50 and Article 32 of the 2014/24/EU Directive.

127 PwC, London Economics and Ecorys for the European Commission (fn 108) 46, 56

128 Ibid, 16, 20.

market".[129] It enables contracting authorities to develop an innovative solution in a long-term partnership with one or more chosen providers and with the option to purchase the outcome of that development process, without going through a further procurement exercise, as long as the final product/service/work corresponds to pre-agreed performance levels and maximum costs.[130] Another key element of this new procurement procedure is that it expressly deals with the structuring of the contractual position after the contract award.[131] Innovation partnership starts with a competitive phase, where any economic operator may submit a request to participate in response to a call for competition, as long as it meets the selection criteria requested by the contracting authority as part of the tender process.[132] The minimum number of candidates eventually invited should be three in order to ensure genuine competition.[133] The most suitable providers are selected as partners based on their skills, abilities and prices. The choice of partner(s) is made on the basis of the competitive procedure with negotiation, which at the option of the contracting authority may be structured in successive stages in order to reduce the number of tenders being negotiated.[134] The contracting authority shall indicate beforehand whether it will use that option, as well as whether it will award the contract at this initial stage or using a staged process. In the latter case, after the competitive phase there will be the Research and Development (R&D) or design stage, followed by the service contract that delivers the final solution (commercial phase). During the R&D phase, the limited number of chosen providers are asked to develop component parts of an overall solution to a complex problem in partnership with the contracting authority. This phase may go through several different stages, during which the innovation partnership may be terminated or the number of partners may be gradually reduced, depending on whether they meet certain pre-determined criteria or milestone requirements.[135] At the next stage, that is, the commercial phase, the contracting authority awards a delivery contract or contracts to the partner(s) that deliver(s) the best solution at that design stage.[136]

In view of the above, the Table 1.1 summarizes the key features of the procurement procedures and the circumstances under which the contracting authorities choose to run them.[137]

129 Article 31, para. 1 of the 2014/24/EU Directive.

130 Recital 59 and Article 31 of the 2014/24/EU Directive.

131 John Bennett "Innovation Partnership – Does It Offer A Genuine Breakthrough?" <http://publicsectorblog.practicallaw.com/innovation-partnership-does-it-offer-a-genuine-breakthrough/> accessed January 25, 2025.

132 Article 31, paras 1 and 6 of the 2014/24/EU Directive.

133 Article 65, para. 2 of the 2014/24/EU Directive.

134 Article 31, para. 5 of the 2014/24/EU Directive.

135 Local Government Lawyer "Horses for Courses" <www.localgovernmentlawyer.co.uk/procurement-and-contracts/308-procurement-features/25892-horses-for-courses> accessed January 25, 2025; LexisPSL Local Government Team "The Innovation Partnership Explained" <https://localgovernmentlawyer.co.uk/lexisnexis/561-lexis-lg/lexis/localgov/procurement/31403-the-innovation-partnership-procedure-explained-2%20:> accessed January 25, 2025.

136 Bennett (fn 131).

137 The table was taken from the website of Bird and Bird "Introduction to EU Public Procurement Law" <www.twobirds.com/~/media/PDFs/Brochures/Public%20procurement/Bird%20%20Bird

Table 1.1 Choice of procurement procedures

PROCEDURE	*KEY FEATURES*	*PERMITTED CIRCUMSTANCES*
Open	• Any interested party may submit a tender, that is, there is no pre-qualification stage. This makes it unsuitable for procurements where a large number of bidders are anticipated. • No negotiation with bidders permitted. • Suitable for tenders that are easy to evaluate.	No restrictions on the use of this procedure.
Restricted	• Pre-qualification stage, that is, only those bidders that meet selection criteria will be invited to tender. • No negotiation with bidders permitted although it is permissible to clarify bids and finalize terms. The scope for amendments to tenders through clarifications and finalization of terms is however very limited. • Minimum of five bidders to be invited following the pre-qualification stage. • Suitable for many procurements, particularly for standard goods or services.	No restrictions on the use of this procedure.
Competitive Dialogue	• Pre-qualification stage, that is, only bidders that meet the selection criteria will be invited to dialogue. • Dialogue is used to develop one or more suitable solutions to the contracting authorities' needs. • Once solutions are identified the dialogue phase is concluded and final tenders are invited. • Once tenders are submitted there is no negotiation of tenders only clarifications and finalization of terms. • Suitable for complex contracts such as major ICT contracts.	This procedure is only available in particular situations, as contemplated in Article 26, paragraph 4 of the 2014/24/EU Directive.
Negotiated	• Only bidders that meet the selection criteria will be invited to negotiate • The negotiation can take place in stages with the number of bidders reduced at each stage.	This procedure is only available in particular situations, as contemplated in Article 26, paragraph 4 of the 2014/24/EU Directive.
Innovation Partnership	• Only bidders that meet the minimum requirements will be invited to submit research and innovation projects and negotiate. • The negotiation can take place in successive stages with the number of partners reduced at each stage.	This procedure is only available where there is a need for an innovative product, service or work that cannot be met by those already available on the market.

Figure 1.2 Key steps of procurement procedures

The key steps of the various procurement procedures are summarized in Figure 1.2.[138]

1.7.3 Procurement Techniques

Apart from procurement procedures, contracting authorities may also use some other common procurement practices, which are called "procurement techniques" under the Directive 2014/24/EU. The procurement techniques that will be discussed in the book are the framework agreements, dynamic purchasing and e-auctions.

Framework agreements were introduced in order to enable contracting authorities to achieve administrative and price efficiencies. In this way, the award of multiple contracts by a single contracting authority or by a central purchasing body[139] ("CPB") is possible without having to repeat the same or similar tendering processes but by establishing an approved list of suppliers that have been enrolled

%20%20Introduction%20to%20EU%20Public%20Procurement%20Law.pdf> accessed January 25, 2025.

138 The figure was inspired by the website of Bird and Bird "Introduction to EU Public Procurement Law" <www.twobirds.com/~/media/PDFs/Brochures/Public%20procurement/Bird%20%20Bird%20%20Introduction%20to%20EU%20Public%20Procurement%20Law.pdf> accessed January 25, 2025.

139 See OECD "Centralised Purchasing Systems in the European Union – SIGMA Papers No. 47" <www.oecd-ilibrary.org/governance/centralised-purchasing-systems-in-the-european-union_5kgkgqv703xw-en> accessed January 25, 2025. CPB is usually organized as a government agency or as a limited non-profit company and acts for or on behalf of several contracting authorities.

in the framework.[140] At the same time, contracting authorities' buying power gets greater.[141] By strengthening their buying power, contracting authorities have the opportunity to pool skills and expertise as well as to share the risks and costs that arise in a procurement process.[142] Here is an example framework with two agreements:[143]

The term of a framework agreement shall not exceed four years, save in exceptional cases duly justified, in particular by the subject of the framework agreement.[144] The implementation of the rules on framework agreements is mandatory for the Member States and contracting authorities can choose to apply more than one type to award the public contract.[145] The standard steps that are usually taken in a framework agreement procedure are the following ones:[146]

(a) An invitation to economic operators to participate in the procedure, which describes the procurement entity's needs, the terms as well as the conditions of the procurement.
(b) The selection of one or more suppliers which was made after the assessment of the economic operators' qualifications and responses.
(c) The procurement entity enters into a framework agreement with the selected supplier(s).
(d) Placing orders with the selected supplier(s) as soon as a particular need arises.

Framework agreements are mainly used for repeat purchases of relatively standard and simple goods, such as office and simple information and communication technology ("ICT") supplies or services, such as maintenance contracts.[147] Apart from the off the shelf supplies and relatively straightforward services markets, framework agreements may be of much wider beneficial application. Indicatively, they may be useful in emergencies and other urgent situations as well as in the case of

140 Rick Canavan "Public Procurement and Frameworks" in Christopher Bovis (ed) *Research Handbook on EU Public Procurement Law* (Edward Elgar Publishing 2016), 119; Marta Andrecka "Clarification or Missed Opportunity? The Provision on Framework Agreements in the 2014 Directive" in Grith Skovgaard Ølykke and Albert Sanchez-Graells (eds) *Reformation or Deformation of the EU Public Procurement Rules* (Edward Elgar Publishing 2016), 216.

141 The fact that contracting authorities have buying power does not mean that they necessarily have market power as competition lawyers might understand it.

142 Andrecka (fn 140), 217.

143 Figure 1.3. The figure was taken from the website Constructing Excellence "What is a Framework?" <http://constructingexcellence.org.uk/tools/frameworkingtoolkit/what-is-a-framework/> accessed January 25, 2025.

144 Article 33, para. 1 of the 2014/24/EU Directive.

145 See Recital 61 of the 2014/24/EU Directive where it is contemplated that contracting authorities should be allowed to obtain specific works, supplies or services covered by the framework agreement, either by requiring them from one of the economic operators, or by awarding a specific contract for the works, supplies or services following a mini competition among the economic operators parties to the framework agreement.

146 Albano and Nicholas (fn 69), 13.

147 Ibid, 5.

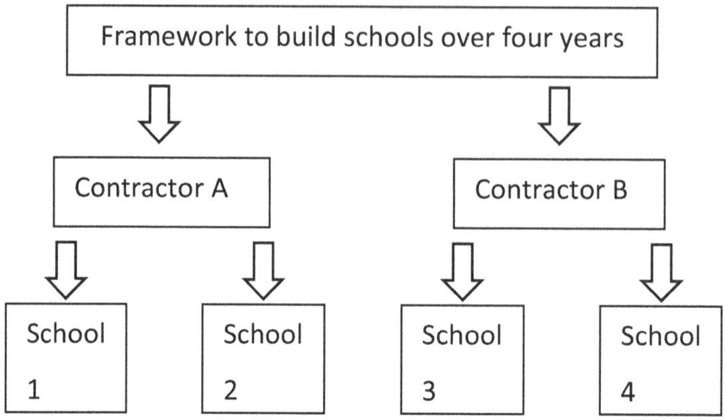

Figure 1.3 Example of framework with two agreements

"specialised items requiring a dedicated production line and/or items that need to be tailored to the needs of the procuring entity, where the need is identified but the time for their request is still unknown".[148] Framework agreements are also used in relatively concentrated markets where repeat procurement is appropriate, though this is not very common. This kind of markets may regard fuel supplies, airline or car rental services, regional janitorial, consulting or advisory services.[149] An illustrative example is the National Fuels framework agreement in the UK which constitutes a "one-stop-shop for all fuels and associated services without the need to trawl through a number of frameworks across multiple professional buying organisations".[150]

Framework agreements are constantly gaining ground in public procurement, as their use since 2006 has been increasing at an average 18% per year.[151] These procurement techniques are rather popular in Northern Europe, while a growth has been noticed in large procurers such as France and Spain.[152] Indicatively, "from 2006 to 2009 the use of framework contracts has increased by almost a factor of four" and "in 2009 over 25.000 framework contracts amounted to about one seventh of the value of all contracts published in the Official Journal of the European Union".[153]

148 Ibid, 5, 28.

149 Ibid, 187, 217.

150 Crown Commercial Service "National Fuels" <https://ccs-agreements.cabinetoffice.gov.uk/contracts/rm3801> accessed January 25, 2025

151 PwC, London Economics and Ecorys for the European Commission (fn 96), 5.

152 Ibid.

153 European Commission "Evaluation Report: Impact and Effectiveness of EU Public Procurement Legislation, Part 1" (2011) <http://ec.europa.eu/transparency/regdoc/rep/2/2011/EN/SEC-2011-853-F1-EN-MAIN-PART-1.PDF> accessed January 25, 2025, 8.

Dynamic purchasing system was first introduced under the old Directive 2004/18/EC on the coordination of procedures for the award of public works contracts, public supply contracts and public service contracts and it is recognized as the most successful type of procedure as far as the attraction of bidders is concerned, because of the "fluid nature of the participants".[154] This means that it is an open system, allowing new suppliers to become parties to it after its conclusion.[155] Since not all terms and conditions are determined beforehand, a second round of competition may be necessary. It is a completely electronically based process for commonly used purchases which are easily available on the market.[156] It takes place as a form of the restricted procedure and its use is rather rare, though it has more than doubled since 2007.[157]

Electronic auctions (e-auctions) are a procurement tool that uses web-based software to allow potential suppliers to compete online, in real time, to provide prices for the goods/services under auction.[158] Specifically, Article 35, paragraph 1(2) of 2014/24/EU Directive contemplates that:

> E-auction is a repetitive electronic process, which occurs after an initial full evaluation of the tenders, enabling them to be ranked using automatic evaluation methods

They are a representative electronic purchasing technique, the use of which has nearly doubled in number during 2009 and 2010.[159] E-auctions can be based on price alone or other criteria such as quality, delivery or service levels.[160] They can take two forms; they can be either reverse or forward. In the former, the contract is awarded to the lowest bidder and in the latter the bidder with the highest price wins the contract, for example when a company bids to purchase paper and magazines for recycling.[161] A typical reverse e-auction starts with a request for quotation ("RFQ") in which buyer's requirements are explained.[162] The suppliers, whose tenders are deemed to be admissible, are then invited to bid against one another in a virtual auction taking place over the internet.[163] During the bidding process, new prices are revised downwards on an on-going basis and/or new values concerning

154 PwC, London Economics and Ecorys for the European Commission (fn 108), 95. See also Rick Canavan (fn 140), 124.

155 Nicholas and Albano (fn 69), 19.

156 PwC, London Economics and Ecorys for the European Commission (fn 108), 23.

157 Ibid, 24 and 38. See also Roger Bickerstaff "E-Procurement Under the New EU Procurement Directives" (2014), 3, *PPLR*, 144.

158 Crown Commercial Service "eAuctions" <www.crowncommercial.gov.uk/information-for-buyers-and-suppliers/start-buying/commercial-agreements/eauctions> accessed January 25, 2025.

159 PwC, London Economics and Ecorys for the European Commission (fn 108), 24

160 Ibid.

161 Ibid.

162 Chi-Bin Cheng "Solving a Sealed-Bid Reverse Auction Problem by Multiple-Criterion Decision-Making Methods" (2008), 56(12), *Computers & Mathematics with Applications*, 3261.

163 Article 35, para. 5(5) of the 2014/24/EU Directive.

certain elements of tenders are presented.[164] In this way, tenders are evaluated automatically without the intervention of contracting authorities.

1.8 Competition Law in a Nutshell

This section provides a brief and general overview of the competition rules which are relevant to the core focus of the book, which is bid rigging. Until the adoption of the 2014 public procurement Directives, collusive practices in public procurement were primarily addressed at the EU level through the lens of competition law. They were seen as a typical example of an agreement between two or more independent market operators, that restricts competition and are prohibited under Article 101 TFEU.

Competition policy has been an integral part of the European Union from its very beginning, as it arose from the need to ensure the good function of the Single Internal Market and the free movement of goods and services throughout the EU. The EU's general competition rules are set out at Articles 101 and 102 TFEU. Article 101(1) TFEU is the principal provision to control anticompetitive behaviour by cartels (including bid-rigging behaviour), so the focus of this section will be only on this provision. Article 102 TFEU prohibits the abuse of a dominant position by one or more undertakings and so it will remain out of the book's scope.[165]

Article 101 TFEU prohibits any agreement or concerted practice made between undertakings (essentially every entity engaged in an economic activity)[166] as well as any decision by associations of undertakings that may affect trade between Member States and that has as its object or effect the prevention, restriction or distortion of competition within the internal market. Article 101 TFEU is only concerned with agreements, concerted practices or decisions made by associations of undertakings which may have an appreciable effect on trade between the European Member States, drawing the line in this way between areas which are covered by EU law and those which are covered by national law. Though nowadays every EU Member State has a domestic equivalent to Article 101 that must be consistent with EU law, this concept is still very important because it has two implications. The first one is that national courts and national CAs must apply EU law, when trade between Member States is affected.[167] The second one is that national courts and

164 Article 35, para. 1 of the 2014/24/EU Directive; François Lichère and Sara Richetto "Framework Agreements, Dynamic Purchasing Systems and Public E-Procurement" in François Lichère, Roberto Caranta and Steen Treumer (eds) *Modernising Public Procurement: The New Directive* (DJØF Publishing, 2014), 207.

165 Although outside the scope of this book, there is a notion of collective dominance in Article 102 TFEU that could potentially apply to bid rigging arrangements. For further information see Félix Mezzanotte "Using Abuse of Collective Dominance in Article 102 TFEU to Fight Tacit Collusion: The Problem of Proof and Inferential Error" (2010), 33(1), *World Competition*, 77–102.

166 Case 41/90, Höfner and Elser v Macroton GmbH (1991) ECRI-1979.

167 Regulation 1/2003, Article 3(1).

national CAs cannot apply a stricter national law than EU law to agreements.[168] Moreover, either an anticompetitive object or effect will suffice to establish an infringement of Article 101(1) TFEU.[169] In order to determine whether a specific conduct is injurious to competition by object, account should be taken of the content of its provisions, the objectives it seeks to ascertain as well as its economic and legal context of which it forms part.[170] Yet, there are some agreements that are always considered to be "by object" restrictions, such as price-fixing, market-sharing and bid rigging.[171] Therefore, bid rigging falls always under the scope of Article 101 TFEU and it is automatically void.

If an agreement is not restrictive of competition by object, it must be examined whether it has restrictive effects on competition. Account must be taken of both actual and potential effects. In other words, the agreement must have likely anti-competitive effects on prices, output, innovation or the variety or quality of goods and services.[172] Such negative effects must be appreciable. Thus, the prohibition rule of Article 101(1) does not apply when the identified anticompetitive effects of an agreement are insignificant for the market.[173] This means that agreements of minor importance are not prohibited. Article 101(2) TFEU lists particular types of prohibited conduct and then Article 101(3) TFEU exempts conduct that falls foul of Article 101(1) TFEU but satisfies four specific criteria found in Article 101(3) TFEU. Hence, the fact that an agreement has an anticompetitive object or effect does not mean that it is automatically prohibited, provided that

> it contributes to improving the production or distribution of goods or to promoting technical or economic progress, while allowing consumers a fair share of the resulting benefit, and which does not:
>
> (a) impose on the undertakings concerned restrictions which are not indispensable to the attainment of these objectives;
> (b) afford such undertakings the possibility of eliminating competition in respect of a substantial part of the products.[174]

168 Ibid, Article 3(2).
169 Case C-56/65 Société Technique Minière (L.T.M.) v Maschinenbau Ulm GmbH (M.B.U.) (1966), ECL:EU:C: 1966:38.
170 Case C-501/06 GlaxoSmithKline Services Unlimited v Commission (2009), ECR I-9291, (2010), 4, CMLR 50.
171 Cases T-374/94 European Night Services v Commission (1998) ECR II-3141, (1998), 5, CMLR 718.
172 Case 23/67 Brasserie de Haecht v Wilkin (1967) ECR 407, (1968) CMLR 26; Case C-234/89 Delimitis v Henninger Brau AG (1991) ECR I-935, (1992), 5, CMLR 210. Helpful guidance on the Commission's approach to the establishment of anticompetitive effects can be found in the Commission's Guidelines on the application of Article 101(3) of the Treaty OJ (2004) C-101/8, paras 24–27 and in its Guidelines on Horizontal Cooperation Agreements OJ (2011) C-11/1, paras 26–47.
173 This is the de minimis doctrine. See Case 5/69 Franz Völk v S.P.R.L. Ets J. Vervaecke (1969) ECLI:EU:C:1969:35.
174 Article 101(3) TFEU.

In virtue of Article 101(3) TFEU, Article 101(1) can be declared inapplicable not only in relation to agreements, but also in relation to categories of agreements, which satisfy a block exemption. The generic authorization of agreements that satisfy the terms of a block exemption provides legal certainty and assurance for firms seeking to engage in lawful and beneficial cooperation, such as the transfer of a technology licence.[175] Yet, severe restrictions of competition are unlikely to fulfil the conditions of Article 101(3) TFEU.[176] Such restrictions are usually black-listed in block exemption regulations or identified as hardcore restrictions in Commission guidelines and notices.[177]

Before completing the general overview of the competition rules which are relevant to the core focus of the book, it is important to underline the prominent role that leniency plays in the EU, when it comes to uncover and investigate cartels under Article 101 TFEU. According to statistical study of 52 European Commission cartel decisions from 2004 to 2014, 94% of these cartel cases came to light thanks to leniency.[178] The high level of fines increases the upside of applying for leniency, as the immunity recipient's fine under leniency programme is reduced to zero, in contrast with the other cartel members.[179] Hence, it makes sense that the book shows particular interest in this competition law enforcement mechanism and how it interplays with procurement remedies, such as the debarment mechanism and self-cleaning defence, in the domain of public procurement markets. In addition to leniency, it is also the Damages Directive 2014/104/EU that plays a significant role in the EU as far as cartels under Article 101 TFEU are concerned. First, it safeguards the public enforcement of competition law by restricting access to evidence provided to CAs by immunity recipients in the context of leniency programmes.[180] Second, it has introduced several improvements in the rules and legal tools for bringing damages claims for infringements of competition law caused by cartels, such as bidding rings.[181]

1.9 Structure of This Book

Now that the overview of public procurement and competition rules is complete, this introductory chapter will finish with an outline of the book structure and

175 Whish and Bailey (fn 49), 168–169.

176 Paragraph 46 of the Communication from the Commission's Guidelines on the Application of Article 81(3) of the Treaty, OJ C 101, 27/4/2004, 97–118.

177 Ibid.

178 Sébastien Broos, Axel Gautier, Jorge Marcos Ramos and Nicolas Petit "Analyse Statistique des Affaires D' Ententes dans l'UE (2004–2014)" (2016), 67 Revue économique 79 at 85; See also Wouter Wils "The Use of Leniency in EU Cartel Enforcement: An Assessment after Twenty Years" (2016), 39(3), *World Competition*, 327–388.

179 Auriol, Hjelmeng and Søreide (fn 85).

180 Barry Rodger, Miguel Sousa Ferro and Francisco Marcos *The EU Antitrust Damages Directive: Transposition in the Member States* (Oxford University Press, 2018).

181 Ibid.

chapters. Although the theme of collusion is central to every chapter of this book, the chapters can also be read individually. The book is divided into ten chapters.

Chapter 1: This chapter explains what bid rigging is, the forms it can take and why it is important to ensure that public contracts are awarded in an open, fair and transparent manner, without being distorted by collusive tendering. It then reviews the existing body of literature and explains the contribution of this book to the ongoing academic and policy debate. The research questions as well as the limitations and methodology of the book are considered. Finally, the chapter outlines EU public procurement rules and provides a brief introduction to EU competition rules to ensure that the book is understandable to both disciplines.

Chapter 2: This chapter introduces the research and provides perspective on the topic. It explains how incentives work in auctions using game theory, a tool commonly used in auction theory, and discusses how different auction formats can impact the risk of collusion. The chapter then identifies the principles of preventing collusion in auction design and explores the possibility of these principles to the procurement context. Finally, the chapter offers recommendations for addressing the issue of collusion in public procurements, drawing on insights from auction theory's approach to tackling in-auction collusion.

Chapter 3: After demonstrating that competition and collusion are crucial factors in auction theory and design, this chapter delves into whether the same holds true for public procurement rules. It retraces the evolution and key milestones of EU procurement rules and explores whether they evolved in conjunction with anti-cartel legislation in Europe or whether they developed independently. As will be shown, little consideration has been given to preventing bid rigging, in the design and development of procurement rules. Though there has been a growing emphasis on the necessity of promoting a pro-competitive design of public procedures at the regulatory level, the systematic and consistent integration of bid rigging prevention into policy design, as seen in auctions, has been lacking. Therefore, this chapter, serving as an introduction to the subsequent analysis, sets the stage before delving into the main argument. This argument asserts that the mechanisms in place to prevent collusion in tender procedures are insufficient, despite the recognition within the public procurement framework of the negative implications of bid rigging and the importance of maintaining fair competition by ensuring equal access to public contracts and preventing market distortion.

Chapter 4: After providing background on Directive 2014/24/EU, the groundwork has been laid for evaluating it from a bid rigging perspective. This chapter focuses on the pre-contractual procurement planning phase. It argues that contracting authorities should first and foremost avoid direct contact with market operators. If engaging with market operators is unavoidable, the chapter recommends that contracting authorities establish a policy for conducting preliminary market consultation. Several recommendations are provided for this purpose. The chapter also explains how the formulation of technical specifications by contracting authorities can increase the likelihood of bid rigging. The final section of this chapter examines collusive practices when the public contract is divided into lots. The two fundamental rules of economic theory are critically analyzed. As it will be shown, they are not applicable in all scenarios. Therefore, it is essential to enhance and strengthen these rules and there is need to make them more robust and effective in the ways suggested in the chapter.

Chapter 5: This chapter discusses the next stage of the procurement process, which is the competitive bidding stage. It argues for the adoption of design features that can significantly reduce the potential for collusive outcomes, thus promoting fair competition for public contracts. The chapter focuses on specific procedures and techniques contemplated under the 2014/24/EU Directive that are at risk of being misused for collusion. It draws conclusions about each of these procedures. Efficient procedures are crucial to ensure that contracting authorities receive the best possible offers while making efficient use of public funds, especially given the severe budgetary challenges faced by many EU Member States. Moreover, efficient procedures benefit all economic operators and make it easier for small and medium-sized enterprises ("SMEs") and cross-border bidders to participate in EU public procurement procedures.

Chapter 6: This chapter also discusses the competitive bidding stage, but this time with a focus on specific techniques contemplated under the 2014/24/EU Directive. It explores the pro-collusive aspects of framework agreements and examines whether there are inherent structural inefficiencies in the design and implementation of the framework agreement procedure. It is suggested that opening framework agreements to new participants could help address these structural inefficiencies. Additionally, the chapter delves into electronic auctions and their pro-collusive elements, offering recommendations to reduce collusion by concealing the prices at which competitors drop out, and limiting the number of valid offers submitted per round. It is also recommended to delay the publication of this information.

Chapter 7: This chapter focuses on the leniency programme, the key mechanism to strengthen the public enforcement of competition law, and its compatibility with the debarment mechanism and self-cleaning measures, which are both procurement remedies. As the chapter will show, procurement remedies interfere with cartel enforcement and the debarment mechanism undermines leniency in public procurement. The fact that firms may be banned from bidding, where there are plausible indications for their participation in agreements aiming at distorting competition, discourages infringing companies from coming forward and self-reporting. Even the self-cleaning measures under the current procurement Directive 2014/24/EU, which aim to help debarred firms to avoid exclusion or minimize its risk, undermine leniency in public procurement. This is particularly true after the recent judgment of the European Court of Justice in case C-124/17 Vossloh Laeis GmbH v Stadtwerke München GmbH. In this case, it was held that a contracting authority must be able to ask a leniency applicant to provide the decision of the competition authority concerning it. This must apply even if there is a pending private action for damages for breach of competition law by the contracting authority against that leniency applicant. In view of the conflicting policy objectives mentioned above, a number of proposals are discussed in order to better align leniency programmes with the mechanism of debarment and self-cleaning policy in public procurement.

Chapter 8: After dealing with leniency programmes, which are a mechanism to strengthen the public enforcement of competition law, it is time to address damages claims for bid rigging, a mechanism to enforce the private enforcement of competition law in the realm of public procurement. Thus, this chapter critically analyzes whether the new Damages Directive 2014/104/EU has facilitated authorities in successfully recovering damages for being overcharged. As will be demonstrated, this is not the case. Therefore, alternative compensatory remedies are discussed, and recommendations are provided to simplify the process contracting authorities seeking damages for bid rigging.

Chapter 9: Even after the Competition Law Damages Directive was passed, it is still difficult for public authorities to get damages for bid-rigging. Therefore, this chapter addresses the function of whistleblowing as a tool for detecting cartels in public procurement and as a way to support National Competition Authorities' enforcement actions against unlawful cartels in public marketplaces. The chapter specifically examines the degree to which the recent EU legal regime for whistle-blower protection (2019/1937 Directive on the protection of persons who report breaches of Union law) encourages whistleblowers to present National Competition Authorities with concrete evidence that will result in the enforcement of competition law in public procurement. Additionally covered in this chapter is the model of the US financial incentive whistleblower programme, which is very successful and provides many benefits when compared to the new programme in Europe. To draw a clearer picture of how the US whistle-blowing programme works in practice, functions and combats bid rigging, interviews were conducted with 12 practitioners in the United States and the relevant findings are discussed in the chapter.

Chapter 10: This chapter summarizes the findings of the preceding chapters and concludes the book, by generally recommending ways to make the current Directive 2014/24/EU on the public sector more effective in limiting and preventing bid rigging. Moreover, recommendations are made in order to enhance the use of competition law enforcement mechanisms in the fight against bid rigging in public procurement.

2 The Significance of Bid Rigging, Its Rationale and the Factors Conducive to It through the Lens of Auction Theory

2.1 Introduction

This chapter outlines the analytical framework of my research, which will be developed using auction theory. It will do so by examining the economic incentives and characteristics that increase the likelihood of bid rigging. Auction theory is defined as "an applied branch of economics which deals with how people act in auction markets and researches the properties of auction markets".[1] Auction theory operates under the assumption that bids are calculated and submitted independently.[2] However, bid rigging contradicts the assumption that bids are made independently, by involving collusion among bidders. This behaviour may occur because firms in a market typically act selfishly or as rational profit-maximizers. They may choose to collude to maximize profits whenever the gains from collusion outweigh the returns from competitive bidding, taking into account the potential benefits for violators of the collusion agreement. Hence, starting from the basic assumptions of auction theory, it will serve as a benchmark in the subsequent chapters to assess the risk of bid rigging in the public procurement process under Directive 2014/24/EU. The goal is to determine whether the current European public procurement regime effectively addresses bid rigging. Before delving into this analysis, this chapter will introduce and explain these underlying assumptions.

Auction theory can be approached from various perspectives, but this chapter will primarily focus on the game-theoretic viewpoint, according to which auctions are games in which:

> The players are the bidders, the actions are the bids and the payoffs depend on whether or not one receives the good and how much one pays for it (and possibly how much one pays for participating in the auction in the first place).[3]

1 Chunxue Zhu "Rationality in Bidding Theory: A Construction Industry Perspective" in Martin Casensky, Vian Ahmed, David Eaton and Monty Sutrisna (eds) *Proceedings BuHu 8th International Postgraduate Research Conference* (The Czech Technical University of Prague, 2008), 257–264.

2 Jonathan Levin "Auction Theory" (2004) Lecture Notes – Unpublished Manuscript, Stanford University <https://web.stanford.edu/~jdlevin/Econ%20286/Auctions.pdf> accessed on January 28, 2025.

3 Steve Tadelis, *Game Theory: An Introduction* (Princeton University Press, 2013), 271.

DOI: 10.4324/9781003359999-2

As already mentioned, there is a branch of auction theory that focuses on private value. One of the fundamental assumptions in a "private values" model is that bidders' valuations are private. Hence, auctions exhibit all the characteristics of a game with incomplete information, since the type of each buyer, their private value, is known only to them and not to the other buyers.[4] In essence, each bidder assesses the auctioned item based on their own criteria and judgment, without considering the bids of others. This information is private, as no bidder can accurately determine how much the auctioned item is worth to the other bidders.

In addition to the "private values" model, there is also a branch of auction theory that examines common value. In the "common value" model, the item for sale has an uncertain valuation, that is the same for all bidders after the auction.[5] Oil tracts serve as a good example.[6] Bidders value the oil tract based on how much oil they can extract from it, and this value is equal for all bidders regardless of the winner. The challenge is that before the auction, no one knows the exact amount of oil present. In this model, bidders receive "signals" about the uncertain value of the item and must base their bids on these signals. However, in this scenario, having knowledge of another bidder's valuation would be highly valuable. Therefore, the common belief in the private values model that each bidder acts independently does not apply here. The exchange of information becomes crucial in common value auctions, indicating that bid rigging may be more likely to occur in such a setting.[7]

For the sake of simplicity and for the purposes of this chapter, public tendering is described as auctions or reverse auctions, as it is commonly referred to in the economic literature. Complications arising during an auction, such as overpayment of the auctioned item by a bidder who overestimated its value,[8] or collusion among

4 Michael Maschler, Eilon Solan and Shmuel Zamir *Game Theory* (Cambridge University Press, 2016), 355, 468; John Harsanyi "Games with Incomplete Information Played by 'Bayesian' Players, I–III, Part I. The Basic Model" (1968), 14(5), *Management Science*, 159–182.

5 Flavio M. Menezes and Paulo K. Monteiro *An Introduction to Auction Theory* (Oxford University Press, 2004).

6 Brit Grosskopf, Lucas Rentschler and Rajiv Sarin "An experiment on first-price common-value auctions with asymmetric information structures: The blessed winner"(2018), 109, *Games and Economic Behaviour*.

7 Francoise Forges and Ram Orzach "Core-stable Rings in Second Price Auctions with Common Values" (2011), 47(6), *Journal of Mathematical Economics*; Charles N. Noussair and Gyula Seres "The Effect of Collusion on Efficiency in Experimental Auctions" (2020), 119, *Games and Economic Behaviour*.

8 This is the phenomenon of the "winner's curse", which is basically the result of overbidding in a common value auction. It exists both in first- and second-price sealed-bid auctions, with important economic consequences as to which auction format may be better at allocating a common value good in an efficient way. In a purely common value setting, the bidders have different prior estimates of the value, but the object is worth the same to all bidders ex post. See Tadelis (fn 3), 284; David J. Salant *A Primer on Auction Design, Management and Strategy* (The MIT Press, 2015), 78. In the "private values" model, overbidding is a complication that may arise. That is the fact that the experimental evidence on auctions shows that bidders typically bid above their valuations in first-price sealed bid auctions (or more generally in sealed-bid auctions). Please see John H. Kagel and Alvin E. Roth, *The Handbook of Experimental Economics* (Princeton University Press, 1995).

bidders,[9] also occur in public tendering. Auction design, which refers to the rules governing each contract put out to tender, can help address these issues, making it more difficult for bidders to collude and creating incentives for cartel members to break their collusive agreement once it is reached.[10] This is why auction design complements antitrust enforcement and substantially prevents or at least reduces the likelihood and effectiveness of collusion.[11] Due to the complementary nature of auction design and antitrust enforcement, auction theory serves as a benchmark in order to suggest the precise design of public tendering and evaluate whether current procurement rules align with the principles of auction theory.

Auction theory has been among the most influential branches of economics,[12] and the fact that it usually inhabits a much simpler environment[13] than public procurement does not negate the robustness of this benchmark. Its robustness is not negated either by the fact that auction theory captures only the economic efficiency, that is, the best value for money, and not strategic aims, such as the protection of the environment and the promotion of sustainable development. Furthermore, it should be noted that in auction theory there are several assumptions, which may be too restrictive and unrealistic in real life situations.[14] For instance, in auction theory it is assumed that the auction bidders' decisions are economically rational, without taking into account the impact of personality features on decision making, the bidders' inclination to take risks or their emotional involvement.[15] Hence, auction theory might be criticized for being unrealistic, but it is very important all the same. Auction theory has a stable theoretical design which can serve as a valuable testing-ground for economic theory, as auctions are "simple and well-defined economic environments".[16] Its primary benchmark and consideration is economic

9 Owen M. Kendler "Auction Theory Can Complement Competition Law: Preventing Collusion in Europe's 3G Spectrum Allocation" (2002), 23(1), *University of Pennsylvania Journal of International Law*, 160.

10 Aniol Llorente-Saguer and Ro'I Zultan "Auction Mechanisms and Bidder Collusion: Bribes, Signals and Selection", Discussion Paper No. 14-06, December 2014 <http://in.bgu.ac.il/en/humsos/Econ/Workingpapers/1406.pdf> accessed on January 28, 2025.

11 Hong Wang and Hong-min Chen "Deterring Bidder Collusion: Auction Design Complements Antitrust Policy" (2016), 12(1), *Journal of Competition Law and Economics*, 62.

12 Paul Klemperer, *Auctions: Theory and Practice* (Princeton University Press, 2004), 39. After all, we should not forget that William Vickrey, the "father" of auction theory, got the Nobel Prize in Economics in 1996 (https://www.nobelprize.org/prizes/economic-sciences/1996/summary/); and Robert Wilson and Paul Milgrom, two of the most influential researchers in the dawn of auction theory, got it in 2020 (https://www.nobelprize.org/prizes/economic-sciences/2020/summary/).

13 Paul Klemperer "Auction Theory: A Guide to the Literature" (1999), 13(3), *Journal of Economic Surveys*, 227–286.

14 Preston McAfee and John McMillan "Auctions and Bidding" (1987), 25(2), *Journal of Economic Literature*, 699–738.

15 Joanna Bialynicka-Birula "Rationality versus Irrationality of Auction Bidders – Interdisciplinary Perspective" (The International Association for Research in Economic Psychology/The Society for the Advancement of Behavioural Economics Conference, Rome, 2008).

16 Paul Klemperer (fn 13), 227.

efficiency[17] and auction theory has been important in developing our understanding of the incentives to collude and/or submit competitive bids. Moreover, auction design informed by auction theory may prevent collusion among bidders more cheaply and efficiently than investigations and prosecutions under competition law.[18]

In this chapter, the focus is particularly on ascending, descending and sealed bid auctions because the current public procurement regime contemplates purchasing processes, which have the same design characteristics as these three auction formats. The chapter investigates their elements, which are critical to the study of collusion and describes the structures that bidding rings use in ascending and sealed bid auctions. It also explains the incentives for collusion embedded in each of these auction formats. The auction formats examined in this chapter will be approached only in the context of public procurement, as the aim of this book is to study the effectiveness of the current public procurement regime in respect of preventing bid rigging and concerted practices in public tendering and make recommendations in order to improve it. By understanding the way that auctioneers design their auctions in order to combat collusion, the procurement agents will be able to make choices that make collusive outcomes difficult to achieve.[19]

However, it should be underlined that the auction design, like procurement rules, cannot successfully deal with the general market collusion, meaning with situations of endemic collusion where firms are generally collusive in nature, interact continuously outside of the auction and tend to collude on most of their dealings.[20] Such situations do not fall within the scope of auction design but rather within the scope of competition law, as collusion will exist under either auction format, regardless of the design of the auction and the actions taken by the auctioneer to limit the possibility of collusion.[21] Auction design can preempt or at least lower the probability and effectiveness of collusion, thus serving as a key complement and alternative to *ex post* competition law enforcement.[22] Yet, it is competition law that prohibits collusion in the marketplace, establishes the consequences of this anticompetitive conduct and ensures sufficient deterrence. Therefore, it is only the type of in-auction collusion that can be addressed by auction design.[23] In-auction collusion is particularly interesting when multiple units are involved and bidders

17 Roger L. Zhan "Optimality and Efficiency in Auctions Design: A Survey" in Chinchuluun A., Pardalos P.M., Migdalas A. and Pitsoulis L. (eds) *Pareto Optimality, Game Theory and Equilibria. Springer Optimization and Its Applications, Vol 17* (Springer, New York, 2008), 437–456.

18 Kendler (fn 9), 160.

19 The issue regarding which is the most profitable auction scheme that enables the seller to best exploit his monopoly positions is closely related to the problem of designing games. See Christian Montet and Daniel Serra, *Game Theory and Economics* (Palgrave 2003), 152.

20 Timothy C. Salmon "Preventing Collusion between Firms in Auctions" in M.C.W Janssen (ed) *Auctioning Public Assets: Analysis and Alternatives* (Cambridge University Press, 2004), 112.

21 Ibid.

22 Kendler (fn 9), 160–161.

23 Ibid, 114.

can win more than one auctioned item[24] or when the same or similar goods/services are procured regularly, like in road maintenance, which may not be in-auction procurement strictly speaking, but very close to it. In view of the division of public contracts into lots under the current Directive on public procurement,[25] this is a topic that also interests procurement authorities and so it falls within the scope of the present study.

In view of the above, the chapter is structured as follows. Section 2.2 sets out the primary motives of firms/ suppliers in public tendering who take part in a bidding ring. Game theory, which is a tool employed in auction theory, and particularly the famous problem in game theory known as the "Prisoner's Dilemma" will help to explain the undertakings' incentives when deciding whether to compete or collude in a public tender and why it is rational for them to deviate from their collusive agreement when trying to maximize profits. Section 2.3 continues with auction theory and Section 2.4 deals with how specific auction formats influence the risk of collusion. Section 2.5 examines the residual risk of collusion, even if the auction system is designed in a way that is consistent with auction theory. Therefore, some principles of good collusion prevention in auction design are identified, with an eye towards providing suggestions to making collusive outcomes less likely.[26] In Section 2.6 concluding remarks are made.

2.2 The Firms' Incentive to Rig Bids and Deviate from Their Collusive Agreements

Bid rigging allows firms to pay less and receive more than they would under market conditions.[27] There are several factors that determine the likelihood of these illegal profits affecting the firms' cost–benefit analysis. These factors are closely tied to their business cycle fluctuations, workload and profitability at the decision is made.[28] Financial conditions, such as depressions, recessions and decreases in market demand tend to favour collusion.[29] For instance, empirical studies show that many collusive agreements over the past 30 years were formed in response to declining demand.[30] Furthermore, after a downturn, firms anticipate tough com-

24 Ibid.

25 Article 46 of 2014/24/EU Directive.

26 Salmon (fn 20), 126.

27 OECD "Guidelines for Fighting Bid Rigging in Public Procurement: Helping Governments to Obtain Best Value for Money" <www.oecd.org/en/topics/sub-issues/competition-enforcement/fighting-bid-rigging-in-public-procurement.html> accessed on January 28, 2025.

28 Anna Zarkada-Fraser "A Classification of Factors Influencing Participating in Collusive Tendering Agreements" (2000), 23, *Journal of Business Ethics*, 273; see also Marshall C. Howard, *Legal Aspects of Marketing* (McGraw-Hill New York 1964) and Campbell R. McConnell, Stanley L. Brue and Sean M. Flynn, *Economics: Principles, Problems and Policies* (McGraw-Hill New York 1993).

29 Walter Bruce Erickson "Economics of Price Fixing" (1969), 2, *Antitrust Law and Economic Review*, 83.

30 Rainer Lindberg, Finnish Competition Authority "Boosting the Crisis Economy – Competition as an Ally" <https://competitionpolicyinternational.com/assets/0d358061c11f2708ad9d62634c6c40ad/Lindberg-JUNE-2009_1_.pdf> accessed on January 28, 2025.

petition that may result in the exit of at least one competitor. This motivates them to engage in collusive behaviour to shield themselves from fierce competition, especially in industries with high sunk costs that make re-entry challenging.[31] The main incentive for participating in a bidding ring is also the opportunity to achieve benefits and progress that would otherwise be unattainable in a market where "the services or products in question are completely new, involve major investments and substantial financial risks and require the pooling of know-how by the relevant undertakings".[32] Hence, under certain financial conditions collusion may be a rational choice for firms as it enables them to coordinate for higher profits.

As will be explained below with the help of the "Prisoner's Dilemma", the firms in a market behave selfishly. So, if the joint profit maximum, in other words the collusive gain, appears to firms more lucrative than their feasible alternatives, that is, the competitive solution, they will try to form a bidding ring. Indeed, bid-rigging is a faster and easier way of increasing profits, than making investments of uncertain length and return, for example.[33] By suppressing the inter-firm rivalry, the colluding firms may charge a high price and earn "a higher than competitive rate of return for a time or permanently", given that the damages they have to pay in case they are found guilty of bid rigging, as well as the punishment and the costs of apprehension and conviction, do not outweigh their profits.[34] Before coming to a collusive agreement, it is also the costs of entering into the collusive agreement as well as the costs of maintaining it that count and determine the decision of the potential bid riggers.[35] So, for a bidding ring to dominate competition, the suppliers must be sure not only about the collusive gain that should exceed the competitive return, but also about the net return to a potential violator of their cartel agreement, which should not be higher than the collusive gain.[36] Otherwise, individual members of the bidding ring will have the incentive to cheat and deviate from the collusive agreement.

31 Andreas Stephan "Price Fixing in Crisis: Implications of an Economic Downturn for Cartels and Enforcement" (2012), 35(3), *World Competition: Law and Economics Review*, 516; Nicolas Schmitt and Rolf Weder "Sunk Costs and Cartel Formation: Theory and Application to the Dyestuff Industry" (1998), 36(2), *Journal of Economic Behaviour and Organisation*, 197–220. However, it should be noted that at the same time, a deterioration of market conditions could also destabilize a cartel as each firm seeks to ensure its own survival. Future gains from the cartel are lower so the benefit from collusion is lower and the short-term gains from deviation could tempt firms to deviate from the collusive agreement.

32 Joined Cases T-374–375, 384 and 388/94 European Night Services and Others v E.C. Commission [1998], 5, CMLR 718, para. 230–231.

33 Robert C. Marshall and Leslie M. Marx, *The Economics of Collusion-Cartels and Bidding Rings* (MIT Press 2012), 22.

34 George J. Stigler, *The Organisation of Industry* (The University of Chicago Press, Chicago 1968), 39, 142; Gary Becker "Crime and Punishment: An Economic Approach" (1968), 76(2), *Journal of Political Economy*, 205–207.

35 Robert H. Porter and J. Douglas Zona "Collusion" (2008), 2, *Competition Law and Policy: ABA Section of Antitrust Law*, 1080.

36 Lester G. Telser *Competition, Collusion and Game Theory* (The Macmillan Press Ltd, 1971), 178.

Economists use game theory, specifically the "Prisoner's Dilemma", to explain why firms collude,[37] and to analyze the behaviour of rival firms in relation to changes in price, output and advertising expenditure. Game theory offers a natural framework for studying strategic behaviour, and the "Prisoner's Dilemma" serves as a model for oligopolistic interactions.[38] Cartels, as a type of oligopoly, attempt to collude like a monopoly by setting prices and output levels that maximize joint profits.[39] The classic "Prisoner's Dilemma", which is a one-shot game, two suspects under arrest for a crime find it in their best interest to confess, resulting in a sentence for both. The optimal outcome would be for neither to confess and both to be released, but individual incentives lead them to confess to avoid a heavier sentence.

This scenario can be applied to pricing in an oligopoly, where both firms would ideally want to set high prices, but fear losing market share if one undercuts the other. The Nash equilibrium in this case is for both firms to choose low prices. However, in repeated games, players can adjust their strategies based in previous outcomes, leading to the possibility of new equilibriums that were not feasible in a one-shot game (not confessing; high prices). Repetition allows players to observe and respond to each other's actions, creating a dynamic environment where cooperation (not confessing; high prices) can be sustained through the threat of punishment for deviations. This type of equilibrium is only achievable in repeated games and highlights the importance of ongoing interactions in strategic decision-making.

The "Nash equilibrium" is named after the mathematician John Nash who was the first to introduce this concept. It is a solution concept of a game involving two or more players, where each player is assumed to know the equilibrium strategies of the others and no player stands to benefit by unilaterally changing their own strategy. If each player has selected a strategy and no player can improve their payoff by changing strategies while the others remain unchanged, then the current set of strategies and payoffs represent a "Nash equilibrium".[40]

The above scenario can be better understood if it is illustrated diagrammatically. Hence, as already assumed, two competing firms in a market choose between a low and a high price:

The numbers in each cell of the table are the payoffs, namely the profits that each firm can make resulting from a price set by each. First number is pay-off for Firm 1 and second number is pay-off for Firm 2. In a one-shot version of this game, each firm will end up setting a low price because if it sets a high price the other firm

37 Mark Jephcott *Law of Cartels* (Jordan Publishing Limited 2011), 8.

38 Joe Chen and Joseph E. Harrington "The Impact of the Corporate Leniency Program on Cartel Formation and the Cartel Price Path" in Vivel Ghosal and John Stennek (eds) *The Political Economy of Antitrust* (Elsevier, 2007), 60.

39 Steven Tomlinson "Understanding a Cartel as a Prisoner's Dilemma" <http://college.cengage.com/economics/0538797274_mceachern/student/lecture/8432.pdf> accessed January 28, 2025.

40 Information Resources Management Association USA, *Game Theory: Breakthroughs in Research and Practice* (IGI Global, USA, 2018), 224; see also Martin J. Osborne and Ariel Rubinstein, *A Course in Game Theory* (MIT Press, 1994).

Table 2.1 Payoff table: Prisoner's Dilemma[1]

	Firm 2 LOW PRICE	*Firm 2 HIGH PRICE*
Firm 1 LOW PRICE	6, 6	12, 0
Firm 1 HIGH PRICE	0, 12	8, 8

1 Ibid, 9.

has an incentive to undercut the price and gain 12 (the entire market). However, both firms are better off if they agree to set a high collusive price and share the monopoly return between them (e.g. 8, 8). Through repeated interactions, the Nash equilibrium of the dynamic game is collusion because if one firm deviates, it knows that the other firm will punish it by pricing at constant marginal cost in perpetuity.[41] Consequently, the deviating firm will be able to capture the entire market only in one period, while it will earn nothing in all subsequent periods in perpetuity. For this reason, it is not in firms' interest to try and undercut each other, but to stick to their collusive agreement.

Given the outcomes above, it is useful for a procurement entity and certainly for policy makers to understand before the initiation of procurement proceedings: (a) the concept of strategy, (b) how an auction can be analyzed as a game in advance to comprehend expected bidder behaviour and predict outcomes from various auction designs, (c) why and when some suppliers may view collusion as their optimal strategy rather than competition and (d) the circumstances under which incentives to cheat the other bidders are either increased or reduced. It is significant for the purpose of deterring and detecting bid rigging, to have a better understanding of the motivations of bid riggers to collude, cheat and deviate from collusive agreements as well as the costs associated with maintaining collusion. In this way, game theory can be a valuable tool in altering the rules of an auction/procurement process to promote competition among bidders and discourage collusion among them.

2.3 Auction Theory

"Auction" is the economic term that refers to the process of procurement through competitive bidding, where the bidders compete for the sale rather than the purchase of products, services or the right to deliver a project or manufacture a product.[42]

41 In theory there is a restriction on the discount factor of firms as well (they need to be "patient enough"). Please see Marc Ivaldi et al. "The Economics of Tacit Collusion: Final Report for DG Competition, European Commission" <https://ec.europa.eu/competition/mergers/studies_reports/the_economics_of_tacit_collusion_en.pdf> accessed on January 28, 2025.

42 Vijay Krishna, *Auction Theory* (Academic Press, 2009, 2nd edition), 1. See also Klemperer "Auction" (fn 13), 4.

Many transactions are conducted through auctions, including the sale of treasury bills foreign exchange,[43] houses, cars, agricultural produce, livestock and art and antiques.[44] Government contracts are awarded through procurement auctions and businesses often use auctions to purchase inputs or subcontract work.[45] In recent years, governments have expanded their use of auctions to allocate spectrum, airport slots, oil drilling rights, timber, land and to procure goods and services from the private sector.[46] In the United States, auctions are the preferred form of procurement in the public sector, according to the Federal Acquisition Regulation.[47] Auctions offer desirable properties, such as transparency and well-defined rules, making them a good benchmark for European procurement rules. This is why their role has been increased in the private sector as well, especially with the rise of e-commerce, government privatizations and public and private outsourcing. In the past, the private sector relied on other procurement arrangements, such as cost-plus contracts negotiated with a single supplier.[48] Hence, it is worth examining the auction rules in order to understand how they attract entry, allocate items to the highest-valuing party, and prevent collusion through well-designed rules that are difficult to manipulate. This study has broad commercial implications for both public procurement and the private sector.

2.4 Auction Formats and Cooperative Strategies

This section, not only introduces the main forms that an auction can take, but also identifies the factors that lead bidders in specific auction formats to choose cooperative strategies, such as collusion, over competition. There is a particular interest in analyzing the profile of bidders' strategies in an auction and their incentives to collude rather than compete in auction formats that closely resemble current public procurement processes. This type of study is crucial because, according to economic theory the incentive for bidders to collude in an auction depends partly on the auction format.[49] The idea that colluding bidders may need to deviate from a

43 R. Preston McAfee, Michael Williams and Kenneth Hendricks "Auctions and Bid Rigging" in Roger D. Blair and D. Daniel Sokol (eds) *The Oxford Handbook of International Antitrust Economics, Vol 2* (OUP, 2015), 498.

44 ibid.

45 ibid.

46 Policonomics: Economics made simple "Game Theory III: Collusion" < http://policonomics.com/lp-game-theory3-collusion/> accessed January 28, 2025.

47 Tadelis (fn 3), 270.

48 Paul Klemperer "Bidding Markets" (2007), 3(1), *Journal of Competition Law and Economics*, 3; Steven Tadelis "Public Procurement Design: Lessons from the Private Sector" (2012), 30(3), *International Journal of Industrial Organization*, 297. See also Patrick Bajari, Robert S. McMillan and Steve Tadelis "Auctions Versus Negotiations in Procurement: An Empirical Analysis" (2009), 25(2), *Journal of Law Economics and Organization*, 372–399.

49 McAfee, Williams and Hendricks (fn 44), 503; Marc S. Robinson "Collusion and the Choice of Auction" (1985), 16(1), *The RAND Journal of Economics*, 141–145; Keith Waehrer "Asymmetric Private Values Auctions with Application to Joint Bidding and Mergers" (1999), 17(3), *International*

bidding ring once formed is also of particular interest. By examining all these bidding strategies, policy makers can more easily design procurement tendering, such as auction mechanisms, in a way that promotes equilibrium strategies benefiting bidders resulting in the highest expected revenue for the public buyer and discouraging collusion, which poses a serious threat to revenue.

In a single auction one or multiple objects may be auctioned, but also each of these objects may have multiple units.[50] Auctions that include only one object are called single-object auctions. The most common forms that a single-object auction can take are the following ones:

(a) Ascending-bid auction (also known as the open, oral or English auction).
(b) Descending-bid auction (also known as Dutch auction).
(c) First-price sealed-bid auction.
(d) Second-price sealed-bid auction (also called the Vickrey auction by economists).

Auctions involving multiple objects are referred to as multiple-object auctions, while those involving objects with multiple units are known as multi-unit auctions. Multi-object and multi-unit auctions are also of interest in this chapter because a contracting authority may choose to divide the supply of a product into multiple contracts or lots, when purchasing several supply contracts of different types or from different geographical areas.[51] Therefore, these types of auctions will also be analyzed in this chapter.

2.4.1 *Ascending-Bid Auctions*

In ascending-bid auctions the price is successively raised until only one bidder remains, ultimately winning the auctioned object at the final price.[52] In other words, in ascending-bid auctions bids are freely announced until no potential buyer wishes to make a higher bid and drops out.[53] Bidders do not always have to agree with the price announced by the auctioneer, but "they can also call out their own price suggestions with larger or smaller increments than is suggested by the auctioneer".[54]

Translated into a procurement setting this would be the inverse. The price, which is what the procurement agency pays the supplier for its services, starts high

Journal of Industrial Organisation, 437–452; Robert C. Marshall and Leslie M. Marx "Bidder Collusion" (2007), 133, *Journal of Economic Theory*, 374–402; Tadelis (fn 3), 285.

50 Ibid.

51 Nicola Dimitri, Riccardo Pacini, Marco Pagnozzi and Giancarlo Spagnolo "Multi-contract Tendering Procedures and Package Bidding in Procurement" in N. Dimitri, G. Piga and G. Spagnolo (eds) *Handbook of Procurement* (Cambridge University Press, 2006), 193–194.

52 Klemperer (fn 13), 11.

53 Salant (fn 8), 29–30; Vicki M Coppinger, Vernon Smith and Jon A Titus "Incentives and Behavior in English, Dutch and Sealed-Bid Auctions" (1980), 18(1), 2.

54 Ibid.

and is lowered until only one supplier is willing to accept the contract at this low price. Though in the domain of public procurement contracting authorities do not use ascending-bid auctions to procure goods/works/services, the current Directive 2014/24/EU on public procurement contemplates in article 35 the use of electronic auctions ("e-auctions") in case of public contracts whose subject-matter involves quantifiable elements[55] and do not require any intervention or appreciation by the contracting authority.[56] E-auctions are a representative electronic purchasing technique, the use of which nearly doubled in number during 2009 and 2010.[57] There has been considerable interest in the use of such auctions in the procurement of goods and services by public sector organizations in the EU, like the NHS in the UK, in order to secure cost savings for public buyers.[58] For this reason, the chapter's interest is in finding out what auction theory has to say regarding equilibrium bidding behaviour and bidders' strategic incentives when it comes to ascending-bid auctions and collusive schemes.

Auction theory suggests that the different types of end time format used in an online auction, that is, whether it is an extended end-time auction or an auction with a hard close, elicit different strategic incentives.[59] For instance, in an auction with a hard close, the bidders have strategic incentive to bid late in order to avoid a bidding war that will raise the final price of the auctioned item or in order to protect information about the item's value that can make a bidder increase his willingness to pay.[60] On the contrary, in an extended end-time auction the strategy of submitting a last-minute bid is not effective, as other bidders will still get more time to respond.[61] This means that the end time rule of an auction can determine when bidders shall bid (e.g. to submit a first bid early or late), how much they shall bid (e.g. to submit a low first bid or a high first bid) and even whether it is optimal

55 This means that they can be expressed in figures or percentages. For example, fuel, vehicles, furniture etc.

56 Recital (67) of the 2014/24/EU Directive. It should be underlined that electronic auctions may also be used for the purchase of a specific intellectual property right.

57 PwC, London Economics and Ecorys for the European Commission "Public Procurement in Europe-Cost and Effectiveness" (2011) <https://op.europa.eu/en/publication-detail/-/publication/0cfa3445-7724-4af5-8c2b-d657cd690c03> accessed on January 28, 2025. See also Penelope Alexia Giosa "Do e-auctions Increase the Risk of Bid Rigging?" (2018), 35, *CCP Research Bulletin*, 6.

58 The Regulatory Policy Institute (RPI) "Reverse e-Auctions and NHS Procurement: Executive Summary" <https://rpiresearchgroup.org/files/eAuctions_Exec_Summary_TME33py.pdf> accessed on January 28, 2025.

59 An extended end time auction has an extension rule that prolongs the auction by a fixed amount of time after each new bid. An auction with a hard close has a fixed and known ending time. See Axel Ockenfels and Alvin E. Roth "The Timing of Bids in Internet Auctions-Market Design, Bidder Behavior, and Artificial Agents" (2002), 23(3), *AI Magazine*, 9–87.

60 ibid.

61 Ryan Timothy O'Regan "A Look at the Game Theory of Online Auctions: The Choice Between End-Time Formats on Yahoo! Auctions" <https://dlib.bc.edu/islandora/object/bc-ir:102332/datastream/PDF/view> accessed on January 25, 2025, 6–7.

for them to collude or not.[62] Different combinations of these strategic options may result in different payoffs for each bidder in an e-auction.[63] In the domain of public procurement, contracting authorities can either close an e-auction at the previously indicated date and time[64] or prolong the auction by a fixed amount of time after they receive no more new prices or new values meeting the requirements concerning minimum differences.[65] Therefore, the conclusions that auction theory draws about extended end-time auctions and auctions with a hard close are particularly significant for public procurement as well, since both types of e-auction are contemplated in the current Directive on public procurement.

It has been empirically proved that e-auctions with a hard close[66] create incentives to bid late even in the simplest case of purely private values.[67] One intuition behind last-minute bidding at equilibrium is that the particular bidders want to avoid a bidding war that raises the expected final price and yields zero profits for all bidders – winner or losers – while there is still time for other bidders to react.[68] For this reason, in e-auctions with a hard close there is an incentive not to bid too high when there is still time for other bidders to react, but to wait until the last minute to bid because there will be positive probability that another bidder's last-minute bid will not be successfully transmitted.[69] This kind of equilibrium is interpreted as a form of conscious parallel conduct because its outcome is the suppression of some bids and the generation of higher benefits for successful bidders who mutually and deliberately delay their bids in the auction.[70] Apart from conscious parallel conduct, e-auctions with a hard close can also favour explicit collusion, because

62 It should be noted that if many bidders observe the strategy of submitting bids in the closing seconds of an auction in order to avoid bidding wars and begin to bid in this way, the result can be compared to collusion among bidders. See O'Regan (fn. 62), 6.

63 Payoffs are measured using the price paid for an item. So, for the winning bidders the payoff is how much they value the auctioned item minus the amount of the payment. See O'Regan (fn 62), 4.

64 See Article 35, para. 8(a) of the 2014/24/EU Directive.

65 According to Article 35, para. 8(b) of the 2014/24/EU Directive, "contracting authorities shall close an electronic auction "when they receive no more new prices or new values which meet the requirements concerning minimum differences, provided that they have previously stated the time which they will allow to elapse after receiving the last submission before they close the electronic auction".

66 This concerns ebay auctions in particular, where you can see what other parties are bidding.

67 Dan Ariely, Axel Ockenfels and Alvin Roth "An Experimental Analysis of Ending Rules in Internet Auctions" (2005), 36(4), *RAND Journal of Economics*, 893.

68 Ibid, 901; Alvin Roth and Axel Ockenfels "Last-Minute Bidding and the Rules for Ending Second-Price Auctions: Evidence from eBay and Amazon Auctions on the Internet" (2002), 92(4), *American Economic Review*, 1095; Axel Ockenfels and Alvin E. Roth "Late and Multiple Bidding in Second Price Internet Auctions: Theory and Evidence Concerning Different Rules for Ending An Auction" (2006), 55, *Games and Economic Behavior*, 308.

69 Ockenfels and Roth "Late and Multiple Bidding in Second Price Internet Auctions" (fn 69), 303.

70 Ibid. See also fn 7 at Alvin Roth and Axel Ockenfels "Last-Minute Bidding and the Rules for Ending Second-Price Auctions (fn 69), where it is clarified that "the probability that some late bids will not be successfully transmitted is a risk for each bidder, but a benefit for his opponents, and it is this "public good" aspect of the risk of bidding late that creates the possibility of a profitable collusive late-bidding equilibrium" in an extended end time auction.

as already explained above, any predictability regarding the duration of an auction facilitates collusion.[71]

On the other hand, auction theory considers that an extended end-time e-auction is essentially an English auction, though generally an online auction is strategically much different from a traditional English auction.[72] This means that extended end-time auctions have the same susceptibility to collusion, such as ascending-bid auctions. Hence, it is indispensable to examine what the auction theory literature says regarding equilibrium bidding behaviour in English auctions and under which circumstances collusion is deemed to be the optimal strategic option for bidders. The findings will also apply to e-auctions with a hard close, as auction theory equates e-auctions having a hard close with ascending-bid auctions, though the former is performed electronically.

In common value, as well as in affiliated value[73] settings, it is rare for a bidder to enter the ascending-bid auction with fixed values for the auctioned item.[74] This is because his strategy depends on the prices at which his competitors drop out, as value in ascending-bid auctions is determined through the escalation of bids.[75] Yet, each bidder has a reservation value when they enter the auction, meaning the maximum price a bidder is willing to pay for the product based on their personal valuation.[76] In an independent private values setting, meaning in an auction where the reservation value is private to each bidder, the unique Nash equilibrium of the English auction has each bidder drop out when the price reaches his reservation value.[77] In equilibrium, English auctions end when "the bidder with the second-highest value drops out, so the winner pays an amount equal to the second highest value".[78] If there are two identical auctioned items in a simultaneous ascending

71 OECD "Guidelines for Fighting Bid Rigging in Public Procurement" <www.oecd.org/en/topics/sub-issues/competition-enforcement/fighting-bid-rigging-in-public-procurement.html> accessed on December 17, 2024, 6; OECD "Competition and Procurement: Key Findings 2011" <www.oecd.org/en/publications/competition-and-procurement-key-findings_c6e6d5ae-en.html> accessed on January 17, 2025, 9, 18–19, 31–32, 85; OECD "Policy Roundtables: Collusion and Corruption in Public Procurement 2010" <www.oecd.org/en/publications/collusion-and-corruption-in-public-procurement_ef957f70-en.html> accessed January 26, 2025, 10–11, 326, 494.

72 This is true, as based on the analysis above it gets apparent that extended end-time e-auctions are strategically different from ascending-bid auctions. See Salant (fn 8), 47.

73 The affiliated values auction model in essence is a mixture of the private values and common values.

74 Peter Cramton "Ascending Auctions" (1998), 42(3–5), *European Economic Review*, 745; Marco Pagnozzi "Bids as a Vehicle for (Mis)Information: Collusion in English Auctions with Affiliated Values (2011), 20(4), *Journal of Economics and Management Strategy*, 1171. However, please note that in private values auction models, each bidder has a private valuation for the good that should not change as the auction progresses.

75 Ibid; Coppinger, Smith and Titus (fn 54), 21.

76 Bharat Bhargava, Mamata Jenamani and Yuhui Zhong "Understanding the Impact of Shill Bidding in Online English Auctions", Technical Report CSD-TR 03-036, Department of Computer Science, Purdue University, 2003, 8 <https://pdfs.semanticscholar.org/eee4/ef16b12e99193ad42bdfead2ffc0163ca7e3.pdf> accessed on October 31, 2024.

77 Ibid; Levin (fn 2).

78 Jonathan Levin (fn 2), 2.

auction, the bidder has an incentive to stop bidding for the second item before its marginal valuation is reached.[79] This means that keeping on bidding for two items makes high the price paid for the first item. Therefore, a bidder that wants to buy only a single unit may outbid the bidder with the highest value for the second item.

The bidding strategy that applies to single-unit ascending auctions, that is, bidding up to the highest valuation in order for the second-highest value to drop out, is also applicable in the presence of a bidding ring in an ascending-auction.[80] Consequently, if a non-ring member wins the auction in the presence of a bidding ring, the auctioneer/seller achieves the same revenue as they would in the absence of the bidding ring.[81] This also implies that collusion in ascending-bid auctions is "self-contained", meaning that if the bidding ring wins, it captures all collusive gains.[82] Conversely, if the bidding ring loses, non-ring bidders do not benefit from collusion, as they must pay the same amount they would without the bidding ring. In the absence of leakage of collusive gains to outside bidders, the incentives for forming a bidding ring are particularly strong in ascending-bid auctions. Additionally, non-ring members have no incentive to stay outside the bidding ring in an ascending-bid auction.[83] Another factor that makes the formation of a bidding ring appealing to bidders in an ascending-bid auction is the difficulty of entry for new bidders, as weaker bidders know that stronger bidders can easily outbid them.[84] This deters weaker bidders from participating in the auction.[85] As we know from auction theory, the deterrence of entry is one of the prerequisites for a successful cartel to flourish.[86] Ascending-bid auctions also favour the creation of bidding rings where ring members can strategically manipulate the information transmitted through their bids to influence the bidding strategies of non-ring members and make them bid less aggressively.[87] As a result, ring members get higher profits.[88] This manipulation can involve dropping out of the auction at a low price to make non-ring members believe the auctioned item's value is lower than it actually is.[89] English auctions facilitate such manipulative behaviour, as bidders

79 Peter Cramton "Simultaneous Ascending Auctions" in Peter Cramton, Yoav Shoham and Richard Steinberg (eds), *Combinatorial Auctions* (MIT Press, 2006), 108.

80 McAfee, Williams and Hendricks (fn 44), 503; Yeon-Koo Che and Jinwoo Kim "Optimal Collusion-Proof Auctions" (2009), 144(2), *Journal of Economic Theory*, 584.

81 McAfee, Williams and Hendricks (fn 44), 503.

82 Robert C. Marshall and Leslie M. Marx, *The Economics of Collusion-Cartels and Bidding Rings* (MIT Press 2012), 176.

83 McAfee, Williams and Hendricks (fn 44), 504.

84 Paul Klemperer "Using and Abusing Economic Theory" (2003), 2–3, *Journal of the European Economic Association*, 280.

85 Ibid.

86 Robert C. Marshall and Michael J. Meurer "Bidder Collusion and Antitrust Law: Refining the Analysis of Price Fixing to Account for the Special Features of Auction Markets" (2004), 72(1), *Antitrust Law Journal*, 93.

87 Marco Pagnozzi (fn 75), 1172.

88 Ibid.

89 Ibid.

can infer their competitors' information on the auctioned item's value by observing their bids.[90]

Collusion is more easily sustained in ascending-bid auctions than in ordinary industrial markets.[91] As already said, throughout each phase of the e-auction, contracting authorities must instantly communicate to all bidders enough information. The reason is that bidders will be able in this way to calculate their relative rankings at any given time.[92] Contracting authorities may also share other information, such as the number of current participants, where this has been indicated previously.[93] When bidders' values are interdependent and signals are positively correlated, more information leads to more aggressive bidding,[94] stimulating competition and creating a reliable process of price discovery. However, the material information that contracting authorities must reveal according to the new European public procurement legislation makes firms' pricing immediately and absolutely observable.[95] This allows bidders to establish and enforce collusive outcomes. Members of a bidding ring can monitor compliance with the collusive agreement and retaliate against any deviation.[96] Even though the current public procurement regime does not permit the disclosure of the bidders' identities during the e-auction, the number of participants agreeing to stay in the auction is observable, making it easy for bidders to identify each other.[97]

In multi-object or multi-unit auctions, the threat of punishment for deviation from the collusive agreement is even easier and quicker, as ring members can raise prices only on objects that the deviator will win.[98] Although the auction formats under discussion refer to single-object auctions, it is essential to consider multi-unit auctions in electronic bidding. The reason is that "ascending-bid auctions are used iteratively to sell multiple objects and this is typically the case at both traditional on-site auctions and in many on line auctions".[99] The multi-object/multi-unit auctions can favour the creation of a bidding ring for two additional reasons. First, in multi-unit ascending auctions the auctioned objects are well defined, making it easier for ring members to share collusive gains. Second, bids in a multi-unit ascending-bid auction can serve as a signal for concluding a collusive agreement and on who should win, at what price and how the allocation of collusive shares

90 Ibid.
91 Paul Klemperer (fn 85), 285.
92 Article 35, para 7 of 2014/24/EU Directive.
93 Ibid.
94 Todd R. Kaplan and Shmuel Zamir "Advances in Auctions" in Petyon Young and Shmuel Zamir (eds) *Handbook of Game Theory with Economic Applications: Vol 4* (Elsevier, 2014), 391–392; Peter Cramton (fn 75), 745.
95 Paul Klemperer (fn 85), 284.
96 Klemperer, ibid, 285; Klemperer (fn 12), 86; Marshall and Marx (fn 83), 200.
97 Article 35, para 7 of 2014/24/EU Directive.
98 Paul Klemperer (fn 85), 284–285.
99 Salant (fn 8), 46.

should be made.[100] Price acts as an assignment device, causing bidders with lower valuations to drop out in response to higher prices.[101]

Therefore, the information provided by the auctioneer during and at the conclusion of the auction makes the mission of a bidding ring to suppress within-cartel rivalry quite effective without the need for previous communication among collusive bidders regarding their values.[102]

2.4.2 Descending-Bid Auctions

Descending-bid auctions work in the opposite way. The auctioneer starts with a high price, higher than expected to receive and then gradually decreases it until the first bidder enters and the auction ends.[103] The first bidder to accept the price wins, and their bid matches the current price. Bidders do not learn about other potential bidders' value for the object during the auction.[104] When bids are private information, collusion is not the best strategic option for bidders, as non-disclosure of bids prevents bidders from using them as signals for collusion. Achieving maximum collusive profits is impossible.[105] Common value uncertainty and bid non-disclosure in descending-bid auctions lead to direct communication among bidders to achieve full collusive gains, which is illegal and easier to detect.[106] Descending-bid auctions can break up collusion and lower prices to near-competitive levels.[107] Non-colluding bidders can quickly win by accepting the auctioneer's price and final bids in a descending-bid auction[108] eliminate retaliation possibilities by other bidders for that round, risking the sustainability of a collusive scheme.[109] Moreover, the finality of bids in descending-bid auctions creates a cost for colluding bidders, even if the punishment of the deviating bidders were possible.[110] Each punishment results

100 Ibid; Klemperer (fn 12), 86; Marshall and Marx (fn 83), 200.

101 Cramton (fn 75), 751.

102 William E. Kovacic, Robert C. Marshall, Leslie M. Marx and Matthew E. Raiff "Bidding Rings and the Design of Anti-Collusive Measures for Auctions and Procurements" in N. Dimitri, G. Piga and G. Spagnolo (eds) *Handbook of Procurement* (Cambridge University Press), 387.

103 Salant (fn 8), 31.

104 David Easley and Jon Kleinberg "Auctions" in D. Easley and J. Kleinberg (eds) *Networks, Crowds, and Markets: Reasoning about a Highly Connected World* (Cambridge University Press, 2010), 252

105 Kovacic, Marshall, Marx and Raiff (fn 103), 402.

106 McAfee, Williams and Hedricks (fn 44), 507; Andrzej Skrzypacz and Hugo Hopenhayn "Tacit Collusion in Repeated Auctions" (2004), 114(1), *Journal of Economic Theory*, 153–169.

107 Alexander L. Brown, Charles R. Plott and Heidi J. Sullivan "Collusion Facilitating and Collusion Breaking Power of Simultaneous Ascending and Descending Price Auctions" (2009), 47(3), *Economic Inquiry*.

108 The bids in a descending-bid auction are final, meaning that once a bidder submits a bid for the auctioned item, he has to purchase it at that value.

109 Brown, Plott and Sullivan (fn 108), 407.

110 ibid.

in a loss if a bidder bids more than their value, as bids are final in descending-bid auctions and prevent outbidding.[111]

The current public procurement regime does not provide for descending-bid auctions because these types of auctions do not have a direct counterpart in procurement practices. In a descending-bid auction, the government would start the tender at a low price and the first bidder to participate would win the public contract at the price they bid. Since this approach is not applicable to public procurement, descending bid auctions are not relevant to public procurement.

2.4.3 First-Price Sealed-Bid Auctions

In first-price sealed-bid auctions only one bid is submitted by each bidder, typically in writing, and always in secret from the other bidders.[112] The auctioneer evaluates the bids after they are all submitted and the highest bidder wins and pays the amount of their bid.[113] In public procurement, the public purchaser would select the lowest bid as the winner, as they will pay that price, unlike in a "normal" auction where the auctioneer receives that price.

In first-price sealed-bid auctions, bidders usually aim to bid just high enough to win the item, shading their bid below their valuation based on what they think other bidders will bid.[114] This means that a bidder's optimal bid in first-price sealed-bid auctions dependents on how others bid. Using game theory terminology, auctions are considered games, and in first-price sealed-bid auctions each player has a strategy (e.g. a price for the item) that maximizes their expected payoff based on what strategies (e.g. prices for the item) they expect others to play.[115] This makes the strategy of each bidder in first-price sealed auctions *weakly dominant* as the optimal choice for each bidder depends on what other bidders choose.[116] Therefore, in first-price sealed-bid auctions the strategy of each bidder is not to bid their true valuation,[117] but to bid slightly less than their valuation.

Applied to procurement auctions, this means that each bidder would bid slightly above their cost. In this case, there is a positive probability that other bids will be

111 ibid.

112 Kovacic, Marshall, Marx and Raiff (fn 103), 387.

113 Ibid; Paul Milgrom, *Putting Auction Theory to Work* (Cambridge University Press, 2004), 112.

114 Joseph Harrington, *Games, Strategies and Decision Making* (Worth Publishers, 2009), 65–66.

115 A player's strategy is what actions or options a player can choose within the game, or situation, where the outcome is dependent on that option. The outcome is also dependent on the actions of the players opponent and their choice in the game. Anthony Kelly, *Decision Making Using Game Theory: An Introduction for Managers* (Cambridge University Press, 2003); Harrington (fn 115).

116 Salant (fn 8), 20; Tadelis (fn 3), 273.

117 If he loses he gets zero and if he wins he pays his valuation, thus getting a payoff of zero. A payoff is a number, also called utility, which reflects the desirability of an outcome to a player, for whatever reason. In other words, it is what players receive at the end of the game. See Theodore Turocy and Bernhard von Stengel "Game Theory" in Hossein Bidgoli (ed) *Encyclopedia of Information Systems* (Elsevier, Amsterdam, 2002), 403; Ilhan Kubilay Geçkil and Patrick L. Anderson, *Applied Game Theory and Strategic Behaviour* (Taylor and Francis Group, 2010), 19.

below their bid, making them the winner of the auctioned object and obtaining a positive payoff, without having to pay a higher price.[118] The fact that the best response of a bidder in first-price sealed-bid auctions depends on beliefs about other bidders' bids makes it difficult to determine Bayesian–Nash equilibrium bidding strategies for this auction type, which is a non-cooperative solution where each bidder's strategy is optimal against their opponents.[119] In fact, in first-price sealed-bid auctions where each bidder knows their own value but not those of other bidders, the unique equilibrium is for each bidder to bid less than their value.[120] Since this non-cooperative behaviour induces "strategic uncertainty"[121] and is not jointly optimal for bidders in this auction format, they may find cooperation through collusive behaviour in their own best interests.[122]

So, let's consider a scenario where a ring is formed in a first-price sealed-bid auction for the reasons mentioned earlier. The bidder chosen by the collusive scheme to win the auction must place a bid lower than what the highest-valuing ring member would have bid if the bidding ring didn't exist.[123] However, the bid made by the bidding ring may present an opportunity for a non-highest valuing cartel member or a non-ring member to participate in the auction and win it.[124] A non-highest valuing cartel member could enter a bid at the auction independently or through a shill, especially if the ring cannot control the bids submitted by their shills.[125] Hence, it appears that in a first-price sealed-bid auction the bidding ring does not fully benefit from its collusive behaviour.[126] This creates an incentive for ring members to break ranks and compete in the auction or for non-ring members to enter the auction and remain outside the ring to potentially earn more profit.[127]

Another reason why first-price sealed-bid auctions do not effectively prevent entry is the "strategic uncertainty" surrounding opponents' strategies, which diminishes the advantage of stronger players. This allows weaker players to take part in the auction and potentially outbid stronger players who may have shaded their bid.[128] Additionally, bidders interested in colluding are less likely to share their

118 Tadelis (fn 3), 276.

119 A Bayesian–Nash equilibrium for first-price sealed-bid auctions is found when each bidder's strategy is to maximize his expected payoff by shading his valuation to such an extent that each bidder may obtain a positive expected value from the auction.

120 See McAfee, Williams and Hendricks (fn 44), 500. This also means that in first-price sealed-bid auctions there is no Nash equilibrium in which each bidder deterministically chooses one of his strategies.

121 "Strategic uncertainty" results from the fact that bidders are not likely to share common priors about distributions of valuations and, even if they do, they may not play Nash equilibrium strategies. See Paul Klemperer (fn 85), 282.

122 Ibid, 501.

123 Llorente-Saguer and Zultan (fn 10); McAfee, Williams and Hendricks (fn 44), 503.

124 Ibid; See also Marshall and Marx (fn 83), 374–402; Robinson (fn 50), 141–145.

125 Marshall and Marx (fn 83), 379, 381.

126 McAfee, Williams and Hendricks (fn 44), 503; Marshall and Marx (fn 83), 176.

127 Ibid.

128 Klemperer (fn 85), 282.

private information about the valuation of the auctioned item with other potential ring members in first-price sealed-bid auctions. This is because if negotiations for forming a bidding ring fail, revealing private information could have significant implications on bidding behaviour.[129] So bargaining over collusive agreements is discouraged in first-price sealed-bid auctions.

First-price sealed-bid auctions are commonly used for government contract submissions.[130] This is why the dominant bidding mechanism in the public procurement sector appears to be the first-price sealed-bid auction,[131] which restricts contracting authorities to using of sealed-bid procedures with the exception of e-auctions.

2.4.4 Second-Price Sealed-Bid Auctions

The second-price auction, like the first-price auction, is a form of sealed-bid tender auctions, where each bidder submits a single bid independently, without having the ability to see others' bids.[132] The object is sold to the bidder with the highest bid and the price the winning bidder pays is the amount offered by the second-highest bidder, meaning the best losing bidder.[133] In a procurement auction, the opposite applies, meaning that the winner has the lowest bid and receives the second lowest bid.

In both the second-price sealed-bid auction and the first-price sealed-bid auction bidders have the strategy of offering an amount for a single available object.[134]Nevertheless, in second-price auctions bidders have an incentive to submit bids, equal to their true valuation of the object.[135] This is because "under the second price rule the bid only determines if the bidder wins the object, but not how much he has to pay when he wins".[136] Therefore, a bid equal to the true valuation of the object guarantees the bidder's win whenever the price determined by the auction is below the bidder's value.[137]

The second-price auction procedure, however, is not frequently used in procurement auctions and the current Directive on public procurement does not consider

129 Shiran Rachmilevitch "Bribing in First-Price Auctions" (2013), 77(1), *Games and Economic Behavior*, 214–228; Llorente-Saguer and Zultan (fn 10).
130 Klemperer (fn 12).
131 Anders Lunander "Procurement Bidding in First-Price and Second-Price, Sealed-Bid Auctions Within the Common-Value Paradigm" (2002), 19, *Computational Economics*, 227.
132 Klemperer (fn 12), 12.
133 Ibid.
134 Salant (fn 8), 47–48.
135 William Vickrey "Counterspeculation, Auctions and Competitive Sealed Tenders" (1961), 16, *Journal of Finance*, 8–37; William Vickrey "Auctions and Bidding Games" in *Recent Advances in Game Theory: Papers Delivered at a Meeting of the Princeton University Conference* (Princeton University Press, 1962), 15–29.
136 Tilman Börgers and Eric van Damme "Auction Theory for Auction Design" in Maarten Janssen (ed) *Auctioning Public Assets: Analysis and Alternatives* (Cambridge University Press, 2004), 42.
137 Ibid.

it at all. Since the first-price auction is well established in public procurement bidding, there must be serious reasons for switching from a first-price auction to a second-price auction, as such a switch requires resources. Yet, the auction theory literature has shown that there is very little gain from replacing first-price auctions with second-price auctions, as the latter is only beneficial in terms of expected procurement cost when there are very few bidders or high dispersion of bidders' signals.[138] Since the public procurer expects a large number of potential bidders with small dispersion of their signals, there is no reason to implement the second-price auction procedure in governmental procurement bidding.[139] Additionally, from the perspective of collusion deterrence, a first-price auction is preferable to a second-price auction, when collusion is a major concern.[140] As it has been proved, a second-price auction allows a bidding ring to suppress all competition among ring members and capture the entire collusive gain. For these reasons, I am not delving further into this auction format and I believe that it is justifiably outside the current public procurement rules' scope.

2.5 Collusion: A Challenge of Designing an Optimal Auction

After explaining why auction design can be used as a yardstick by public entities to assess the risk of collusion in procurement procedures, it is now time to address collusion itself, a design problem that typically arises in auctions. The designers of public tenders can draw interesting lessons from auction theory (a) by understanding how auctioneers design their auctions to minimize or deter collusion and (b) by designing auctions to deter collusion may impact other goals set by the tendering authorities. While no single auction may be suitable for all industries or commodities, well-designed auction provides the best outcome for the minimizing or deterring collusion.[141] As Motta aptly states "it is better to try to create an environment that discourages collusion in the first place than trying to prove unlawful behaviour afterwards".[142]

Collusion is a serious problem in many auction markets, as it reduces competition and therefore the revenue obtained by the auctioneer.[143] Before identifying principles of good collusion prevention in auction design with the help of auction literature, two parameters need clarification. First, when designing a mechanism to combat collusion, the auctioneer may inadvertently sacrifice revenue or auction efficiency.[144] For this reason, many suggestions discussed below to minimize collusion in auction design will be balanced against other valuable qualities of the

138 Anders Lunander (fn 132), 230, 243–244.
139 ibid, 243–244.
140 Marshall and Marx (fn 83), 401–402.
141 Kendler (fn 9), 169.
142 Massimo Motta *Competition Policy: Theory and Practice* (Cambridge University Press, 2004).
143 Hong Wang and Hong-min Chen (fn 11), 31.
144 Timothy Salmon (fn 20), 127.

auction in the concluding remarks of this chapter.[145] The second parameter is that different auction formats serve different purposes, with some being more efficient in procurement contexts than others. Therefore, many suggestions in this chapter about auction methods that reduce collusion will also be balanced against this consideration.

One of the most basic proposals in auction literature to address collusion is to prefer the sealed bid design over ascending auctions, when designers are particularly concerned about collusion.[146] As explained earlier, ascending auctions are more susceptible to collusion, compared to sealed bid auctions, which eliminate the ability of bidders to retaliate against other bidders within the auction for not complying with a collusive split.[147] In the realm of public procurement, however, e-auctions are increasingly popular, as they simplify contract publication, increase efficiency and enhance transparency in the procurement process. Moreover, they offer advantages in terms of transaction costs and administrative burden. Therefore, suggesting the complete replacement of e-auctions with sealed bid auctions whenever bid rigging is a concern would be unreasonable.

Thus, alternative suggestions can be made, such as adopting the Anglo-Dutch hybrid auction,[148] which combines both the ascending and sealed-bid formats.[149] This auction begins as an ascending auction and switches to a final sealed bid round when all but two bidders have dropped out.[150] The switchover point is unknown to prevent bidders from engaging in parking behaviour.[151] In the final sealed bid round the two remaining bidders must submit final sealed bids that are not lower than the current asking price.[152] The winner pays their bid. The benefit of this auction design is that its second phase makes collusion more difficult by making the exchange of information and the explicit or tacit co-ordination among bidders more

145 Ibid.

146 Hong Wang and Hong-min Chen (fn 11), 62; Robinson (fn 50), 141–145.

147 Ibid, 115. See also Lawrence M. Ausubel and Jesse A. Schwartz "The Ascending Auction Paradox" (1999) <https://pdfs.semanticscholar.org/93f2/3466c138b557223cf6c4dd4a26dd5e34fec1.pdf?_ga=2.161674872.597724635.1541881262-1783031146.1541881262> accessed on January 10, 2025 and Richard Engelbrecht-Wiggans and Charles M. Kahn "Low-Revenue Equilibria in Simultaneous Ascending-Bid Auctions" (2005), 51(3), *Management Science*, 508–518. These papers paint a dismal picture of ascending auctions, as according to them, in an ascending auction the collusive strategy is the only strategy that proves to be a subgame perfect Nash equilibrium.

148 Brazil is a classic example of hybrid design of the bidding process in electricity auctions.

149 This auction format was firstly proposed by Paul Klemperer. See Paul Klemperer "Auctions with Almost Common Values: The 'Wallet Game' and its Applications" (1998), 42, *European Economic Review*, 759–769; Paul Klemperer "What Really Matters in Auction Design" (2002), 16(1), *Journal of Economic Perspectives*, 169–190.

150 Dan Levin and Lixin Ye "Hybrid Auctions Revisited" (2008), 99(3), *Economics Letters*, 592.

151 Parking refers to bidding on licences or objects that do not genuinely interest bidders, but the latter bid on them in order to draw attention away from the licences or objects they are really interested in. See Salmon (fn 20), 124.

152 Levin and Ye (fn 151), 592.

challenging.[153] It also eliminates the ability of bidders to punish strategies in case of any deviation from the collusive scheme, thus destroying any collusive equilibrium.[154] The advantage of the Anglo-Dutch hybrid auction over the ascending auction in preventing opportunities for collusion, is crucial in the domain of public procurements, where the risk of collusive behaviour is high. E-auctions, which are essentially ascending auctions, are commonly used in negotiated and restricted public procurement procedures, where only a few bidders hold a significant share of the supply.[155] Therefore, the Anglo-Dutch hybrid auction could be a good alternative to e-auctions, which are increasingly used in public procurement.

The Amsterdam second-price auction could also be an alternative solution in order to reduce collusion in ascending auctions. This hybrid auction has two phases; in the first phase, the auctioneer can raise the price successively until all but two bidders have dropped out.[156] In the second phase, the bottom price is set as the bid of the third-highest bidder who dropped out in the first phase and the remaining bidders submit sealed bids that must be at least as high as the bottom price.[157] The highest bidder wins and pays the second-highest sealed bid.[158] Both bidders in the second phase receive a premium equal to the difference between the lowest sealed bid and the bottom price.[159] The second-price Amsterdam auction is more appealing to weaker bidders encouraging them to compete aggressively to receive a premium and set a higher reserve price for stronger bidders in the second stage.[160] The aggressive bidding of weaker bidders prompts stronger bidders to bid more aggressively as well.[161] Therefore, with more entries and rigid competition among bidders the Amsterdam auction is less susceptible to collusion.[162]Another reason collusion is less likely in second-price Amsterdam auctions is that members of a

153 International Renewable Energy Agency (IRENA) and Clean Energy Ministerial (CEM) "Renewable Energy Auctions: A Guide to Design" (2015) <www.irena.org/-/media/Files/IRENA/Agency/Publication/2015/IRENA_RE_Auctions_Guide_2015_5_winner_selection.pdf?la=en&hash=F45C1A24BD68F9AF3F52A264AF6C7B7E11940177> accessed on January 12, 2025, 16.

154 Salmon (fn 20), 115; International Renewable Energy Agency (IRENA) and Clean Energy Ministerial (CEM), (fn 154), 16–17.

155 PwC, London Economics and Ecorys for the European Commission (fn 58), 25.

156 Jacob K. Goeree and Theo Offerman "The Amsterdam Auction" (2004) 72 *Econometrica*, 283; Audrey Hu, Theo Offerman and Sander Onderstal "Fighting Collusion in Auctions: An Experimental Investigation" (2011), 29, *International Journal of Industrial Organization*, 85; McAfee, Williams and Hendricks (fn 44), 518.

157 Ibid.

158 Ibid.

159 Ibid.

160 Goeree and Offerman (fn 157), 284; Dejan Trifunovic and Bojan Ristic, *Optimality of English and First-Price Auction in Serbian Privatisation* Conference: From Global Crisis to Economic Growth. Which Way to Take? Belgrade, Faculty of Economics, September 20–22, 2012 <www.researchgate.net/publication/316473330_OPTIMALITY_OF_ENGLISH_AND_FISRT-PRICE_AUCTION_IN_SERBIAN_PRIVATISATION> accessed on January 12, 2025.

161 Trifunovic and Ristic (fn 161), 5.

162 Goeree and Offerman (fn 157), 302; Hu, Offerman and Onderstal (fn 157), 85.

bidding ring have a strong incentive to deviate from their collusive agreement to receive the premium offered in the second phase of this auction format.[163]

As already demonstrated in the case of the second-price Amsterdam auction, premium auctions make collusion less attractive. This is because they encourage bidders outside of the cartel to compete for the premium and members of the cartel to cheat in order to obtain the premium.[164] This is especially beneficial for small and medium enterprises, as it gives them a fair chance of winning auctions against stronger competitors. The auction literature also suggests offering bidding credits to smaller bidders to help them compete against larger firms and discourage collusion in auction rules.[165] Bidding credits are "percentage discounts on the final payment given to qualifying bidders".[166] This practice has been successful in auctions held by the United States Federal Communications Commission ("FCC"), where bidders qualifying for these credits have won many licences. Yet, it is important to be cautious with this pro-competitive measure, as there is a risk of "shell" companies being used as fronts for larger companies rather than truly small and medium enterprises.[167] Setting the credits at an appropriate level requires a careful study of how small and medium enterprises are disadvantaged in credit markets and how much inefficiency the auctioneer is willing to accept in the original allocation to increase competition.[168]

The second basic proposal of the auction literature to combat collusion is to increase the number of bidders relative to the number of items being auctioned. This includes including bidders whose interests overlap or involve large complementarities across items.[169] With more bidders, competition becomes the primary driver until the values of enough bidders have been surpassed, leaving only a few bidders remaining.[170] With fewer bidders, it is easier for them to signal collusive outcomes, interpret these signals correctly and come to quick agreements.[171] However, as the number of bidders increases, it becomes more challenging for them to find amicable splits and reach agreements without using side payments.[172]

163 Trifunovic and Ristic (fn 161), 6.

164 Hu, Offerman and Onderstal (fn 157), 85; Milgrom (fn 114); Trifunovic and Ristic (fn 161), 6.

165 Timothy Salmon (fn 20), 118.

166 Timothy C. Salmon "Spectrum Auctions by the United States Federal Communications Commission" in M.C.W. Janssen *Auctions and Beauty Contests: A Policy Perspective* (Cambridge University Press, 2004), 109.

167 Ibid, 109.

168 Ibid, 110.

169 Large complementarities tend to hinder collusion because they give each bidder a strong incentive to buy multiple synergies rather than just one. On the contrary, it is more likely for bidders with preferences that are diverse in terms of the items they are mainly interested in and possess a low degree of complementarity across items to end up colluding. Hong Wang and Hong-min Chen (fn 11), 57; Salmon (fn 167), 114, 117, 127.

170 Salmon (fn 167), 114.

171 Ibid.

172 Sandro Brusco and Giuseppe Lopomo "Collusion via Signalling in Simultaneous Ascending Bid Auctions with Heterogeneous Objects, with and without Complementarities" (2002), 69(2), *The Review of Economic Studies*, 407–436; Antony M. Kwasnica and Katerina Sherstyuk "Collusion

Side payments increase the risk of prosecution by Contracting Authorities, making it more likely for collusion to be detected.[173] In cases where the auctioneer acts as a buyer, such as in public procurements, and offers multiple contracts for sale, side payments are not necessary to achieve efficiency gains. Even without side payments, cartel agreements can still result in nearly maximum expected payoffs per contract.[174] This is because with a large number of contracts for sale, the ranking of contracts based on each bid rigger's cost becomes more precise and determines the position in the joint distribution more accurately, leading to more accurate estimations of bidder costs.[175] Therefore, an effective strategy to combat collusion should combine the increased number of bidders with the sufficiently small number of contracts offered for sale.

Whenever there is suspicion of collusion in a market, it is preferable for the auction designer to offer a project as a single contract rather than splitting the market into many small contracts and holding many auctions.[176] Additionally, it should be emphasized that it is not only the number of participating bidders that matters, but also the type of bidders included in an auction. Specifically, it has been shown that the inclusion of new players in the auction who were not bidders initially and possess a common value signal may facilitate collusion, as this inclusion allows for pooling more information about the common value[177] of the auctioned object.[178] Since information symmetry facilitates the form and feasibility of bid rigging, there is a need for an auction designer to ensure common value uncertainty, in order to cause the breakdown of the cartel.[179]

In the same vein, the auction literature has repeatedly emphasized the necessity for auction designers to carefully decide how much information to reveal to bidders during each round of the auction. As Stigler observed in his classic article on collusion "collusion is always more effective when the market is more transparent".[180] While it is beneficial for an auctioneer to provide information about the auctioned object to reduce the winner's curse issues and informational asymmetries among

via Signalling in Multiple Object Auctions with Complementarities: An Experimental Test" (2002) <https://pdfs.semanticscholar.org/9417/75cd81f58097e3f45883299d2fc6819634eb.pdf?_ga=2.66081262.1511037327.1541978821-1783031146.1541881262> accessed on January 11, 2025.

173 Martin Pesendorfer "A Study of Collusion in First-Price Auctions" (2000), 67, *Review of Economic Studies*, 387.

174 Ibid, 384. The model used was a first-price procurement auction in which a buyer simultaneously offered a number of contracts for sale. Bidder costs for the contracts were known privately and the buyer imposed a fixed reserve price.

175 Ibid, 385.

176 Ibid, 406; Kovacic, Marshall, Raiff and Marx (fn 103), 406.

177 "In a common value auction, the value of the item up for auction is the same for all bidders, but that value is unknown to the bidders before the auction. Prior to bidding, bidders receive different private signals about the true value of the object". See Hendricks, McAfee and Williams (fn 44), 499.

178 Gyula Seres "Auction Cartels and the Absence of Efficient Communication" (2017), 52, *International Journal of Industrial Organization*, 303–305.

179 Ibid, 283.

180 George Stigler "A Theory of Oligopoly" (1964), 72, *Journal of Political Economy*, 44–61; See also Seres (fn 179), 312.

bidders that may cause duplicative expenditures, this is not the case when it comes to information about the bidders and their bids, especially in a collusive market.[181] The literature on repeated auctions shows that bidders do not need direct and illegal communication, such as side payments, in order to implement efficient bid rotation schemes, if the information on the bids, such as the prices or the identities of the losing bidders is public, as they can easily propose and enforce a division of the auctioned items.[182]

If the auctioneer discloses the identity of the winner and the price paid at the auction, the operation of a bidding ring will be more efficient and less risky for it to be detected.[183] Moreover, if an auctioneer in a first-price sealed-bid auction discloses the amounts of the bids of all the bidders, it is easier for a bidding ring to police the bids of its members.[184] On the other hand, concerted practices in first-price or second-price sealed-bid auctions, which are held sequentially over time cannot achieve first-best collusive profits when bids are private information, but only profits which are substantially smaller than the ones in an efficient bidding ring.[185] The non-disclosure of bids urges bidders to communicate in order to get the full gains from the collusive scheme, which is illegal and makes a bidding ring easier to detect.[186] Hence, a strategic auctioneer discloses information that makes a competitive process easier but conceals information that is apt to favour collusion.[187]

Another auction rule that discourages bidders from colluding is that the auctioneer may impose a reserve price, meaning the lowest price at which the auctioned object will be sold.[188] In procurement auctions, it has been proved that "if the buyer cannot or does not credibly impose a reserve price, or simply has a large value relative to the sellers' costs, then collusion likely can be sustained for a wide range of discount factors".[189] For this reason, "even mildly sophisticated reserve price selection can dramatically shrink the set of discount factors for which collusion is sustainable", as it may have a significant effect on the profitability of the collusive

181 Wang and Hong-min Chen (fn 11), 38; Gyula Seres "Collusion Mechanisms in Auctions with Private and Common Values" <https://editorialexpress.com/cgi-bin/conference/download.cgi?db_name=EWM2014&paper_id=182> accessed on December 17, 2024, 2.

182 Hedricks, McAfee and Williams (fn 44), 507–509; Cramton (fn 75), 754.

183 Kovacic, Marshall, Raiff and Marx (fn 103), 402.

184 Ibid; Hong Wong and Hong-min Chen (fn 11), 38.

185 Hedricks, McAfee and Williams (fn 44), 507.

186 Ibid, 507; Skrzypacz and Hopenhayn (fn 107), 153–169.

187 Cramton (fn 75), 751; Hendricks, McAfee and Williams (fn 44), 509.

188 Daniel A. Graham and Robert C. Marshall "Collusive Bidder Behavior at Single-Object Second-Price and English Auctions"(1987), 95(6), *Journal of Political Economy*, 1217–1239; Peter Cramton and Jesse A. Schwartz "Collusive Bidding: Lessons from the FCC Spectrum Auctions" (2000), 17(3), *Journal of Regulatory Economics*, 229–252; Paul Klemperer "What Really Matters in Auction Design" (2002), 16(1), *Journal of Economic Perspectives*, 169–190; Hu, Offerman and Onderstal (fn 157), 84.

189 Charles J. Thomas "Using Reserve Prices to Deter Collusion in Procurement Competition" (2005), 53(3), *The Journal of Industrial Economics*, 303.

scheme and the severity of the punishment for any deviation of bid riggers from the collusive scheme.[190] For instance, a well-chosen reserve price may induce the deviation of a cartel member from the collusive scheme, if it ensures the cartel member that the short-term gain from this deviation will be large relative to the per-period loss from rival firms' retaliatory measures to that deviation.[191] In the same vein, a deterrent reserve price strategy may cause difficulties even for a strong cartel.[192] Furthermore, setting a reserve price is like fixing the minimum revenue for the auctioneer who may reduce the harm from any collusive splits agreed early in the auction, as this is somehow a compensation for the lack of competition between bidders.[193]

According to Graham and Marshall, the ideal way to respond to the formation of a bidding ring is to set a reserve price that increases as the number of bidders in the bidding ring increases.[194] In this way, each bid rigger's collusive gain decreases as the reserve price increases.[195] A reserve price more aggressive than what would be used, if bidders were not suspected of collusion may be a good strategic option for an auctioneer.[196]Nevertheless, such a measure must always be used with great care because sometimes reserve prices are set too high, which may disincentivize potential bidders from entering the auction and submitting a bid.[197] As previously explained, the smaller the number of bidders, the more likely collusion will occur.

Another proposal to deter collusion in auctions is to hold auctions at irregular and longer intervals for relatively large items, such as packages of separate items.[198] This strategic option by the auctioneer would increase the costs for bid riggers to create and maintain their ring, while any gains from defection would be larger than collusive gains.[199] "Package" bidding is also a possibility under the current Directive on public procurement, as contracting authorities may award contracts combining several or all lots if they reserve the possibility to do so and indicate the lots or groups of lots that may be combined in the contract notice or invitation to confirm interest.[200] Hence, large suppliers in public procurement have the opportunity to bid for large sets of contracts if they have positive complementarities. However, in cases involving significant complementarities between public contracts divided into lots or licences in auctions, there is always a risk of collusion

190 Ibid, 301, 302.
191 Ibid, 303.
192 A deterrent reserve price strategy is to set the lowest reserve price for which the public buyer's expected profit versus static Nash equilibrium price-setting, using that reserve price, is equal to the public buyer's expected profit versus collusive price-setting, using the optimal reserve price versus collusive price-setting. See Thomas (fn 190), 312–313, 323.
193 Salmon (fn 20), 92; Hong Wong and Hong-min Chen (fn 11), 38.
194 Graham and Marshall (fn 189), 1217–1239; Hendricks, McAfee and Williams (fn 44), 504.
195 Ibid.
196 Kovacic, Marshall, Raiff and Marx (fn 103), 401.
197 Salmon (fn 20), 92.
198 Hendricks, McAfee and Williams (fn 44), 518.
199 Ibid.
200 Article 46, para. 3 of 2014/24/EU Directive.

as demand reduction strategy may be an equilibrium that brings colluding bidders larger surplus.[201]

In order to address collusive behaviour, auction literature suggests adopting a combinatorial auction design. This design allows bidders to place a single bid that is "all or nothing" on combinations or packages of items.[202] By doing so, the demand reduction strategy will no longer be an equilibrium, as "the winner determination will be performed by finding the set of mutually exclusive bids that yield the highest revenue".[203] While combinatorial bidding can eliminate the aforementioned collusive equilibrium, it may also result in lower revenue for the auctioneer or contracting authority. For this reason, if the auctioneer or public buyer is most concerned about collusion, they must accept the lower revenue as a consequence.

A final proposal to prevent collusion in auctions is to retain all available information from the auction for an extended period and make this bid data publicly available after the auction. This will help facilitate the prosecution of collusion by public enforcement authorities and/or private litigants.[204] Not only winning bids, but also losing bids may contain relevant information for inferring collusion.[205] This is particularly true in the case of a bidding ring that is not all-inclusive, where the bids of ring members may be sequential and very close to one another, indicating the existence of a bidding ring and the identity of its members.[206] For this reason, it is advisable to record and document the announcement of the auction or procurement, the entities invited to bid, the entities that actually submitted bids, the losing bids and all discussions and conversations that occur during an auction or procurement process.[207]

201 Imagine a situation in which there are two bidders bidding on two lots. Bidder B wants either the first or the second lot but not both while bidder A wants both of them. If bidder A were to reduce his demand to only a single item, then he could end up with a surplus much larger than the one he would get if he won both items at a price lower than his value, because by adopting the demand reduction strategy both bidders can just bid a minimum price on alternate items. For more details see Salmon "Spectrum Auctions by the United States Federal Communications Commission" (fn 167), 167.

202 For instance, if bidder A submitted a package bid on lots 1 and 2 of 20 pounds, in order for bidder B to submit a bid for lot 1 that would win, it would have to be at least 21 pounds. So, if bidder A wants to win both lots, he has to submit a package bid for both which is higher than bidder B would be willing to bid for either item individually. For more see Timothy Salmon "Preventing Collusion between Firms in Auctions" (fn 20), 100–101; Timothy Salmon "Spectrum Auctions by the United States Federal Communications Commission" (fn 167), 165.

203 Salmon (fn 20), 100.

204 Kovacic, Marshall, Raiff and Marx (fn 103), 402–403; Hong Wong and Hong-min Chen (fn 11), 39.

205 Ibid; Marshall and Marx (fn 83), 31.

206 Kovacic, Marshall, Raiff and Marx (fn 103), 402.

207 Ibid.

2.6 Concluding Remarks

This chapter has explained incentives in auctions, by utilizing game theory, a tool employed in auction theory. It also discussed the most common types of auctions, which have a significant impact on the incentives to rig a bid. The chapter also addressed the importance of good auction design, which complements competition law enforcement in deterring bidder collusion. It identified circumstances under which collusive outcomes may be Nash equilibria in common types of auctions, similar to current public procurement processes. Finally, the chapter made recommendations regarding the issue of collusion in public procurements, based on how auction theory addresses the challenge of collusion in auctions. Nevertheless, some recommendations from auction theory may not be entirely realistic in the context of public procurement and contracting authorities may resist them for the reasons explained below.

First, it was recommended that in cases where collusion is a concern, hybrid auctions, such as the Anglo-Dutch hybrid auction or the Amsterdam second-price auction, should be preferred over e-auctions. Despite the benefits of the Anglo-Dutch hybrid auction in combatting collusion, it should be carefully considered alongside its drawbacks. One drawback is that participants may underbid to win the auction leading to economic losses.[208] Another downside is the potential complexity of the auction format, which could hinder the simplification of procedures.[209] Implementing the second phase of the Anglo-Dutch hybrid auction, especially when multiple products are auctioned, can be challenging for procurers.[210] Additionally, in auctions with a large number of diverse items and markets, it may be unclear how to properly implement an unknown switchover point,[211] as this design is more effective in auctions with a small number of similar items.[212] Therefore, procurers should receive additional education and training on the implementation and communication of the Anglo-Dutch hybrid auction. Moreover, contracting authorities should only use this auction format for small and standardized purchases of works and goods that do not involve multiple units to avoid implementation difficulties.

Regarding the second-price Amsterdam auctions, it should be noted that they are not efficient in all procurement contexts. For instance, a series of experiments showed that in symmetric environments the second-price Amsterdam auction performs particularly poorly, resulting in low revenue.[213] In contrast, in asymmetric situations where auctions or public tenders attract a diverse group of bidders, it

208 International Renewable Energy Agency (IRENA) and Clean Energy Ministerial (CEM) (fn 154), 15.

209 International Renewable Energy Agency (IRENA) and Clean Energy Ministerial (CEM) (fn 154), 17.

210 Luiz Maurer and Luiz Barroso *Electricity Auctions: An Overview of Efficient Practices* (World Bank, Washington DC, 2011), 19.

211 Theoretically this sounds like an easy fix, but when an auction has many market areas, it would be difficult for procurers to determine how to implement any such variable switchover rule.

212 Salmon (fn 20), 124.

213 Goeree and Offerman (fn 157), 293.

yields significantly higher revenues than standard formats and only slightly less revenue than the optimal auction.[214] Due to these differences and the need to raise taxes to finance the second-price Amsterdam auction which awards *ex-post* premiums to bidders in the second phase of the process, this hybrid auction is typically controversial and hard to justify.[215]

The second recommendation was that a good collusion fighting technique combines an increased number of *a priori* bidders with a sufficiently small number of contracts offered for sale, whenever there is suspicion of collusion in a market. In practice, however, auctions with an increased number of bidders take a long time and impose relatively high costs on auctioneers/ contracting authorities. Besides, it is not always realistic to have more bidders available, especially when there is complexity in what is being procured and many possible variants that need to be considered. Contracts in the area of commodities also receive the lowest number of bids.[216] What is more, the increased number of bidders presupposes that the procedural aspects are not cumbersome to the extent of discouraging bidders and that direct calls for competition are used, which are correlated with a higher number of bids.[217]

The third recommendation was to hold auctions at irregular and longer intervals and for relatively large items, like packages of separate items. It was also suggested that common value uncertainty should be ensured by avoiding the inclusion of new players in the auction, who were not bidders *a priori* and possess a common value signal. Yet, this recommendation from auction theory does not quite align with the tendency for procurers to divide contracts into lots to make tenders more accessible to SMEs.[218] Similarly, under the reform of public procurement legislation achieved by the enactment of the current Directives, one of the objectives is to broaden the potential supplier base of contracting authorities, by making it easier for new players in the market to participate in public tenders.[219] Thus, the strong involvement of SMEs in public procurement is promoted as a counterbalance to incumbent firms which are the dominant market players.

In the same vein, it was argued that first-price auctions are preferable to second-price actions, when collusion is a major concern. The latter may be used only where there are very few bidders or a high dispersion of bidders' signals. It was

214 Ibid.

215 Arno Schmöller "Bidding Behaviour, Seller Strategies, and the Utilization of Information in Auctions for Complex Goods", Munich Dissertations in Economics, University of Munich, Department of Economics (2010) <https://edoc.ub.uni-muenchen.de/11175/1/Schmoeller_Arno.pdf> accessed on December 12, 2024, 130.

216 PwC, London Economics and Ecorys for the European Commission (fn 58), 8

217 Ibid, 9, 64.

218 European Commission "EU Public Procurement Reform: Less Bureaucracy, Higher Efficiency" (2016) <https://ec.europa.eu/docsroom/documents/16412/attachments/1/translations/en/renditions/native> accessed on December 13, 2025.

219 SIGMA-OECD "Small and Medium-Sized Enterprises (SMEs) in Public Procurement" (2016) <www.sigmaweb.org/publications/Public-Procurement-Policy-Brief-33-200117.pdf> accessed on December 13, 2025.

also argued that the non-disclosure of bids in descending-bid auctions deters concerted practices and that the philosophical commitment to making auctions and procurement processes as transparent as possible increases the risk of collusion. In the case of public procurement, it could be argued that the European legislator has complied to some extent with the recommendations of auction theory about transparency,[220] but this is only a coincidence, otherwise further measures would be taken in a more systematic way. There is still a high degree of transparency in procurement processes, which has a profound effect on the feasibility of bid rigging. Indicatively, it shall be mentioned that in contract award notices the public buyer announces the number of tenders received with respect to each award, the name and personal information of the successful tender(s), the value of the successful tender(s) or the highest tender and lowest tender taken into consideration for the contract award(s).[221] Moreover, in the case of e-auctions the public buyer shall instantaneously communicate to all tenders at least sufficient information to enable them to ascertain their relative rankings at any moment. Other information regarding other prices or values submitted may also be announced by the public buyer, whenever he thinks it is appropriate, as well as the number of participants in that phase of the auction.

Based on the conclusions drawn from the analysis of bidder collusion in auctions, it is recommended that in contract award notices only the high tender should be published without reference to the tenderer that submitted it and without mentioning the lowest tender. In addition, if collusion is a major concern, the contracting authorities should withhold information during the course of an e-auction that regards the number of bidders, the prices or values submitted, and the current high bid because as explained above, such information may support bid signalling and allow members of a bidding ring to detect deviations from their collusive agreement. Particularly in the case of repeated auctions, any information concerning past bids may be helpful to sustain a certain amount of profitable collusion.[222]

The next recommendation from auction theory is to set an aggressive reserve price if collusion among bidders is suspected. However, in the realm of public procurement, the use of reserve prices can be problematic. This is not only because they must be very competitive to ensure potential bidders are not discouraged, but also because there is no officially approved methodology for calculating them. These factors, combined with the need for thorough market research, make it challenging for procurement officers to set appropriate reserve prices to limit collusion. Another dilemma is whether to reveal the reserve price or not. Some academics argue that reserve prices are susceptible to corruption, as officials have discretion

220 The limited compliance with auction theory mainly refers to e-auctions, regarding which the Directive 2014/24/EU contemplates that in no case may contracting authorities disclose the identities of the tenderers. See Article 35, para. 7 of 2014/24/EU Directive.

221 Annex V, Part D of 2014/24/EU Directive.

222 Hong Wong and Hong-min Chen (fn 11), 39.

over setting them.[223] Therefore, setting reserve prices in public tendering requires additional education and training for procurement officers to handle this task effectively.

After discussing the recommendations from auction theory, it becomes clear that there is no one-size-fits-all solution for public tendering at the EU level. The next step is to outline the legislative background of the current EU procurement regime to analyze its internal logic regarding competition and anticompetitive activities, such as bid rigging. This examination is essential before evaluating the consistency of Directive 2014/24/EU with the goal of preventing and combatting bid rigging in public procurement.

223 Procurement officers may choose reserve prices far higher than competitive prices to ensure higher final prices for their preferred sellers. See Sümeyra Atmaca, Koen Schoors and Elena Podkolzina "Corrupt Reserve Prices" (2018) <https://editorialexpress.com/cgi-bin/conference/download.cgi?db_name=EEAESEM2018&paper_id=2464> accessed on December 13, 2024.

3 The Historical Background of EU Public Procurement Rules and the Role of Competition

3.1 Introduction

Many economic transactions at the interface between the public and private sector are governed by public procurement rules. In the European Union, contracting authorities spend nearly 14% of GDP on public procurement each year, totalling more than €1.9 trillion.[1] Therefore, given the budgetary constraints resulting from the economic crisis, it is essential to ensure that procurement markets remain open across Europe and that public funds are used efficiently.[2] Holding a competition in the public market, where all interested firms have equal opportunity to participate, helps secure the best terms and highest quality goods, works and services at competitive prices. Competition allows public contracts to be awarded to the best tenderer offering the best value for the procuring entity "in line with its commercial and horizontal objectives".[3] However, competition for public contracts is declining continuously, partly due to collusion in procurement markets.[4]

The previous chapter outlined the theoretical framework for preventing bid rigging in procurement situations, emphasizing the importance of competition and collusion in auction theory and design. Policy makers in public procurement can gain valuable insights from auction theory on preventing bid rigging. This chapter retraces the development and key points of EU procurement rules, exploring whether they evolved alongside anti-cartel legislation in Europe or developed

1 European Commission "European Semester Thematic Factsheet-Public Procurement, 2017" <https://policycommons.net/artifacts/2035650/european-semester-thematic-factsheet/2788093/> accessed on December 3, 2024.

2 European Commission "Europe 2020-A Strategy for Smart, Sustainable and Inclusive Growth" <http://eur-lex.europa.eu/legal-content/EN/TXT/PDF/?uri=CELEX:52010DC2020&from=EN> accessed December 3, 2024;

3 Sue Arrowsmith "Understanding the Purpose of the EU's Procurement Directives: The Limited Role of the EU Regime and Some Proposals for Reform" in KONKURRENSVERKET – Swedish Competition Authority (ed) *The Cost of Different Goals of Public Procurement* (Konkurrensverket, 2012). See also Irena Georgieva *Using Transparency Against Corruption in Public Procurement* (Springer International Publishing AG, 2017), 5.

4 Albert Sanchez-Graells "Competition and Public Procurement" (2018), 9(8), *Journal of European Competition Law & Practice*, 551–559.

DOI: 10.4324/9781003359999-3

independently. It examines if early procurement rules mentioned cartels or bid rigging and whether public procurement was addressed in early EU anti-cartel legislation?

As will be demonstrated, the public procurement regime primarily focuses on regulating the conduct of contracting authorities rather than bidders. Therefore, little consideration has been given to preventing bid rigging, in the design and development of procurement rules, despite the significance of Article 101 TFEU in public procurement, as it governs the behaviour of providers participating in public procurement procedures.[5] It is therefore, valid to assess whether the public procurement regime facilitates bid rigging. Over the years, the procurement regime has incorporated numerous explicit provisions to ensure that public contracts do not impede future competition for government needs.[6] It also acknowledges the negative impact of bid rigging by imposing restrictions on the duration of agreements, prohibiting anticompetitive behaviour and allowing the exclusion of firms that have violated competition law.[7] Additionally, it emphasizes the importance of maintaining fair competition by promoting equal access to public contracts and preventing market restrictions. The broader EU system aims to safeguard competition among companies.[8] It is crucial to determine whether one aspect of EU law enables potential bidders to breach another. From a taxpayer's perspective, it is equally essential to evaluate the extent to which the public procurement regime facilitates bid rigging, as discussed in Chapter 1 of this book.

Therefore, this chapter serves as an introduction to the subsequent analysis, setting the stage for the argument that the safeguards against collusion in tender procedures are inadequate, despite competition being an objective of the procurement Directives and the recognition of the negative consequences of bid rigging within the procurement regime. Building on this foundation, the following chapters will further assert that the current public procurement rules should be scrutinized from the perspective of bid rigging lens, with relevant recommendations being proposed.

5 Sue Arrowsmith *The Law of Public and Utilities Procurement Volume 1: Regulation in the EU and UK* (Sweet & Maxwell, 2014), para. 4–117; Office of Fair Trading (OFT) "Assessing the Impact of Public Sector Procurement on Competition" <https://webarchive.nationalarchives.gov.uk/20140402182823/http://www.oft.gov.uk/shared_oft/reports/comp_policy/oft742a.pdf> accessed on December 3, 2024; Stefan Weishaar *Cartels, Competition and Public Procurement: Law and Economic Approaches to Bid Rigging* (Edward Elgar, 2013); John Temple Lang "Subsidiarity and Public Purchasing: Who should Apply Competition Law to Collusive Tendering and How Should They Do It?" (1998), 4(1), EPL, 55; Peter Trepte *Regulating Procurement: Understanding the Ends and Means of Public Procurement Regulation* (OUP, 2004), 115–118; Gian Luigi Albano, Paolo Buccirossi, Giancarlo Spagnolo and Matteo Zanza "Preventing collusion in procurement" in N. Dimitri, G. Piga and G. Spagnolo (eds) *Handbook of Procurement* (CUP, 2006), 347; Robert D. Anderson and William Kovacic "Competition Policy and International Trade Liberalisation: Essential Complements to Ensure Good Performance in Public Procurement Markets" (2009), 18, *PPLR*, 67.

6 Arrowsmith (fn 5), para. 4–107.

7 Indicatively see Articles 32(2), 33(7) and 55(8) of Directive 2004/18/EC.

8 There are substantive provisions in the Treaty on the Functioning of the European Union (TFEU) that seek to protect competition. Indicatively, see Articles 101, 102, 103(2), 106, 108, 109 and 119(1) TFEU.

In view of the above, the chapter is structured as follows. Sections 3.2–3.6 provide a historical, as well as critical, overview of the European public procurement regime in relation to the overall legislative developments in the EU competition regime. The procurement directives under investigation are categorized into five generations, based on their date of enactment and the evolution stages of the single/internal market in Europe. Moreover, these sections explain how political parameters, such as the case of the "eurosclerosis" period from the mid-1960s to the mid-1980s influenced government policy. Subsequently, the rationale shifted to prioritizing the liberalization and integration of financial markets to help Member States of the European Economic Community overcome stagnation and reboot economic progress in Europe. Section 3.7 concludes the chapter by summarizing key issues and findings and introducing the next chapters.

3.2 The Development of Procurement Directives

3.2.1 The First Generation of Public Procurement Regime

In 1957 the Treaty of Rome established the European Community (EC), marking the first time that non-discrimination and freedom of movement for goods and services of Member States were considered. This meant that trade could occur across internal EC borders, as if it were domestic trade.[9] Initially, this goal was achieved by eliminating visible trade barriers, such as customs duties on manufactured goods, and implementing a common external tariff.[10] The next step was to address non-tariff barriers, such as national public purchasing regimes and technical standards that favoured domestic products.[11]

Before the provisions of the Rome Treaty, official restrictions between European governments after the two world wars hindered trade.[12] Cartel agreements had also emerged from the exchange of manufactured goods among industrial leaders such as France, Germany, Great Britain and the Low Countries (the Netherlands).[13] Cartelization was a significant aspect of the German economy and society before the First World War, driven by rapid industrialization, heavy industry concentration and state unification.[14] Cartelization was also seen as a beneficial national industrial

9 Stephen Martin and Keith Hartley "Public Procurement in the European Union: Issues and Policies" (1997), 2, *Public Procurement Law Review*, 92.

10 ibid.

11 Andrew Cox, The Single Market Rules and the Enforcement Regime After 1992 (Earlsgate Press, 1993), 32.

12 These restrictions used to take the form of tariffs, quotas and licences.

13 Kalypso Nicolaidis and Raymond Vernon "Competition Policy and Trade Policy in the European Community" in Edward Graham (ed) *Competition Policy in a Changing World Economy* (Institute for International Economics, Washington, 1997), 274.

14 Christopher Harding and Julian Joshua "A Narrative of Cartel Regulation in Europe, 1970 to the Present Time" in C. Harding and J. Joshua (eds) *Regulating Cartels in Europe* (Oxford University Press, 2010), 65–69.

policy before the Second World War, allowing for a rationalized approach to goods production during economic crises.[15]

The ratification of the Treaty of Rome and the European Coal and Steel Treaty marked a crucial moment in the spread of antitrust legislation and the establishment of an administrative-based anti-cartel regime.[16] Competition policy became essential for the European Common Market's success, leading to the regulation of cartels as a key aspect of this new competition policy and law framework.[17] Hence, Article 85(1) of the Treaty of Rome was introduced, prohibiting "all agreements between undertakings, decision by associations of undertakings and concerted practices which may affect trade between Member States and which have as their object or effect the prevention, restriction or distortion of competition within the common market". Practices by bidding participants were subsequently covered under Article 85(1), as long as they met the provision's legal requirements.

Against this background, the Council of Ministers adopted the General Programme on the abolition of restrictions on freedom of establishment and the General Programme for the abolition of restrictions on freedom to provide services in 1962. However, neither General Programmes addressed the deterrence of cartel activity in public procurement, as no provisions were included on this issue. This lack of focus on cartels may be attributed to the fact that the first cartel decision in the *Quinine*[18] case was not made until 1969. Prior to this, the European Commission had not pursued cartel cases, which may have given the impression that cartels in public markets were not a significant form of anticompetitive activity that could lead to price increases and reduced competition.

At the time the General Programmes were implemented in public procurement, Regulation 17/62 was also introduced in the context of EU competition law. This regulation was the first procedural regulation to enforce Articles 85 and 86 of the Treaty of Rome, during a time when competition law was still in its early stages.[19] The procurement market was not addressed in Regulation 17/62, indicating that it was developed independently of the procurement regimes of that time.

15 Bruce Wardhaugh *Cartels, Markets and Crime: A Normative Justification for the Criminalisation of Economic Collusion* (Cambridge University Press, 2014), 169. For instance, the International Steel Cartel has been one of the most powerful cartels of pre-war Europe. See Nicolaidis and Vernon (fn 13), 275.

16 Ibid; Mark Jephcott *Law of Cartels* (Jordan Publishing, 2011, Bristol), 7.

17 Harding and Joshua (fn 14), 110.

18 Case 45/69, Boehringer Mannheim v Commission (Quinine cartel) [1970] ECR 769; this cartel was relevant to the division of national markets as well as to price-fixing and quotas for the export of quinine and quinidine, which are used particularly in the manufacture of medicines for the treatment of malaria and certain cardiac illnesses.

19 Matthew Gream "An Overview of EC Regulation 1/2003 as the New Implementing Regulation for the Rules on Competition Laid Down in Articles 81 and 82 of the EC Treaty" <http://matthewgream.net/Professional/IntellectualProperty/overview_ec-reg-1-2003_paper.pdf> accessed on December 14, 2024.

To implement the General Programmes, the Council of Ministers adopted several Liberalization Directives, including Directives 64/427/EEC, 64/428/EEC, 64/429/EEC and 70/32/EEC.

3.2.1.1 The Early Directives

The general Liberalisation Directives 64/427/EEC, 64/428/EEC and 64/429/EEC liberalized the market in specific industries by abolishing discriminatory treatment based on nationality for establishment and service provision.[20] These directives, following the General Programmes, did not address the need to prohibit cartel agreements in public markets to maintain a competitive economy.

After a few years, the Commission introduced Directive 66/683/EEC, which eliminated all differences between the treatment of national products and that of imported products.[21] Directive 70/32/EEC extended the rules of Directive 66/683/EEC by prohibiting any quantitative restrictions on public procurement, reiterating in this way the need for Member States to abolish discriminatory rules in their national procurement systems.[22] This Directive was the first to regulate the supply of goods applying to both domestic good and imported goods from third countries that freely circulated in the common market.[23]

From the overview of the Liberalisation Directives above, it is clear that the of market access and completion focused on eliminating discrimination and barriers to entry into the European Community's common market, moving away from national preferential purchasing. Anti-cartel provisions were not yet considered essential to complete the internal market.

The Liberalisation Directives were followed by comprehensive secondary legislation known as the Coordination Directives 71/304/EEC, 71/305/EEC and 77/62/EEC. Unlike the earlier Liberalisation Directives, these directives aimed to coordinate procurement award procedures in each member state.[24] These Directives included a *de minimis* rule, meaning they only applied to procurement contracts above a certain financial value.[25] The purpose of introducing a value threshold was

20 Directive 64/427/EEC of July 1964, OJ 117, 23/07/1964, 1863–1870; Directive 64/428/EEC of July 7, 1964, OJ 117, 23/07/1964, 1871–1880; Directive 64/429/EEC of 7 July 1964, OJ 117, 23/07/1964, 1880–1892; Peter Trepte *Public Procurement in the EU-A Practitioner's Guide*, 2007, 28–29.

21 Directive 66/683/EEC of 7 November 1966, OJ 220, 30/11/1966, 3748–3750.

22 Directive 70/32/EEC of 17 December 1969, OJ L 13, 19/01/1970, 1–3; M. E. Comba "Variations in the Scope of the New EU Public Procurement Directives of 2014: Efficiency in Public Spending and a Major Role of the Approximation of Laws" in F. Lichère, R. Caranta and S. Treumer (eds) *Modernising Public Procurement: The New Directive* (Djøf Publishing 2014), 32; Christopher Bovis *EU Public Procurement Law* (Elgar European Law, 2007), 18.

23 Recital of Directive 70/32/EEC (fn 22); Christopher Bovis (fn 22), 18.

24 Directive 71/304/EEC of 26 July 1971 OJ L 185/1, 16/08/71, 678–681; Directive 71/305/EEC of 26 July 1971 OJ L 185/5, 25/08/71, 682–692; Directive 77/62EEC of 21 December 1976, OJ L 13/1, 15/01/77.

25 Article 7, para. 1 of Directive 71/305/EEC (fn 24); Article 5, para. 1(a) of Directive 77/62/EEC (fn 24).

to identify contracts of Community interest. Contracts below the *de minimis* limit were considered to lack a Community dimension and were not relevant to the internal market, as they would not impact trade and competition between EU Member States. Regulating low-value contracts without the *de minimis* limit would have negative consequences, such as increased transaction costs for both the contracting authority and tenderers.[26] Moreover, requiring competitive public tendering for all minor activities would not benefit the internal market, but it would delay contract awards and hinder cross-border services.[27]

It is important to note that even low-value contracts fall under European Community law. While some contracts may not be covered by Community directives on public procurement, contracting authorities must still adhere to fundamental Treaty rules and general principles, such as non-discrimination, equality of treatment, transparency and proportionality.[28] This means that some degree of advertising is necessary to ensure fair competition and review of procurement procedures.[29] Transparency requirements dictate that advertising must occur before a public contract is awarded to allow undertakings from others member states access to relevant information.[30] The same rules apply to below-threshold contracts according to the CJEU.[31]

Directive 71/305/EEC was the first directive to explicitly refer to the development of competition in the field of public contracts by requiring the advertisement of contract awards throughout the European Community. In Recital 9, it was contemplated that "contract notices drawn up by the authorities of Member States awarding contracts should be advertised throughout the Community".[32] This directive aimed to coordinate legislative and administrative provisions among Member States to promote the free movement of services and approximate these provisions.[33]

26 Erik Pijnacker Hordijk and Maarten Meulenbelt "A Bridge Too Far: Why the European Commission's Attempts to Construct an Obligation to Tender Outside the Scope of the Public Procurement Directives Should Be Dismissed" (2005), 3, *PPLR*, 123–130.

27 Ibid; David McGowan "Clarity at Last? Low Value Contracts and Transparency Obligations" (2007), 4, *PPLR*, 274–283.

28 C-275/98, Unitron Scandinavia and 3-S [1999], ECR I-8291, para. 31; C-324/98 Telaustria and Telefonadress [2000], ECR I-10745 paras 60–62; Vestergaard [2001] ECR I-9505, para. 19–20; C-264/03, Commission v French Republic [2005] ECR I-8831, para. 32.

29 C-324/98 Telaustria and Telefonadress [2000], ECR I-10745 para. 62; C-450/03 Parking Brixen GmbH v Gemeinde Brixen and Stadtwerke Brixen AG [2005] ECR I-8585, para. 49; Case C-410/04 Anav v Comune di Bari (2006) ECR I-3303, para. 21.

30 C-231/03 Consorzio Aziende Metano (Coname) v Comune di Cingia de' Botti [2005] ECR I-7287, para. 21.

31 C-6/05 Medipac-Kazantzidis v Venizeleio-Pananeio [2007] ECR I-4557; [2007]3 CMLR, 16, para. 33; C-507/03 Commission v Ireland [2007] ECR I-97777; [2008], 1 CMLR, 34, paras 30–32; C-412/04 Commission v Italian Republic [2008] ECR I-619, para. 66.

32 Recital 9 of Directive 71/305/EEC (fn 24).

33 Articles 57(2), 66 and 100 of the Treaty Establishing the European Economic Community; Comba (fn 22), 31.

The direct mention of competition in Directive 71/305/EEC indicated that it was a key objective of the Directive. However, the Directive had limitations as it did not introduce new tendering procedures or replace existing national practices with Community rules.[34] Moreover, Recital 3 of the Directive did not include competition as a principle for coordinating national procedures for awarding public works contracts. There was also lack of focus on addressing cartels in public procurement, as bid rigging was not identified as a concern. The European legislator merely provided for the prohibition of technical specifications that had a discriminatory effect, the adequate advertising of contracts, the fixing of objective criteria for participation and the introduction of a procedure of joint supervision to ensure the observation of these principles. The deliberate failure to refer to the principle of competition in order to base the co-ordination of national procedures for the award of public works contracts favours the argument that competition was not still seen as an objective but rather as a means of ensuring the aforementioned principles that governed the Directive 71/305/EEC.

Having almost the same provisions as the Works Directive 71/305/EEC, Directive 77/62/EEC came into force in order to regulate the public supplies contracts. However it did not apply to public supplies contracts by public utilities, due to their different legal status. Another reason for the non-application of the Directive to the utilities industries was that the rising unemployment marking the 1970s in Europe rendered inappropriate to restructure at that period of time the major employing sectors, such as the utilities industries.[35] Competition and cartels in public procurement still were not considered to be major issues, though in the meantime bid-rigging practices emerged in public procurement markets, taking the form of "cover bids", submitted by tenderers in order to create the impression of genuine competition among the participants in the procedure.[36] Moreover, back to April 1972 the European Commission had issued its First Report on Competition policy, emphasizing in this way that competition policy was an important means for achieving the aims of the Treaties establishing the Communities and that it must be directed towards the creation and proper operation of the common market.[37] No special mention was made in this report of the practices that jeopardized competition in public procurement, even if other prohibited horizontal agreements among enterprises, such as price-fixing, quota and market-sharing agreements, were thoroughly examined.

34 Bovis (fn 22), 21.

35 Stephen Martin, Keith Hartley and Andrew Cox "Public Procurement Directives in the European Union: A Study of Local Authority Purchasing" (1999), 77(2), *Public Administration*, 393.

36 See Decision 73/109/EEC of 2 February 1973 (IV/26 918– European sugar industry) [1973] OJ L 140/17.

37 European Commission "First Report on Competition Policy – Annexed to the Fifth General Report on the Activities of the Communities" <https://publications.europa.eu/en/publication-detail/-/publication/418817dc-c69b-42b1-a787-013fd545017d/language-en> accessed on December 15, 2024.

The Supplies Directive 77/62/EEC aimed to establish equal conditions of competition to prevent discrimination in public contracts.[38] It sought to ensure transparency to prevent discriminatory behaviour and ensure the prohibition of any restrictions on the free movement of goods in respect of public supplies. Like the Works Directive 71/305/EEC, it set common advertising rules for Member States to promote transparency and non-discrimination. It also contemplated the prohibition of technical specifications capable of discrimination.[39] Both directives viewed competition as a means to achieve transparency and prevent discrimination. Moreover, both directives prohibited the splitting of contracts into smaller lots s to keep them below threshold levels.[40]

After the European Community approved the General Agreement on Tariffs and Trade (GATT) and the Agreement on Government Procurement (GPA) by the World Trade Organization (WTO), Directive 77/62/EEC was replaced by Directive 80/767/EEC. The aim of the latter was to apply to products imported from outside the European Community. The purpose of Directive 80/767/EEC was "to establish an international framework of balanced rights and obligations with respect to government procurement with a view to achieving liberalisation and expansion of world trade".[41] The conditions outlined in this Directive were considered more liberal than those of Directive 77/62/EEC. Some procedural obligations within the procurement framework were changed to ensure they were as favourable to tenderers as those under the GPA.[42] An example of these changes is the requirement for Member States to report each time they chose not to use the open tendering procedure.[43] Also the minimum time limit for receiving tenders was extended.[44] Both amendments were closely tied to the European Community's efforts to create a competitive public procurement market.

3.3 The Second Generation of Public Procurement Regime

3.3.1 Political Background – The Thrust of European Efforts

Due to the numerous legal instruments in place, a complex body of Community rules was created, which made it difficult for them to be incorporated into the law of the Member States.[45] Furthermore, statistics demonstrated a "minimal application of the Directives" across the entire Community and "the tendency of the authorities

38 Recital 2 of Directive 77/62EEC of 21 December 1976, OJ L 13/1, 15/01/77.

39 Recital 4 and Article 9 of Directive 77/62/EEC of 21 December 1976 [1977] OJ L 13/1; Bovis (fn 22), 20.

40 Martin, Hartley and Cox (fn 35), 394.

41 Recital 1 of Directive 80/767/EEC of 22 July 1980 [1980] OJ L 215/1.

42 Ibid, Recital 5; Amy Ludlow, *Privatising Public Prisons – Labour Law and the Public Procurement Process* (Hart Publishing, 2017), 112.

43 Article 5 of Directive 80/767/EEC (fn 41); Ludlow ibid.

44 Article 6 of Directive 80/767/EEC (fn 41); Ludlow ibid.

45 Communication by the Commission to the Council, COM (84), 717, Vol. 1984/0259, 7.

concerned to keep their purchases and contracts within their own country".[46] These disappointing conclusions gave rise to serious cause for concern and discussions with Member States in order to "stimulate a wider opening up of tendering for public contracts" by improving the Directives.[47] Otherwise, European companies would be unable to compete against more efficient market players from the United States and Japan.[48]

Meanwhile, from the mid-1960s to the mid-1980s, growth in the EU Member States started falling behind that of international competitors, due to the high unemployment and economic stagnation experienced in Europe at that time. After the initial burst of prosperity that emerged from the founding of European Community, an era of "eurosclerosis" began.[49] This term, which alludes to the medical term "sclerosis", was first used by the German economist Herbert Giersch in his paper "Eurosclerosis", written in October 1985.[50] Through this term, Giersch attempted to "diagnose" Europe's disease first manifested in the mid-1960s, when essential members of the European Economic Community had become "too rigid to permit a quick and painless adjustment", in view of European integration.[51] An illustrative example was France, then under the presidency of Charles de Gaulle. French President de Gaulle had a state-centric approach and "a very definite view of France's place in the world, as a nation-state not beholden to any other entity (be it a European organisation or a transatlantic multilateral security organisation)".[52]

The budgetary powers granted to the European Parliament, along with its enhanced position in the EEC following the provision for its direct election managed to shift the loyalty of Member States to some extent to the European level.[53] Another determining factor was the role played by the European Court of Justice (ECJ) in European integration through its landmark rulings that established a clear supranational legal framework and protected the internal market from any attempts to undermine[54] After the period of "eurosclerosis", government policy changed. The rationale was that all Member States could benefit if they completed the internal market to overcome stagnation and reinvigorate the economic progress in Europe. To address this situation, proposals were made to increase the Directives' coverage and enhance the political commitment to an open procurement market. For example, suggestions included lowering the financial contractual value threshold below

46 White Paper on Completing the Internal Market, COM (85), 310, 14 June 1985, para. 83.

47 Ibid, 85.

48 Martin, Hartley and Cox (fn 35), 393; Cox (fn 11), 6–58.

49 Anil Awesti "The Myth of Eurosclerosis: European Integration in the 1970s" (2009), 353–354(3), L' Europe en Formation, 39, <https://shs.cairn.info/revue-l-europe-en-formation-2009-3-page-39?lang=fr&ref=doi> accessed on January 6, 2025

50 Herbert Giersch "Eurosclerosis" (1985), Kiel Discussion Papers 112, Kiel Institute for the World Economy (ifW) <https://www.econstor.eu/bitstream/10419/48070/1/025296167.pdf> accessed on January 6, 2025.

51 Ibid.

52 Anil Awesti (fn 49), 4.

53 ibid, 6–9, 17.

54 ibid, 14–16.

which Directives do not apply and extending the scope of Directives to include the utilities industries.[55] The Cecchini report[56] in 1988 and particularly the Atkins Report[57] – The Costs of Non-Europe in Public Sector Procurement – played a key role in this shift.

The Cecchini report identified "healthy competition" as one of the benefits resulting from completing the internal market.[58] It explained that the gains from competitive integration in product markets and the increased competition pressures would be significant. It also emphasized that opening public markets to competition would be a major effect of the internal market programme.[59] Government procurement would see substantial price reductions from the competitive integration of product markets.[60] The report also stressed the need to effectively enforce competition policy to prevent barriers from being replaced by other anticompetitive practices.[61]

The Atkins report highlighted that opening up public procurement should be a priority, along with liberalizing and integrating of financial markets to achieve a well-functioning internal market in Europe. Cox and Furlong pointed out that if there were rules governing the demand side of the market to ensure transparency and liberalization in awarding public contracts to non-national suppliers, three effects would occur in European public and utility supply markets in the short, medium and long terms. First, in the short term the costs of public buyers would decrease, as they would begin to purchase goods, works and/or services from the cheapest supplier rather than from the preferred local or national supplier. This effect was called "the static price effect". Second, in the medium-term competition would increase, as the low prices from foreign companies would urge preferred and protected national suppliers to increase their productivity, invest in new technology or lower their prices so as not to exit from the market. This effect was called "the competition effect". Third, in the long term the increased competition would cause the fundamental restructuring of key industrial sectors dominated by public purchasing, as the least efficient firms would be urged to exit the market and large players would be encouraged to compete and provide significant economies of scale. This effect was called "the restructuring effect".[62]

55 Ludlow (fn 42), 113.
56 Commission of the European Communities "Europe 1992, The Overall Challenge" SEC (88), 524 final, Brussels April 13, 1988, 4–5.
57 W.S. Atkins Management Consultants (Epsom), *The Costs of Non-Europe in Public Sector Procurement* (E.C. Luxembourg, 1988).
58 Commission of the European Communities (fn 56), 1.
59 Ibid, 4, 5, 6.
60 Ibid, 4.
61 Ibid, 7.
62 Andrew Cox and Paul Furlong "Cross-Border Trade and Contract Awards – The Intellectual Myopia at the Heart of the EU Procurement Rules" (1997), 3(1), *European Journal of Purchasing and Supply Management*, 10.

Similarly, the 1985 White Paper[63] underlined that community-wide liberalization of public procurement was essential for the future of the Community economy. It suggested amendments for improving the Directives, such as reviewing the current threshold levels and prioritizing a system of prior information, publication of intentions to use single tender procedures and publication of contract awards.[64] For the utilities sector, it recommended expanding Directives' coverage to include energy, transport, water and telecommunications in the case of supply contracts.[65]

Within the overarching scheme of launching the internal market, the Single European Act (SEA) was adopted, with the aim of completing the internal market. With the enactment of the SEA, the legal basis for the Procurement Directives became the new Article 100a, according to which "the Council shall adopt the measures for the approximation of the provisions laid down by law, regulation or administrative action in Member States which have as their object the establishment and functioning of the internal market".[66]

3.3.2 Public Supply and Public Works Directives

Despite the White Paper and the changes made to the Internal Market provisions of the Treaty introduced by the 1986 Single European Act, a research programme launched by the Commission showed that national procurement practices were "almost hermetically-sealed", as only 0.14% of Gross Domestic Product (GDP) was awarded in public procurement contracts to firms from other Member States of the Community.[67]

In light of the shortcomings of the first-generation Directives and as part of the drive towards achieving a single market by 1992, Directive 88/295/EEC was adopted in the sector of public supplies along with the Directive 89/440/EEC in the sector of public works. Both Directives aimed to extend the scope of first-generation Directives and increase the transparency of procedures and practices for the award of public contracts by setting stricter transparency requirements and developing conditions for effective Community-wide competition.[68]

Directive 88/295/EEC identified the necessity to develop conditions for effective competition for public supply contracts, while Directive 89/440/EC ascertained the need to eliminate practices that restrict competition. Nonetheless, no special mention was made of bid rigging and its anticompetitive outcome. Both Directives improved advertising rules, particularly through Prior Information Notices (PINs)

63 White Paper from the Commission to the European Council (fn 46).

64 Paolo Cecchini *The European Challenge 1992: The Benefits of a Single Market* (Wildwood House, London, 1988); see also White Paper from the Commission to the European Council (fn 46), para. 85.

65 White Paper from the Commission to the European Council (fn 46), para. 86.

66 Article 100(a) of the Single European Act.

67 Ludlow (fn 42), 113.

68 Recital 5 and 7 of the Directive 88/295/EEC of 22 March 1988 [1988] OJ L 127/1; Recital 6 and 14 of the Directive 89/440/EEC of 18 July 1989 [1989] OJ L 210.

to inform contracting authorities' purchasing programmes for the entire budgetary year.[69] Moreover, they required that conditions under which contracts were awarded be made public, offering debriefing to unsuccessful tenderers and publishing contract award notices to attract more suppliers in the Community.[70]

Both Directives also adopted a negotiated procedure for certain contracts previously exempt altogether and in exceptional cases to "limit the use of the single-tender procedure".[71] Directive 89/440 established that open or restricted procedures should be the norm, while Directive 88/295 had a more open default tendering process and allowed the restricted procedure only in justified cases, such as maintaining a balance between contract value and procedural costs or when the specific nature of the products required it.[72]

Another significant amendment in the public works sector was the expansion to include consortia of tenderers for the first time.[73] Directive 89/440 recognized the growing importance of concession contracts in the public sector economy and incorporated rules on the publicity of concession contracts as part of its regime expansion.[74] This adjustment reflected the evolving nature of public procurement, with the market on more responsibilities that were traditionally handled by the State. Additionally, Directive 89/440 raised the threshold level for works contracts to accommodate the increasing costs of construction work and the interest of SMEs in bidding for medium-sized contracts.[75]

All the aforementioned amendments were made not only to align the European public procurement regime with the GATT Agreement on Government Procurement (AGP) but also to facilitate stricter enforcement of the prohibition of restrictions on the free movement of goods, which formed the basis of these Directives, as stated in the pre-amble of Directive 88/295/EEC.[76] The primary objective of these Directives was to introduce transparency to support free movement and to closely monitor compliance with the prohibition of restrictions on freedom of establishment and freedom to provide services, with competition being a key tool to achieve this goal. Despite these efforts, there were no specific provisions in place to detect or deter collusion in public tendering, indicating a somewhat lenient attitude of the European legislator towards this risk. This leniency is highlighted by the fact that the European Commission was actively prosecuting major cartels during the decade between the mid-1970s and mid-1980s.[77]

69 Recital 15 of the Directive 88/295/EEC (fn 68); Recital 19 of the Directive 89/440/EEC (fn 68).
70 Recital 5 of the Directive 88/295/EEC (fn 68); Recital 19 of the Directive 89/440/EEC (fn 68).
71 Recital 12 of the Directive 88/295/EEC (fn 68); Recital 15 of the Directive 89/440/EEC (fn 68).
72 Article 7 of the Directive 88/295/EEC (fn 68).
73 Recital 20 of the Directive 89/440/EEC (fn 68).
74 Recital 11 of the Directive 89/440/EEC (fn 68).
75 Recital 13 of the Directive 89/440/EEC (fn 68).
76 Recital 5 of the Directive 88/295/EEC (fn 68).
77 Harding and Joshua (fn 14), 130–131.

3.3.3 Utilities Directives

In the utilities sector, Directive 88/301/EEC was issued regarding competition in the markets for telecommunications terminal equipment, while Directive 90/531/EEC focused on the procurement procedures of entities operating in the water, energy, transport and telecommunications sectors. Prior to this, contracts awarded in these sectors were excluded from Directive 71/305/EEC, which coordinates procedures for public works contracts, and Directive 77/62/EEC, which coordinates procedures for public supply contracts. The exclusion was due to the varying legal statuses of entities providing such services.[78] Nonetheless, it was determined that identification of these entities should not be based solely on legal status to promote market opening and fair application of procurement rules in the utilities sector.[79]

Despite similarities with Supplies and Works Directives, Directives 88/301/EEC and 90/531/EEC had key differences. Contracting entities were allowed to choose their preferred procedures for contract awards, as long as competition was fair.[80] The provisions of Directive 90/531/EEC were influenced by ongoing Uruguay GATT negotiations,[81] aiming to align with the GATT Agreement and expand procurement practices to previously excluded sectors, promoting to EC-wide or intra-community competition.[82] The Directive also addressed products from third countries, allowing their inclusion if lawfully circulated in at least one member state.[83] Nevertheless, if products from third countries exceeded 50% of the tender value, the contracting authority could reject the tender.[84] Additionally, if the price of tenders with European products did not exceed 3% of tenders with third-country products, authorities could prefer European products.[85]

3.3.4 Remedies Directives

All the efforts made so far to open up public procurement to the European Community would be meaningless without enforcement measures to guarantee transparency and non-discrimination.[86] The first EEC substantive public procurement directives enacted in 1971 included enforcement measures to protect public budgetary interests, but lacked provisions for safeguarding individual rights. The Commission had limited resources and could not oversee thousands of procurement procedures in the then 28 Member States.[87] Hence, it seems that "the existing

78 Recital 8 of the Directive 90/531/EEC of 17 September 1990 [1990] OJ L297/1.
79 Ibid, Recital 9.
80 Ibid, Article 15, para.1.
81 Bovis (fn 22), 29–30.
82 Ibid, 33.
83 ibid, 33–34.
84 Article 29, para. 2 of the Directive 90/531/EEC (fn 78).
85 Ibid, Article 29, para. 3.
86 Recital 3 of the Directive 89/665/EEC of 21 December 1989 [1989] OJ L 395.
87 Ibid; See also Kris Wauters "Public Procurement Review Bodies" in M. Trybus, R.Caranta and G. Edelstam (eds) *EU Public Contract Law* (Bruylant 2013), supra at 1, 353 ff.

arrangements at both national and Community levels for ensuring their application were not always adequate to ensure compliance with the relevant Community provisions, particularly at a stage when infringements could be corrected".[88]

Directive 89/665/EEC was introduced to ensure the effective implementation of public procurement directives and the prompt correction of any infringements during the awarding of public supply and public works contracts.[89] The opening-up of public procurement to the European Community competition necessitated the establishment of efficient and swift remedies for law violations in the public procurement domain. Without such measures, Community undertakings would be discouraged from submitting tenders in Member States unable to rectify the situation.[90]

3.4 The Third Generation of Public Procurement Regime

3.4.1 Public Services Directives

For the first time in the legal history of Europe, services in public markets were open to intra-community competition and liberalization, with the enactment of the first directive on services, that is, Directive 92/50/EEC which undertook the coordination of procedures for the award of public services contracts. In its preamble, it is contemplated that one of the Directive's objectives is to develop effective competition by eliminating practices that restrict competition in general and participating in contracts by other Member States' nationals in particular.[91] Having the same principles as the other Directives, such as advertising rules for public contracts and prohibition of any discrimination that may arise due to technical specifications, Directive 92/50/EEC had still some differences. The most indicative of these differences was that it introduced to a new award procedure, the design contest which "enabled the contracting authority to acquire a plan or design selected by a jury after being put out to competition with or without the award of prizes".[92] This was mainly in the fields of area planning, town planning, architecture and civil engineering or data processing.

3.4.2 Public Supply and Public Works Directives

In order to bring uniformity to the regulatory landscape regarding public procurement, Directives 93/36/EEC and 93/37/EEC were enacted to consolidate numerous directives. Directive 93/36/EEC focused on coordinating procedures for awarding public supply contracts while Directive 93/37/EEC focused on coordinating procedures for awarding public works contracts. Both directives emphasized the

88 Recital 2 of the Directive 89/665/EEC (fn 86).
89 Ibid, Recital 8.
90 Ibid, Recital 3–4.
91 Recital 20 of the Directive 92/50/EEC of 18 June 1992 [1992] OJ L 209/1.
92 Article 1(g) of the Directive 92/50/EEC (fn 92).

importance of ensuring genuine competition by inviting an adequate number of candidates to tender in a restricted procedure.[93] It could be said that the European legislator indirectly acknowledged that a small number of tenderers could lead to collusive behaviour in public procurement and thus sought to prevent this by requiring sufficient competition. The provisions of these directives aimed to promote the freedom of movement of goods and establishment, eliminate restrictions and coordinate national procedures for awarding public supply and works contracts.[94]

The amendments made in these directives were not surprising, as they were based on common sense and aimed to ensure compliance with related directives.[95] Transparency played a key role as a monitoring tool, with effective competition being directly cited as a reason for certain provisions related to advertising contract notices.[96] Hence, provisions regarding information and advertising were expanded compared to transparency provisions, and Directive 93/37/EEC introduced "a special, mitigated regime" for the award of concession contracts.[97]

3.4.3 Utilities Directives – Enforcement Directives

In the sector of utilities, Directive 92/13/EEC was adopted which apart from coordinating the legal instruments that regulate the procurement procedures of entities operating in the water, energy, transport and telecommunication sectors, it also addressed the issue of enforcement mechanisms and introduced a slightly more flexible regime for public utilities.

3.5 The Fourth Generation of Public Procurement Regime

3.5.1 Public Services, Supplies and Works Directive

Ten years after the enactment of the 1993 Directives, the European Union introduced a new set of rules in order to coordinate the procedures for the award of public works contracts, public supply contracts and public service contracts. Apart from the classical objectives dated back to 1970s (i.e. freedom of movement of goods, of establishment as well as freedom to provide services), the new Directive 2004/18/EC pursued the simplification, clarification and modernization of the existing directives.[98] The 2004/18/EC Directive also referred to the opening-up of public procurement to competition as one of its objectives and clearly stated that its coordinating provisions should be interpreted in accordance with this rule as well as with the freedom of movement of goods, freedom of establishment, freedom

93 Article 19, para. 2 of the Directive 93/36/EEC of 14 June 1993 [1993] OJ L199/1; Article 22, para. 2 of the Directive 93/37/EEC of 14 June 1993 [1993] OJ L 199/55.

94 Recital 5 of the Directive 93/36/EEC (fn 94); Recital 2 of the Directive 93/37/EEC (fn 94).

95 Christian Servenay "The New Provisions of Supplies Directive 93/36" (1994), 5, *PPLR*, 169.

96 Recital 14 of the Directive 93/36/EEC (fn 94); Recital 10 of the Directive 93/37/EEC (fn 94).

97 Bovis (fn 22), 45; Trepte (fn 20), 36–37; Recital 14 of Directive 93/36/ (fn 94); Recital 10 and Article 3 of the Directive 93/37/EEC (fn 94).

98 Rhodri Williams "The New Procurement Directives of the European Union" (2004), 4, *PPLR*, 153.

to provide services and the principles of equal treatment, non-discrimination and transparency.[99] The contracts had to be awarded on the basis of objective criteria which ensured compliance with the above principles that guaranteed the assessment of tenders in conditions of effective competition.[100] What is more, for the first time in the history of public procurement directives, there was direct reference to the distortion of competition in relation to private tenderers. A number of provisions were made in order to ensure that new procurement procedures, such as the competitive dialogue,[101] and new procurement techniques, such as framework agreements,[102] dynamic purchasing systems[103] and electronic auctions,[104] did not hinder, limit or distort competition. This was the first kind of constraint in the design and implementation of procurement procedures and techniques with a view to secure undistorted competition, away from collusive behaviour and practices. The Public Sector Directive also included express requirement to limit the duration of framework agreements.[105]

3.5.2 Utilities Directive

In the sector of utilities, the Directive 2004/17/EC was enacted which regulated procurement of entities in water, energy, transport and postal services. In the same line as Directive 2004/18/EC, it was adopted under the EU's internal market provisions and it contemplated that contracts had to be awarded on the basis of objective criteria that ensured compliance with the principles of transparency, non-discrimination and equal treatment and that guaranteed the assessment of tenders in conditions of effective competition.[106]

3.5.3 Enforcement Directive

In December 2007, Directive 2007/66/EC was adopted to improve the effectiveness of review procedures regarding the award of public contracts. This new Directive made progress in combatting illegal direct awards of public contracts. First, it established a "standstill" period of at least ten days between contract award and contract conclusion. Second, it introduced the new sanction of ineffectiveness of the public contract in case (i) of awarding a contract without prior publication of a contract notice in the Official Journal of the European Union, (ii) of failure to apply the standstill clause and (iii) if there have been particular infringements of the substantive Directives in large contracts awarded based on framework agreements and

99 Recital 2 of the Directive 2004/18/EC of 31 March 2004 [2004] OJ L, 134.
100 Ibid, Recital 46.
101 Ibid, Article 29, para. 6.
102 Ibid, Article 32, para. 2.
103 Ibid, Article 33, para. 7.
104 Ibid, Article 55, para. 8.
105 Ibid, Article 32, para. 2.
106 Ibid, Recital 55.

dynamic purchasing systems.[107] Ineffectiveness was found to be the most effective way to restore competition and to create new business opportunities for economic operators who were illegally deprived of their chance to compete.[108]

3.6 The Fifth Generation of Public Procurement Regime

In March 2010, the European Commission launched Europe 2020 – a strategy for smart, sustainable and inclusive growth,[109] with the aim of boosting the economy of Member States in a post-crisis scenario. In this policy paper the European Commission clearly stated that public procurement policy must ensure the most efficient use of public funds and that procurement markets must be kept open EU-wide. Almost a year later, the Green Paper on the modernization of EU public procurement policy "Towards a more efficient European Procurement Market"[110] was published, reiterating the objective of the Europe 2020 Strategy. In this context, three Directive proposals were presented by the European Commission on December 20, 2011.[111] They were approved in the first reading by the European Parliament as well as by the Council and the Directives were eventually published on March 28, 2014.

In general, it is said that the new package of EU Directives on Public Procurement is "within a logic of continuity with Directives 2004/17/EC and 2004/18/EC"[112] and for the first time the European legislator took a step forward and consolidated the significant role of competition in the EU procurement regime in Article 18(1) of the Directive 2014/24/EU.[113] Specifically, Article 18(1) of the Directive 2014/24/EU contemplates that:

> The design of the procurement shall not be made with the intention of excluding it from the scope of this Directive or of artificially narrowing competition. Competition shall be considered to be artificially narrowed where the design of the procurement is made with the intention of unduly favouring or disadvantaging certain economic operators.

107 Article 2d of the Directive 2007/66/EC of 11 December 2007[2007] OJ L 335/31.

108 Ibid, Recital 14.

109 COM (2010) 2020 final, Brussels, 3.3.2010 <https://eur-lex.europa.eu/legal-content/EN/TXT/PDF/?uri=CELEX:52010DC2020&from=EN> accessed on December 14, 2024.

110 COM (2011) 15 final, Brussels, 27.1.2011 <https://eur-lex.europa.eu/legal-content/EN/TXT/PDF/?uri=CELEX:52011DC0015&from=EN> accessed December 14, 2024.

111 COM (2011) 895 final, Brussels, 20.12.2011; COM (2011) 896 final, Brussels, 20.12.2011; COM (2011) 897 final, Brussels, 20.12.2011.

112 Rui Medeiros "The New Directive 2014/24/EU on Public Procurement: A First Overview" In L. V. Tavares, R. Medeiros and D. Coelho (eds) *The new Directive 2014/24/EU on Public Procurement.*

113 Directive 2014/24/EU of the European Parliament and of the Council of 26 February 2014 on public procurement and repealing Directive 2004/18/EC [2014] OJ L 94/65.

The explicit consideration of competition as an objective and as "a manifestation of the equal treatment principle"[114] in the 2014/24/EU Directive demonstrates an increased recognition of the role of competition in public procurement. Along the same lines, the European legislator introduced new provisions that empower Member States to preserve competition in the public market and prevent of distortions in the dynamic competitive processes.[115] One of the most notable provisions is the debarment mechanism, which allows contracting authorities to exclude firms that have violated competition law[116] as well as the authority of contracting authorities to restrict the number of lots that can be awarded to a single bidder.[117]

3.7 Concluding Remarks

This chapter outlines the legislative background of the current European procurement regime, tracing the critical junctures of EU procurement rules and exploring whether they were influenced by anti-cartel legislation in Europe or developed independently. The analysis reveals that the public procurement regime primarily focuses on regulating the conduct of contracting authorities rather than bidders. As a result, little consideration has been given to preventing bid rigging, in the design and development of procurement rules. However, Article 101 TFEU plays a crucial role in public procurement, as it can render public contracts unlawful due to anticompetitive agreements between providers. The founding fathers of European public procurement did not initially prioritize competition as an objective *per se* of the Directives but rather as a means to uphold the principles of non-discrimination and transparency to prevent restrictions on the free movement of goods. Over time, this perspective has shifted, especially since the Cecchini report in 1988, which emphasized the importance of effectively enforcing competition policy in government procurement.

The significant changes came with the enactment of the 2004/18/EC Directive. For the first time in the history of public procurement directives, there were numerous provisions directly addressing the distortion of competition in relation to private tenderers. These provisions aimed to ensure that public contracts are not structured in a manner that hinders future competition for government requirements. Specifically, the new procurement procedures, such as the competitive dialogue, and the new procurement techniques introduced by this Directive, such as framework agreements, dynamic purchasing systems and electronic auctions, should not impede, restrict or distort competition. This marked the first instance of constraints being placed on the design and implementation of procurement procedures and

114 Arrowsmith (fn 5), para. 7.28.

115 Ibid, para. 4.107; Recitals (31), (49), (61) and (96). See also Article 24 about conflicts of interest, Article 30 about the competitive dialogue, Article 40 about the preliminary market consultations, Article 41 about the prior involvement of candidates or tenderers and Article 57 about the exclusion grounds.

116 Article 57, para. 4(d) of the Directive 2014/24/EU.

117 Article 46 of the Directive 2014/24/EU.

techniques to secure undistorted competition, moving away from collusive behaviour and practices.

Building on this, the European legislator further emphasized the role of competition in the EU public procurement by consolidating it in Article 18(1) of the subsequent Directive 2014/24/EU. The legislator also acknowledged the undesirability of bid rigging by incorporating provisions that promote the prevention of distortions in dynamic competitive processes, such as excluding firms that have violated competition law and allowing contracting authorities to limit the number of lots awarded to a single bidder. Yet, the prevention of bid rigging was not systematically and consistently integrated into the policy design of the current EU public procurement Directives contrary to auction theory and design principles. Additionally, EU procurement rules did not align with EU anti-cartel legislation and vice versa. Consequently, it is argued that the current public procurement rules do not adequately address anticompetitive practices such as bid rigging, despite their detrimental impact on public spending. While Directive 2014/24/EU acknowledged bid rigging as a significant problem, it did not go far enough in ensuring that public procurement rules are designed and implemented in a manner that avoids distorting competition.

Based on the findings above, it is apparent that there is need for more dialogue between institutional actors at the EU level. However, the fact that public procurement and competition belong to different policy departments tends to inhibit the achievement of this goal. Public procurement falls within the portfolio of the Directorate-General (DG) for Internal Market, Industry, Entrepreneurship and SMEs, whereas competition falls within the portfolio of the DG for Competition. By that very fact, this means that the policy spheres are distinct; therefore, the institutional priorities of these DGs may not always converge, especially in light of the different interests and values of the officials working for each of them. The variety of Commission activities and policy spheres do not guarantee neat dovetailing and cohesion between the DGs.[118] Taking this weakness into account, the European Commission pursued cooperation with the national competition agencies of the EU Member States through the European Competition Network (ECN).[119] In this way, a consistent and uniform application of EU competition legislation and case law across the EU Member States is guaranteed, while the European Commission, through the ECN, can more easily reach the national procurement bodies and make

118 Damian Chalmers, Gareth Davies and Giorgio Monti *European Union Law – Text and Materials* (Cambridge University Press, 2019), 66. See also Laura Cram "The European Commission as a Multi-Organization: Social Policy and IT Policy in the EU" (1994), 1 (2), *Journal of European Public Policy*, 195; Hussein Kassim, John Peterson, Michael W. Bauer, Sara Connolly, Renaud Dehousse, Liesbet Hooghe and Andrew Thompson *The European Commission of the Twenty First Century* (Oxford University Press, 2013), 115–118.

119 International Competition Network (ICN) "Anti-Cartel Enforcement Manual April 2015 – Chapter on Relationships between Competition Agencies and Public Procurement Bodies" <www.internationalcompetitionnetwork.org/wp-content/uploads/2018/05/CWG_ACEMPublicProcurement.pdf> accessed on December 15, 2024.

them aware of its competition decisions and interpretation of EU competition legislation.[120]

In view of the above discussion and analysis, the next chapters will assess to what extent the provisions of the current Directive 2014/24/EU deter collusion effectively in public tenders or rather facilitate it. In order to make this assessment, each stage of a public procurement process will be separately examined, as contemplated by the Directive 2014/24/EU. It will be investigated whether they are appropriate enough to ensure fair competition for public contracts or rather consolidate – and even aggregate – collusive schemes among public tenderers. As explained in the previous chapter, this assessment will be made using as a benchmark the auction theory literature, in which competition and collusion are considered important.

120 Ibid, 26.

4 Procurement Planning under Directive 2014/24/EU

Are Its Provisions Suitable for Preventing the Development of Bid Rigging?

4.1 Introduction

In the previous chapter, the internal logic of the EU public procurement regime was examined from the time of the Liberalisation Directives to the Fifth Generation of public procurement directives. It was demonstrated that very little thought has been given to preventing bid rigging in the design and development of procurement rules. The prevention of bid rigging was not factored into policy design in a systematic and consistent way, drawing on what we know from economic theory. However, looking at public procurement rules from a bid rigging point of view is necessary, as bid rigging is a very deliberate breach of the law that results in overspending of public funds—taxpayer's money that could otherwise be invested in public services. The significance of this issue is even more apparent when considering that bid rigging leads to higher artificial prices than other anticompetitive activities, such as price fixing and market sharing.[1] Moreover, the scale of the bid rigging problem faced by EU Member States makes this approach necessary. For example, in Germany the Federal Statistics Office reported 297 convictions and 42 suspended prison sentences for bid rigging from 1998 to 2013, whilst the French Competition Authority issued more than 220 decisions for collusion cases in public procurement resulting fines for over 750 different firms.[2] In addition, any shortcomings in the enforcement of Article 101 TFEU not only hinder the achievement of competition goals, such as better allocation of resources, greater economic efficiency, increased innovation and lower prices, but also negatively influence the functioning of the internal market, which relies on a system of undistorted competition.[3]

1 Stephen Davies and Adrian Majumdar *The Development of Targets for Consumer Savings Arising from Competition Policy* (Office of Fair Trading, 2002), 3; see also Marsela Maci, "Bid Rigging in the EU Public-Procurement Markets: Some History and Developments" (2011), 32, *ECLR*, 406.

2 Florian Wagner-von Papp "Compliance and Individual Sanctions in the Enforcement of Competition Law" in Paha (ed), *Competition Law Compliance Programs-An Interdisciplinary Approach* (Springer, 2016), 155; John Moore "Cartels Facing Competition in Public Procurement: An Empirical Analysis", September 2012 <http://chaire-eppp.org/files_chaire/moore_2013_-_cartels_facing_competition.pdf> accessed January 10, 2025.

3 Commission "Impact Assessment Report – Damages Actions for Breach of the EU Antitrust Rules", COM (2013) 404 final <http://ec.europa.eu/competition/antitrust/actionsdamages/impact_assess-

DOI: 10.4324/9781003359999-4

Having already set the current Directive 2014/24/EU in context, the groundwork has been laid for its assessment from a bid rigging perspective. The chapter begins with an assessment of the pre-contractual procurement planning stage. The procurement planning stage, which is the preparation phase of the entire procurement process, is critical in determining the fight against bid rigging in later stages. Furthermore, it is essential in addressing the research question: should public procurers adjust their current procurement strategies to combat anticompetitive practices or not? If so, it is important to identify what legislative or soft law instruments are needed to prevent the development of collusion among economic operators interested in participating in a public tender. When assessing the procurement planning stage from a competition standpoint, this chapter will utilize the benchmark framework developed in Chapter 2, focusing on the conditions that favour collusion according to auction theory.

As previously mentioned, procurement planning is the initial phase of the public procurement process, during which decisions are made regarding which goods or services to purchase and when. Section 4.2 will address the preliminary market consultations (Article 40) as well as the prior involvement of candidates and tenderers in the preparation of the procurement procedure (Article 41). It will explore the scenarios in which the participation of private sector market participants in the contract development and award process could lead to bid rigging in later stages. Section 4.2 will also evaluate how effectively the current Directive has tackled this issue and propose suggestions for improvement.

The next issue, in Section 4.3, concerns the technical specifications (Article 42) and whether the way they are formulated by contracting authorities creates conditions that facilitate bid rigging. It will be demonstrated that this is indeed the case and the chapter will then explore the extent to which the current Directive has addressed this problem.

Section 4.4 will shift focus to the division of contracts into lots. Much of the discussion has centred on the opportunities it provides for SMEs to participate in public contracts competition.[4] Nevertheless, the division of contracts into lots

ment_en.pdf> accessed January 13, 2025, 18.

4 This is implied by the fact that Recital (78) of the 2014/24/EU Directive, after stating that the design of public procurement should be "SME sensitive", goes on immediately to talk about division into lots; see also European Commission by PwC, ICF GHK and Ecorys "SMEs' Access to Public Procurement Markets and Aggregation of Demand in the EU" (2014) <https://op.europa.eu/en/publication-detail/-/publication/c0681db7-e56e-11e5-8a50-01aa75ed71a1> accessed on January 15, 2025; Manuel Zimmermann "Economic Efficiency and the Division of Large Procurement Contracts Into Lots: An Analysis" (2017), 4, *EPPPL*; Veronika Grimm, Riccardo Pacini, Giancarlo Spagnolo and Matteo Zanza "Division in Lots and Competition in Procurement" in Nicola Dimitri, Gustavo Piga and Giancarlo Spagnolo (eds) *Handbook of Procurement* (Cambridge University Press, 2006; Miguel Assis Raimundo "Aiming at the Market You Want: A Critical Analysis of the Duties on Division Into Lots Under Directive 2014/24/EU" (2018), 4, *PPLR*; Ignacio Herrera Anchustegui "Division Into Lots and Demand Aggregation – Extremes Looking For The Correct Balance?" in Grith S. Ølykke and Albert Sanchez-Graells (eds) *Reformation or Deformation of the EU Public Procurement Rules* (Edward Elgar Publishing, 2016).

can also have undesirable effects on competition, if contracting authorities do not adhere to fundamental economic principles each time they implement this measure. Therefore, these principles will be examined, and their practical effectiveness will be assessed. Suggestions will be offered on how the bidding process for lots can be improved to prevent bid rigging. Section 4.5 will serve as the conclusion to the chapter.

4.2 Preliminary Market Consultations and Prior Involvement of Candidates or Tenderers – Analysis of Bid Rigging Issues and Recommendations

As shown in Appendix 1, where Articles 40 and 41 of Directive 2014/24/EU are referenced, the Directive now includes explicit provisions about the ability of contracting authorities to conduct market consultations before tendering. This allows contracting authorities to inform economic operators of their procurement plans and requirements ensuring there are interested suppliers for future procurement processes.[5] The previous public sector Directive 2004/18/EC briefly mentioned the use of "technical dialogue" between the public buyer and market in Recital 8,[6] but the new provision in Directive 2014/24/EU aims to promote innovation in public procurement.[7] However, it is important to note that in certain circumstances not covered by the Directive, market consultations may increase the risk of supplier collusion.

Article 40 of the current Directive does not provide specific instructions on how market consultations with market operators should be carried out. Each contracting authority must decide whether technical dialogue with market operators will be open or closed, through public sessions or private discussions.[8] Some practices that contracting authorities may use for preliminary market consultations include:[9] (a) conducting market sounding exercises through questionnaires or crowd-sourcing,

5 Spyros Panagopoulos "Strategic EU Public Procurement and Small and Medium Size Enterprises" in Christopher Bovis (ed) *Research Handbook on EU Public Procurement Law* (Edward Elgar Publishing 2016), 284–285.

6 Ibid.

7 Bengt-Ale Lundvall "Product Innovation and User-Producer Interaction" < https://vbn.aau.dk/files/7556474/user-producer.pdf> accessed on January 15, 2025; Oana S. Pantilimon Voda "Innovative and Sustainable Procurement: Framework, Constraints and Policies" in Christopher Bovis (ed) *Research Handbook on EU Public Procurement Law* (Edward Elgar Publishing 2016), 219–221.

8 Johanna Sammalmaa "The Application of the EU Foundational Principles in the Preparation Phase of Public Procurement – A Research Plan" (paper presented at the 7th Public Procurement Research Students Conference, University of Nottingham, September 8–9, 2016).

9 Katriina Alhola, Marja Salo, Riina Antikainen and Annukka Berg "Promoting Public Procurement of Sustainable Innovations: Approaches for Effective Market Dialogue" in Khi V. Thai (ed) *Global Public Procurement Theories and Practices* (Springer International Publishing 2017), 70–71; Cabinet Office "Procurement Policy Note-Procurement Supporting Growth: Supporting Material for Departments, Action Note 04/12" (May 9, 2012) <www.gov.uk/government/uploads/system/uploads/attachment_data/file/62097/PPN-Procurement-Supporting-Growth.pdf> accessed on January 15, 2025; Abby Semple "Guidance for Public Authorities on Public Procurement of Innovation" <www

(b) holding product surgery sessions where potential suppliers present solutions, (c) organizing face-to-face meetings with stakeholders, (d) hosting procurement forums for direct communication between procurers and potential suppliers, (e) arranging matchmaking events for information sharing, (f) holding "buyer-supplier" events or industry boot camps (industry days) to discuss best practices and challenges, (g) conducting research projects or pilots, (h) establishing networks of procuring units to share experiences and practices in public procurement and (i) utilizing collaborative platforms or solutions exchange, for co-designing and exchanging solutions in public procurement.

Based on the list above, direct communication channels between procurers and potential suppliers are widespread and common practice in market dialogues. Though there is no empirical survey yet on the most frequent procedure adopted by procurers in preliminary market consultation, it is argued that direct engagement of contracting authorities with economic operators is preferable for complex and innovative projects, or to complement information acquired through questionnaires or web-based portals.[10] Direct engagement saves time and effort, allowing contracting authorities to evaluate budget, cost issues, contract risks and market capacity more accurately.[11] The frequency of direct communication procedures in market analysis is confirmed by OECD's 2015 survey on the implementation of the relevant Recommendation.[12] The survey noted that "respondents may face challenges in reconciling aspects of the pre-tender dialogue with suppliers and *the requirement to reduce the opportunities for bidders to meet*"[13] (emphasis added). Even the European Central Bank, the only European institution with a policy to undertake market consultation before starting the formal procurement procedure, prefers holding informal meetings with both incumbent and potential contractors for preliminary market consultation.[14]

The inclination of contracting authorities for market dialogue procedures that procurers and potential suppliers work together, could be justified by the fact that "useful (market) dialogue is, by definition, an informal rather than a formal process

---

.oneplanetnetwork.org/sites/default/files/from-crm/ppi-platform_guide_new-final_download.pdf> accessed on January 15, 2025.

10 SIGMA "Market Analysis, Preliminary Market Consultations and Prior Involvement of Candidates/Tenderers – Brief 32" (September 2016) <www.sigmaweb.org/publications/Public-Procurement-Policy-Brief-32-200117.pdf> accessed on January 15, 2025.

11 Ibid, 6.

12 OECD (2015), "Draft report to the Council on Implementation of the 2012 Recommendation on Fighting Bid Rigging in Public Procurement" (Note by the Secretariat prepared for the Working Party No. 2 on Co-operation and Enforcement, June 15, 2015).

13 OECD "Fighting Bid Rigging in Public Procurement – Report on Implementing the OECD Recommendation" (2016) <www.oecd.org/en/publications/2016/09/fighting-bid-rigging-in-public-procurement-report-on-implementing-the-oecd-recommendation_5cf813ae.html> accessed January 15, 2025, 13.

14 European Court of Auditors (ECA) "Special Report – The EU Institutions Can Do More to Facilitate Access to Their Public Procurement" <www.eca.europa.eu/Lists/ECADocuments/SR16_17/SR_PROCUREMENT_EN.pdf> accessed on January 15, 2025, 27.

(...) and any organised opportunities for dialogue do not exclude *ad hoc* opportunities for dialogue with the private sector".[15] Considering the contracting authorities' tendency to engage directly with potential suppliers in market dialogue and the absence of clear guidelines in the 2014/24/EU Directive on what contracting authorities should and should not do when dealing directly with economic operators before launching a procurement procedure, it is argued that there are cases where market consultations facilitate bid rigging.

For example, let's consider a contracting authority that issues a consultation announcement to procure innovative supplies with high technical and financial complexity. This is a common practice, as market consultations are essential for complex procurements that involve significant preparation and the acquisition of innovative solutions.[16] Market consultations are also used to determine if a specific product or technology is already available on the market, needs further development or requires customization that has not been previously done.[17] In the case of innovative markets with high specialization and complexity, the barriers to entry are expected to be high, making them vulnerable to collusion. Imagine the contracting authority invites all market operators to live events spread out over three months[18] to discuss the upcoming contract and help map the competitive landscape. Live events and direct contact between procurers and economic operators are common in complex and innovative procurements, such as the one we are discussing. In contrast, simple desk-based market analysis is sufficient for standard and commoditized procurements.[19]

Considering the innovative and highly specialized nature of the market in our scenario, which does not easily attract new entrants, meetings and live events facilitate interaction among incumbent firms. Pre-auction discussions and alliances between firms can lead to bidder cartels or rings forming before the auction begins, as discussed in Chapter 2, but it cannot be faced by using an auction design.[20] Even if we suppose that despite the barriers to enter the market, there are still new firms that eventually express their interest in participating in the technical dialogue with the relevant contracting authority, open meetings make potential tenderers be identified and known to the competitors.[21] Even if new firms express interest in

15 UNCTAD "Survey of Good Practice in Public–Private Sector Dialogue, 2001" <http://unctad.org/en/docs/iteteb4_en.pdf> accessed on January 15, 2025, 21.

16 European Commission "Prior Market Consultations-Simplification and Efficiency" <https://ec.europa.eu/regional_policy/policy/how/improving-investment/public-procurement/e-library_en> accessed on January 20, 2025.

17 Oana S. Pantilimon Voda (fn 7), 220.

18 The time usually needed for the consultation process is between three and six months. See European Commission (fn 16).

19 Sigma (fn 10), 3.

20 Timothy C. Salmon "Preventing Collusion between Firms in Auctions" in M.C.W Janssen (ed) *Auctioning Public Assets: Analysis and Alternatives* (Cambridge University Press, 2004), 98.

21 Abby Semple – Public Procurement Analysis "Legal Considerations for Market Engagement" <https://ec.europa.eu/environment/gpp/pdf/24_11_2015/Webinar%20slides_Semple.pdf> accessed on January 20, 2025, 5.

participating in the technical dialogue with the contracting authority, open meetings can expose potential tenderers to competitors. Incumbent firms will know who their potential competitors and entrants are and so they will have the time and opportunity either to monitor the procurement practices of the latter before the contracting phase takes place or to approach them in order to persuade them to merge or drop out.[22] This means that even if a bidding ring is not all-inclusive, it may be sustainable under such circumstances, since the bidding behaviour of the outsiders can be easily predicted or controlled by the cartel members. While there is no empirical evidence that technical dialogues increase collusion, the possibility is a concern, considering the lack of focus on collusion in EU public procurement regulations.

Another aggravating factor in scenarios like the one mentioned above is that when dealing with innovative works, supplies or services that have a high technical, financial or contractual complexity, contracting authorities will inevitably engage with potential contractors during preliminary market consultations. A small group of market operators specializing in such works, supplies or services, does not allow contracting authorities to hire advisors who only act as technical advisors and not as tenderers in the subsequent competition for the contract. This gives an extra incentive for market operators participating in the technical dialogue, to use the information provided to form a bidding ring during the contracting phase. When market operators take part in preliminary market consultations, they usually have an interest in the resulting contract.[23] Additionally, according to the 2024 flash Eurobarometer survey on corruption in business, six out of ten companies state that bidder involvement in designing specifications is one of the most common corrupt practices in public procurement (61%).[24]

Given the above, a general ban on open and public sessions during preliminary market consultations can be recommended, if collusion or incumbent interference is a risk. In such cases, a web-based contact or private face-to-face discussions between the contracting authority and each economic operator may be proposed. However, a "one-size-fits-all" approach may not be preferable, as there could be instances where a contracting authority cannot afford to develop an electronic support platform or where face-to-face discussions with an economic operator could

22 This happened prior to the Netherlands 3G auction in 2000 of five licences. Apart from mergers, firms which are considered strong potential entrants may enter a partnership with an incumbent or be co-opted into joint ventures with incumbents. See Paul Klemperer "Bidding Markets" (2007), 3(1), *Journal of Competition Law and Economics*, 22–23.

23 See the empirical research that was conducted during a two-year research project called TOPNETS Developing Partnerships and Networks in Public Procurement by University of Turku Faculty of Law and University of Vaasa Faculty of Business Studies Department of Management. For further information about the project, see Johanna Sammalmaa's paper "The Application of the EU Foundational Principles in the Preparation Phase of Public Procurement – A Research Plan" (presented at the 7th Public Procurement Research Students Conference, University of Nottingham, September 8–9, 2016).

24 European Commission "Businesses' Attitudes towards Corruption in the EU – Flash Competitive 543" <https://europa.eu/eurobarometer/surveys/detail/3180> accessed on January 20, 2025.

increase the risk of bid rigging. This could occur when procurement officers lack the necessary experience and commercial instinct to conduct a technical dialogue with a market operator. Therefore, a knowledgeable and skilled market operator could pressure them into disclosing confidential information about the works, supplies or services they wish to procure or misuse this face-to-face discussion to alter terms or specifications for a cartel purposes. This confidential information or modified terms or specifications can later be used by the market operator to gain a clear advantage in the subsequent competition over the other firms or to sustain a cartel that already exists among some of the participating market operators. In successful cartel monitoring mechanisms, it is likely that a market operator would share any confidential information obtained during preliminary market consultations with other cartel members to avoid retaliation or punishment. It would also make sense for a market operator involved in a cartel to suggest correction(s) or modifications to specifications during face-to-face discussions with procurement officers, ensuring that the specifications align with products or services marketed by cartel members.

Let us consider the worst-case scenario where procurement officers are corrupt and disclose confidential bid information in private discussions with a specific economic operator. Collusion between procurement officers and bidding companies is not uncommon among administrative elites responsible for identifying needs, budgeting and designing tenders before launching them.[25] An example of bid rigging involving bribed public officials is when they provide favoured firms with exclusive information giving them a competitive advantage in tailoring their bids and increasing their chances of winning contracts.[26] Mis-assessment of needs[27] at the stage of procurement planning is a common corruption technique,[28] limiting competition and facilitating rent capture.[29] Collusion and corruption often occur *in*

25 Jason P Matechak and Centre for International Private Enterprise "Fighting Corruption in Public Procurement" < https://www.cipe.org/legacy/publication-docs/matechak.pdf> accessed January 20, 2025.

26 Kari K. Heggstad and Mona Frøystad *The Basics of Integrity in Procurement* (Bergen, Norway: U4 Anti-Corruption Resource Centre Chr. Michelsen Institute – CMI, 2011), 9.

27 This means procuring goods and services which are not necessary for a contracting authority or procuring them in a size and quantity excessive compared to the actual needs.

28 Ibid; Eitan Goldman, Jörg Rocholl and Jongil So "Political Connections and the Allocation of Procurement Contracts" <http://idei.fr/sites/default/files/medias/doc/conf/icied/papers_2011/goldman.pdf> accessed on January 20, 2025; Transparency International *Handbook for Curbing Corruption in Public Procurement* (Berlin, Transparency International, 2006); Vito Tanzi and Hamid Davoodi "Corruption, Public Investment, and Growth – A Working Paper of the International Monetary Fund" <www.imf.org/external/pubs/ft/wp/wp97139.pdf> accessed on January 20, 2025; Mihály Fazekas, István János Tóth, Lawrence Peter King "Corruption Manual for Beginners: 'Corruption Techniques' in Public Procurement with Examples from Hungary" <www.crcb.eu/wp-content/uploads/2013/12/Fazekas-Toth-King_Corruption-manual-for-beginners_v2_2013.pdf> accessed on January 20, 2025.

29 Fazekas, Tóth and King (fn 28), 15.

tandem and they have mutually reinforcing effect, with bid rigging accompanying kickback schemes to ensure the selection of corrupt firms.[30]

Article 41 addresses the exchange of information between contracting authorities and candidates or tenderers during preliminary market consultations. Yet, the only reference it makes to competition law issues, which in a sense may regard bid rigging concerns as well, is that in case of prior involvement of candidates or tenderers in the preparation of the procurement procedure, the contracting authority shall take appropriate measures to ensure that competition is not distorted by the participation of that candidate or tenderer. Paragraph 2 of Article 41 further clarifies that such measures shall include the communication to the other candidates and tenderers of relevant information exchanged in the context of the technical dialogue and the fixing of adequate time limits for the receipt of tenders.

The explicit contemplation of these measures ensures that the principles of equal treatment and non-discrimination of economic operators apply and competition among them is neither precluded nor distorted. However, it is argued that these measures are not adequate and appropriate to deal with bid rigging concerns as the ones described above. First, they do not deal with the concern of open and public sessions and the inevitable interaction of market operators in the context of these open meetings. Second, they do not handle the selective information provision, which is an illustrative corruption technique, as explained in the scenario above. The communication to the other candidates and tenderers of the information exchanged during the technical dialogue presupposes that procurement officers are not corrupt and they do their job in the right way. Yet, 27% of companies report that corruption has hindered their ability to win public tenders or contracts.[31] Public procurement-related corruption costs the EU over €5 billion annually (across all sectors),[32] affecting all Member States to varying degrees. The European Commission acknowledges that "there are no corruption-free zones in the EU".[33]

In the case of bribed procurement officers, as presented in the scenario above, the 2014/24/EU Directive remains silent. It does not suggest any possible mechanism or legislative instrument that would control procurement officers and ensure that all relevant information exchanged in the technical dialogue will be communicated to

30 OECD "Policy Roundtables – Collusion and Corruption in Public Procurement 2010" <https://www.oecd.org/en/publications/collusion-and-corruption-in-public-procurement_ef957f70-en.html> accessed on January 20, 2025, 9; Michael Kramer and International Anti-Corruption Resource Center "The Most Common Procurement Fraud Schemes and their Primary Red Flags" <http://iacrc.org/procurement-fraud/the-most-common-procurement-fraud-schemes-and-their-primary-red-flags/> accessed January 20, 2025.

31 European Commission "Businesses' Attitudes towards Corruption in the EU – Flash Eurobarometer 543" <https://europa.eu/eurobarometer/surveys/detail/3180> accessed on January 20, 2025.

32 European Parliament "The Cost of Non-Europe in the Area of Organised Crime and Corruption – Annex II – Corruption" <www.europarl.europa.eu/RegData/etudes/IDAN/2016/558779/EPRS_IDA%282016%29558779%28ANN2%29_EN.pdf> accessed on January 20, 2025.

33 Piotr Bakowski and Sofija Voronova "Corruption in the European Union – Prevalence of Corruption, and Anti-Corruption Efforts in Selected EU Member States" <www.europarl.europa.eu/RegData/etudes/STUD/2017/608687/EPRS_STU(2017)608687_EN.pdf> accessed on January 20, 2025.

other candidates and tenderers. Additionally, there is no specific reference to what kind of information should be communicated to the other candidates and tenderers. This determination is left to procurement officers' discretion as to which information is relevant and which is not. However, when procurement officers are rather inexperienced and without commercial instinct, they can miss out some points raised in their discussion with the market operators and consequently may fail to disclose them to other candidates and tenderers, even though they should definitely share this information.

Another provision under the current Directive that deals indirectly with competition concerns in the context of preliminary market allocation is Article 58, paragraph 4. According to this article,

> A contracting authority may assume that an economic operator does not possess the required professional abilities where the contracting authority has established that the economic operator has conflicting interests which may negatively affect the performance of the contract.

This conflict of interests pertains to the actions of economic operators that may inappropriately influence the performance of a public contract. It should be differentiated from Article 24 of Directive 2014/24/EU, which governs situations where the conflict of interests arises from the contracting authority. According to Article 24, Section 2 of the current Directive,

> The concept of conflicts of interest shall at least cover any situation where staff members of the contracting authority or of a procurement service provider acting on behalf of the contracting authority who are involved in the conduct of the procurement procedure or may influence the outcome of that procedure have, directly or indirectly, a financial, economic or other personal interest which might be perceived to compromise their impartiality and independence in the context of the procurement procedure.

Article 58, paragraph 4 should also be distinguished from cases where collusive activities unduly affect a tender, as "the existence of conflicting interests does not necessarily imply any wrongdoing".[34] Therefore, according to Article 58, paragraph 4 of the current Directive, contracting authorities may reject the tender of an economic operator, if that economic operator has taken on conflicting roles during the market dialogue phase. This could give them an unfair advantage over other bidders in the later stages of the procurement process, or could distort their advice to the contracting authority. This measure aims to stop bid rigging activities that are supported and facilitated by an economic operator's inappropriate involvement in preparing the procurement procedure. Furthermore, if a contracting

34 Abby Semple and Marta Andrecka "Classification, Conflicts of Interest and Change of Contractor: A Critical Look at the Public Sector Procurement Directive" (2015), 3, *European Procurement and Public Private Partnership Law Review*, 180–181.

authority determines that an economic operator has conflicting interests that negatively impact contract performance, the operator cannot regain trust by providing evidence or taking corrective actions. This is because the self-cleaning defence[35] (Article 57, paragraph 6 of the current Directive) only applies to conflicts of interest on the contracting authority's side, not the economic operator's side.[36]

Yet, there is still legal uncertainty under the current Directive about the procedural treatment of conflicts of interests that arise on in the contracting authorities' side. There are no provisions detailing the extent of the contracting authorities' duty to investigate, the threshold of proof required, the actions to take if a conflict of interest is found or the legal consequences that may follow.[37] This uncertainty undermines efforts to deter bid rigging practices that begin in the procurement planning stage. Therefore, it is essential for the European Commission to offer practical guidance to procurement agents on these matters. The need for such guidance is evident given the significant discretion contracting authorities have in determining whether an economic operator possesses the necessary professional abilities due to conflicting interests. While ECJ judgments in cases such as *Fabricom*,[38] *Michaniki*[39] and *Assitur*,[40] as well as the General Court's judgment in the *Intrasoft*[41] case provide some insight into the ECJ's general approach to conflicts of interest involving economic operators, they do not address application of the 2014/24/EU Directive.

In all these cases, it was determined that the blanket exclusion of contractors who have previously performed related work is not supported by the European legal regime. Even if a tenderer acted as an advisor in pre-tender work, or had individual links to media organizations, or ownership links to other bidders or drafted documentation used in the procurement, it cannot be automatically excluded from the process but each time the relevant authority has to consider and assess the evidence and facts of the case. These court cases confirm not only the great flexibility given to contracting authorities as far as conflict of interest on the part of economic operators is concerned, but also the high degree of probability that there must exist on the part of contracting authorities when rejecting bids or annulling their decisions for this reason. Nonetheless, misjudgements by contracting authorities are possible because they must make their assessment promptly, without delaying the

35 The procurement rules provide the possibility for a tenderer to demonstrate its reliability and take part again in procurement procedures, despite the existence of a ground for exclusion.

36 Deividas Soloveičik and Karolis Šimanskis "The Evolving Concept of Conflict of Interests in the EU Public Procurement Law" (2017), 2, *EPPPL*, 118; Abby Semple and Marta Andrecka (fn 34), 182.

37 Javier Miranzo Díaz "The Procedural Treatment of Conflicts of Interest in EU Public Procurement" in G. Ferrari, G. Garau and J. Mondéjar-Jiménez (eds) *Tourism, Economy and Environment: New Trends and Research Perspectives* (Chartridge Books Oxford, 2017), 203.

38 Joined cases C-21/03 and C-34/03 Fabricom SA v état belge (2005), ECR I-01559.

39 Case C-213/07 Michaniki AE v Ethniko Simvoulio Radiotileorasis (2008), ECR I-9999.

40 Case C-538/07 Assitur Sri v Camera di Commercio, Industria, Artigianato e Agricoltura di Milano (2009) ECR I-04219.

41 Case T-403/12 Intrasoft International v European Commission, EU:T:2015:774.

determination for any reason.[42] Lengthy procurement procedures are costly and create uncertainty for both the public procurer and bidding firms.[43] Furthermore, statistics show that procurement officers are often involved in corruption.

Many academics in the corruption literature link corrupt practices with the discretion granted to public officers in a procurement entity.[44] Corrupted procurement officers may use their discretion in a biased manner to exclude tenders that meet competition conditions and instead favour a small network of bidding firms. Limiting the number of bidders is a primary way to avoid competition during the submission phase.[45] Hence, procurement officers using their discretion in a biased manner can lead to collusive activities, such as bid rigging in later stages of the procurement process, where the same market participants act as candidates or tenderers. Therefore, Article 58, paragraph 4 of the current Directive has not effectively addressed bid rigging concerns in the context of market consultations.

The weaknesses of the aforementioned articles under the current Directive, which aim to deter bid rigging practices initiated or sustained at the procurement planning stage illustrate the need for a clearer and more accurate approach to considering the conduct of preliminary market consultations. While a "one-size-fits-all" approach may not be preferable, there should be some recommendations from the European Commission regarding how contracting authorities should make decisions and act when organizing and conducting a technical dialogue with private stakeholders. This should depend on factors such as (a) the experience and vulnerability of the contracting authority to corruption, (b) the nature of the market, (c) the nature of the required supplies/works/services and (d) the cost and complexity of the communication tools needed for conducting prior market consultations. Currently, Member State is responsible for issuing guidance notes on how market analysis should be conducted, such as the Action Note 04/12 from the English Government[46] and the online resource "Procurement Journey Scotland"[47] from the Scottish Government. Both provide step-by-step guide on preliminary

42 Joined cases C-21/03 and C-34/03 Fabricom SA v état belge (2005) ECR I-01559, paras [9]–[11], [43].

43 Marko Šostar and Ana Marukić "Challenges of Public Procurement in EU Funded Projects" (2017), 22(2), *Journal of Contemporary Management Issues*, 104.

44 Andre Saddy "Front-line servants, discretion and corruption" in Gabriella M. Racca and Christopher R. Yukins (eds) *Integrity and Efficiency in Sustainable Public Contracts: Balancing Corruption Concerns in Public Procurement Internationally* (Bruylant, Brussels 2014), 353; see also John Gardiner "Defining Corruption" in Arnold J. Heidenheimer and Michael Johnston (eds) *Political Corruption: Concepts and Contexts* (Transaction Publishers, 2005) and Mark Philp "Conceptualizing Political Corruption" in Arnold J. Heidenheimer and Michael Johnston (eds) *Political Corruption: Concepts and Contexts* (Transaction Publishers, 2005).

45 Mihály Fazekas, István János Tóth and Lawrence Peter King "An Objective Corruption Risk Index Using Public Procurement Data" (2016), 22, *European Journal on Criminal Policy & Research*, 372.

46 Cabinet Office (fn 9).

47 Scottish Procurement "The Procurement Journey" <www.procurementjourney.scot/procurement-journey> accessed February 8, 2019; see also Sigma (fn 10), 3.

market consultation, helping contracting authorities find the right balance between exchanging information and maintaining market integrity.

It is important to note from the guidance notes mentioned above that whenever a contracting authority engages directly with economic operators as part of a market analysis, the process must be carefully planned and managed to avoid distorting subsequent competition.[48] Details are not provided on how this goal can be achieved, leaving room for suggestions. One suggestion is that contracting authorities should have a policy for conducting preliminary market consultation before starting the formal procurement procedure. They should create checklist templates for procurement officers to use during market analysis and keep a record of the market analysis process, including the reasons for choosing a particular process, such as direct engagement with economic operators to conduct the market dialogue.[49]

For the first suggestion to yield realistic results, it is further recommended that contracting authorities should draft and submit a report at the end of every market analysis process. This report will outline the issues considered, the research resources and information used and obtained during the market dialogue as well as the main conclusions drawn.[50] This is particularly significant in the case of face-to-face discussions with an economic operator, for the reasons explained above. During face-to-face discussions, procurement officers should be exceptionally careful to gather and classify the remarks and comments made by each economic operator. They should avoid committing themselves to any suggestions made by the latter. After the completion of the preliminary market consultation there should be ample time for the entire procurement team to understand the remarks of all economic operators, examine their substance and express an opinion about the possibility or need to accept them. In addition, it is suggested that this report should be published and sent to interested economic operators, without revealing the identity and number of the economic operators that responded to the invitation to participate in the technical dialogue. Disclosing such information could facilitate cartel formation, by enabling cartel members to monitor the compliance of each other with the collusive agreement, especially when web-based contact took place or private face-to-face discussions were conducted during the preliminary market consultation. In the same vein, the report should not include the specific points of the tender documents that the contracting authority intends to modify after the preliminary market consultation, because this would facilitate cartel redistributions which may be made to resolve any deviation from the collusive agreement until the publication of the contract notice and of the final tender documents. Instead, the report should consist of an updated self-declaration confirming that the procurement officers conducting the preliminary market consultations acted in accordance with the guidelines of their authority, communicated to all candidates and tenderers

48 Sigma (fn 10), 4.
49 ibid.
50 ibid.

the information exchanged during or resulting from the market dialogue phase and did not get involved in corrupt practices. In this way, public officers will have the fear of being subject to prosecution under national law in case of misrepresentation. This will serve as an additional incentive for public officers to conduct preliminary market consultations carefully and appropriately.

In addressing the issue of corrupted procurement officers during face-to-face meetings, an additional suggestion would be to include at least one neutral observer during any face-to-face discussions with economic operators. This neutral person could be an employee from the relevant contracting authority that procured the product, work or service at issue. Also, a "Chinese wall" should be built between the procurement officers conducting face-to-face discussions and launching a preliminary market consultation and those assessing the bids and awarding the contract. This strict separation would guarantee their integrity throughout the procurement procedure and help reduce the risk of corruption that facilitates collusion.

Another suggestion aimed at limiting the interaction of market operators and their contact with procurement officers during the procurement planning stage is the cooperation of contracting authorities with Competition Authorities (CAs), who possess information about the relevant market. Under certain circumstances, it may be beneficial for contracting authorities to share information with CAs instead of engaging directly with economic operators. While it is understandable that contracting authorities are interested in the capabilities of economic operators as well as the technical, financial, legal and operational perspectives of a contract/project, they may need to contact the market operators directly to assess these parameters. Yet, when contacting authorities want to gather general market information, they should not engage directly with market operators. Instead, they should consult publicly available reports from CAs that have the necessary data.

CAs have extensive experience in investigating competition in an industry, as they are often tasked with examining individual firm behaviour and broader structural or behavioural market problems, according to Article 17, paragraph 1 of Regulation 1/2003.[51] An illustrative example is the Competition and Markets Authority (CMA) in the UK, which conducts market investigations. For conventional authorities, such exercises may resemble merger regulation or antitrust enforcement. Contracting authorities can benefit from CAs' information on the number of suppliers available for effective competition,[52] previous suppliers for the proposed public contract and the number of economic operators needed to deliver it.[53] This information can aid in strategic decisions such as dividing a public contract into lots, selecting a procurement procedure or promoting SME participation.

51 Niamh Dunne "Between Competition Law and Regulation: Hybridized Approaches to Market Control" (2014), 2(2), *Journal of Antitrust Enforcement*, 228.

52 Whether the number of suppliers is sufficient to ensure effective competition or not depends each time on demand, minimum efficient scale of production and other factors. This means that it may not always be efficient for there to be more than a small number of bidders.

53 Yet, if there is a secret bid rigging cartel, there is always the risk that the competition authority may wrongly conclude that the market is operating well, when in fact it is rigged.

CAs' contribution is especially crucial in innovative or high-technology markets, where defining market boundaries and assessing competition is complex, because a reliable market definition must factor in both performance and potential competition. As already explained, in innovation markets procurement officers often conduct preliminary market consultations and engage directly with the relevant economic operators, increasing the risk of bid rigging and corruption. Therefore, promoting cooperation between CAs and contracting authorities to make informed decisions on information sharing can limit opportunities for market operators to interact and contact procurement officers.

When deciding on conflict of interests involving economic operators, contracting authorities are granted a high level of discretion. It is important to recommend that the principle of accountability be applied in these cases. Both the contracting authorities and the public procurement officers should be held accountable if they only partially exercise their discretion. Accountability can be ensured through internal control and audits within procurement entities, as well as by implementing effective mechanisms for filing complaints and challenging procurement decisions.[54]

4.3 Technical Specifications – Analysis of Bid Rigging Issues and Recommendations

After covering the conduct of preliminary market consultations, this section moves on to discussing whether the way technical specifications are formulated by contracting authorities creates conditions facilitating bid rigging. The focus will be on provisions that favour the restriction of market participation because, as explained in Chapter 2, deterring entry is a prerequisite for a successful cartel to flourish.[55]

According to Recital (74) of the 2014/24/EU Directive, technical specifications drawn up by public purchasers need to allow public procurement to be open to competition. They should be drafted in a way that avoids artificially narrowing competition through requirements that favour a specific economic operator. To this end, the current Directive adopts an anti-formalistic approach, allowing for the use of performance or functional specifications instead of detailed *ad hoc* specifications and references unfamiliar or inaccessible standards.[56] As a result of this new functional approach, Article 42, paragraph 4 contemplates that:

> Unless justified by the subject-matter of the contract, technical specifications shall not refer to a specific make or source, or a particular process which characterises the products or services provided by a specific economic

54 See Fazekas, Tóth and King (fn 28), 8.

55 Robert C. Marshall and Michael J. Meurer "Bidder Collusion and Antitrust Law: Refining the Analysis of Price Fixing to Account for the Special Features of Auction Markets" (2004), 72(1), *Antitrust Law Journal*, 93.

56 Sue Arrowsmith "The Law of Public and Utilities Procurement: Regulation in the EU and UK", (2nd edition, Sweet & Maxwell, 2005), 1147.

> operator, or to trade marks, patents, types or a specific origin or production with the effect of favouring or eliminating certain undertakings or certain products. Such reference shall be permitted on an exceptional basis, where a sufficiently precise and intelligible description of the subject-matter of the contract pursuant to paragraph 3 is not possible. Such reference shall be accompanied by the words "or equivalent".

The point worth analyzing from a competition point of view in Article 42, paragraph 4 of the current Directive, is the obligation to accompany any listed technical specifications with the words "*or equivalent*". Failure to include the words "or equivalent" after specifying a particular product in the contract documents cannot only discourage economic operators who use similar systems from participating in the procurement process, but also hinder the flow of imports in intra-Union trade. This is because it limits the contract to suppliers who plan to use the specifically identified product.[57] However, the 2014/24/EU Directive does not define or clarify the meaning of the concept "*equivalent*", leaving contracting authorities free to decide each time at their discretion whether specific supplies, services or works are equivalent to the ones they set. This legal uncertainty may result in a lower number of responses than usual for similar tenders, as many undertakings may be discouraged from participating in the procurement process, especially new entrants or SMEs due to the high participation costs, time investment and lack of certainty about returns on investments. The impact of "context-related" uncertainties[58] on the bidding strategy of an undertaking at the competitive bidding stage has also been empirically confirmed.[59] As explained by auction theory in Chapter 2, in tenders with a low number of response, where there is a small and manageable group of bidders and a certain level of lock out, collusion thrives.[60]

In addition, it is important to consider the overall bias of stakeholders towards product substitution, also known as "equivalent" products, and their mistaken belief that deviating from brand specifications negatively impacts the project. The general distrust in product substitution, as evidenced by empirical survey, makes it risky to grant contracting authorities the discretion to define and set limits for what constitutes an "*equivalent*" product. A narrow interpretation of this concept

57 Vestergaard, C-59/00, EU:C:2001:654, para. 22.

58 Uncertainties related to the service requirements as well as the product specifications and performance.

59 Melanie E. Kreye, Linda B. Newnes and Yee Mey Goh "Uncertainty in Competitive Bidding – A Framework for Product-Service Systems" (2014), 25(6), *Production Planning & Control – The Management of Operations*, 462–477.

60 Spend Network for Competition and Markets Authority (CMA) "Report on Bid-Rigging Algorithms – The Use of Public Sector Procurement Information to Identify Bid-Rigging in Public Procurement Markets" (2016) < https://assets.publishing.service.gov.uk/government/uploads/system/uploads/attachment_data/file/627670/Report_on_bid-rigging_algorithms.pdf> accessed on January 20, 2025; see also OECD "Guidelines for Fighting Bid-Rigging in Public Procurement" (2009) <www.oecd.org/en/publications/2009/02/guidelines-for-fighting-bid-rigging-in-public-procurement_d4a5f7a8.html> accessed on January 20, 2025.

can hinder new entrants from participating in the market. When barriers to entry are high and there is a lack of supply diversity, residual competition in the public market becomes weak. This is due to the limited number and strength of outsiders to the collusive agreement, who cannot offer competitive prices compared to cartel members. This weakness in combination with the incumbency advantages of leading undertakings makes collusion a likely market outcome.

The Specification Report 2017 from NBS (National Building Specification), a UK-based system providing innovative specification and information solutions to construction professionals for over 40 years, supports this argument. The Report indicates that over half of respondents face challenges to using "*or equivalent*" for brands and standards.[61] Fifty-seven percent believe that difficulties in producing or using specifications arise from the substitution of specified materials.[62] This belief has been present since 2013 in the construction industry, where there is a strong emphasis on the importance of specifications in project design intent, making product substitution a potential risk.[63] The importance of this empirical research should not be underestimated just because it regards only the construction industry. From a competition point of view, construction is a benchmark sector in public procurement because (a) it receives the highest number of bids along with business services, (b) contracts in the construction sector attract most competition, (c) construction comprises nearly 38% of the total value of contract award notices and (d) in the construction sector, the open procedure is used for 80% of the procurements.[64] Therefore, the construction industry is representative of how stakeholders in public procurement think and act regarding equivalent products.

Professor Sue Arrowsmith shared her perspective on the meaning of "*equivalent*" stating that it aligns with the general principle in the Treaty that purchasers cannot reject products or services that offer *exactly the same functional performance as those specified* or *exceed* it (emphasis added).[65] This interpretation is supported by the author of this monograph for two main reasons. First, public purchaser have the right to accept bids that meet their functional needs and correspond to their choices, even if they do not match the technical specifications exactly. Second, from a competition law standpoint, not adopting this interpretation could lead to collusion. The exclusion of products, services or service providers from other Member States that do not meet exactly the same technical requirements as those specified by contracting authorities, but do offer the same functional performance or exceed it, could limit the market, create a certain level of lock out and result in a small and manageable group of suppliers. This group of suppliers would

61 NBS "Specification Report 2017" <www.thenbs.com/knowledge/nbs-specification-report-2017> accessed on January 17, 2025.

62 Ibid.

63 Ibid.

64 PwC, London Economics and Ecorys for the European Commission "Public Procurement in Europe-Cost and Effectiveness" (2011) <https://op.europa.eu/en/publication-detail/-/publication/0cfa3445-7724-4af5-8c2b-d657cd690c03> accessed on December 3, 2024, 8, 46 and 99.

65 Arrowsmith (fn 56), 1144–1145, 1107.

probably consist of incumbent undertakings, as they would be the only ones in the market feeling confident to deliver on the relevant contract. Under such circumstances, in a limited market with few suppliers, the chances of bid rigging are enhanced, as already explained in Chapter 2.[66]

Hereafter, two illustrative examples are needed to demonstrate the importance of interpreting the concept "*equivalent*" in the aforementioned way. The first example is when a contracting authority divides a contract into lots and simultaneously sets high technical specifications, to distinguish serious bidders from weak bidders.[67] The second example is when procurement officers are corrupt and seek unwanted bidders by manipulating assessment criteria.[68] In both cases, the number of bidders is limited, competition decreases and a concentrated market is created unnecessarily. Consequently, the risk of collusion increases, as it is easier for a small number of bidders to signal collusive outcomes, interpret them correctly and reach quick agreements, as already explained in Chapter 2.[69] Therefore, in situations like these, the concept of "*equivalent*" should include bids that offer the same functional performance as specified or exceed it to maintain the competitive tension in the market. At this point, it is worth referring to the recent judgment of the CJEU, which held that the material of which a product is made cannot be classified as a "performance" or "functional requirement" according to Article 42(3)(a) of Directive 2014/24/EU.[70] While a material may enhance the performance of a product or help it meet a functional requirement, it does not, on its own, represent a "performance" or "functional requirement".[71] Therefore, contracting authorities cannot specify, in the technical specifications of a public works contract, the materials of which the products proposed by the tenderers must be made, without adding the words "or equivalent".[72] This is unless the use of a specific material is essential to the contract's subject matter, and no alternative based on a different technical solution can be considered.[73]

In light of the recent CJEU judgment, the significance of the concept "equivalent" becomes evident as well as the need for the CJEU to interpret this concept explicitly. Alternatively, the European legislator can provide guidelines on how

66 Spend Network (fn 60), 7.

67 The example is taken from real life. See the facts of the Italian Auction (October 2000) as presented by Paul Klemperer in his article "How (not) to run auctions: the European 3G Telecom Auctions" (2002), 46(4–5), *European Economic Review*, 834–835.

68 Fazekas, Tóth and King (fn 28), 26–27; according to the 2024 flash Eurobarometer survey on corruption relevant to business, six in ten respondents (61%) say that tailor-made criteria for specific companies is one of the most common corruption practices occurring in public procurement practices. See European Commission "Businesses' Attitudes towards Corruption in the EU – Flash Eurobarometer 543" <https://europa.eu/eurobarometer/surveys/detail/3180> accessed on January 20, 2025.

69 Salmon "Preventing Collusion between Firms in Auctions" (fn 20), 114.

70 Case C-424/23 DYKA Plastics NV v Fluvius System Operator CV, ECLI:EU:C:2024:749.

71 Ibid.

72 Ibid.

73 Ibid.

the concept "*equivalent*" should be defined in a procompetitive manner, rather than allowing contracting authorities to determine its content at their discretion, as empirical evidence has shown they may be corrupted or biased towards product substitution.

Another concern arising from Article 42 regarding market participation, is the contracting authorities' discretion to assess whether the works, supplies or services proposed by a tenderer can meet the requirements defined by the technical specifications in an equivalent manner (Article 42, paragraph 5). Specifically, paragraph 5 contemplates that:

> Where a contracting authority uses the option of referring to the technical specifications referred to in point (b)of paragraph 3, it shall not reject a tender on the grounds that the works, supplies or services tendered for do not comply with the technical specifications to which it has referred, once the tenderer proves in its tender by any appropriate means, including the means of proof referred to in Article 44, that the solutions proposed satisfy in an equivalent manner the requirements defined by the technical specifications.

It is true that the 2014/24/EU Directive has made significant progress in this area compared to the old Directive 2004/18. Article 23, paragraph 5 of the old Directive used to require that "the tenderer must prove *to the satisfaction of the contracting authority* and by any appropriate means that the work, product or service in compliance with the standard meets the performance or functional requirements of the contracting authority" (emphasis added). In the current Directive, the subjective wording "to the satisfaction of the contracting authority", is no longer used. Additionally, Article 44, paragraph 2 clarifies that contracting authorities must accept other appropriate means of proof, such as a technical dossier from the manufacturer, in addition to those expressly referred to in paragraph 1. However, some scholars believe that contracting authorities still have considerable discretion when it comes to evaluating evidence under the 2014/24/EU Directive, potentially undermining its functional approach.[74] For this reason, it is recommended that when evaluating the equivalence of a proposed solution with the technical specifications, alternative forms of proof should not be employed. Only the means of proof explicitly stated in paragraph 1 of Article 44 should be utilized. To implement such a measure, the 2014 Directive would need to be revised and also overturn the principle established in *Max Havelaar*,[75] according to which contracting authorities are not allowed to refer to specific labels when selecting the most economically advantageous tender.

74 Albert Sanchez Graells, *Public Procurement and the EU Competition Rules* (Oxford: Bloomsbury, 2015, 2nd edition), 334–335.

75 Case C-368/10 European Commission v Kingdom of the Netherlands, ECLI:EU:C:2012:284.

Another important point in Article 42 of the 2014/24/EU Directive is the shift towards performance-based specifications in Article 42.[76] The ability of contracting authorities to stipulate less prescriptive requirements in terms of outputs and functionality descriptions promotes competition, by attracting more bidders, such as suppliers of substitute products.[77] However, little attention has been given to the competition law challenges that arise from using performance-based specifications at the bidding and evaluation stages. The first challenge is the low number of bidders that performance-based specifications may attract. Performance-based specifications are generally considered innovative and unfamiliar procurement models, as their success relies on the full understanding contracting authorities may struggle to understand what the market offers or clearly articulate their needs.[78] This miscommunication, coupled with some public procurers being ill-informed, often leads to a lack of bidders and a failure to maintain competitive tension in the procurement process.[79] As discussed in Chapter 2, when the supply side is dominated by a few firms, there is a risk of bid rigging in the market.[80]

The second challenge involves the relationship between performance-based specifications and preliminary market consultations. Transitioning to performance-based specifications requires a strong connection with the market consultation process.[81]Contracting authorities need to gather input from the market to define performance indicators and later monitor the supplier's work and the quality of the offered service.[82] However, the current Directive does not adequately regulate pre-

76 "Performance-based specifications describe a desired performance level or performance target to be achieved, but do not make specific demands on how that level/target is reached. Instead of prescribing the need in terms of inputs, it is described in terms of outputs". See Laura Turley, Mariana Hug Silva, Scarlett Benson and Carlos Dominguez for International Institute for Sustainable Development "Performance Based Specifications: Exploring When They Work and Why" (2014) <www.iisd.org/sites/default/files/publications/performance-based-speculations-exploring-when-they-work-and-why.pdf> accessed on October 14, 2017, 3.

77 OECD "Fighting Bid Rigging in Public Procurement – Report on Implementing the OECD Recommendation" (fn 12); see Sanchez Graells (fn 74), 328.

78 Ibid.

79 Turley, Hug Silva, Benson and Dominguez (fn 76), 37–38.

80 Joe S. Bain, *Industrial Organisation* (John Wiley 1968), 462–463; George J. Stigler "A Theory of Oligopoly" (1964), 72(1), *The Journal of Political Economy*, 44, 51–56; Edward Hastings Chamberlin *The Theory of Monopolistic Competition: A Re-Orientation of the Theory of Value* (Cambridge Mass: Harvard University Press, 1966), 46–51; a slightly different approach by Demsetz and Weiss who argue accordingly that collusion accompanied by superior performance is facilitated by market concentration and that besides concentration, there are also many other variables conducive to collusion, see Harold Demsetz *The Market Concentration Doctrine – An Examination of Evidence and A Discussion of Policy* (AEI-Hoover Policy Studies, 1973), 20, and Leonard W. Weiss "The Structure-Conduct: Performance Paradigm and Antitrust" (1979), 127(4), *University of Pennsylvania Law Review*, 1118.

81 Laura Turley – International Institute for Sustainable Development "Moving towards Performance-Based Specifications in Public Procurement" (2013) <www.iisd.org/sites/default/files/publications/specs_public_procurement.pdf> accessed on October 14, 2017.

82 Sustainable Technology for Older People-Get Organised "Overview Open Market Consultation" <http://stopandgoproject.eu/wp-content/uploads/2017/04/STOPandGO_OMC_Report_v1.2.pdf> accessed on November 10, 2017.

liminary market consultations in terms of maintaining effective competition. This lack of regulation poses a risk when formulating and drafting performance-based specifications with input from market operators who may have a vested interest in the contract or engage in anticompetitive activities such as bid rigging. The risk is that performance-based specifications may be unduly influenced by market operators, leading to the exclusion of non-members or new entrants who may not have the capacity to meet artificially high performance standards set by the contracting authority. This could result in limited competition in the tender process.

Market operators are drawn to performance-based specifications, because they can leverage their expertise in products and markets to innovate.[83] However, the technical and financial expertise required to develop and draft the performance-based specifications leaves contracting authorities vulnerable to manipulation. There is a risk that market operators may influence the specifications to exclude competitors who are not part of their bidding rings or new entrants who may struggle to meet artificially high performance standards set by the contracting authority. Additionally, "specifications based on outputs and functionality descriptions are more prone to relative and subjective judgments".[84] This makes it challenging for contracting authorities to determine if these specifications create unjustified obstacles to competition. The subjective nature of performance-based specifications allows corrupt procurement officers to use their discretion unfairly, favouring bid rigging schemes and hindering fair competition.[85]

4.4 Division of Contracts into Lots (Article 46 of 2014/24/EU Directive) – Analysis of Bid Rigging Issues and Recommendations

After explaining how the formulation of performance-based specifications by contracting authorities can facilitate bid rigging, it is now necessary to address the division of public contracts into lots. During the procurement planning stage, contracting authorities have the option to decide whether to divide a contract into lots. Article 46, paragraph 1 of Directive 2014/24/EU allows contracting authorities the discretion to determine if a contract will be awarded in separate lots and gives them the freedom to define the size and scope of each lot. Member States also have the choice to make the splitting of public contracts mandatory.[86] In cases where this option is not exercised, as seen in countries such as the UK, the Netherlands, and Belgium,[87] contracting authorities must provide reasons for not dividing the contract into lots, known as the "Divide or explain formula".[88] This means that in the

83 Turley – International Institute for Sustainable Development (fn 81), 4–5; Turley, Hug Silva, Benson and Dominguez (fn 76), 7.

84 Turley, Hug Silva, Benson and Dominguez (fn 76), 11.

85 Fazekas, Tóth and King (fn 28), 21–22.

86 Article 46, para. 4 of the Directive 2014/24/EU.

87 Zimmermann (fn 4), 423.

88 Martin Trybus and Marta Andrecka "Favouring Small and Medium Sized Enterprises with Directive 2014/24/EU?" (2017), 3, *EPPPL*, 229; Herrera Anchustegui (fn 4), 126.

absence of a mandatory provision, the default approach is to divide contracts into lots and any decision to the contrary must be justified by the contracting authority by providing the main reasons in the procurement documents or an individual report as required under Article 84 of the 2014/24/EU Directive.[89]

There has been a long-standing belief that dividing large public contracts into lots expands the supplier and provider base to small-medium enterprises (SMEs), thereby enhancing competition in both the short and long term.[90] However, aside from promoting competition, dividing contracts into lots can also facilitate anticompetitive activities such as bid rigging. This occurs because when the same contracting authority awards multiple lots simultaneously, it allows economic operators, who typically bid on all lots, to "share the pie".[91] This ensures that each operator will possess at least one lot. Even in cases where the awarding of multiple lots is done sequentially rather than simultaneously, collusion among economic operators can still be encouraged, as they can "identify defections from the collusive agreement and react quickly within the same sequential award".[92] Additionally, the frequent interactions between economic operators bidding on multiple lots, and the pre-announcement of tenders for awarding lots can increase the likelihood of collusive practices like bid rigging.[93]

The significance of addressing collusive practices, such as bid rigging, lies in their detrimental impact on the purpose of dividing contracts into lots. Bid rigging can reduce allocative efficiency, which refers to the allocation of a procurement to the economic operators who can provide the goods or service at the highest value/price ratio.[94] If, due to bid rigging, economic operators awarded lots of a public contract do not offer the highest value/price ratio but instead submit artificially inflated prices to maximize profits, the public sector fails to achieve the best value

89 SIGMA and OECD "Brief 36 – Division off Contracts into Lots" <www.sigmaweb.org/publications/public-procurement-policy-brief-36-200117.pdf> accessed January 25, 2025, 4.

90 Martin Trybus "The Promotion of Small and Medium Sized Enterprises in Public Procurement: A Strategic Objective of the New Public Sector Directive?" in François Lichère, Roberto Caranta and Steen Treumer (eds) *Modernising Public Procurement: The New Directive* (Djøf Publishing 2014), 268; Laura Carpineto, Gustavo Piga and Matteo Zanza "The Variety of Procurement Practice: Evidence From Public Procurement" in Nicola Dimitri, Gustavo Piga and Giancarlo Spagnolo (eds) *Handbook of Procurement* (Cambridge University Press, 2006), 21–22; Albert Sanchez Graells "Prevention and Deterrence of Bid Rigging: A Look from the New EU Directive on Public Procurement" in Gabriella M. Racca and Christopher R. Yukins (eds) *Integrity and Efficiency in Sustainable Public Contracts. Balancing Corruption Concerns in Public Procurement Internationally* (Bruylant, Brussels, 2014), 12.

91 Gherghina Simona "Public Investments and the Application of Articles 101 and 102 TFEU" in Adrianna Almăşan and Peter Whelan (eds) *The Consistent Application of EU Competition Law: Substantive and Procedural Challenges* (Springer, 2017), 99.

92 SIGMA and OECD "Brief 2 – Economic Issues in Public Procurement" (January 2011), <www.sigmaweb.org/publications/Economic_Issues_Public_Procurement_2011.pdf> accessed on January 20, 2025.

93 OECD "Policy Roundtables – Competition in Bidding Markets 2007" <www.oecd.org/en/publications/competition-in-bidding-markets_af4c1b4b-en.html> 35 accessed on January 20, 2025

94 Zimmermann (fn 4), 425.

for money. This is especially concerning when contracts are split into lots, as it not only hinders value for money, but also leads to increased transaction costs. These costs are associated with managing multiple award procedures and conducting separate evaluations for each lot procured.[95] As a result, the combination of increased transaction costs and payments to undeserving suppliers results in losses to the government's budget, ultimately burdening taxpayers.

In order to prevent collusive practices when a public contract is split into lots, economic theory has emphasized that two vital rules should always apply. These rules are based on auction theory, similar to many findings in Chapter 2 of this book. After examining the purpose and content of these two intuitive rules of economic theory, we will assess their effectiveness in combatting bid rigging. The analysis will focus on the weaknesses that still need to be addressed when implementing these rules prescriptions, using hypothetical case scenarios from various markets and industries. It will be demonstrated that the aforementioned rules of economic theory are not a cure for all situations. They require further refinement and adjustments, especially considering that the weaknesses they present are not addressed by the 2014/24/EU Directive. Therefore, recommendations will be proposed to enhance their effectiveness.

4.4.1 The Number of Lots Should Be Smaller Than the Expected Number of Participants

The first recommendation is that the number of lots should be smaller than the expected number of participants.[96] This aligns with the analysis in Chapter 2, which suggests increasing the number of bidders relative to the number of auctioned items. This strategy aims to include bidders with overlapping interests and large complementarities across items,[97] preventing firms from dividing lots as if they were spoils at a low price.[98] Essentially, the goal of this criterion is to make it difficult for colluding tenderers to coordinate and share the rewards, as the discrepancy between participants and lots will deter bid riggers from profiting. However, this rule has limitations, as it does not consider the market composition or firms operating in multiple markets.[99] Additionally, the rule does not account for the "numerical and

95 ibid, 427.

96 Paul Klemperer "What Really Matters in Auction Design" (2002), 16(1), *Journal of Economic Perspectives*, 169–189; Paul Klemperer "How (Not) to Run Auctions: the European 3G Telecom Auctions" (2002), 46(4–5), *European Economic Review*, 829–845; Paul Klemperer *Auctions: Theory and Practice* (Princeton University Press, 2004); Grimm, Pacini, Spagnolo and Zanza (fn 4), 183–185.

97 Wang and Chen "Deterring Bidder Collusion: Auction Design Complements Antitrust Policy" (2016), 12(1), *Journal of Competition Law and Economics*, 57; Salmon (fn 20), 114, 117, 127.

98 Klemperer (fn 96), 177–178

99 Grimm, Pacini, Spagnolo and Zanza (fn 4), 183–185.

dimensional distribution of lots", in other words the lots' exact configuration.[100] When lot sizes vary and there is asymmetry in lot values, the potential for market sharing agreements may decrease[101] for two reasons.

First, splitting the contract into high and low-value lots can lower barriers to entry, allowing SMEs, to participate.[102] Second, greater asymmetry in lot values leads to differences in the contributions of ring members to collusive gains. Since the payoffs from participation in the ring are based on individual contributions to the profitability of the ring,[103] cooperative payoffs may vary among ring members. This discrepancy can challenge the sustainability of a bidding ring, especially if ring members are symmetric. A ring member receiving a small and low-value lot, may have reduced pay-offs, incentivizing deviation from the collusive agreement to secure additional profits.[104]

Despite the reasons mentioned above, the current rule of economic theory does not play a role in determining the optimal lot sizes and values. These decisions are left to the contracting authorities who have significant autonomy under the 2014/24/EU Directive. They determine the size and subject-matter of the lots,[105] making the rule secondary to the contracting authorities' freedom to decide autonomously, without administrative or judicial supervision.

Moreover, the rule cannot address effectively other forms of bid rigging, such as cover bidding, bid rotation and subcontracting arrangements. Let's first consider cover bidding. For example, if a ministry is furnishing a new office and splits the contract into lots for desks, chairs, storage units and meeting room furniture,[106] one or more of the tenderers may intentionally submit high offers or offers with special terms not specified in the contract notice. As a result, the contracting authority may reject these offers and award all or several of the contract lots to the designated winner. This scenario is possible under the 2014/24/EU Directive, which in Recital 79 allows for package bidding, where a bidder can offer a single price for a set of items.

Package bidding is allowed when after evaluating tenders based on the award criteria laid down for each lot, the contracting authorities compare those tenders with a bidder's submission for a specific combination of lots and find that the combined bid meets the relevant award criteria better than the individual bid for each

100 Ibid.

101 OECD "Hearing on Auctions and Tenders: Further Issues – Working Party No. 2 on Competition and Regulation" <https://one.oecd.org/document/DAF/COMP/WP2(2015)1/en/pdf> accessed January 20, 2025.

102 OECD, Second Public Procurement Review of the Mexican Institute of Social Security (IMSS): Reshaping Strategies for Better Healthcare (OECD Publishing, Paris 2018), 151.

103 Robert C. Marshall and Leslie M. Marx *The Economics of Collusion-Cartels and Bidding Rings* (MIT Press), 2012, 63.

104 Gian Luigi Albano and Giancarlo Spagnolo "Asymmetry and Collusion in Sequential Procurement: A 'Large Lot Last' Policy" (2010), 10(1), *The B.E. Journal of Theoretical Economics*.

105 Recital (78) of the Directive 2014/24/EU.

106 The scenario is taken from the Public Spend Forum. Please see Peter Smith "Five Alternative Approaches to Lots Lotting for Contracts" <www.publicspendforum.net/blogs/peter-smith/2017/03/15/contracts-lots-lotting-public-procurement-uk-europe> accessed on January 20, 2025.

lot.[107] Article 46, paragraph 2 of 2014/24/EU Directive along with Recital 79, supports this approach and requires contracting authorities to indicate in the procurement documents the objective and non-discriminatory criteria or rules they intend to apply, if one bidder is awarded more lots than the maximum number of lots specified in the contract notice or in the invitation to confirm interest.

Now, let's discuss bid rotation in the context of a hospital seeking to re-tender a management contract covering various non-medical services, such as cleaning, security, maintenance and catering. While a single facilities management contract is an option, separate competitions for each service may be chosen.[108] For example, if the hospital is not satisfied with a previous joint venture winner or wants to involve SMEs. In this scenario, shorter durations, like two years, may be set for individual service contracts to facilitate re-tendering.[109] This could lead to bidders rotating the lowest bids on a regular basis. Simply fixing the ratio between the number of potential bidders and the number of lots to increase competition, without considering the timing and scope of contract division may not prevent such anti-competitive practices.

Regarding the third form that bid rigging can take, namely subcontracting arrangements made as a payback ("*quid pro quo*"), imagine a public contract based on the most economically advantageous offer (MEAT) and split into two lots. For the first lot, tenderer A submits an offer of €200,000, tenderer B submits an offer of €180,000, and tenderer C submits an offer of €190,000. For the second lot tenderer B submits an offer of €160,000, while tenderer C submits an offer for €130,000. While economically tenderer B should win the first lot and tenderer C should win the second lot, the contracting authority decides that tenderer C's offer for the first lot is better based on the best price-quality ratio. Therefore, tenderer C agrees to perform both lots in accordance with Recital 79 and Article 46, paragraph 2 of the 2014/24/EU Directive. After being awarded the contract, tenderer C subcontracts part of the services to an undertaking that would have bid for the first lot, acting as tenderer D. However, tenderer D did not bid because they had an agreement with tenderer C to subcontract part of the contract to them. Simply dividing the contract into two lots with three participants does not prevent rigging through subcontracting arrangements.

Apart from the above, the rule that relates the number of bidders to the number of lots cannot be applied in the case of public contracts that need to be awarded quickly. In order to predict the *expected* number of participants (emphasis added), a contracting authority needs ample time to go to market, conduct research and plan the procurement process. For example, a health authority in the UK seeking solutions for low carbon ward lighting had to issue a procurement call two years

107 Recital (79) of the Directive 2014/24/EU.

108 Ibid.

109 For the usual duration of facilities management contracts, please see Hannah Davis "Deciding the Duration of a Facilities Management Contract" <www.fgould.com/uk-europe/articles/deciding-duration-facilities-management-contract/> accessed on January 20, 2025.

before the lighting was needed.[110] When urgent needs arise in public contracts, contracting authorities do not have the time to predict the number of undertakings that would be expected to take part in the procurement process.

Procurements for innovative solutions can be even more complex. It can be challenging for a contracting authority to map the competitive landscape and determine if similar contracts have been delivered on the market before. For this reason, in these cases, calculating the expected number of participants requires preliminary market consultations, which typically take three to six months to complete.[111] Moreover, until recently "most EU institutions had no policy for preliminary market consultations prior to starting the formal procurement procedure".[112] A legal basis clarifying the regime for a preliminary market consultation has only been introduced by the modifications of the Financial Regulation and Rules of Applications and entered into force in January 2016.[113] Hence, it is not always practically possible to gauge or to gauge timely and successfully the expected number of participants in a public procurement process in order to adjust beforehand the number of lots in which the contract will be divided.

Last but not least, there are procurements where "the technical aspects of supply require a very large number of lots", such as in the case of medicines.[114] In these markets, it may not always be feasible to define the number of lots in accordance with the expected number of participants, as priority is to procure a great variety of innovative medicines that will be readily available in the hospital pharmacies, regardless of the number of participating suppliers.

4.4.2 At Least One Lot More Than the Number of Incumbents, Reserved to New Entrants

The second recommendation is that contracting authorities should define at least one additional lot more than the number of incumbent firms and reserve it for new entrants.[115] This special treatment of new entrants acts as an incentive, encourag-

110 Luke Georghiou, Jakob Edler, Elvira Uyarra and Jillian Yeow "Policy Instruments for Public Procurement of Innovation: Choice, Design and Assessment" (2014), 86, *Technological Forecasting and Social Change*, 6.

111 European Commission (fn 16).

112 European Court of Auditors "The EU Institutions Can do More to Facilitate Access to Their Public Procurement – Special Report No 17" <www.eca.europa.eu/Lists/ECADocuments/SR16_17/SR_PROCUREMENT_EN.pdf> accessed January 20, 2025, 8; Nikola Komšić "Big Data for Procurement – The Importance of Correctly Acquiring and Using Information in Public Procurement" in Gustavo Piga and Tünde Tátrai (eds) *Law and Economics of Public Procurement Reforms* (Routledge, 2017).

113 European Court of Auditors (fn 112), 61.

114 Grimm, Pacini, Spagnolo and Zanza (fn 4), 183.

115 ibid, 169–170; Paul Klemperer "What Really Matters in Auction Design" (fn 96), 169–189; Ken Binmore and Paul Klemperer "The Biggest Auction Ever: The Sale of the British 3G Telecom Licences" (2002), 478(112), *The Economic Journal*, C74–C96; Paul Milgrom *Putting Auction Theory to Work* (Cambridge University Press, 2004).

ing the participation of weaker bidders in the public procurement process. They now have a reasonable chance of success by being able to bid on specific parts of the project. This can also increase the competitiveness of stronger bidders, as the entry of new bidders seeking to improve the procurement outcome can drive down prices on all lots, even if those new bidders are ultimately unsuccessful. This fosters competition not only in the short term but also in the long term, as the experience gained by new bidders make them significant competitors in future tenders.

Despite its good intentions, the effect and application of this rule are rather limited in practice. The main reason for this is the broad margin of discretion given to contracting authorities by the current Directive, which means that it is up to them whether and to what extent they will apply the rule. The significance of this parameter becomes obvious when considered in combination with the overall tension of the European Member States not to secure preferential treatment for SMEs. Data from the **European Public Accountability Mechanisms (EuroPAM)** in the area of public procurement supports this.[116] Before proceeding to the assessment of EuroPAM data, it is important to highlight the fact that in an empirical study by PricewaterhouseCoopers **(PwC)** commissioned by the European Commission in 2014 proved that "breaking tenders down into lots is one of the most important tools to help SMEs access public contracts", while a scatter diagram in the same study suggested that "there was some marginal correlation between the median value of single awards (lots) and the proportion of these contracts won by SMEs in the EU".[117] This conclusion is also supported by Piga and Zanza[118] who conclude that SME participation in public procurement processes is mainly achieved by splitting tenders into lots that can be bid for separately, as well as by Sandholm.[119] However, in another empirical study that regarded only the sector of defence, it was found that splitting a public contract into lots does not automatically increase the chances of successful SME participation, because some aspects of the tender,

116 EuroPAM is an "observatory of European transparency legislation, similar to national procurement portals" and one of the areas it covers is public procurement. It is also one of the watchdog tools that DIGIWHIST (Digital Whistleblower) project has to identify systemic vulnerabilities in the respective legislations and their implementation. To see more about the project, follow the link <http://digiwhist.eu/about-digiwhist/> accessed on January 20, 2025.

117 Gunnar Wessel Thomassen, Pernille Orderud, Ivar Strand, Máté Péter Vincze, Patrick de Bas, Maarten van der Wagt and Anastasia Yagafarova "SMEs' Access to Public Procurement Markets and Aggregation of Demand in the EU-February 2014" <https://publications.europa.eu/en/publication-detail/-/publication/c0681db7-e56e-11e5-8a50-01aa75ed71a1> accessed January 20, 2025, 52–53.

118 Gustavo Piga and Matteo Zanza "An Exploratory Analysis of Public Procurement Practices in Europe" in Thai KV et al. (eds) *Challenges in Public Procurement: An International Perspective* (Boca Raton, Florida 2005), 185, 187–188.

119 Tuomas Sandholm "Expressive Commerce and Its Application to Sourcing: How We Conducted $35 Billion of Generalized Combinatorial Auctions" (2007), 28(3), *AI Magazine*, 49.

such as SMEs' competence in matters of procedure for participation in public tenders, should get improved.[120]

Regarding the data from EuroPAM, the investigation focused on the database relevant to the public procurement rules of each European Member State in 2020. Specifically, the focus was on whether there was preferential treatment for SMEs in every EU Member State.[121] After studying the answers provided on this issue based on the legislation of each Member State, it was concluded that only 7 out of 28 European Member States actually had preferential treatment for SMEs in 2020. Most of these seven EU countries had not implemented specific measures to ensure this preferential treatment, relying instead on general provisions. Greece, Cyprus and the Netherlands serve as illustrative examples. This raises the question of whether and to what extent contracting authorities will reserve lot(s) of public contracts for SMEs, given their discretion under the current Directive not to do so.

Furthermore, the rule above may face practical hindrances. First, the special treatment of SMEs may raise fairness issues and could potentially violate state aid rules and the principle of equal treatment.[122] Second, reserving one or more lots for new market entrants may reduce the number of lots available for incumbents potentially weakening competition for all lots.[123] Strong bidders may exit the market altogether if they are unable to secure a share of significant procurement contracts.[124] Third, defining just one lot more than the number of incumbents and reserving it for new entrants does not guarantee that the market will not still be dominated by incumbents. The possibility of awarding multiple lots to the same tenderer, as outlined in the current Directive (Recital (79) and Article 46, paragraph 2), along with a bidder's right to withdraw their tender at any time, may incentivize either collusion between incumbents and new entrants or lead to blackmail of the latter by the former.

The fewer and weaker the new players in a market, the easier it is for incumbent firms to blackmail them or make them an offer of side-payment for the latter to withdraw their tender, so the remaining lots are shared by the incumbents. Similarly, in the Netherlands, the weak entrant was not able to participate in the procurement process until the end because it was threatened by an incumbent.[125]

120 Michael Eßig and Andreas H. Glas "Considering Small and Medium-Sized Suppliers in Public Procurement – The Case of the German Defence Sector" in Dirk Mattfeld, Thomas Spengler, Jan Brinkmann and Martin Grunewald (eds) *Logistics Management – Contributions of the Section Logistics of the German Academic Association for Business Research, 2015, Braunschweig, Germany* (Springer International Publishing, Switzerland 2016), 30.

121 The dataset is available in the following link: <http://europam.eu/?module=data-downloads> accessed on January 20, 2025. See particularly Qual-26 in the Microsoft Excel document.

122 OECD "Policy Roundtables: Competition in Bidding Markets" (fn 93), 35.

123 Gian Luigi Albano, Nicola Dimitri, Isabelle Perrigne and Gustavo Piga "Fostering Participation" in Nicola Dimitri, Gustavo Piga and Giancarlo Spagnolo (eds) *Handbook of Procurement* (Cambridge University Press, 2006), 287.

124 Ibid.

125 See more about the Netherlands Auction (July 2000) in the article of Paul Klemperer "How (not) to run auctions: the European 3G Telecom Auctions" (fn 96), 833–834.

Although the new entrant complained to the government, the government took no action, "perhaps because excluding the incumbent firm would have ended the auction immediately and it might have been hard to impose a meaningful fine".[126] Things were worse in the case of Italy where even a strong bidder (and not just a weak one) withdrew its tender at the last minute, supposedly because there had been collusion by which the firm at issue took part in the auction only to avoid invoking the rule reducing the number of licences.[127] Apart from Europe, the United States also suffered from the undesirable use of bid withdrawals as a strategic device. Indicatively, in spectrum auctions conducted by the **Federal Communications Commission (FCC)**, it was revealed that most of the bid withdrawals were used for undesirable bid signalling and in order to "acquire near the end of the auction more preferred licenses that seem to free up after the decline of another bidder".[128]

For all these reasons above, the intuitive rules of economic theory that were just analyzed are not a panacea for all cases. In order to render them more effective, particular attention should be paid to the transparency rules that govern the procurement procedure when a public contract is split into lots. The less information is concealed about the bidder identities, the better the aforementioned rules can apply in practice, as it will be less likely for cover bidding, bid rotation and sub-contracting arrangements to take place. As already explained, these are the main forms of bid rigging schemes that do not fall within the scope of the first rule of economic theory, as the optimal number of lots does not affect their implementation.

Bid withdrawals are another issue that needs to be addressed in order to discourage insincere bidding in public contracts that are divided into lots. This would help maintain optimal asymmetry between lots and economic operators throughout the procurement process. One possible solution could be to allow bidders to withdraw their bids in at most two rounds of an auction, similar to what the FCC in the United States already does.[129] However, this approach may not always be applicable all procurement procedures outlined in the 2014/24/EU Directive, such as electronic auctions (Article 35 of the Directive). Another potential solution, inspired by the legal system in the United States, could involve imposing penalties for withdrawing a high bid.[130] The penalty could be the difference between the withdrawn bid and the final sale price, compensating the public purchaser for any damages incurred.[131] However, European systems of tort or delict often do not recognize the deterrent or penal function of civil liability, unlike the US legal

126 Ibid.
127 ibid, 834–835.
128 Peter Cramton "Simultaneous Ascending Auctions" in Peter Cramton, Yoav Shoham and Richard Steinberg (eds), *Combinatorial Auctions* (MIT Press, 2006), 112–113.
129 ibid.
130 Ibid, 105.
131 Ibid. See also David P. Porter "The Effect of Bid Withdrawal in a Multi-Object Auction" (1999), 4(1), *Review of Economic Design*, 73–97.

system.[132]Additionally, many civil law jurisdictions are hesitant to award damages due to public policy concerns.[133]

Punitive damages are considered contrary to public policy in Europe because they deviate from the civil law's compensatory logic, which aims to restore the injured party to their initial state (*in integrum restitution*) without providing additional enrichment.[134] Moreover, punitive damages are seen as "a *quasi* criminal sanction"[135] even though they are awarded in civil or administrative proceedings, as is the case here. Despite this, the **Court of Justice of the EU (CJEU)** has taken a bold step towards formally authorizing punitive damages in cases of intellectual property infringement, by stating that the Member States are not prohibited from introducing punitive damages as a measure where an intellectual property right has been infringed.[136] Hence, it could be said that a similar approach could be taken for bid withdrawals.

In the further alternative, it may be suggested to completely prohibit bid withdrawals, unless they are sufficiently justified by the relevant economic operators and supported by adequate evidence. Drawing examples from US legislation, valid justifications for bid withdrawal could include a clerical or mechanical error made in good faith (*bona fide*), not due to gross negligence, that materially alters the bid from the bidder's original intent.[137] Another acceptable reason for bid withdrawal could be unforeseen circumstances arising after submitting the bid. In either case, it is recommended that the mistake be clearly outlined in a written notice within strict deadlines from the bid withdrawal request. Obvious mistakes, such as typographical, arithmetical, transposition errors or errors in extending unit price, should be corrected rather than leading to bid withdrawal.[138]

A last issue that should be clarified by the European legislator is the pricing strategy bidders can employ when bundling lots is allowed; otherwise it could encourage incumbents to engage in illegal practices and disadvantage SMEs in the procurement process, as seen in examples from the Netherlands and Italy. In subparagraph 1 of Article 46, paragraph 2, the 2014/24/EU Directive does not clarify whether a bidder can offer a lower price for all lots or a combination of lots compared to individual lots. If this is the case, this may promote multiple bidding and value for money for the public purchaser. Yet, at the same time concerns about competition intensity and SME participation in the market emerge. This could

132 Gerhard Wagner "Punitive Damages in European Private Law" in Jürgen Basedow, Klaus J. Hopt, Reinhard Zimmermann and Andreas Stier (eds) *Max Planck Encyclopedia of European Private Law* (Oxford University Press, 2012)

133 Csongor István Nagy "Recognition and Enforcement of US Judgments Involving Punitive Damages in Continental Europe" (2012), 30(1), *Netherlands Internationaal Privaatrecht (NIPR)*, 5.

134 ibid.

135 ibid.

136 Wagner (fn 132).

137 Massachusetts General Laws, Chapter 149, Section 44B (3) and (4) <https://malegislature.gov/Laws/GeneralLaws/PartI/TitleXXI/Chapter149/Section44B> accessed January 20, 2025.

138 Code of Maryland Regulations, Title 21.05.02.12 "Mistakes in Bids" < http://mdrules.elaws.us/comar/21.05.02.12> accessed January 20, 2025.

favour incumbents but also incentivize them to use illegal methods, such as side-payments or blackmail, to eliminate weaker market players and secure lot awards for themselves. For this reason and to uphold the initial objective of involving SMEs public procurement, this interpretation should be explicitly rejected, even if it comprises value for money.

4.5 Conclusion

This chapter has undertaken a critical review of the first phase of the EU public procurement process, specifically the procurement planning phase which involves determining which goods or services are to be purchased by a contracting authority and when. It has addressed the conduct of preliminary market consultations, the formulation of technical specifications as well as the decision made by contracting authorities on whether to divide the public contract into lots. The analysis reveals that the current Directive has failed to consider conditions and incentives that increase the likelihood of bid rigging outcomes.

First, the direct engagement of contracting authorities with market operators in the context of market dialogue raised bid rigging concerns. The opportunities for potential suppliers to meet are many and the collusion between public officers and undertakings may sustain bidding rings that already exist. To address this issue, the chapter argued that contracting authorities should refrain from contacting market operators during the procurement planning stage where cooperation with Competition Authorities is possible. Instead, cooperation should only occur when market consultation is necessary to gather information about the market structure, such as the availability of suppliers for effective competition, whether there are past suppliers of similar contracts, and the number of economic operators required for delivery of the relevant contract.

If direct engagement with market operators is inevitable, it is suggested that contracting authorities should have a policy for conducting preliminary market consultations. The chapter recommended using checklist templates and keeping a record of the market analysis process, as well as drafting a report at the end of each market analysis. This report should outline the issues considered and the main conclusions drawn. Additionally, the report should include an updated self-declaration confirming that procurement officers conducting the preliminary market consultations followed the guidelines of their authority, shared information with all candidates and tenderers and avoided corrupt practices. The report should be published and sent to interested economic operators, without revealing the identity or number of economic operators involved in the technical dialogue, to prevent cartel formation or the implementation of a cartel existing among economic operators. The report should also not disclose specific points of the tender documents that the contracting authority intends to modify after the preliminary market consultation, because this would facilitate cartel redistributions. When procurement officers have face-to-face discussions with economic operators, it is important to have at least one neutral person present. The procurement officers conducting the preliminary market consultation should be different from those evaluating the bids and awarding public contracts.

Another factor that could increase the likelihood of bid rigging is how technical specifications are formulated by contracting authorities. The chapter pointed out the uncertainty surrounding the term "*equivalent*" that must accompany any listed technical specifications and its impact on the number of competing bidders at the bidding stage. It was also underlined that it is quite risky to give contracting authorities too much discretion in evaluating the equivalence or not of a solution proposed by tenderers with the technical specifications. This evaluation should be done using only the means of proof explicitly mentioned in paragraph 1 of Article 44. If a contracting authority abuses its discretionary power or does not conduct the equivalence evaluation in a flexible and procompetitive manner, it can narrow the field of competition in that market, increasing the risk of bid rigging. Therefore, it was recommended that the 2014 Directive be revised and the principle established in *Max Havelaar* be overturned, allowing contracting authorities to refer to specific labels when selecting the most economically advantageous tender.

Another point that was raised regarding technical specifications was that the shift towards performance-based specifications may deter many economic operators from bidding because of their innovative nature which is still unknown to the majority of undertakings. In a concentrated market with a narrow field of competition such as this one, the effectiveness of collusion increases. The situation may be further exacerbated due to the inevitable interrelation of performance-based specifications with the preliminary market consultations, whose conduct is not properly and adequately regulated by the current Directive in terms of competition law.

The last section of this chapter was dedicated to collusive practices when the public contract is split into lots. The two basic rules of economic theory were critically reviewed, and it was examined to what extent they can successfully address bid rigging or if they need further elaboration and amendments. As it was shown, the intuitive rules of economic theory are not applicable in all cases and there is a need to make them more robust and effective by minimizing the amount of information disclosed about the bidder identities when a public contract is split into lots as well as by regulating the issue of bid withdrawals more strictly. The chapter's analysis suggests that one possible measure could be to completely forbid bid withdrawals if they are not sufficiently justified by the relevant firms that request it and if their request is not accompanied by adequate evidence. It was also highlighted that the European legislator should not leave unaddressed the issue regarding the pricing strategy that a bidder can adopt when bundling of lots is permissible. If it is officially interpreted that the price which a bidder can offer for all the lots (or a combination of some) can be lower than the one he offers for the individual lots, the public purchaser will benefit in the short term by achieving value for money. Nevertheless, in the long term this means the encouragement of big incumbent firms in the market to bid and exhaust all possibilities of winning multiple lots in the relevant procurement process to the detriment of SMEs. One of the means that may be used in order to achieve their goal is the circumvention of the division of public contracts into lots, as already explained below through several illustrative examples.

As long as the aforementioned concerns and questions are not entirely overcome, bid rigging is likely to take place both at this procurement stage and at the next one, that is, contracting phase. Since the procurement planning considers when and how the processing steps of a public tender will be conducted, it makes sense to investigate next in the book the procurement procedures and techniques. Therefore, in the next chapter we will see how a procurement planning stage susceptible to bid rigging can constitute the ground for new or sustainable bid rigging practices at the competitive bidding stage. Specifically, the next chapter will examine the design of the contracting phase under the current Directive in order to identify the aspects of procurement procedures and techniques that heighten the likelihood of bid rigging and concerted practices which is already evident from the procurement planning.

5 Contracting Phase I

Are the Procedures under 2014/24/EU Directive the Most Effective Toolkit for Preventing Bid Rigging?

5.1 Introduction

As demonstrated in the previous chapter of this book, the initial phase of the public procurement process, known as pre-contractual procurement planning, is structured in a manner that gives rise to several competition law concerns. The involvement of private sector economic operators in the development and awarding of contracts can facilitate bid rigging under certain circumstances. This is also true for the formulation of technical specifications and the division of public contracts into lots by contracting authorities. Chapter 4 outlined strategies to make bid-rigging schemes more difficult to execute during the preparation phase design.

This finding has important ramifications for the analysis in the current chapter. Due to structural weaknesses and questions that are still to be overcome by the European legislator, there is a higher risk of bid rigging in the second phase of the public procurement process, namely the contracting phase. Bid rigging in the contracting phase can lead to the exclusion of potentially more efficient competitors from the bidding process and reduce suppliers' incentive to improve quality or make innovations. This does not benefit the community, nor does it ensure that taxpayers' money is spent in the most effective way, as the best value for money is not achieved. Studies show that collusion among suppliers adds at least 20% to the price that would otherwise be paid.[1] This is public money that could otherwise go to public services, health or paying off national debt. Hence, this chapter focuses on the procedures provided by the 2014/24/EU Directive. It scrutinizes the specific procedures which present a particular risk of being misused for collusion. It is argued that there is a need to adopt design features that significantly reduce the scope for collusive outcomes, with the aim of ensuring fair competition for public contracts and optimal procurement outcomes. Efficient procedures that ensure contracting authorities obtain the best possible offer with efficient use of public funds are crucial in the context of severe budgetary constraints and economic difficulties

1 Robert D. Anderson and William Kovacic "Competition Policy and International Trade Liberalisation: Essential Complements to Ensure Good Performance in Public Procurement Markets" (2009), 18, *Public Procurement Law Review*, 71. See also Luke M. Froeb, Robert A. Koyak and Gregory J. Werden "What is the Effect of Bid Rigging on Prices?" (1993), 42(4), *Economic Letters*, 419.

DOI: 10.4324/9781003359999-5

in many EU Member States.[2] Moreover, efficient procedures benefit all economic operators and make it easier for SMEs and cross-border bidders to participate in EU public procurement procedures.[3] This objective will be achieved by assessing the tender provisions of the current Directive against the conditions that favour bid rigging according to auction theory, as already outlined and analyzed in Chapter 2. This will be the overarching methodological framework of this chapter.

Therefore, the chapter is structured as follows. Section 5.2.1 discusses open and restricted procedures and highlights the risk of bid rigging when public procurers have the discretion to choose between the open and restricted procedure without considering the values and circumstances of each Member State. The chapter recommends that the open procedure should be the default procurement method, with specified exceptions. Section 5.2.2 addresses the negotiated procedure without prior publication and the innovation partnership which follows the procedural rules of the competitive procedure with negotiation. There is a risk of bid rigging when contracting authorities use this procedure to award a public contract to a consortium of economic operators for technical reasons. Due to the absence of competition, the high-level technologies involved, as well as the fact that procurement officers usually abuse negotiated procedures in order to favour particular economic operators, it is very likely that "sham" consortia between potential competitors will arise, which serve no other purpose than to hide a damaging bidding ring. To address this, the use of "voluntary ex ante transparency notice" (VEAT) is recommended.

In Section 5.2.3 the competitive dialogue is discussed, noting that there can only be two participants in the post-dialogue phase. To prevent bid rigging, it is suggested that at least three candidates be selected for the post-dialogue phase to ensure genuine competition. If this is not possible, contracting authorities should assess the vulnerability of the remaining candidates to coordinated conduct. Section 5.2.4 briefly touches on the innovation partnership, highlighting the importance of providing precise information in the competitive phase to avoid narrowing competition unnecessarily. The accountability of contracting authorities and procurement officers in drafting minimum requirements for tenders in an innovation partnership procurement and when assessing the capacity of candidates at the competitive stage is emphasized. Finally, Section 5.3 concludes with some final remarks.

5.2 Choice of Procedures (Articles 25–30 of Directive 2014/24/EU)

This section discusses specific primary procedures that have been inherited from previous procurement directives and are currently available to all procurers. The

2 European Commission "Green Paper on the Modernisation of EU Public Procurement Policy towards a More Efficient European Procurement Market, Brussels 27.2011", COM (2011) 15 final, 3 <https://eur-lex.europa.eu/legal-content/EN/TXT/PDF/?uri=CELEX:52011DC0015&from=EN> accessed on February 10, 2024.

3 Ibid, 4.

chapter's focus is on identifying where the danger of bid rigging lies in their context and how this issue should be addressed.

5.2.1 Open and Restricted Procedures – Analysis of Bid Rigging Issues and Recommendations

As explained in Chapter 1, the open procedure is primarily used for low-value purchases, where the requirement is simple and the procurer is seeking the cheapest supplier.[4] In the open procedure, contracting authorities and entities publish a contract notice and any interested economic operator can submit a tender. From these tenderers who meet the criteria for qualitative selection, the contracting authority chooses the tender that best fulfils the award criterion indicated in the contract notice (lowest price or most economically advantageous tender).[5]

The restricted tender is the procedure that contracting authorities use when they prioritize shorter time frames, reducing wasted transaction costs,[6] or minimizing bid and evaluation costs for complex procurements with limited tender spread due to their specialized nature.[7] In the restricted procedure, all economic operators can respond to the contract notice to express interest in participating, but only selected candidates meeting the criteria indicated in the notice, are invited to submit tenders.[8]

Under the 2014/24/EU Directive, public procurers have the freedom to choose between the open and restricted procedures. Article 26(2) contemplates that "Member States shall provide that contracting authorities may apply open or restricted procedures as regulated in this Directive". This freedom means that Member States cannot restrict the use of these procurement procedures to specific circumstances or types of procurement.[9] The 2014/24/EU Directive allows contracting authorities to define open and restricted procedures independently of the values and factual circumstances of each Member State. However, the choice of the restricted procedure over the open one can be risky in terms of collusion. Restricted procedures are more likely to lead to collusive behaviour than open procedures.[10] This is due to their higher costs for

4 PwC, London Economics and Ecorys for the European Commission "Public Procurement in Europe-Cost and Effectiveness" (2011) <https://op.europa.eu/en/publication-detail/-/publication/0cfa3445-7724-4af5-8c2b-d657cd690c03> accessed on December 3, 2024, 5.

5 European Commission (fn 2), 13.

6 Transaction costs occur when economic operators submit expression of interest for public contracts which are not relevant or attractive to them.

7 Abby Semple *A Practical Guide to Public Procurement* (Oxford University Press, 2015), 73–75.; Sue Arrowsmith *The Law of Public and Utilities Procurement: Regulation in the EU and UK*, (3rd edition, Sweet & Maxwell, 2014), 608–609.

8 European Commission (fn 2), fn 28, 13.

9 Arrowsmith (fn 7), 611–612.

10 Ibid, para. 7.03.

bidding firms,[11] fewer offers received[12] and lower likelihood of cross-border bids compared to open procedures.[13] The selection stage in restricted procedures, which involves assessing all economic operators responding to the notice, can cause delays and costs that may deter supplier participation.[14] Moreover, shorter submission periods[15] in restricted procedures leave less time for bidders to prepare their bids,[16] potentially limiting competition, especially when this is combined with early information provision to the desired bidder(s).[17] These factors, combined with rules favouring large firms and deterring new market entrants, make the restricted procedure less attractive for SMEs and more conducive to cartel behaviour.[18] In view of these parameters, the restricted procedure does not attract new market entrants very easily. In light of auction theory discussed in Chapter 2, deterring entry is key factor for cartels to thrive.[19] Moreover, with fewer bidders in restricted procedures, it becomes easier for them to signal collusive outcomes to other bidders, interpret signals and reach agreements quickly.[20]

At this point, it should be noted that corruption can increase the risks of the restricted procedure being used for improper purposes. Corrupt procurers may choose the restricted procedure over the open procedure when they are bribed to favour specific bidders and ignore collusive schemes, especially in markets with anticompetitive structures.[21] As demonstrated in Chapter 4, public procurement is a vulnerable area for unethical business practices, such as corruption. The Stockholm

11 PwC, London Economics and Ecorys for the European Commission (fn 4), 79–80.
12 Ibid, 95.
13 Ibid.
14 Arrowsmith (fn 7), para. 7.03.
15 The time period between the publication of call for tenders and the deadline for submitting the bids.
16 Mihály Fazekas, István János Tóth and Lawrence Peter King "Corruption Manual for Beginners: 'Corruption Techniques' in Public Procurement with Examples from Hungary" <www.crcb.eu/wp-content/uploads/2013/12/Fazekas-Toth-King_Corruption-manual-for-beginners_v2_2013.pdf> accessed on February 11, 2024. See also Charles Kenny and Maria Musatova "Red Flags of Corruption in World Bank Projects: An Analysis of Infrastructure Contracts – Policy Research Working Paper 5243, 2010", World Bank, Washington DC, 14, <https://openknowledge.worldbank.org/bitstream/handle/10986/3731/WPS5243.pdf?sequence=1&isAllowed=y> accessed on February 11, 2024; OECD *Integrity in Public Procurement. Good Practice from A to Z* (OECD, 2007), <https://read.oecd-ilibrary.org/governance/integrity-in-public-procurement_9789264027510-en#page1> accessed on February 11, 2024.
17 Fazekas, Tóth and King (fn 16), 34.
18 Arrowsmith (fn 7), para. 7.03.
19 Robert C. Marshall and Michael J. Meurer "Bidder Collusion and Antitrust Law: Refining the Analysis of Price Fixing to Account for the Special Features of Auction Markets" (2004), 72(1), *Antitrust Law Journal*, 93.
20 Timothy C. Salmon "Preventing Collusion between Firms in Auctions" in M.C.W Janssen (ed) *Auctioning Public Assets: Analysis and Alternatives* (Cambridge University Press, 2004), 114.
21 The waste disposal market, the construction sector, the IT-supply sector, the electricity market as well as the market for certain postal services in a number of EU Member States are illustrative examples of oligopolistic markets which are prone to cartel-building. See European Commission (fn 2), 30, fn 66.

Programme[22] also highlights public procurement as a key area in the fight against corruption.[23] Therefore, the wide discretion given to contracting authorities in choosing the procurement procedure allows corrupt public procurers to opt for the restricted procedure to limit competition and exclude certain bidders.

To address this issue, it is suggested that the current EU procurement rules incorporate a provision similar to Articles 28 and 29 of the Model Law on Public Procurement 2011, as adopted by the **United Nations Commission on International Trade Law (UNCITRAL).**[24] Recognizing the discretionary decision-making involved in procurement by government entities and the potential for abuse, at all levels but also a risk of abuse, the 2011 Model Law mandates the use of the open procedure as the default method of procurement, unless specific exceptions apply.[25] The 2011 Model Law contemplates that a procuring entity may engage in procurement by means of restricted tendering when:[26]

(a) The subject matter of the procurement, by reason of its highly complex or specialised nature, is available only from a limited number of suppliers or contractors; or
(b) The time and cost required to examine and evaluate a large number of tenders would be disproportionate to the value of the subject matter of the procurement.

Moreover, if the procuring entity uses a method of procurement other than open tendering, it shall state the reasons and circumstances upon which it relied to justify the use of that method.[27] Thus, contrary to what was suggested in the previous chapter about the call for less transparency when a public contract is split into lots, the observance of the transparency principle at this point of the procurement cycle is essential. Transparency will ensure that the decisions of public procurers do not reduce competition, nor do they enhance the likelihood of cartelization in public markets.

22 Council document 17024/09 adopted by the European Council on December 10–11, 2009.
23 European Commission (fn 2), 48.
24 This is a Model Law which provides a template for the design and development of regulatory rules on public procurement. It is used by many countries, such as Egypt, India, Kazakhstan, the Russian Federation and Thailand, as well as by international organizations, such as the African Development Bank, the Asian Development Bank, the European Bank for Reconstruction and Development, the Inter-American Development Bank, the Organisation for Economic Co-Operation and Development (OECD) and the World Bank. It assumes that states will regulate procurement through legally binding rules. See United Nations Commission on International Trade Law "Status: UNCITRAL Model Law on Public Procurement (2011)" <https://uncitral.un.org/en/texts/procurement/modellaw/public_procurement/status> accessed July 30, 2024.
25 UNCITRAL Model Law on Public Procurement 2011 <www.uncitral.org/pdf/english/texts/procurem/ml-procurement-2011/2011-Model-Law-on-Public-Procurement-e.pdf> accessed June 1, 2017, Article 28 of the 2011 UNCITRAL Model Law on Public Procurement.
26 Ibid, Article 28, para. 1.
27 Ibid, Article 28, para. 3.

Alternatively, it could probably be argued that there should be an explicit provision under the current Directive listing the grounds for using open and restricted procedures in specific market conditions, by analogy with the list of grounds for the use of competitive dialogue and competitive procedure with negotiation (Article 26, paragraph 4 of the current Directive). Nonetheless, this suggestion is questionable, as we cannot be sure whether the situations in which open and restricted procedures shall be available to contracting authorities will be successfully captured by such criteria without the danger of pigeonholing. In addition, by restricting the authorities' use of these procedures and by removing their discretion to choose, we may ultimately eliminate the officials' ability to shape and complete their priorities, as procurement officials are particularly competent to assess and prioritize the needs of the authority they serve. "Excellence requires the ability to demonstrate distinctiveness" and so rule-bound procurement entities with officers deprived of discretion and flexibility to react strategically may result in lack of good sense and judgement.[28]

The choice to use either the open or the restricted procedure reflects the different values and priorities that each contracting authority has. Hence, it is not outlandish to suggest that additionally to the adoption of provisions similar to Articles 28 and 29 of the 2011 Model Law, there is need to invest in procurement officers and recognize them as professionals who have adequate knowledge, training and experience to make informed decisions regarding the use of open or restricted procedures. This presupposes a solid grounding in competition law as well as the development of a clear set of values and integrity standards in which procurement officers must be trained in order to ensure that they have a good understanding of markets, risks of corruption and collusive behaviour by bidders. Furthermore, procurement officers should be incentivized to work efficiently and maximize their utility in the administration by getting bonuses and salaries as high as those in the private sector.[29] It has been empirically proved that public wages have a significant negative effect on the index of corruption,[30] but this does not necessarily apply to developing countries, where higher public wages can generate a bad selection

28 Steven Kelman "Procurement and Public Management: The Fear Of Discretion and the Quality of Government Performance" (AEI Press 1990), 9, 28.

29 OECD (fn 16), 18.

30 Indicatively, it has been proved that experienced low-wage officials accept bribes 91% of the times whereas the proportion is reduced to 38% among experienced high-wage officials. Experienced high-wage public officials are also 27% points less likely to choose the corrupt option. See R. van Veldhuizen "The Influence of Wages on Public Officials' Corruptibility: A Laboratory Investigation" (2013), 39, *Journal of Economic Psychology*, 346, 352; Caroline Van Rijckeghem and Beatrice Weder "Bureaucratic Corruption and the Rate of Temptation: Do Wages in the Civil Service Affect Corruption and by How Much?" (2001), 65(2), *Journal of Development Economics*, 307–331; Nadeem Ul Haque and Ratna Sahay "Do Government Wage Cuts Close Budget Deficits? Costs of Corruption" (1996), 43(4), *Staff Papers (International Monetary Fund)*, 754–778.

effect resulting in highly motivated workers being crowded out by individuals susceptible to be corrupted.[31]

5.2.2 Negotiated Procedure without Prior Publication – Bid Rigging Issues and Recommendations

As previously discussed in Chapter 1, the competitive procedure with negotiation is a type of procedural process that typically receives only a few offers.[32] Therefore, it is only utilized in specific situations, which are common to both the competitive procedure with negotiation and competitive dialogue, as outlined in Article 26(4) of the 2014/24/EU Directive. When this procedure is employed without a call for competition, meaning without prior publication of a contract notice, it can have significant negative effects on competition. Consequently, negotiated procedures without prior publication are reserved for exceptional circumstances, such as natural disasters that necessitate immediate action.[33] In cases where contracting authorities invoke this exception, they are required to provide justifications as to why there are no reasonable alternatives, substitutes or functionally comparable works, supplies and services available for procurement.[34]

In the subsequent subsection, I will elaborate on how the current regulatory framework of the negotiated procedure without prior publication can facilitate bid rigging.

5.2.2.1 Only One Possible Provider for Technical Reasons (Article 32, Paragraph 2(b)(ii))

According to Article 32, paragraph 2(b)(ii) of the 2014/24/EU Directive:

> The negotiated procedure without prior publication may be used for public works, supplies and service contracts…where the works, supplies or services can be supplied only by a particular economic operator… as competition is absent for technical reasons.

If there is no interest from other undertakings because the contract can only be carried out by a single business, the contracting authority is permitted to negotiate with only one supplier, without publishing an OJEU notice advertising that the relevant contracting authority is commencing procurement for goods, services or works. This is an exceptional case that should only apply when no reasonable

31 Timothy Besley and John McLaren "Taxes and Bribery: The Role of Wage Incentives" (1993), 103(416), *The Economic Journal*, 119–141; Van-Ha Le, Jakob de Haan and Erik Dietzenbacher "Do Higher Government Wages Reduce Corruption? Evidence Based on a Novel Dataset" (2013), *CESifo Working Paper 4254*, CESifo Group Munich <https://papers.ssrn.com/sol3/papers.cfm?abstract_id=2274648> accessed on February 18, 2024.

32 PwC, London Economics and Ecorys for the European Commission (fn 4), 94.

33 Recital 80 of the 2014/24/EU Directive.

34 Ibid, Recital 50 and Article 32.

alternative or substitute exists and the absence of competition is not the result of an artificial narrowing down of the parameters of the procurement.[35] In the same vein, before the introduction of the current Directive, the CJEU has used a twofold test to assess if the negotiated procedure without prior publication of a contract notice should apply on the grounds of technical reasons. First, it assesses whether the existence of "technical reasons" was established or not and second it asks for proof that these "technical reasons" made it absolutely necessary to award that contract to a particular contractor.[36] Hence, the exclusivity due to technical reasons should be rigorously justified on a case-by-case basis, to ensure that enough competition is triggered, despite the absence of an advert placed in OJEU.[37]

Yet, the fact that contracting authorities have the right to award the public contract to a *consortium*[38] of economic operators, when exclusivity arises from technical reasons, raises bid rigging concerns, despite the aforementioned safeguards (emphasis added).[39] As a general rule, bidding consortia are set up for commercial reasons, such as raising sufficient capital to participate in a public tender or spreading the risk across a number of participants, without necessarily reducing competition and/or causing a price effect. However, when a procurement procedure is moved out of the more transparent domain and aims to award technologically complicated contracts, it becomes easier for a few relatively homogeneous suppliers with similar technology and inputs to use the consortium arrangement as a cover to eliminate competitive pressure and reduce the number of competitors to one, without having legitimate commercial reasons to cooperate.[40] This is because in

35 Ibid, Article 32, para. 2(b).

36 Case C-57/94 Commission v Italy (Acoli-Mare) [1995] ECR I-1249, para. 24; C-385/02 Commission v Italy [2004] ECR I-8121, para. 19; C-394/02 Commission v Greece [2005] ECR I-4713, para. 34.

37 Preamble (50) of Directive 2014/24/EU.

38 In the procurement context, consortium refers to two or more entities that have come together specifically for the purpose of bidding for appointment as a supplier and can include those parties establishing a special purpose vehicle to be the prime contracting party with the contracting authority". See Mills and Reeve "Glossary" <www.procurementportal.com/procurements-started-before-24-february-2025/public-contracts-regulations-2015-glossary/> accessed on January 10, 2025.

39 The formation of consortia and the award of public contracts to them in the context of negotiated procedures without prior publication is a practice adopted by several contracting authorities in EU Member States. Indicatively see case C-199/85, Commission v Italy (1987) ECR and case C-394/02, Commission v Greece [2005] ECR I-4713.

40 A joint bidding consortium as a bid rigging device to eliminate competition is not a theoretical consideration. Bidding consortia among potential competitors, temporary or otherwise, are quite common in public and private procurement. See Penelope Giosa "Bidding Consortia: Critical Assessment of the Revised Horizontal Guidelines" (2023), 18, *European Procurement and Public Private Partnership Law Review*; James L. Smith "Joint Bidding, Collusion and Bid Clustering in Competitive Auctions" (1983), 50(2), *Southern Economic Journal*, 355–368; Gian Luigi Albano, Giancarlo Spagnolo and Matteo Zanza "Regulating Joint Bidding in Public Procurement" (2009), 5(2), *Journal of Competition Law and Economics*, where several examples are mentioned. Indicatively, in the United States this practice has been used by some oil companies in auctions for offshore leases and by four companies operating school buses (FTC v B&J School Bus Services, Inc., 116 FTC 308 (1993). In Europe, the Norwegian Supreme Court held that submitting a joint bid breaches

cases where there is no transparency and a call for competition and the public contracts involve a multitude of high-level technologies, it is challenging to identify the undertakings that provide the relevant services in the market as well as those capable of entering it without incurring significant additional costs, even if they are not yet present in the market. As a consequence of the contracting authorities' difficulty in adequately analyzing the relevant market, it is also challenging for them to evaluate whether the consortium members are actual or potential competitors. The same difficulty arises when assessing whether each consortium member is capable of submitting an individual bid or if have manufacturing incapacity and an inability to finance the entire expenditure required to perform the contract.

The concerns mentioned above are not unfounded. A few years ago, the European Commission confirmed the existence of a collusive scheme among firms regarding technical development. In 2021, five car manufacturers were found

---

competition law, where two independent undertakings are capable of submitting individual bids or they could easily attain such a position (Case E-3/16, Ski Taxi SA, Follo Taxi SA and Ski Follo Taxidrift AS and the Norwegian Government, 22 December 2016) <https://eftacourt.int/wp-content/uploads/2019/01/3_16_Judgment_EN.pdf> accessed on July 30, 2024. The Lithuanian Competition Authority and the Vilnius Regional Administrative Court held that joint bids of two Lithuanian construction companies Panevežio statybos trestas (PST) and Irdaiva in 24 public tenders restricted competition "by object", as both firms were capable to bid separately. For more information see Competition Council of the Republic of Lithuania "Vilnius Regional Administrative Court: Joint Bidding by Construction Companies Restricted Competition" <https://kt.gov.lt/en/news/vilnius-regional-administrative-court-joint-bidding-by-construction-companies-restricted-competition> accessed on July 30, 2024 and concurrences "The Lithuanian Competition Authority Fines Two Construction Firms for Bid Rigging in the Market for Renovation and Modernisation of Schools and Kindergartens (IRDAIVA)" <www.concurrences.com/en/bulletin/news-issues/december-2017/the-lithuanian-competition-authority-fines-two-construction-firms-for-bid> accessed on July 31, 2024; The Spanish Competition Authority fined the hospital waste management companies Consenur, Cespa, Interlun and Sistemas Integrales Sanitarios €2 M for having entered into market-sharing agreements and for knowingly submitting joint bids in cases that this was not technically or economically necessary. See Resolución no S/0014/07, de January 18, 2010, de Comisión Nacional de los Mercados y la Competencia <https://doctrina-administrativa.vlex.es/vid/-314545990> accessed on July 30, 2024; Richard Burton-Concurrences "The Spanish Competition Authority Fines € 2 M Hospital Waste Management Companies For Market-Sharing Arrangement (Consenur/Cespa/Interlun/Sistemas Integrales Sanitarios)" <www.concurrences.com/en/bulletin/news-issues/january-2010/The-Spanish-Competition-Authority-41648> accessed on July 30, 2024; The Finnish Supreme Administrative Court imposed on an association of taxi drives (Kuopion Taksiautoilijat ry) a fine of €5,000 for forbidden cooperation in a tender arranged by the city of Kuopio. The association of taxi drivers made a joint bid for managing the city service, but due to the large number of members (93) behind the joint tender, few outside bids were received. The unlawful collaboration of the taxi drivers weakened considerably the possibilities of Kuopio city to get savings through the tender. See Finnish Competition and Consumer Authority "Bidding Cartels" <www.kkv.fi/en/facts-and-advice/competition-affairs/competition-restraints/cartels-and-other-horizontal-agreements/bidding-cartels/> accessed on July 30, 2024. Also, in Denmark there has been increased focus on competition rules in relation to consortia agreements. Therefore, the Danish Competition and Consumer Authority published thorough Guidelines in April 2018 in order to explain to businesses in which situations cooperative agreements to submit joint bids restrict competition. See Danish Competition and Consumer Authority "Joint Bidding Under Competition Law-Guidelines 2018" <www.en.kfst.dk/media/50765/050718_joint-bidding-guidelines.pdf> accessed on February 16, 2024.

guilty of colluding on the technical development of nitrogen oxide cleaning and failing to meet minimum pollution standards, despite having the technology to do so.[41] Hence, collusion on a product characteristic is always a potential danger that should not be underestimated.

Moreover, the fact that procurement officers often engage in corruption by invoking special exceptions to avoid an ordinary competitive bidding procedures, suggests a tolerance for "sham" consortia in negotiated procedures without prior publication.[42] The abuse of negotiated procedures is considered one of the most common corrupt practices in public procurement (46%) by Eurozone companies, according to the 2024 Eurobarometer survey.[43] The lack of a contract notice limits[44] the possibility of procurement review procedures and prevents interested third parties from proving that consortium members could supply the works, supplies or services individually as potential competitors.

As previously mentioned, there are several efficiency-enhancing justifications for forming and operating of a consortium, such as dispersing transaction risks or pooling expertise and technical resources to fulfil a contract.[45] Therefore, a blanket prohibition on consortia would be undesirable. Instead, the widespread use of the VEAT is recommended. A contracting authority can voluntarily publish its intention to directly award a public contract without a contract notice in the Official Journal of the European Union using a VEAT.[46] When a VEAT is published, the contracting authority must observe a standstill period of at least ten days before concluding the public contract.[47] This allows interested persons to decide whether to challenge a contract award before the national review body with full knowledge of the relevant facts.[48] The standard VEAT form is outlined in Annex XII to Commission Implementing Regulation (EU) 2015/1986, requiring justification for

41 European Commission "Antitrust: Commission fines car manufacturers €875 million for restricting competition in emission cleaning for new diesel passenger cars" <https://ec.europa.eu/commission/presscorner/detail/en/ip_21_3581> accessed on June 13, 2023.

42 This is a recognized corruption technique. Please see Tina Søreide "Corruption in Public Procurement, Causes, Consequences and Cures", Chr. Michelsen Institute, Bergen 2002 <www.cmi.no/publications/843-corruption-in-public-procurement-causes> accessed on February 15, 2024; Jessica Schultz and Tina Søreide "Corruption in Emergency Procurement", 32(4), *Disasters*, 516–536; OECD (fn 16); Fazekas, Tóth and King (fn 16).

43 European Commission "Businesses' Attitudes towards Corruption in the EU – Flash Eurobarometer 543", 36 <https://europa.eu/eurobarometer/surveys/detail/3180> accessed on January 10, 2025.

44 Yet, a third interested party can still request a review of a public contract that was awarded without being put to tender, if it thinks that a tender should have been published.

45 Slaughter and May "Private Equity and Competition Law" <www.slaughterandmay.com/media/odhn4oip/private_equity_and_competition_law_consortium_bids_1212pdf.pdf >accessed on June 6, 2024.

46 Article 2d(4) of Directive 89/665/EEC.

47 Ibid.

48 Case C-19/13 Ministero dell'Interno v Fastweb SpA [2014] pub. electr. EU:C::2014:2194.

awarding the contract without prior publication of a contract notice in the OJEU among other information.[49]

Nonetheless, the fact that this notice is published only on a voluntary basis, depending each time on the discretion of contracting authorities, raises concerns as it was empirically shown that the majority of VEAT notice usage across the 27 Member States from 2010 to 2012 was by France, Poland, Denmark and the United Kingdom.[50] The other 23 Member States combined were responsible for just over 10% of the total VEAT notices.[51] Moreover, another empirical study has shown that procurement officers usually abuse negotiated procedures and they do so for the benefit of a corrupt network.[52] This suggests that under such circumstances, corrupt procurement officers may not be willing to use VEAT notices. Thence, I suggest that the ex ante transparency notices should be made mandatory every time public contracts are awarded under a negotiated procedure without prior publication, where competition is absent for technical reasons.

Publishing a VEAT notice in the OJEU in order to notify the market of the contracting authority's intention to conclude a specific public contract may have some implications for the timeliness of public contracts, as publishing takes time. However, as already mentioned, the contracting authority stands still and does not proceed to the signing of the contract for ten days after the publication of VEAT notices. For this time period, the day after the publication of the VEAT notice is the first day.[53] This is a reduced time limit that protects contracting authorities from the risk of a procurement challenge on the grounds of ineffectiveness,[54] which has a much longer time period from 6 months to 30 days after the public contract is entered into.[55] This suggestion aligns with the Commission's policy choice, which

49 Implementing Regulation (EU) 2015/1986 of 11 November 2015 establishing standard forms for the publication of notices in the field of public procurement [2015] OJ L296.

50 Europe Economics and Milieu for the European Commission "Economic Efficiency and Legal Effectiveness of Review and Remedies Procedures for Public Contracts – Final Study Report MARKT/2013/072/C, April 2015" <www.osservatorioappalti.unitn.it/viewFile.do?id=1452091689514&dataId=8234&filename=Testo.pdf> accessed on January 10, 2025, 100. It should be noted that from the 25,000 published VEAT notices in EU Member States, France published the most ones (21,102 contracts).

51 Ibid.

52 See European Commission (fn 42); Ada Popescu, Mihaela Onofrei and Christopher Kelley "An Overview of European Good Practices in Public Procurement" (2016), 7(1), *Eastern Journal of European Studies*, 85.

53 Article 2a of the Remedies Directive 2007/66/EC.

54 The ground of ineffectiveness (Article 2d(4) of the Directive 2007/66/EC) applies where an above threshold contract has been awarded without prior publication of a contract notice. However, VEAT notices can provide an absolute defence to a claim for a declaration of ineffectiveness.

55 Trevor Watt-Bevan Brittan "Procurement: Validity of a VEAT Notice (Voluntary Ex Ante Transparency Notice) and Limitation Periods" <www.bevanbrittan.com/insights/articles/2019/procurement-validity-of-a-veat-notice-voluntary-ex-ante-transparency-notice-and-limitation-periods/> accessed on July 30, 2024; Government Computing "Use of VEAT Notices to Avoid Contract Competition Grows" <www.techmonitor.ai/digital-economy/government-computing/use-of-veat-notices-to-avoid-contract-competition-grows> accessed on July 30, 2024; Eversheds Sutherland LLP "Ever-

was made based on the consideration that among pre- and post-contractual types of remedies, pre-contractual remedies are the most effective.[56] Moreover, the use of the negotiated procedure without prior publication in case that competition is absent for technical reasons does not entail extreme urgency on the part of the contracting authority. The 2014/24/EU Directive has a separate provision for the use of the negotiated procedure without prior publication for reasons of extreme urgency.[57]

5.2.3 *Competitive Dialogue-Bid Rigging Issues and Recommendations*

After identifying the aspects of the competitive procedure involving negotiation that may be exploited by economic operators in the absence of prior publication of a contract notice and having provided recommendations regarding bid rigging concerns, it is now necessary to address the next procurement procedure outlined in the Directive 2014/24/EU: the competitive dialogue. Competitive dialogue is a two-stage procedure which is contemplated under Article 30 of Directive 2014/24/EU according to which:

> Any economic operator may submit a request to participate in response to a contract notice by providing the information for qualitative selection that is requested by the contracting authority.
>
> ...Only those economic operators invited by the contracting authority following the assessment of the information provided may participate in the dialogue.

The award criteria are set out in a descriptive document and after the publication of the contract notice, interested economic operators have 30 days to request participation in the process. The contracting authority must invite at least three economic operators to an open dialogue in which the final technical, legal and economic aspects are defined.[58]

Once the dialogue phase is complete, the selected candidates submit their final tenders. At this post-dialogue stage, bid rigging concerns arise because there are cases where only two participants are able to submit final tenders.[59] Article 66 of

shed's Procurement ebriefing: Can Contracting Authorities Mitigate the Risk of An Ineffectiveness Claim?" <www.eversheds-sutherland.com/global/en/what/articles/index.page?ArticleID=en/Public_Procurement/Procurement_ebrief_Contracting_authorities_mitigate_the_risk_050411> accessed on July 30, 2024.

56 Commission "Impact Assessment Report-Remedies in the field of Public Procurement", SEC (2006), 557, 23.

57 Article 32, para. 2(c) of Directive 2014/24/EU.

58 Article 65, para. 2 of Directive 2014/24/EU.

59 This has happened in several projects. Indicatively see London Borough of Havering "Invitation to Continue Dialogue – Havering Estate Regeneration Partner Project" <http://democracy.havering.gov.uk/documents/s27129/5.%20LBH%2012%20Sites%20Regeneration%20Procurement%20-%20ITCD.pdf> accessed on February 18, 2024; FMG Consulting & Nabarro LLP "Lessons

2014/24/EU Directive does not expressly provide for three final tenders at the post tender stage of the competitive dialogue procedure, but it only contemplates that in the final stage the number arrived at shall make for genuine competition in so far as there are enough tenders, solutions or qualified candidates. Moreover, there are scholars who consider that two is a sufficient number of economic operators invited to submit final tenders, for the purposes of competition.[60] The fact that there may be only two bidders able to submit final tenders can be easily explained, as the competitive dialogue is the procurement route for **Public Private Partnerships (PPP)**[61] and **Private Finance Initiative (PFI)**[62] projects that range from leases to concessions and which are characterized by high barriers to entry. When bidding for a PFI or PPP project, there are a lot of high participation costs as well as costs relevant to the assembling and setting up of the consortium.[63] PPP and PFI works also require specific skills and strong balance sheets that the private contractor should have regarding the design, building, finance, operation, services and

---

Learnt from the National Sports Centres – Procurement of New Operating Contracts – Sport England" <www.whatdotheyknow.com/request/323120/response/811144/attach/6/Lessons%20Learned%20Report%20Sport%20England%20070911.doc?cookie_passthrough=1> accessed on February 18, 2024.

60 Arrowsmith (fn 7), 16-917; Adrian Brown "The Impact of the New Procurement Directive on Large Public Infrastructure Projects: Competitive Dialogue or Better The Devil You Know?" (2004), 4, *PPLR*, 171; See also Sue Arrowsmith and Richard Craven "Competitive Dialogue in the United Kingdom", Chapter 3 in S. Arrowsmith and S. Treumer (eds) *Competitive Dialogue in EU Procurement Law* (Cambridge University Press, 2012).

61 A Public Private Partnership is "a long-term contract between a private party and a government entity, for providing a public asset or service, in which the private party bears significant risk and management responsibility, and remuneration is linked to performance". See World Bank Group "What are Public Private Partnerships?" <https://ppp.worldbank.org/public-private-partnership/what-ppp-defining-public-private-partnership> accessed on January 10, 2024.

62 Private Finance Initiative "involves and infrastructure project (e.g. hospital, health centre, school, leisure centre, social housing, street lighting, road or prison) being funded by private sector equity and debt funding and then being paid for by the public sector 'customer' through monthly payments over the life of the project". PFI is now replaced by PF2. See LexisNexis "PFI (Private Finance Initiative)/PPP (Public Private Partnerships) and Procurement" <www.lexisnexis.com/uk/lexispsl/bankingandfinance/document/391289/5D5H-YTC1-F185-X42J-00000-00/PFI-(Private-Finance-Initiative)-PPP-(Public-Private-Partnerships)-and-procurement#> accessed on February 19, 2024.

63 Ekene I. Ezulike, John G. Pery and Kamel Hawwash "The Barriers to Entry into the PFI Market" (1997), 4(3), *Engineering, Construction and Architectural Management*, 185–186; Frederic Marty and Arnaud Voisin "Partnership Contracts, Project Finance and Information Asymmetries: From Competition for the Contract to Competition within the Contract?" Seminar of Economic Analysis of Public Law and Policies, Chaire MADP, Sciences Po., Paris, Dec 2011, Paris, France, 14–15; Timo Välilä "How Expensive Are Cost Savings? On the Economics of Public–Private Partnerships" (2005), 10(1), *European Investment Bank Papers*, 109–110; See also Oliver E. Williamson, *The Economic Institutions of Capitalism – Firms, Markets, Relational Contracting* (The Free Press, New York, 1985) and Oliver E. Williamson "Transaction Cost Economics and Organisation Theory" in O. Williamson (ed) *Organisation Theory: From Chester Barnard to the Present and Beyond* (Oxford University Press, New York, 1990).

long-term maintenance of the asset over a concession period.[64] In addition to these, the project values and the risk that PPP and PFI markets involve are so high that they reduce competition in comparison with the conventional contracts.[65]

The role of entry deterrence in sustaining collusion was previously discussed in Chapter 2. Additionally, successful cartels actively create barriers to entry.[66] In the case of PFI and PPP markets, an empirical study in the UK[67] has shown a variety of barriers, such as high transaction and bidding costs, that affect organizations' participation in PFI projects.[68] Under these circumstances, the two selected candidates asked to submit final tenders can easily reach agreements on price, quantity and quality.[69] Alternatively, they may engage in bid suppression schemes, by agreeing not to submit final tenders, to refrain from submitting a final tender or to withdraw a previously submitted solution to benefit one of them, the designated winner.[70]

The risk of collusion at the post dialogue stage, where only two selected candidates are invited to submit final tenders, is heightened by the possibility that the candidates may know each other from the dialogue or pre-dialogue phases. During the pre-dialogue phase, the contracting authority may organize industry days to explain the project to potential bidders.[71] Additionally, at the dialogue stage, apart

64 Ezulike, Pery and Hawwash (fn 61), 184–185; P.M. Carillo "A Knowledge Transfer Framework: the PFI Context" (2006), 24(10), *Construction Management and Economics*, 1054–1055.

65 Ezulike, Pery and Hawwash (fn 61), 187–188; Marty and Voisin (fn 61), 4.

66 Margaret C. Levestein and Valerie Y. Suslow "What Determines Cartel Success?" (2006), 44(1), *Journal of Economic Literature*, 43–95; Robert Clark, Decio Coviello, Jean-Francois Gauthier and Art Shneyerov "Bid Rigging and Entry Deterrence in Public Procurement: Evidence from an Investigation into Collusion and Corruption in Quebec" (2018), 34(3), *Journal of Law, Economics & Organization*, 304.

67 "Off-balance-sheet public-private partnerships, such as PFI, represent 1.7 per cent of Britain's gross domestic product, the third highest ratio in Europe, behind Portugal and Hungary", Henry Mance and George Parker – Financial Times "UK Finance Watchdog Exposes Lost PFI Billions", January 18, 2018 <www.ft.com/content/db1b5c66-fba7-11e7-9b32-d7d59aace167> accessed on February 18, 2024.

68 Patricia Carrillo, Herbert Robinson, Peter Foale, Chimay J. Anumba and Dino Bouchlaghem "Participation, Barriers and Opportunities in PFI: The United Kingdom Experience" (2008), 24(3), *Journal of Management in Engineering*, 138–145. See also Ekene I. Ezulike "The Barriers to Entry into the PFI Market" (1997), 4(3), *Engineering, Construction and Architectural Management*, 179–193 where it was also shown that construction contractors face barriers to entry when approaching the PFI market.

69 Martin Pesendorfer "A Study of Collusion in First-Price Auctions" (2000), 67, *Review of Economic Studies*, 387.

70 Withdrawal of bids is a straightforward way to remove competition and it leads to the same outcome as using faulty or overpriced bids. See Bence Tóth, Mihály Fazekas, Agnes Czibik and István János Tóth "Toolkit for Detecting Collusive Bidding in Public Procurement – With Examples from Hungary" (2015), Working Paper Series: CRC-WP/2014:02, 28 <www.crcb.eu/wp-content/uploads/2015/04/Toth-et-al_CRCB_WP_v2_150413.pdf> accessed on February 18, 2024; OECD "The 2023 Recommendation of Fighting Bid Rigging in Public Procurement and the Guidelines" <https://legalinstruments.oecd.org/en/instruments/OECD-LEGAL-0396> accessed on January 10, 2025.

71 HM Treasury "Competitive Dialogue in 2008-OGC/HMT Joint Guidance on Using the Procedure", 15 <https://assets.publishing.service.gov.uk/government/uploads/system/uploads/attachment_data/file/225317/02_competitive_dialogue_procedure.pdf> accessed on February 20, 2024.

from conducting dialogue sessions on a one-to-one confidential basis with individual bidders, the contracting authority may hold forums or a bidders' day to communicate important information to all bidders, such as the structure of the dialogue phase and how individual sessions will be conducted.[72]

Another factor conducive to bid rigging in competitive dialogue with only two candidates at the final stage is that the name of the successful candidate and the value of the successful final tender will be available not only to the unsuccessful candidate but also to the unsuccessful economic operators through the contract award notice.[73] As explained in Chapter 2, this high degree of transparency strengthens a bidding ring, as it helps its members to effectively coordinate their illegal agreement. They can monitor compliance with the collusive agreement and take retaliatory measures against any member that deviates from it.[74]

The standstill period, which suspends the conclusion of the public contract to give tenderers time to review the contract award decision and decide whether to start a review procedure, favours prompt punishment for deviation from the collusive agreement. While the standard threat to prevent deviations from the bidding ring is a return to non-collusive play, targeted punishment such as initiating a review procedure, can also be effective.[75] Threatening litigation can support the submission of fully collusive bids and deter cheating among bid riggers.[76] The European Commission has recognized this practice by introducing the term "nuisance complaints" to cover unnecessary actions, frivolous claims and nuisance appeals.[77] Hence, some suppliers exploit the standstill period to delay the contract signature and impose costs on the winning bidder both by delaying profits and income streams from the disrupted contract award and by keeping resources on hold.[78] Unnecessary actions or nuisance complaints are the most commonly cited reason why the Remedies Directive[79] is used inappropriately.[80]

To ensure genuine competition, the number of selected candidates submitting final tenders must be sufficient to ensure genuine competition. Article 65 (2) of the 2014/24/EU Directive sets a minimum of five candidates in the restricted procedure and three candidates in procedures such as competitive dialogue to ensure genuine

72 Ibid, 22.
73 Article 50, para. 1 and Annex V, Part D, Sections 12–23 of 2014/24/EU Directive.
74 Robert C. Marshall and Leslie M. Marx *The Economics of Collusion-Cartels and Bidding Risks* (MIT Press, 2012), 200; Clark, Coviello, Gauthier and Shneyerov (fn 64), 302.
75 Marshall and Marx (fn 74), 200.
76 Robert C. Marshall, Michael J. Meurer and Jean-Francois Richard "Litigation Settlement and Collusion" (1994), 109(1), *Quarterly Journal of Economics*, 211–240.
77 European Commission "Impact Assessment Report-Remedies in the Field of Public Procurement", COM (2006), 195, <https://eur-lex.europa.eu/legal-content/EN/TXT/?uri=celex%3A52006SC0557> accessed on February 21, 2024, 30.
78 Ibid; Europe Economics and Milieu for the European Commission (fn 49), 24.
79 Directive 2007/66/EC amending the remedies directives covering the public sector (Directive 89/665/EEC) and the utilities sector (Directive 92/13/EEC).
80 Thirty-five percent of Contracting Authorities/entities and 20% of suppliers support this. See Europe Economics and Milieu for the European Commission (fn 49), 77.

competition. Therefore, a minimum of three final tenders should be required in competitive dialogues. Nevertheless, the number of competitors may not always lead to efficient competition, especially in complex or expensive procurements, such as pharmaceuticals. Having a small number of bidders with the capacity to invest in product development may lead to a more efficient outcome, despite the risk of bid rigging. So, if the current Directive forces a higher number of competitors at the final stage of competitive dialogue, as suggested above, they may not be able to develop or produce the product as efficiently because they will enjoy fewer economies of scale or may not have sufficient capital to invest in the development of the product. After all, increasing the number of competitors may not always be feasible, especially in markets with a naturally small number of competitors.[81]

Since it is not always possible to increase the number of competitors at the final stage of a competitive dialogue, contracting authorities should first determine if the two remaining firms are susceptible to coordinated conduct. To do this, it is recommended that contracting authorities should examine each time a number of parameters regarding the two remaining competitors. First, they should examine if the two competitors are symmetric and if their products are homogeneous. When competitors are symmetric, they have similar cost structures and functions, capacity constraints, market shares, efficiency and access to the credit market.[82] This means that all the relevant firms have a common view about how they should act, common interests to serve and they have more to gain from colluding rather than competing with each other.[83] Symmetric firms reach an agreement quite easily, while in case of firms with product and cost heterogeneity joint-profit maximization may not be a reasonable goal.[84] Second, they should investigate if the two remaining firms compete in a single or multimarket setting. Multi-market contact makes easier the exchange of information and the awareness of the firms' positioning in terms of market share, which both favour their coordinated conduct.[85] It also

81 See for example a public authority in a rural area. Competitors in other regions may find it prohibitively expensive to take up the public contract.

82 Stephen Martin, *Industrial Organization in Context* (Oxford University Press Inc., New York, 2010), 189; Antonio Lopez Mino "Contracting Authorities Inability to Fight Bid Rigging in Public Procurement: Reasons and Remedies" in Racca G.M, Yuki C. and Cavallo Perin R. (eds) *Promoting Integrity in Public Procurement: Accountability and Transparency* (Bruylant 2014) 203; Gian Luigi Albano "Demand Aggregation and Collusion Prevention in Public Procurement" in Racca G.M, Yuki C. and Cavallo Perin R. (eds) *Promoting Integrity in Public Procurement: Accountability and Transparency* (Bruylant 2014), 162; Gian Luigi Albano, Paolo Buccirossi, Giancarlo Spagnolo and Matteo Zanza "Preventing Collusion in Procurement" in Nicola Dimitri, Gustavo Piga and Giancarlo Spagnolo (eds) *Handbook of Procurement* (Cambridge University Press 2006), 356; Carmen Estevan de Quesada "Competition and Transparency in Public Procurement Markets" (2014), 5, *PPLR*, 234.

83 Martin (n 80), 190.

84 Alexis Jacquemin and Margaret Slade "Cartels, Collusion and Horizontal Merger" in R. Schmalensee and R. Willig (eds) *Handbook of Industrial Organization* (Elsevier 1989), 1, 418.

85 John Lipczynski, John O.S. Wilson and John Goddard *Industrial Organization: Competition, Strategy and Policy* (Pearson Education Limited 2013), 182. See also D.P. O'Brien and Dennis Swann *Information Agreements, Competition and Efficiency* (Macmillan 1969).

enables the suppliers both to observe the strategies of their competitors more easily and to respond more effectively to any deviations in case of collusive agreements.[86] Third, contracting authorities should check if one of the two remaining firms is known to be disruptive to the market, for instance by pricing aggressively or by innovating regularly. In such a case, the likelihood of a collusion is quite small, as the past behaviour of this firm in the market does not favour the stability of any collusive schemes.

Thus, where there are fewer than three competitors at the post-dialogue phase of the competitive dialogue and the contracting authority ascertains that the remaining firms are vulnerable to coordinated conduct, it will be necessary for the contracting authority to review the use of the competitive dialogue and restart the process from the dialogue phase. In this way, both competition and value for money will be ensured. In any other case, that is, where it turns out that the two remaining competitors are not vulnerable to coordinated conduct, the contracting authority should balance the aforementioned disadvantages of forcing a higher number of competitors at the final stage of the competitive dialogue with the likelihood of collusion and decide accordingly, depending on its priorities.

5.2.4 Innovation Partnership – Bid Rigging Issues and Recommendations

Having addressed the competitive dialogue and bid rigging concerns that arise when the relevant industry is vulnerable to bid rigging and only two selected candidates compete with each other at the post-dialogue phase, the current section focuses on the innovation partnership. As previously explained in Chapter 1, the innovation partnership is a new procurement procedure introduced by the 2014/24/EU Directive. It is intended to be used when there is a need for "an innovative product, service or work that cannot be met by those…already available on the market".[87] This procedure allows contracting authorities to develop an innovative solution in a long-term partnership with one or more chosen providers. They also have the option to purchase the outcome of that development process, without going through a further procurement exercise, as long as the final product/service/work meets pre-agreed performance levels and maximum costs.[88] Since the innovation partnership is based on the procedural rules of the competitive procedure with negotiation[89] and the grounds for using it overlap with those for competitive dialogue or competitive procedure with negotiation,[90] there is little to be said about this procurement procedure in terms of bid rigging and concerted practice, as these issues have already been covered in the aforementioned sections.

86 Estevan de Quesada (n 80), 234–235; Albano (n 80).
87 Article 31, para. 1 of the 2014/24/EU Directive.
88 Recital 59 and Article 31 of the 2014/24/EU Directive.
89 Recital (49) of the 2014/24/EU Directive.
90 That is, innovation, complexity or inability of contracting authorities to establish the technical specifications with sufficient precision.

In particular, what should be emphasized in this section about innovation partnerships is that contracting authorities may not always be able to provide sufficiently precise information in the competitive phase to make a well-informed decision about the most suitable candidates to invite to participate in the procedure. It can be challenging for the contracting authority to identify, cost and describe (even in outline terms) the need for an innovative solution, as innovative products, services or works are still in the discussion phase during the competitive phase. According to Article 31(2) of the 2014/24/EU Directive, the new solution is crystallized and developed in collaboration with the contracting authority after the research and innovation process, and the results are provided in the commercial phase. While highly specialized selection criteria and advanced skills on the capacity side are acceptable for purchasing products with a high degree of technical specialism, in the public sector setting a high standard in the competitive phase of an innovation partnership, may unduly narrow competition by excluding potentially suitable candidates without substantial proof that the invited candidates can develop a more suitable solution. This could increase the likelihood of bid rigging, as a small number of bidders make it easier to form and monitor bid rigging cartels,[91] reducing the incentive for cartel members to engage in secret price-cutting.[92] This issue is particularly relevant in innovation partnerships, where bidding competition is already very low. Data from all innovation partnership procurements published EU-wide in the TED database up to May 2019 shows that the average number of offers received is 1.2.[93] Moreover, only 9% of innovation partnership procurements award contracts to more than three vendors, indicating low competition in product development.[94] The fact that only 14% of vendors win a contract for the first time with the procurer and only 6% are start-ups confirms collusion concerns. These factors suggest that the innovation partnership procurement market is slow to evolve and does not attract new entrants, operating mainly with the incumbent firms.[95] Economic theory, as discussed in Chapter 2, suggests that higher entry barriers, make it easier for bidding rings to succeed, as there are no new players to disrupt the cartel's operation.[96] Hence, it is unlikely that "an upstart or expanding company will suddenly enter the field and outbid the designated low bidder,

91 Edward Hastings Chamberlin *The Theory of Monopolistic Competition: A Re-Orientation of the Theory of Value* (Cambridge Mass: Harvard University Press, 1966), 46–51.

92 George J. Stigler *The Organisation of Industry* (The University of Chicago Press, Chicago 1968), 46, 51–56.

93 Lieve Bos – DG CONNECT F3 unit ("Digital Innovation and Blockchain") "Update on Results from Completed and Ongoing FP7 and Horizon 2020 funded Pre-Commercial Procurement (PCP)" <www.agid.gov.it/sites/agid/files/2024-05/resultseufundedpcpsstatusjan2020pdf.pdf> accessed on August 15, 2024.

94 Ibid.

95 Albano, Buccirossi, Spagnolo and Zanza (fn 80), 353–354.

96 Martin (fn 80), 190; Massimo Motta *Competition Policy: Theory and Practice* (Cambridge University Press 2004), 143.

defeating in this way any collusive agreement" that may exist in the relevant market.[97] This lack of new entrants allows incumbent firms to collude freely, as there is no competition to challenge their agreements.

In view of the above, contracting authorities should be especially cautious when drafting the minimum requirements for all tenders in an innovation partnership procurement. They should also carefully assess the capacity of candidates to develop and implement innovative solutions during the competitive phase of the procedure. Public procurement officers need a high level of expertise and a good market knowledge to articulate specialized and complex needs. This helps avoid excluding potentially suitable candidates from innovation partnership negotiations. Achieving this requires internal training, targeted recruitment, reliance on external experts and consultants or pooling expertise with other public procurers.[98] Innovation brokers can be particularly valuable consultants. They can establish connections between public procurers and innovative SMEs or start-ups offering innovative solutions.[99] Innovation brokers can advise public procurers on defining their needs for innovative ideas, identifying promising innovative solutions in the market and organizing networks of public procurers to share knowledge and best practices in innovation procurement, such as in the case of innovation partnerships.[100] Cooperative procurement can also benefit innovation partnerships, by providing public procurers with critical expertise for innovative goods and services, facilitating mutual learning and the exchange of best practices. This is achieved by enabling the engagement of professional staff with the necessary skills and experience.[101] The most structured form of cooperation is typically through central purchasing bodies that manage the public procurement process for other procurers.[102] Less structured forms of cooperation include public buyers' networks and associations that collaborate on an ad-hoc basis, such as for a specific innovation procurement.[103]

Regarding the very low level of competition in bidding for innovation partnerships, the solution is to attract high-tech start-ups and innovative SMEs to public procurement of innovation. The 2014/24/EU Directive has already taken the first steps by stating that contracting authorities shall accept the European Single Procurement Document (ESPD), as preliminary evidence at the time of submitting requests to participate or tenders. ESPD is an updated self-declaration that confirms the bidders meet all administrative requirements, replacing the need

97 Kara L. Haberbush "Limiting the Government's Exposure to Bid Rigging Schemes: A Critical Look at the Sealed Bidding Regime" (2000), 30(1), *Public Contract Law Journal*, 112.

98 European Commission "Commission Notice – Guidance on Innovation Procurement (2021/c 267/01) <https://eur-lex.europa.eu/legal-content/EN/TXT/PDF/?uri=CELEX:52021XC0706(03)&rid=6> accessed on January 10, 2024.

99 Ibid, 28.

100 Ibid.

101 Ibid, 19.

102 Ibid.

103 Ibid.

for certificates.[104] To facilitate cross-border tendering, the 2014/24/EU Directive also introduced an online repository of certificates (e-Certis), which serves as a mapping service of evidence from all European Member States.[105] These measures reduce the administrative burden and simplify the procurement process for start-ups and SMEs. Additionally, under the new Directive economic operators are no longer required to have a yearly turnover higher than two times the estimated contract value, unless there are valid reasons to justify it.[106] This change makes it easier for start-ups and SMEs to participate in public procurement of innovation. Nevertheless, further financial measures would be beneficial, as innovation partnerships involve high risks and project values, and start-ups and SMEs often lack the financial stability of larger companies. For this reason, it is recommended that payment schemes, friendly to high-tech start-ups and innovative SMEs be developed to ensure these firms are paid early and regularly.[107] Advance payments for direct contractors, direct payments by the public purchaser, or shorter payment periods for subcontractors would be crucial in encouraging start-ups and SMEs to engage in innovation partnerships.

5.3 Conclusion

This chapter has undertaken a comprehensive critical review of the second phase of the EU public procurement process, which is the contracting phase. It has been shown that several provisions relevant to the procurement procedures either increase the risk of bid rigging or contribute to its sustainability. Therefore, the procedures under 2014/24/EU Directive are not the best possible toolkit for preventing bid rigging, as procurers should seek to adjust them in order to combat these anticompetitive practices. This conclusion raises further questions about what kind of adjustments are needed. For this reason, policy-oriented suggestions were made. First, regarding the freedom of public procurers to choose between the open and restricted procedure, it was argued that EU procurement rules should include provisions similar to those of the 2011 Model Law. These provisions provide for the use of the open procedure as the default procurement method, unless specified exceptions apply. The restricted procedure should only be used under specific conditions and each time the contracting authority adopts a method of procurement other than the open procedure, there should be relevant justification. Additionally, it was argued that procurement officers should have a grounding in competition law. They should be incentivized to work efficiently and reject the use of corrupt practices and acts of bribery by receiving bonuses and salaries as high as those in the private sector.

104 Article 59 of the 2014/24/EU Directive.
105 Article 61 of the 2014/24/EU Directive.
106 Article 58, para 3, Section 2 of the 2014/24/EU Directive.
107 European Commission (fn 98), 27.

Regarding the bid rigging concerns that arise in negotiated procedures without prior publication, a possible solution is to make the VEAT mandatory. This should be done each time competition is absent for technical reasons and public contracts are awarded under a negotiated procedure without prior publication. The protection of contracting authorities from the risk of a procurement challenge on the ground of ineffectiveness outweighs any implication that the publication of a VEAT notice in the OJEU may have for the timeliness of public contracts.

In the event of a competitive dialogue, where only two selected candidates compete with each other in the post-dialogue phase, there should be a requirement of at least three participants in the relevant process to ensure genuine competition. However, increasing the number of competitors may not always be the most efficient solution, and at times it may not be feasible to add more competitors at the final stage of a competitive dialogue. Therefore, before implementing such a measure, contracting authorities should assess whether the two remaining firms are susceptible to coordinated conduct, considering a number of suggested parameters. If it is found that the two firms are vulnerable to collusion, the use of the competitive dialogue should be re-evaluated and the process should restart from the dialogue phase. In other cases, the contracting authority should weigh the disadvantages of adding more competitors at the final stage of the competitive dialogue against the risk of collusion and decide accordingly.

Regarding innovation partnerships, the chapter highlights the challenges faced by contracting authorities in identifying, costing and describing the need for an innovative solution at the early competitive stage, when the innovative products, services or works are still in the conceptual phase. This can lead to unnecessarily high standards being set, which may limit competition. The limited number of bidders can also make it easier for bid rigging cartels to form, especially in innovation partnership procurements, where competition in bidding is already low and there are few new entrants. Hence, recommendations were made to help public procurement officers gain and market knowledge to articulate specialized and complex needs and avoid excluding potentially suitable candidates from innovation partnership negotiations. Suggestions included internal training, targeted recruitment and the use of external experts and consultants, such as innovation brokers. Additionally, cooperative procurement was seen as beneficial for innovation partnerships, as it could pool expertise and it could enable mutual learning as well as exchange of best practices. To address the issue of low competition in bidding for innovation partnerships, the chapter proposed ways to attract high-tech start-ups and innovative SMEs to public procurement of innovation. It identified the strengths of the 2014/24/EU Directive in this regard and acknowledged the need for additional financial measures. The chapter recommended payment schemes that are favourable to high-tech start-ups and innovative SMEs, to ensure that these firms are paid promptly and consistently.

6 Contracting Phase II

Are the Procurement Techniques under 2014/24/EU Directive the Most Effective Toolkit for Preventing Bid Rigging?

6.1 Introduction

In the previous chapter, we answered the research question what aspects of procurement procedures increase the likelihood of bid rigging and may be exploited by potential suppliers. We then recommended specific legislative and soft law instruments to deter collusion when contracting entities utilize these procurement procedures. Now, we will address the techniques and instruments for electronic and aggregated procurement and answer the same research questions. The study of these instruments is necessary due to their interaction with procurement procedures, as they facilitate the progression and completion of procurement procedures. Although these instruments precede subsequent procurement procedures, the book does not address them before discussing procurement procedures. This is because the book follows the structure of the 2014/24/EU Directive, which prioritizes procurement procedures before electronic and aggregated procurement techniques and instruments.

The structure of this chapter is as follows: Section 6.2 will discuss procurement techniques and specifically focus on the pro-collusive elements of framework agreements. This section will examine whether there are inherent structural inefficiencies in the way the framework agreement procedure is designed and implemented under the 2014/24/EU Directive. It is recommended that framework agreements be open to new participants to address these structural inefficiencies. In Section 6.3, electronic auctions and their pro-collusive elements will be discussed, with recommendations to reduce collusion by concealing the prices at which competitors drop out, as well as limiting the number of valid offers submitted per round. Also delaying the publishing of this information is recommended. Section 6.4 will present the main conclusions.

6.2 Techniques and Instruments for Electronic and Aggregated Procurement

The term "techniques", which is used in Directive 2014/24/EU, is not a legally defined term, but rather a terminology that explains common procurement

DOI: 10.4324/9781003359999-6

practices.[1] The particular procurement techniques which will be discussed below are framework agreements, dynamic purchasing systems and e-auctions.

6.3 Framework Agreements – Bid Rigging Issues and Recommendations

The old Directive 2004/18/EC was the first legislative document that authorized and regulated the use of framework agreements in the EU as a flexible tool for aggregated procurement. According to Article 1(5) of this old Directive, which is the same as Article 33(1) of the current Directive, framework agreement is:

> An agreement between one or more contracting authorities and one or more economic operators, the purpose of which is to establish the terms governing contracts to be awarded during a given period, in particular with regard to price and, where appropriate, the quantity envisaged.

The standard steps typically taken in a framework agreement procedure are as follows:[2]

1. An invitation to economic operators to participate in the procedure, outlining the procurement entity's needs, terms and conditions.
2. Selection of one or more suppliers based on assessment of economic operators' qualifications and responses.
3. Procurement entity enters into a framework agreement with the selected supplier(s).
4. Placing orders with the selected supplier(s) as needs arise.

The first three steps make up the first stage of the procedure, while the fourth is the second stage of the framework agreement procedure.[3] When all terms and conditions of a framework agreement are established in the first stage, no further arrangements with the supplier(s) are necessary. This type of framework agreement is known as a "framework contract".[4] Framework contracts involve arrangements with one supplier and are concluded either when a purchase order is issued or accepted, without the need for a second round of competition among potential

1 PwC, London Economics and Ecorys for the European Commission "Public Procurement in Europe-Cost and Effectiveness" (2011) <https://op.europa.eu/en/publication-detail/-/publication/0cfa3445-7724-4af5-8c2b-d657cd690c03> accessed on December 3, 2024, 22.

2 Gian Luigi Albano and Caroline Nicholas "Description, Taxonomy and Motivations for Using Framework Agreements" in Gian Luigi and Caroline Nicholas (eds) *The Law and Economics of Framework Agreements: Designing Flexible Solutions for Public Procurement* (Cambridge University Press, 2016), 13.

3 Ibid.

4 Ibid, 16–17.

suppliers.[5] Like all forms of framework agreements, framework contracts are closed systems, meaning new contracting authorities or suppliers cannot be added during their lifetime.[6] The use of framework contracts is limited to specific procuring entities.[7]

The second form of a framework agreement involves two rounds of competition among suppliers, both in the first and second stages of the procedure. This form allows for more than one supplier, with a minimum of three economic operators, as required by Article 32(4) of the old Directive. However, under the new legislative regime, a framework agreement can be entered into with only two economic operators, even if other eligible tenders were submitted.[8] Appendix 2 contains a diagram further explaining the process.

At the first stage of the procedure, only a part of the framework agreement's terms and conditions is established. This necessitates a secondary competition or "mini-tender" phase to identify the suppliers with whom the procuring entity will ultimately enter into the public contract.[9] Until the second stage of the procedure, no awardees are selected, only a limited number of suppliers with the best offers to enter into a framework agreement with the procuring entity. The reason for this award procedure is that sometimes a procuring entity is unable to predict the quantity, nature or timing of its needs over a period of time. Therefore, it prefers to define these parameters later, as the need arises.[10] This is a *stricto sensu* framework agreement and operates as a closed system.[11]

In addition to the aforementioned award procedure, in this type of framework agreement the procuring entity also has the option to decide whether specific works, supplies or services will be acquired through a reopening of competition or directly based on the terms outlined in the framework agreement.[12] The possibility for a *stricto sensu* framework agreement to include both types of award procedures was initially discussed in case law in Denmark and Sweden[13] before Directive 2014/24/EU clarified this point. This flexibility provided to procuring entities is particularly important for central purchasing bodies that must accommodate the diverse needs

5 Ibid; Sue Arrowsmith "An Assessment of the New Legislative Package on Public Procurement" (2004), 41, *Common Market Law Review*, 1293.

6 Carina Risvig Hamer "Regular Purchases and Aggregated Procurement: The Changes in the New Public Procurement Directive regarding Framework Agreements, Dynamic Purchasing Systems and Central Purchasing Bodies" (2014), 4, *PPLR*, 202.

7 Albano and Nicholas (fn 2), 17.

8 Carina Risvig Hamer "Regular Purchases and Aggregated Procurement: The Changes in the New Public Procurement Directive Regarding Framework Agreements, Dynamic Purchasing Systems and Central Purchasing Bodies" (2014), 4, *PPLR*, 202.

9 Article 33, para. 4(c) of the Directive 2014/24/EU.

10 Albano and Nicholas (fn 7), 4.

11 European Commission, Directorate General Internal Market and Services "Explanatory Note-Framework Agreements – Classic Directive" (2005) <https://ec.europa.eu/docsroom/documents/15474/attachments/1/translations/en/renditions/pdf> accessed on January 10, 2025.

12 Article 33, para. 4(b) of the Directive 2014/24/EU.

13 Risvig Hamer (fn 8), fn 22.

of multiple contracting authorities and manage public contracts of varying complexity and value.[14] Appendix 3 includes a diagram outlining the types of award procedures in the case of *stricto sensu* framework agreements.

6.3.1 The Closed Nature of Framework Agreements

The first concern regarding bid rigging involves the "closed" system of the two types of framework agreements, namely the framework contract and the *stricto sensu* framework agreement. In both cases, new bidders cannot participate in the process or join the agreement after it has been concluded, as orders are placed only by reference to the tenders submitted the suppliers to access the framework. This creates a significant barrier to entry, restricting the market for the subject of the framework agreement, as external competitors are excluded for the entire duration of the agreement.[15] This situation is familiar to economic operators whenever a framework agreement procurement technique is utilized. Therefore, companies entering into such agreements are aware in advance of their interdependence and the fixed number and composition of participants throughout the agreement's duration. An illustrative example of a bidding ring facilitated by the limited number of competitors in tenders for a three-year framework agreement is the Arro, Caverion and Pettersen bid rigging cartel in Norway.[16] These three companies were the only bidders allowed in restricted tenders for electrical services to a health enterprise ("Vestre Viken Helseforetak").[17] They engaged in collusive bidding by dividing contracts among themselves, deceiving the contracting authority into believing the bidding process was competitive.[18] Consequently, the bid riggers could offer any price to the health enterprise knowing they would not be outbid.[19] The recognized interdependence and high barriers to entry or expansion are essential conditions for an oligopolistic market.[20] Therefore, in a closed framework agreement the market can be described as static and oligopolistic,[21] "erecting a protective ring around

14 Ibid, 203.

15 G.L. Albano and Caroline Nicholas "Integrity Concerns in Framework Agreements" in Gian Luigi and Caroline Nicholas (eds) *The Law and Economics of Framework Agreements: Designing Flexible Solutions for Public Procurement* (Cambridge University Press, 2016), 193, 187; see also Ignacio Herrera Anchustegui "Centralizing Public Procurement and Competitiveness in Directive 2014/24" (July 2015) <https://dx.doi.org/10.2139/ssrn.2633445> accessed on November 17, 2024.

16 Global Competition Review, Jan Magne Juuhl-Langseth, Mona Søyland and Anders Thue Simonsen Vogt Wiig AS "Norway: Overview" <https://globalcompetitionreview.com/review/the-european-middle-east-and-african-antitrust-review/the-european-middle-eastern-and-african-antitrust-review-2017/article/norway-overview> accessed on January 10, 2025.

17 Ibid.

18 Ibid.

19 Ibid.

20 OECD "Policy Roundtables-Oligopoly"(1999) <www.oecd.org/daf/competition/1920526.pdf> accessed on November 17, 2024, 20.

21 Framework agreements may establish an oligopoly in the sense that the use of long-term framework agreements and the absence of second-stage competition might be seen as partitioning off or insulating part of the demand in the market, reducing in this way the area in which competitive forces

those few vendors that hold standing agreements with the Government".[22] This is particularly evident, as on average, a multi-provider framework involves 4.4 suppliers.[23] Once firms acknowledge their interdependence they cannot be expected to ignore it when determining their competitive behaviour".[24] Coordination becomes possible due to the small number of market players who are familiar with each other, assuming standard transparency mechanisms are in place.

There are several obstacles that can facilitate collusion between firms within a framework agreement. First, it can be challenging for a contracting authority to seek new contractors outside the framework agreement, for better value for money, if there are significant price differences between the framework suppliers and the market prices. Holding a new tendering procedure and advertising in the Official Journal if the contracting authority disagrees with the prices from framework suppliers, undermines the administrative convenience that framework agreements aim to provide. Repeating this process can be time-consuming and costly for the public sector, potentially outweighing the high prices paid to framework suppliers.

The only way for a contracting authority to request price changes within the original framework, without a new procurement procedure, is through a price revision clause, if it is included in the agreement.[25] The clause must be "clear, precise and unequivocal" outlining the scope of modifications and conditions for use.[26] Without a well-defined clause, parties may interpret the clause differently, leading to arbitration or legal disputes, adding further costs to procurement entities. Additionally, price revision clauses can bring costs to procurement entities because a form of retainer must usually be paid to a framework supplier so as to remain capable to deliver at all times under the framework agreement, despite the risk of market fluctuations.[27] In some cases, despite a price revision clause, a supplier within a framework agreement may still have control over pricing, especially if they are the only one able to meet a specific call-off.[28]

The high barriers to entry, due to the closed system of framework agreements, create significant barriers to entry for SMEs, which are often involved in framework

can apply. Whether this creates anticompetitive structure in the market will also depend upon the proportion of the market that the particular public buyer has in the market.

22 Christopher R. Yukins "Are IDIQs Inefficient? Sharing Lessons with European Framework Contracting"(2008), 37(3), *Public Contract Law Journal*, 557

23 PwC, London Economics and Ecorys for the European Commission (fn 1), 146, fn 109.

24 ibid, 19; see also Dennis Yao and Susan S. DeSanti "Game Theory and the Legal Analysis of Tacit Collusion" (1993), 38(1), *The Antitrust Bulletin*, 117.

25 Article 72, para 1(a) of Directive 2014/24/EU; Steen Treumer "Contract Changes and the Duty to Retender under the New EU Public Procurement Directive" (2014), 3, *Public Procurement Law Review*; see also Denfleet International Ltd v NHS Purchasing and Supply Agency and others (2005) EWHC 55 (Admin).

26 Article 72, para 1(a) of Directive 2014/24/EU.

27 Rick Canavan "Public Procurement and Frameworks" in Christopher Bovis (ed) *Research Handbook on EU Public Procurement Law* (Edward Elgar Publishing 2016), 145.

28 ibid.

agreements, particularly in services sectors, while they are increasingly present in technology-intensive industries, such as information and communications technology and biotechnology.[29]

6.3.2 Incompleteness of Framework Agreements' Terms

Framework agreements *stricto sensu*, are characterized as incomplete compared to framework contracts. This is because not all terms and conditions are defined in the master contract during the initial stage of the procedure. Some terms are left to be determined before the second round of competition. The number of quality dimensions that need to be identified initially varies depending on whether the products/services require customization to meet specific needs and market conditions.[30] European legislation is one system that focuses a significant amount of effort on the first round of competition. This ensures that only a limited number of suppliers are selected for the framework agreement, resulting in minimal competition during the second stage.[31] Specifically, according to Article 33(2) of the current Directive:

> Contracts based on a framework agreement may under no circumstances entail substantial modifications to the terms laid down in that framework agreement…

Additionally, some of the most experienced central purchasing agencies in European Member States such as the Crown Commercial Service in the United Kingdom, BBG in Austria, SKI in Denmark and Hansel in Finland provide most of the contractual terms and conditions at the outset.[32]

The establishment of most of the contractual terms and conditions in the framework agreement implies that call-off contracts will be homogeneous and vary only slightly from each other in terms of quality and technical characteristics.[33] Products that do not differ in intrinsic attributes, such as quality, do not present vertical differentiations.[34] "Vertical differentiations can be likened to cost asymmetries" because "a firm that offers better quality is positioned as if it were enjoying a cost advantage".[35] In the case of call-off contracts under a framework agreement this

29 OECD "Policy Brief-Small and Medium-Sized Enterprises: Local Strength, Global Reach" (June 2000) <www.oecd.org/cfe/leed/1918307.pdf> accessed on November 20, 2024.

30 World Bank Group "Guidebook for Setting-Up and Operating Framework Agreements – 2021" <https://documents1.worldbank.org/curated/en/958921624026529503/pdf/Guidebook-for-Setting-up-and-Operating-Framework-Agreements.pdf> accessed January 10, 2025.

31 Albano and Nicholas (fn 2), 18.

32 Ibid, 70.

33 Ibid, 196.

34 Gian Luigi Albano, Paolo Buccirossi, Giancarlo Spagnolo and Matteo Zanza "Preventing Collusion in Procurement" in Nicola Dimitri, Gustavo Piga and Giancarlo Spagnolo (eds) *Handbook of Procurement* (Cambridge University Press 2006), 356–57.

35 Ibid.

means that in the absence of vertical differentiations, potential suppliers participating in the second round of competition will find themselves bidding in a cost symmetric environment.[36] Cost symmetry is believed to enhance collusion because the problem of coordinating on a collusive price can be easily overcome. As a result, competition at the second stage of the framework agreement procedure will be primarily price-driven and if potential suppliers want to collude, it will be relatively easy for them to agree on a common pricing policy. This is in the nature of framework agreements, as product and service homogeneity plays a central role when it comes to the framework agreements' ability to effectively aggregate demand, thus leveraging buying power, and producing the expected effects on economies of scale.[37] In any other case, the mission of the framework agreement as a flexible tool for aggregated procurement is not successfully accomplished.

6.3.3 Duration of Framework Agreements

The general principle is that framework agreements should not exceed four years (Article 33, paragraph 1 of Directive 2014/24/EU). However, the length of framework agreements may be exceeded in exceptional cases that are duly justified. Recital 62 of Directive 2014/24/EU clarifies that such cases may arise where economic operators need to dispose of equipment with an amortization period longer than four years, which must be available at any time over the entire duration of the framework agreement. Regarding individual contracts based on a framework agreement, they may be longer than the framework agreement itself, considering the time needed for their performance, equipment maintenance and staff training (Recital 62).

Despite the above clarification, there is still uncertainty about how much longer than four years framework agreements may be extended and how long the call-off contracts may last.[38] The fact that in practice framework contracts may have duration of seven years or more adds to this concern. For example, the Council of the European Union recently concluded six framework contracts with durations ranging from seven to ten years.[39] This also applies to contracts related to buildings.[40]

The longer the duration of framework agreements, the more call-offs there will be for the subsequent conclusion of individual contracts.[41] On average, there are

36 Albano and Nicholas (fn 15), 197.

37 OECD, Public Procurement in Chile: Policy Options for Efficient and Inclusive Framework Agreements (OECD Public Governance Reviews, OECD Publishing, Paris, 2017), 34.

38 Marta Andrecka "Clarification or Missed Opportunity? The Provision on Framework Agreements in the 2014 Directive" in Grith Skovgaard Ølykke and Albert Sanchez-Graells (eds) *Reformation or Deformation of the EU Public Procurement Rules* (Edward Elgar Publishing 2016), 228.

39 European Court of Auditors (ECA) "Special Report – The EU Institutions Can Do More to Facilitate Access to Their Public Procurement" <www.eca.europa.eu/Lists/ECADocuments/SR16_17/SR_PROCUREMENT_EN.pdf> accessed on November 21, 2024, 33.

40 Ibid, 64.

41 Albano and Nicholas (fn 15), 194.

15 call-offs over the lifetime of a framework agreement.[42] This means that the framework's awardees have frequent interactions throughout the life of the framework, which may lead to collusion instead of healthy competition. As highlighted in Chapter 2 of the book, when circumstances favour collusion in a market, it is preferable for the auction designer to offer a project as a single contract rather than split the market into many small contracts and hold multiple auctions.[43] With a minimum duration of four or more years for framework agreements in practice, firms have enough time to make collusive arrangements in an oligopolistic market.

Moreover, the literature on repeated auctions shows that bidders do not need direct and illegal communication, such as side payments, to implement efficient bid rotation schemes. If information on bids, such as prices or identities of losing bidders is public, bidders can easily propose and enforce a division of the auctioned items.[44] If the auctioneer discloses the identity of the winner and the price paid at the auction, the operation of a bidding ring will be more efficient and it will be less risky for it to get detected.[45] This is the case in framework agreements, where after the award of each call-off contract, the value of the successful tender and the name of the successful tenderer are disclosed through the contract award notice.[46]

To address this concern, the number of call-offs could be minimized to limit potential suppliers' interactions and opportunities to collude. However, this may not be a viable solution if the number of call-offs determines the cost of a framework agreement. Research has shown that "where a framework is used to satisfy only a small number of call-offs, the cost of the framework is higher than the cost of running separate competitions".[47] Therefore, it would be cost-effective for a procuring entity to conclude a framework agreement for a small number of call-offs.

In addition to the above, suppliers who frequently interact in a market that has been static and narrow for four or more years in exceptional cases, as in the case of a framework agreement, can more easily reach a collusive agreement. As explained in Chapter 2 of the book, repeated interactions lead to a Nash equilibrium of collusion because if one firm deviates, it knows the other firm(s) will punish it by pricing at a constant marginal cost indefinitely. Therefore, it is not in the firms' interest to undercut each other. Additionally, according to auction theory, when there are few bidders who interact frequently, it is relatively easier for them to signal collusive outcomes to other bidders, interpret these signals correctly and quickly come to

42 PwC, London Economics and Ecorys for the European Commission (fn 4), 85.

43 Martin Pesendorfer "A Study of Collusion in First-Price Auctions" (2000), 67, *Review of Economic Studies*, 406; William E. Kovacic, Robert C. Marshall, Leslie M. Marx and Matthew E. Raiff "Bidding Rings and the Design of Anti-Collusive Measures for Auctions and Procurements" in N. Dimitri, G. Piga and G. Spagnolo (eds) *Handbook of Procurement* (Cambridge University Press), 406.

44 Preston McAfee, Michael Williams and Kenneth Hendricks "Auctions and Bid Rigging" in Roger D. Blair and D. Daniel Sokol (eds) *The Oxford Handbook of International Antitrust Economics, Volume 2* (Oxford University Press, 2014), 507–509; Peter Cramton "Ascending Auctions" (1998), 42(3–5), European Economic Review, 754.

45 Kovacic, Marshall, Raiff and Marx (fn 43), 402.

46 See Annex V, Part D of the Directive 2014/24/EU.

47 PwC, London Economics and Ecorys for the European Commission (fn 4), 147.

quick agreements without explicitly colluding.[48] The large number of second-stage competitions/call-offs during the framework agreement may provide opportunities to send signals through prices to each other.

Another factor that raises collusion concerns is the duration of framework agreements, especially when they are repeated in a market because they are considered particularly suitable and appropriate for it. This may discourage new entrants and competitors outside the framework agreement from entering or remaining in the market. The longer framework agreements last, the more likely it is that outside competitors will leave the market because they cannot afford to be excluded for four or more years, especially when the procuring entity is a dominant buyer or the use of the framework is obligatory/repeated.[49] As known from auction theory, deterring entry is essential for a successful cartel to thrive.[50] Additionally, competitors outside the framework agreement may fear the incumbency advantages enjoyed by the framework awardees in future agreements, leading to market concentration or cartelization.[51]

Given the pro-collusive features of framework agreements, procuring entities need to be extremely cautious when they deciding to use a framework. The need for caution becomes evident when considering that the current Directive does not address how the relevance of a contracting authority can be questioned or the accountability of procurement officers. Professor Sue Arrowsmith has also highlighted that the older Directive 2004/18/EC does not specify how frameworks should be used leaving it up to each Member State to achieve their regulatory goals.[52] Since then, the discretion given to Member States has remained the same. Furthermore, an empirical study has shown that contracting authorities have a limited perception of the risk of collusion[53] so it should not be assumed that procurement officers will take measures to address collusion at the planning stage of a framework agreement. In such circumstances, defining the market and conducting a basic survey to determine if the market for a specific framework agreement is susceptible to collusion either at either the first or second stage of the procedure would be a good starting point for procurement officers.

Market studies and market definition can be challenging and costly for procurers. Therefore, contracting authorities should carefully consider whether the

48 Timothy C. Salmon "Preventing Collusion between Firms in Auctions" in M.C.W Janssen (ed) *Auctioning Public Assets: Analysis and Alternatives* (Cambridge University Press, 2004), 114.

49 In the same way, long-term supply agreements in private sector by dominant firms can foreclose the market.

50 Robert C. Marshall and Michael J. Meurer "Bidder Collusion and Antitrust Law: Refining the Analysis of Price Fixing to Account for the Special Features of Auction Markets" (2004), 72(1), *Antitrust Law Journal*, 93.

51 Albano, Buccirossi, Spagnolo and Zanza (fn 34), 353–354.

52 Sue Arrowsmith (ed) *Public Procurement Regulation in the 21st Century: Reform of the UNCITRAL Model Law on Procurement* (St Paul, Thomson-West, 2009), 15–16.

53 Office of Fair Trading "Assessing the Impact of Public Sector Procurement on Competition" (2004) <http://webarchive.nationalarchives.gov.uk/20140402182823/http://www.oft.gov.uk/shared_oft/reports/comp_policy/oft742a.pdf> accessed on November 21, 2024.

benefits of conducting such studies outweigh the costs. One way to avoid these costs is to collaborate with national Competition Authorities that have expertise in this area. In a stable competitive environment where factors such as price structure, cost structure, technology or market geography remain constant, frequent market studies may not be necessary. Updates with transaction costs may suffice, especially for framework agreements used for repeat purchases of standard and simple goods, which are criticized for being "insufficiently responsive in practice to technological change and dynamic markets".[54]

After conducting a market survey, contracting authorities should adjust their procedures accordingly, especially in high-risk markets such as construction and road infrastructure. To prevent collusion, framework agreements should be designed to create asymmetry between suppliers and call-offs so that any colluding framework awardees may find it difficult to coordinate and share the pie between them. Since "the sequence of call-offs could, in principle, be assimilated with a public contract split into several lots",[55] the prescription of the economic theory that the number of lots should be smaller than the expected number of participants may apply to the framework agreement call-offs as well. In practice, the average number of suppliers with whom a multi-provider framework is concluded is 4.4.[56] So, before determining the number of call-offs, it is good for the relevant procurement officers to make themselves aware of this empirical evidence and determine accordingly the number of call-offs.

The number and value of contracts awarded at the call-off stage can also impact the risk of collusion. Symmetric suppliers, namely firms with similar bargaining power, are more likely to collude when contracts are similarly valued, because it is easier for them to allocate contracts between them.[57] Asymmetric suppliers, on the other hand, are vulnerable when contracts are differently valued. For this reason, contracting authorities should adjust contract values based on the symmetry or asymmetry observed among framework awardees. However, implementing these recommendations may require significant market knowledge and resources. Smaller procuring bodies may find it challenging to gather this information due to the associated costs. Collaboration with national Competition Authorities with relevant expertise is crucial in these cases.

In the same vein, contracting authorities are recommended to opt for the price-quality ratio version allowed under the **most economically advantageous tender (MEAT)** criterion,[58] when awarding public contracts under a framework agreement, rather than solely focusing on price. By requesting technical requirements from suppliers that ensure a specific standard of quality for the products/services procured, it increases the asymmetry between them, acting as a deterrent

54 Albano and Nicholas (fn 15), 166, 173.
55 Ibid, 193.
56 PwC, London Economics and Ecorys for the European Commission (fn 4), 146, fn 109.
57 Albano and Nicholas (fn 15), 205.
58 Article 67, para 2 of Directive 2014/24/EU.

to collusive schemes. This is particularly true for framework agreements with two stages of competition for awarding procurement contracts. Suppliers receive a specific technical score in the first stage of competition, making them "score-heterogeneous" before the second-stage competition.[59] This makes it difficult for them to agree on a collusive scheme, as bidders with a higher technical score may not want to join a bidding ring. Even if they do, they have an incentive to deviate and win the public contract for themselves.

The life of bid riggers can become even more challenging in a framework agreement if, in addition to the recommended measures, contracting authorities vary the call-off methods used for awarding public procurement contracts. This suggestion endorsed by academics and professionals in the public procurement sector aims to create an unstable environment for prospective collusive bidders. The surprise effect of adopting a call-off method unknown to framework agreement awardees hinders their plans to allocate forthcoming contract opportunities among themselves.[60] This aligns with auction theory, which generally recommends uncertainty[61] to prevent collusive behaviour. According to the explanatory note of the European Commission, one way to choose between different economic operators is the "cascade method", where the economic operator with the best tender for the framework agreement is contracted first. If they are unable or unwilling to provide the goods, services or works, the next-ranked supplier is considered.[62] However, this method may concentrate public contracts in the hands of the highest-ranked supplier. Besides the "cascade" method, contracting authorities can use other direct award methods for call-off contracts, such as rotation between suppliers, percentage allocation or random selection.[63]

Another aspect that requires consideration from the European legislator is the closed nature of framework agreements which excludes economic operators who were not initially parties to it. The closed system of framework agreements can lead to a cartelized market once the first stage is completed.[64] Suggestions have

59 Albano and Nicholas (fn 15), 197.

60 Sue Arrowsmith and Caroline Nicholas "Regulating Framework Agreements under the UNCITRAL Model Law", Chapter 2, in Sue Arrowsmith (ed) *Reform of the UNCITRAL Model Law on Procurement: Procurement Regulation for the 21st Century* (Eagan, MN: West, 2009); Peter Arden "Legal Regulation of Multi-provider Framework Agreements and the Potential for Bid Rigging: A Perspective from the UK Local Government Construction Sector" (2013), 5, *PPLR*, 177–178; Procurement Lawyers' Association "The Use of Framework Agreements in Public Procurement" <www.procurementlawyers.org.uk/wp-content/uploads/2017/07/PLA_Paper-on-Frameworks.pdf> accessed on January 10, 2025, 35–36.

61 Indicatively, in Chapter 2 of the book it was explained why auction theory suggests uncertainty regarding the common value of the auctioned object or the point at which an ascending auction may switch to a final sealed bid round.

62 Commission (fn 10).

63 Procurement Lawyers' Association (fn 60), 35.

64 Albano and Nicholas (fn 15), 179; Albano, Buccirossi, Spagnolo and Zanza (fn 34) 351; Albert Sanchez-Graells *Public Procurement and the EU Competition Rules* (Oxford Hart, 2015, 2nd ed), 298–299.

been made to introduce a mechanism, such as dynamic purchasing systems, to allow new entrants during the framework agreement's lifespan.[65] This prevents an incumbency advantage that weakens competition and disrupts any collusive scheme. While concerns about transaction costs and firms' incentives to enter a framework agreement exist, the openness to new joiners should not be a limiting factor as awardees have the opportunity to improve their offers throughout the agreement's duration. This already applies in many dynamic purchasing systems, which allow suppliers to improve their offers at any time during the period when the framework agreement is in operation.[66] This type of framework agreements is commonly encountered outside the EU. Regarding transaction costs, policy makers are concerned about the suggestion of allowing new entrants during call-off bidding in the second stage. To address this, new entrants should only be permitted if certain conditions are met cumulatively:

(a) There is a divergence in the prices requested by the bidders admitted to the framework agreement at the first stage of the procedure, when the framework agreement is concluded and when the need arises.
(b) There is a discrepancy between the prices stipulated by the awardees in the framework agreement and the prices requested by suppliers in the market outside the framework agreement.

If the discrepancy in price between the first stage of the process and when the need arises is caused by market shocks and demand fluctuations, then market prices will also change. Therefore, it is reliable benchmark to determine whether this difference is justified. Also, as previously mentioned, dealing with price disparities is exceptionally costly, time-consuming and challenging for the contracting authority to conduct a completely new tendering process along with a new advertisement in the Official Journal to ensure better value for money from new contractors outside the framework agreement. By including a provision for new entrants in the current Directive during the second-stage competition when the specified conditions are met, the administrative convenience that framework agreements primarily aim for is maintained, while reducing the potential for anticompetitive behaviour that closed framework agreements can have. Additionally, this provision acts as an incentive for framework awardees to keep their prices at or below commercial prices at the call-off stage, or else face intense competition with the participation of new entrants in the framework agreement market. Allowing outside parties to enter the second stage of the framework agreement under these circumstances should be open to any economic operator that meets the relevant selection criteria.

65 Peter Arden "Legal Regulation of Multi-provider Framework Agreements and the Potential for Bid Rigging: A Perspective from the UK Local Government Construction Sector" (2013), 5, *PPLR*, 177–178.

66 Albano and Nicholas (fn 2), 20.

The risk of collusion during the second stage of framework agreements could be further reduced if economic operators outside the framework agreement were able to challenge the call-offs or awards of procurement contracts. This is currently impossible under the Procurement Remedies Directive 2007/66/EC which contemplates in its Recital, paragraph (17) that:

> A review procedure should be available at least to any person having or having had an interest in obtaining a particular contract and who has been or risks being harmed by an alleged infringement.

In other words, the provision mentioned above does not give legal standing to tenderers who are not involved in the contract award process. The situation is similar for contracting authorities looking to initiate a review procedure. The CJEU clarified in the *Simvoulio* case that while aggrieved private parties can bring a claim, contracting authorities may not always have the same legal standing. However, Member States are allowed to include contracting authorities in the group of individuals who can access review procedures.[67] Given this, it could be argued that the current legal framework does not support challenging procurement contracts awarded in the second stage of a framework agreement, which already faces market limitations and exclusivity. Therefore, it may be suggested that special provisions be made as an exception for framework agreements to prevent collusion risks. Specifically, it could be recommended that any economic operator eligible to bid for procurement contracts under a framework agreement should have legal standing to challenge the process. This would serve as deterrent against collusive agreements and ensure that public contracts are awarded to the most competitive bidders, maintaining the integrity of the procurement process. This suggestion has been made by the European Commission in the past regarding the ability to bring proceedings under the Procurement Remedies Directive.[68] However, the Council has maintained restrictive language,[69] to protect the procedural laws of Member States, which require for a legitimate interest in the outcome of the award process

67 Case C-570/08 Simvoulio Apokhetefseon Lefkosias v Anatheoritiki Arhi Prosforon, ECLI:EU:C:2010:621, paras 35–36; Folkert Wilman *Private Enforcement of EU Law Before National Courts: The EU Legislative Framework* (Edward Elgar, 2015), 90–91.

68 Wilman, (fn 67), 90.

69 "The review procedures are available…at least to any person having or having had an interest in obtaining a particular contract and who has been or risks being harmed by an alleged infringement", Article 3, para. 3, Directive 2007/66/EC.

to bring legal action.[70] Despite this, some Member States allow associations or non-economic bodies to start review procedures.[71]

A broad scope for legal standing, such as the one suggested above, raises concerns that framework agreements may become less appealing to contracting authorities. This is because the interests of economic operators (and even associations/bodies that do not act as economic operators) in ensuring the effectiveness of public procurement law may not be balanced with contracting authorities' interest in limiting frivolous litigation and meeting their needs promptly. This argument holds especially true when considering that the most common type of remedy is setting aside decisions, followed by interim measures and the removal of discriminatory specifications.[72] Therefore, it is recommended that there should not be an automatic suspension of the procurement procedure if a procurement contract concluded at the second stage of a framework agreement is reviewed. The contracting authority should be able to request permission from the review body each time to continue the procurement procedure. In some countries, such as Germany, this is allowed, and even the public contract can be concluded during the review proceedings if the negative consequences of the automatic suspension outweigh its benefits.[73] In terms of costs to a contracting authority defending a review case, this may not be a significant issue. The Commission has reported that the costs of defending such cases, as well as the costs for suppliers bringing forward a review case, vary widely across the EU and only account for 0.4–0.6% of the contract value.[74] However, this suggestion also has weaknesses. It may be challenging for economic operators outside the framework agreement market to discover collusive agreements between the framework awardees and gather evidence to challenge them. To address this evidential hurdle, economic operators outside the framework agreement could use the review procedure initiated by them through an interlocutory procedure before or after the conclusion the call-off contract. This would allow them to seek a review with the relevant contracting authority to correct any alleged infringement, without being able to refer to the competent review body to set aside the relevant contract.

Last but not least, it should not be forgotten that in the case of framework agreements, collusion is an inherent risk. Contracting authorities should work diligently

70 Ibid. See also Commission, Proposal for Utilities Remedies Directive 92/13, COM (90) 297, 17; Commission, Communication on the Council's position on the Proposal for Public Sector Remedies Directive 89/665, SEC (89), 1196, 7; Council, Common Position on the Amended Proposal for a Council Directive on the Co-ordination of the Laws, Regulations and Administrative Provisions Relating to the Application of Review Procedures to the Award of Public Supply and Public Works Contracts, doc. 7834/89 ADD1, 7.

71 European Commission "Report on the Effectiveness of Directive 89/665/EEC and Directive 92/13/EEC, as Modified by Directive 2007/66/EC, Concerning Review Procedures in the Area of Public Procurement", COM (2017) 28 final, 4.

72 ibid, 5.

73 OECD Integrity in Public Procurement. Good Practice from A to Z (OECD, 2007) <https://read.oecd-ilibrary.org/governance/integrity-in-public-procurement_9789264027510-en#page1> accessed on January 11, 2025, 113.

74 Commission (fn 10), 6.

to enhance competition and market access. This can be achieved, for instance by expressing their needs in technical and functional terms, rather than detailed *ad hoc* specifications. This issue has already been addressed in Chapter 4 of the book, when discussing technical specifications.

6.4 Electronic Auctions – Analysis of Bid Rigging Issues and Recommendations

In an attempt to maximize the efficiency of public spending in an era of austerity and continuing cuts to public purchasing, there is a trend towards the use of electronic communications by public bodies when buying supplies and services or when tendering public works (e-procurement). E-procurement offers a number of benefits such as simplified and shortened processes, reductions in red-tape and administrative burdens as well as significant savings for all parties.[75] Electronic auctions (e-auctions) are a representative electronic purchasing technique which, as already explained in Chapter 1, uses web-based software to allow potential suppliers to compete online, in real time, to provide prices for the goods/services under auction.[76]

The absence of discretionary evaluation by contracting officials, the contracting authority's saving advantage through increased price competition as well as the fact that compliance with electronic protocols renders the relevant purchasing procedure fully accountable are some of the main reasons why e-auctions were adopted and clarified under the 2014/24/EU Directive.[77] In addition to these benefits, it was noted that e-auctions reduce entry barriers, as they entail high costs for authorities but not for firms and it is enough for a tenderer to make its offer online, without having to be physically present.[78] Though this is true, at the same time the use of technological tools may be a disincentive for SMEs to take part in the process, due to their unfamiliarity with information and communications technology (ICT) procurement.[79]

75 European Commission "E-Procurement" <http://ec.europa.eu/growth/single-market/public-procurement/e-procurement_en> accessed on February 23, 2024.

76 Crown Commercial Service "eAuctions" <www.gov.uk/guidance/eauctions> accessed on July 6, 2024.

77 Nicola Dimitri, Federico Dini and Gustavo Piga "When Should Procurement Be Centralized?" in N. Dimitri, G.Piga and G. Spagnolo (eds) *Handbook of Procurement* (Cambridge: Cambridge University Press), 74; Michael H. Rothkopf and Andrew B. Whinston "E-Auctions for Procurement Operations" (2007), 16(4), 404.

78 PwC, London Economics and Ecorys for the European Commission (fn 4), 78; Laura Carpineti, Gustavo Piga and Matteo Zanza "The Variety of Procurement Practice: Evidence from Public Procurement" in N. Dimitri, G.Piga and G. Spagnolo (eds) *Handbook of Procurement* (Cambridge: Cambridge University Press), 23.

79 "SMEs co-exist with global players and often face difficulties in adopting state of the art ICT technologies and accessing finance", European Commission "Support the Growth of ICT Innovative Creative Industries SMEs" <https://ec.europa.eu/info/funding-tenders/opportunities/portal/screen/opportunities/topic-details/ict-18-2014> accessed on July 31, 2024; see also Hannes Selhofer, Stefan Lilischkis, Georgios Karageorgos and Peter O'Donnell "The European e-Business Report

The main characteristic of the e-auction system under the 2014/24/EU Directive is that information must be communicated to all tenderers throughout each phase of an e-auction. This allows tenderers to determine their position relative to other participants. This information may include details about prices or values submitted by other bidders as well as the number of participants in each phase of the auction. Another significant element of the current Directive is that e-auctions may occur in several successive phases. Additionally, the current Directive allows contracting authorities to close an electronic auction at a pre-determined date and time or when a specified number of auction phases have been completed. This concern applies to all auctions, not just e-auctions.

Though the European legislator has implemented important measures to address collusion in e-auctions, such as the non-disclosure of tenderers' identities (Article 35, paragraph 7 of the 2014/24/EU Directive), there are still some elements that increase the risk of collusion. Therefore, in this section, I will first identify all the elements that make coordination among tenderers more likely and sustainable.

6.4.1 Dissemination of Information

As previously mentioned, positive steps to limit the information disclosed to tenderers in an e-auction about their competitors. The most significant step is that the identities of the tenderers will not be revealed at any point during the electronic auction. However, even with anonymous identities, collusion can still occur among participants in an e-auction for the reasons explained below.

Article 35(7) of Directive 2014/24/EU states that during each phase of an electronic auction, enough information should be provided to all tenderers to allow them to determine their ranking compared to other participants. This enables them to understand their chances of winning the contract in relation to other bids. Contracting authorities may also share additional information such as other prices or values submitted, as well as the number of participants in each phase of the auction.

The dissemination of the aforementioned information allows bidders in an e-auction to track the prices at which competitors drop out and the valid offers submitted in each round. This enables members of a bidding ring to verify if their co-conspirators fulfilled their promise to submit, for example "cover bids", which are artificially high bids or bids that don't secure the contract award. Therefore, firms involved in bid rigging can monitor any deviations from their collusive agreement. Since bidders' identities are not revealed, the bidding ring cannot use targeted punishments against a defector in the same auction. However, the bidding ring will still be effective in suppressing rivalry among members because of the knowledge that one or several bidders deviated. The general threat of ending the collusive

2006/07 edition – A Portrait of e-business in 10 sectors of the EU Economy 5th Synthesis Report of the e-Business Watch" <http://aei.pitt.edu/54204/1/2006-2007.pdf> accessed on July 31, 2024, according to which only about 15% of small firms and 30% of medium-sized firms have their own ICT department.

agreement and reversing to competitive behaviour for the remainder of the e-auction serves as the most severe for the deviating firm. Additionally, all firms would receive lower non-collusive profits. The disclosure of information mandated by the current Directive, makes deviations from a pre-arranged collusive agreement observable, albeit anonymized, enhancing the stability of bidding rings and making e-auctions more prone to collusion.

The risk of collusion due to information disclosure in e-auctions, as outlined above, is further heightened when multiple contracts/lots are awarded. In such cases, concerted practices may merge as bidders can "exploit the openness of the auction format and signal through prices".[80] What is more, when the value of products/services procured through an e-auction is low, particularly in the case of awarding multiple contracts/lots, ring members have little motivation to deviate from the collusion since the benefits of doing so are minimal compared to the risk of future retaliation.[81]

6.4.2 Multi-Round Format and Price as an Award Criterion

Under Article 35(5) of 2014/24/EU Directive, it is specified that e-auctions may occur in several consecutive phases. The multi-round format of an e-auction can improve the sustainability of a bidding ring, particularly in markets where collusion is a concern. According to auction theory, collusion is more likely to happen when auctions are held regularly, allowing the same group of bidders to participate repeatedly.[82] This same principle applies to e-auctions with multiple phases/rounds. The ongoing interaction among bidders, even in an online setting where identities are hidden, provides opportunities to observe price trends and detect any deviations from collusive agreements. Information tends to flow easily in industries with few suppliers, making it relatively simple to identify anonymous bidders. Additionally, the short time-intervals between rounds in a multi-round e-auction strengthen the enforcement mechanisms within a bidding ring. Any member deviating from the agreement may face immediate retaliation in the next stage of the e-auction.[83]

In addition to the multiple rounds in e-auctions under the current Directive, concerns about collusion are also raised by the criterion of selecting the lowest

80 Albano and Nicholas (fn 15), 201; G.L. Albano, N. Dimitri, R. Pacini and G. Spagnolo "Information and Competitive Tendering" in N. Dimitri, G. Piga and G. Spagnolo (eds) *Handbook of Procurement* (Cambridge: Cambridge University Press), 160.

81 Robert C. Marshall and Leslie M. Marx, *The Economics of Collusion-Cartels and Bidding Risks* (MIT Press, 2012), 206.

82 Ibid, 205–206; Ohad Soudry "Promoting Economy: Electronic Reverse Auctions under the EC Directives on Public Procurement" (2004), 4(3), 362; Masaki Aoyagi "Bid Rotation and Collusion in Repeated Auctions" (2003), 112(1), *Journal of Economic Theory*, 79–105; Srabana Gupta "The Effect of Bid Rigging on Prices: A Study of the Highway Construction Industry" (2001), 19(4), *Review of Industrial Organization*, 455.

83 P. Klemperer, *Auctions: Theory and Practice* (Princeton University Press, 2004); Albano, Buccirossi, Spagnolo and Zanza (fn 34) 358.

price. According to Article 35, paragraph 3 of 2014/24/EU Directive, e-auctions are based on one of the following elements of the tenders:

(a) Solely on prices where the contract is awarded on the basis of price only.
(b) On prices and/or on the new values of the features of the tenders indicated in the procurement documents where the contract is awarded on the basis of the best price-quality ratio or to the tender with the lowest cost using a cost-effectiveness approach.

In an environment where competition is driven solely by price considerations, such as in the case of e-auctions under Article 35(3) (a) of the current Directive, where bidders compete on a "level" playing field, bidding firms find it easier to agree on a collusive scheme due to their symmetry in the products/services they offer.[84] Their values for the products/services procured are very similar, making it easy to determine which ring member wins the public contract and what payments should be made between each ring member. On the contrary, when the contract is awarded based on either the best price-quality ratio or cost-effectiveness, the bidders competing in each round of the e-auction will be score-heterogeneous, leading to difficulties in colluding.[85] That is because the weighting of each criterion used to determine the most economically advantageous tender varies.[86] Price competition with different qualities could be seen as price competition among bidders with different costs.[87] Bidders with different cost structures and functions typically do not have a shared view on how to act or common interests to pursue. Therefore, forming a bidding rig under such circumstances is challenging. Conversely, the ring mechanism enables a cartel to eliminate all ring competition, making the allocation structure of the bidding ring much simpler.[88] This concept was also highlighted in Chapter 2 of the book, stating that symmetric firms can easily reach an agreement, while firms with product and cost heterogeneity cannot realistically aim for joint-profit maximization.[89] Therefore, when bidders only compete on price in a multi-round e-auction, without considering the quality of their products/services or their cost-effectiveness, it is akin to a group of similar suppliers competing in multiple auction rounds increasing the risk of collusion.

The situation worsens when examining how things operate in practice. Empirical research suggests that in dynamic purchasing and e-auctions, the most

84 Albano and Nicholas (fn 15), 198.
85 Ibid.
86 See Article 35, para 6 of the 2014/24 Directive.
87 Ibid, 197.
88 Marshall and Marx (fn 81), 189, 191–192. See also R. Preston McAfee and John McMillan "Bidding Rings" (1992), 82(3), *The American Economic Review*, 579–599.
89 Alexis Jacquemin and Margaret Slade "Cartels, Collusion and Horizontal Merger" in R. Schmalensee and R. Willig (eds) *Handbook of Industrial Organization* (Elsevier 1989), 418.

economically advantageous criterion is often overlooked, with price being the predominant factor considered.[90]

6.4.3 The Way an E-Auction Can Close

According to Article 35, paragraph 8 of 2014/24/EU Directive, contracting authorities shall close an electronic auction in one or more of the following manners:

(a) At the previously indicated date and time.
(b) When they receive no more new prices or new values which meet the requirements concerning minimum differences, provided that they have previously stated the time which they will allow to elapse after receiving the last submission before they close the electronic auction.
(c) When the previously indicated number of phases in the auction has been completed.

The Organisation for Economic Co-Operation and Development (OECD) has found that having predictable procurement schedules and in general any predictability regarding the timing of tenders can facilitate collusion.[91] However, in e-auctions that use hard-close ending rules, namely fixed deadlines, collusion cannot be sustained, even with two bidders.[92] This is because sniping dominates collusion.[93] Sniping, also known as last-minute bidding in auctions, is the strategic behaviour of bidding as late as possible.[94] In auctions that use hard-closed ending rules, that is, fixed deadlines, experienced bidders are motivated to maximize their payoff as the auction deadline approaches.[95] This is because other bidders have limited time to respond, making collusion less likely. However, it has been shown that in infinitely repeated simultaneous e-auctions with a soft-close ending rule, as outlined in Article 38(8)(b) of Directive 2014/24/EU, collusive behaviour is possible,

90 PwC, London Economics and Ecorys for the European Commission (fn 4), 59.

91 OECD "Guidelines for Fighting Bid Rigging in Public Procurement" <www.oecd.org/en/publications/guidelines-for-fighting-bid-rigging-in-public-procurement_8cfeafbb-en.html> accessed on January 10, 2025, 6; OECD "Competition and Procurement: Key Findings 2011" <www.oecd.org/en/publications/competition-and-procurement-key-findings_c6e6d5ae-en.html> accessed on January 10, 2024; OECD "Policy Roundtables: Collusion and Corruption in Public Procurement" <www.oecd.org/en/publications/collusion-and-corruption-in-public-procurement_ef957f70-en.html> accessed on January 10, 2025.

92 Sascha Fullbrunn "Collusion or Sniping in simultaneous ascending Auctions – A prisoner's dilemma" <https://journals.ub.ovgu.de/index.php/FEMM-WPS/article/view/109/107> accessed January 12, 2025.

93 Ibid.

94 Zhigang Cao, Yunlong Wang, Xiaoguang Yang and Lin Zhao, "Does Soft-Close Eliminate Sniping in Online Auctions? An Attention-Based Explanation" (December 27, 2023) <https://ssrn.com/abstract=4676973 or http://dx.doi.org/10.2139/ssrn.4676973> accessed January 12, 2025.

95 Ibid.

particularly when there are few bidders and/or markets, leading to a lack of coordination challenges.[96]

Directive 2014/24/EU has not adequately addressed the pro-collusive elements of e-auctions mentioned above. Therefore, recommendations are needed to reduce the susceptibility of e-auctions to anticompetitive practices. The current Directive promotes transparency by facilitating the exchange of information among all bidders to prevent corruption, such as collusion between bidders and procurement officers. The phrase used in paragraph 7 of Article 35 of 2014/24/EU Directive, that the contracting authorities shall instantaneously communicate to all tenderers *at least sufficient information* to enable them to ascertain their relative rankings at any moment, is characteristic of the approach that the European legislator has adopted (emphasis added). Yet, as already shown, the minimum amount of information about the bidding history of other auctioneers should be made available, in order to hinder the observation of any deviation, even the anonymous one, from the pre-arranged collusive agreement in case of a bidding ring. Many academics argue for reduced information flow during multi-round e-auctions to make collusion more difficult.[97] To achieve this, auctioneers should not be informed of the prices at which their competitors dropped out or the number of valid offers submitted per round. It should be enough for auctioneers to know if their bid is the leading and the price of the top bid to determine their next offer.[98] Moreover, delaying the publication of information as much as possible can also deter collusion, as it makes punishing defectors more challenging once the e-auction has ended.[99] This approach increases the benefits of breaking the collusive agreement while jeopardizing its stability.

In addition to the above, it is suggested that in markets where collusion is a concern, preference should be given to e-bids over e-auctions. The one-round format of e-bids makes it difficult to manipulate bidder strategies, making it an effective anti-cartel measure".[100] When it comes to closing an e-auction closes, if there are few bidders or markets, contracting authorities should avoid closing the e-auction when no further valid bids are submitted within a specific period. This can lead to outbidding the leading bid and increase the possibility of collusion. On the other hand, closing the auction at a predetermined time or after a set number of rounds is preferable in terms of preventing collusion when there are few bidders or markets.

96 Fullbrunn (fn 92); Anthony M. Kwasnica and Katerina Shertyuk "Collusion and equilibrium selection in auctions" (2007), 117(516), *Economic Journal*, 120–145.

97 R. Preston McAfee, Michael Williams and Kenneth Hendricks "Auctions and Bid Rigging" in Roger D. Blair and D. Daniel Sokol (eds) *The Oxford Handbook of International Antitrust Economics, Volume 2* (Oxford University Press, 2014), 518; Srabana Gupta, Indranil Ghosh and Ido Millet "An Empirical Study of Collusion Potential Metrics and their Impact on Online Reverse Auction Success" in Diane H. Parente (ed) *Best Practices for Online Procurement Auctions* (IGI Global, 2008), 245.

98 Albano and Nicholas (fn 15), 243–244.

99 Albano, Buccirossi, Spagnolo and Zanza (fn 34), 352–353.

100 Albano and Nicholas (fn 15), 199; see also OECD (fn 91), 7.

This method reduces the chance of collusive schemes and encourages sniping over collusive strategies.

6.5 Conclusion

This chapter has conducted a thorough critical review of the second phase of the EU public procurement process, specifically focusing on procurement techniques and instruments. Regarding framework agreements, there should be guidance on how each Member State should utilize them, along with provisions for questioning decisions made by contracting authorities. It was suggested that procurement officers should assess the vulnerability to collusion in the market for a specific framework agreement either in the first or the second stage of the procedure. Close collaboration between procurement officers and national CAs was recommended to address this issue. Asymmetry among suppliers and call-offs was also suggested to disrupt potential collusive behaviour among framework awardees. Close cooperation with the national CAs is needed to make this suggestion work. However, these suggestions may be feasible for smaller procuring bodies, due to the high cost of obtaining such information. Cooperation with national CAs may not yield significant improvement, if the issue of who will cover the costs of collecting market information remains unresolved.

Adjusting the value of contracts awarded in the second stage of framework agreements based on the level of symmetry between framework awardees was recommended. Applying the MEAT criterion for awarding public contracts can also ensure asymmetry between supplier, as suppliers with varying technical scores are less likely to form collusive bidding rings. Utilizing various call-off methods, such as the cascade method or random selection, was suggested to prevent collusive behaviour among framework awardees.

To address the closed nature of framework agreements, allowing new joiners was suggested to reduce barriers to entry. However, this openness may discourage firms from entering into framework agreements. Therefore, framework agreements should be open to new tenderers if the framework awardees can improve their offers anytime the framework agreement is in operation, while meeting specific conditions related to price divergence and discrepancy. Granting legal standing to economic operators entitled to tender for the award of procurement contracts under a framework agreement was proposed. This would allow them to challenge collusive agreements, with the review procedure initiated by these operators serving as a means to prevent collusion.

The chapter also discussed e-auctions and identified factors that promote coordination among tenderers. Recommendations were made to limit the disclosure of bidding history and delay the publication of certain information to prevent collusion. The use of e-bids instead of e-auctions was suggested, in cases of collusion concerns, as the one-round format of e-bids is less susceptible to manipulation. Closing the auction at a predetermined time or after a set number of rounds was recommended, when there are few bidders or markets. This method reduces the likelihood of collusive schemes.

In conclusion, this chapter highlighted that current European procurement rules are not do not align with economic theory and may contribute to bid rigging. Auction theory was proposed as a benchmark to assess collusion risks and suggest strategies to combat cartel formation in competitive bidding. In this way, it is emphasized that contracting authorities need to invest more resources in making procurement procedures more collusion proof and raising awareness among procurement officers. The next chapter will explore how competition regulators address bid rigging in public procurement through leniency programmes, essential tools for detecting and combatting cartels.

7 Debarment, Self-Cleaning and Leniency

Friends or Foes?

7.1 Introduction

So far, this thesis has conducted a thorough study of the latest European Directive 2014/24 on procurement and offered a bid rigging perspective on the current procurement rules. It has been demonstrated that the procedures, techniques and instruments for electronic and aggregated procurement provided by the current Directive are not entirely suitable to combat collusive behaviour in public procurement. Therefore, it has been suggested that bid rigging primarily and secondarily concerted practices can be addressed under the current Directive, as long as procurement agents are given guidance on how to prevent them. Additionally, specific legislative and soft law instruments need to be implemented to assist contracting authorities in better protecting themselves against this anticompetitive behaviour. Moreover, the previous chapters have identified particular instruments in the current Directive that pose a risk of being misused for collusion and recommendations have been made on how to make them more collusion-proof.

Even if the design of the procurement process is improved to make collusion less likely, determined bid riggers may still enter into such agreements. For this reason, after assessing of the relevant provisions in the latest Directive on public sector, it is worth examining the policies that competition regulators bring to the area of public procurement in an attempt to deter bid rigging. This chapter focuses on the leniency programme, which is a key mechanism to strengthen the public enforcement of competition law, as well as on the debarment mechanism and self-cleaning measures, which are both procurement remedies. As will be shown, procurement remedies interfere with cartel enforcement and this chapter will explore this issue, arguing that the vulnerability of leniency recipients to the mechanism of debarment and self-cleaning provisions makes the leniency policy of CAs unworkable in the domain of public procurement.

Leniency has become a "weapon of mass dissuasion" and detection in the arsenal of CAs worldwide, in their efforts to identify, prosecute and dismantle cartels, which are considered the ultimate evil in antitrust.[1] Leniency

1 Antonio Capobianco and Yonatan Cwikel "Roundtable on Ex Officio Cartel Investigations and the Use of Screens to Detect Cartels" (OECD, November 4, 2013) <www.oecd.org/en/publications/ex-officio-cartel-investigation_4089581e-en.html> accessed January 13, 2024; Wouter P.J. Wils "Leni-

DOI: 10.4324/9781003359999-7

programmes[2] offer undertakings that defect from a cartel the opportunity to receive an award, if they provide information about the cartel. This incentivizes both undertakings and their employees to disclose the violation, offering evidence to CAs against other cartel members in exchange for reduced penalties or immunity from sanctions. For example, in the EU, nearly two-thirds of cartel investigations completed since 2001 were initiated because a cartel member chose to cooperate with CAs in exchange for immunity from fines.[3] The importance of insider reporting in detecting competition law violations has also been acknowledged through the recent Whistleblower Protection Directive, which was approved by the European Parliament on April 16, 2019. This Directive aims to enhance protection to individuals and organizations that report violations of EU law and, including Union competition law.[4]

Despite the significant importance of leniency programme in cartel enforcement, the number of leniency applications in Europe has decreased by almost 50% in recent years.[5] In 2014, the European Commission received 46 leniency applications but by 2016, only 24 applications were submitted.[6] While it is not wise to draw definitive conclusions based solely on three years of data, this decline is a concerning trend that should be carefully considered to prevent a weakening of the EU leniency policy. Additionally, an empirical survey revealed that practitioners with extensive experience in leniency programmes have noticed a decrease in their clients' interest and motivation to apply for leniency in recent years.[7] The survey participants identified the increased risk of civil damages claims as the primary

ency in Antitrust Enforcement: Theory and Practice", 30(1), *World Competition: Law and Economics Review*, 19–26.

2 According to Article 2(15) of the European Directive 2014/104/EU leniency programme means a programme concerning the application of Article 101 TFEU or a corresponding provision under national law on the basis of which a participant in a secret cartel, independently of the other undertakings involved in the cartel, cooperates with an investigation of the competition authority, by voluntarily providing presentations regarding that participant's knowledge of, and role in, the cartel in return for which that participant receives, by decision or by a discontinuation of proceedings, immunity from, or a reduction in, fines under a leniency programme, not including pre-existing information. See also UNCTAD Secretariat "The Use of Leniency Programmes as a Tool for the Enforcement of Competition law against Hardcore Cartels in Developing Countries" (UNCTAD August 26, 2010) <http://unctad.org/en/docs/tdrbpconf7d4_en.pdf> accessed January 13, 2024.

3 Andreas Stephan "Cartels" in Ioannis Lianos and Damien Geradin (eds) *Handbook on European Competition Law* (Edward Elgar Publishing 2013), 227.

4 European Commission "Proposal for a Directive of the European Parliament and of the Council on the protection of persons reporting on breaches of Union law", April 23, 2018, COM (2018) 218 final-2018/0106 (COD), Recital 15 <https://eur-lex.europa.eu/legal-content/EN/TXT/?uri=celex:52018PC0218> accessed on May 11, 2024.

5 Johan Ysewyn and Siobhan Kahmann "The Decline and Fall of the Leniency Programme in Europe" Concurrences No 1-2018, 45.

6 Ysewyn and Kahmann (fn 5), ibid.

7 Survey prepared by Brussels Matters for its meeting "The European Antitrust Leniency Calculus c. 2016: Still Worth It?" (Brussels June 16, 2016) <http://www.brusselsmatters.eu/index.html?page=489&sz_event=Leniency16> accessed on May 11, 2024; see also Wouter P.J. Wils "Private Enforcement of EU Antitrust Law and Its Relationship with Public Enforcement: Past, Present and Future" (2017), 40(1), *World Competition: Law and Economics Review*, 42.

reason for this decline.[8] In fact, during the presentation titled "Is there Life After Leniency?" at the 67th ABA (American Bar Association) Antitrust Section Spring Meeting, 46% of attendees voted in favour of completely shielding leniency applicant from civil liability to incentivize more leniency applications.[9]

In the realm of public contracts, the situation remains the same. The implementation of the leniency programme to detect bid rigging is quite challenging. It has been argued that this difficulty stems from the strong stability of cartels in public procurement markets. A company that benefits from the high profits of a robust cartel has no incentive to report its existence and request leniency.[10] The scenario would be different if the cartel was weak and disintegrated on its own. In such cases, the most favourable option for a company is to come forward and self-report, to receive the immunity or, at the very least, a reduction in fines. Another reason for the challenge in applying leniency programmes is that many cartels are typically exposed during a merger between two companies. The acquiring company often discovers the anticompetitive behaviour of the acquired company. However, in public procurement, bid rigging companies are usually small, so mergers between them do not meet the turnover threshold required to trigger a merger notification under EU law.[11] Additionally, the potential reputational damage, which could negatively impact future procurement processes, serves as a disincentive for companies involved in bidding rigging to apply for leniency.[12] Furthermore, research has shown that leniency programmes do not effectively deter firms from forming new bidding rings and inflating transaction prices. An experimental study conducted at the Kyoto Sangyo University Experimental Economics laboratory observed real conversations among bid riggers before bidding in a repeated procurement auction game.[13] The study revealed that leniency programmes lack the power to discourage companies from engaging in bid rigging and driving up prices.[14]

8 Ibid.

9 Eduardo Frade, Susan Jones, Lisa M. Phelan and Brent Snyder "Is There Life After Leniency?" American Bar Association (ABA) Antitrust Section Spring Meeting (Washington DC, March 27, 2019).

10 Alberto Heimler "Cartels in Public Procurement" (2012) *Journal of Competition Law and Economics*, 859; International Competition Network (ICN) "Anti-Cartel Enforcement Manual: Relationships between Competition Agencies and Public Procurement Bodies" <www.internationalcompetitionnetwork.org/wp-content/uploads/2018/05/CWG_ACEMPublicProcurement.pdf> accessed on January 13, 2025.

11 Heimler (fn 10) 859.

12 Ibid.

13 Yasuyo Hamaguchi et al., *An Experimental Study of Procurement Auctions with Leniency Program*, CPRC Discussion Paper Series CPDP-24-E January 2007 <www.semanticscholar.org/paper/An-experimental-study-of-procurement-auctions-with-Hamaguchi-Ishikawa/646fe57a46e5481525e4f170ca7727b56444a2e4> accessed January 13, 2025; Catarina Moura Pinto Marvão and Giancarlo Spagnolo, "What do we know about the Effectiveness of Leniency Policies? A Survey of the Empirical and Experimental Evidence" in Caron Beaton-Wells and Christopher Tran (eds) *Anti-Cartel Enforcement in a Contemporary Age – Leniency Religion* (Hart Publishing, 2015), 77–78.

14 Hamaguchi and Kawagoe (fn 13), 3–4.

This chapter argues that in addition to other reasons, it is primarily the vulnerability of leniency recipients to the mechanism of debarment and self-cleaning provisions that hinders the success of leniency policies in the realm of public procurement. While debarring bidders may appear to be a reasonable solution for procurement lawyers, scholars and policy makers, it lacks sense from a competition law perspective. Excluding firms from bidding on public contracts for a significant period of three years, through the debarment mechanism makes the leniency programme less appealing to colluding companies. Moreover, debarred companies must prove that they have taken appropriate remedial actions to prevent future occurrences, as required by self-cleaning provisions, which entails full cooperation with government agencies. This cooperation involves disclosing information that falls under the definition of leniency statements outlined in Directive 2014/104/EU on rules governing actions for damages resulting from competition law violations (the **Damages Directive**).[15] This confidential information may later be used by the same government agencies to seek damages for the overcharge they experienced due to bid rigging conspiracies. Consequently, self-cleaning provisions increase the risk of debarred firms facing civil litigation, altering the leniency calculation and necessitating a more nuanced assessment of whether to seek leniency. While the following chapter of the thesis will advocate for local authorities and government departments to more frequently seek damages for being overcharged by collusive tenderers, this does not imply that private enforcement should compromise leniency. As Chapters 6 and 7 will demonstrate, granting contracting authorities access to leniency documents is not the primary method to protect or enhance their right to compensation for antitrust harm. In fact, Chapter 6 will illustrate that providing contracting authorities with the confidential version of leniency decisions undermines the viability of leniency programme in public procurement as well as the "blanket ban" imposed by the Damages Directive on disclosing files and documents submitted by the first leniency applicant. Hence, Chapter 6 aligns with Chapter 7, despite initial appearances to the contrary.

In view of the above, this chapter is divided into five sections. The first section serves as an introduction. Section 7.2 outlines the current rules regarding the mechanism of debarment in public procurement as well as the provisions on the EU's self-cleaning policy. Section 7.3 critically analyzes and sheds light on the recent judgment of the European Court of Justice (CJEU), C-124/17 Vossloh Laeis GmbH v Stadtwerke München GmbH,[16] delivered on October 24, 2018. This court decision demonstrates that self-cleaning provisions undermine the leniency programme because the full collaboration required of the infringing firm by the contracting authority makes it easier for the latter to access information from the leniency file, such as the full decision of a CA, and file damages claims for bid rigging. Hence, a discussion is held on whether the Vossloh Laeis GmbH v Stadtwerke München GmbH case is compatible with the 2014/104/EU Damages Directive provisions on

15 Directive 2014/104/EU of 26 November 2014 [2014] OJ L 349, 1–19.
16 ECLI:EU:C:2018:855.

the disclosure of evidence, some of which include leniency statements.[17] Moreover, it is examined to what extent it is appropriate to prioritize the interest of parties injured by the infringement over the interest associated with public enforcement, specifically the protection of leniency programmes. Section 7.4 discusses several proposals to better align leniency programmes with the mechanism of debarment and the self-cleaning policy in public procurement. Finally, Section 7.5 concludes the chapter with a summary.

7.2 Debarment Mechanism, Self-Cleaning Defence and Leniency in Public Procurement: Conflicting Policy Objectives

With the goal of safeguarding public funds from underperformers and wrongdoers, the European Union has implemented the debarment mechanism in public procurement.[18] The debarment mechanism was first introduced in 1884, when the US Congress passed a law stating that contracts should only be awarded to the lowest "responsible" bidder. In European public procurement, debarment is seen as an administrative tool used by governments to disqualify contractors from receiving public contracts or extensions to existing contracts.[19] This helps protect public budgets and other interests in contract performance, as economic operators on the exclusion list are considered to be at a higher risk of not being able to properly execute the contract.[20] It wasn't until the early 2000s that the scope of debarment expanded, allowing public procurement agencies to exclude suppliers based on reasonable doubt of their integrity, regardless of any criminal justice proceedings in the case.[21] According to Recital 101 of the Procurement Directive 2014/24/EU contracting authorities should "be able to exclude candidates or tenderers whose performance in earlier public contracts has shown major deficiencies with regard to substantive requirements".[22] The Directive also outlines mandatory and discretionary exclusion grounds for suppliers posing integrity risks. Under discretionary exclusion grounds, a contracting authority can exclude a tenderer from a

17 Article 6, para 6 of the Directive 2014/104/EU on certain rules governing actions for damages under national law for infringements of the competition law provisions of the Member States and of the European Union.

18 Collin Swan and Belita Manka "Risky Business: Does Debarring Poor Performers Mitigate Future Performance Risk?" (paper submitted to the Third International Conference on Public Procurement Law Africa, organized by the African Procurement Law Unit at Stellenbosch University) (Cape Town, November 1–2, 2018).

19 Steven Schooner "The Paper Tiger Stirs: Rethinking Suspension and Debarment" (2004), 13, *Public Procurement Law Review*, 211; Sarah Schoenmaekers "The EU Debarment Rules: Legal and Economic Rationale"(2016), 3, *Public Procurement Law Review*, 94.

20 Sue Arrowsmith, Hans-Joachim Prieβ and Pascal Friton "Self-Cleaning as a Defence to Exclusions for Misconduct: An Emerging Concept in EC Public Procurement Law" (2009), 18, *Public Procurement Law Review*, 270–275; Schoenmaekers (fn 19), 99.

21 Emmanuelle Auriol and Tina Soreide "An Economic Analysis of Debarment" 2017, (50), *International Review of Law and Economics*, 37.

22 Recital 101, Directive 2014/24/EU of 26 February 2014 [2014] OJ L 94/65.

procurement procedure for up to three years from the relevant event. Some of these grounds involve competition law infringements by the tenderer, such as suspected agreements with other tenderers to distort competition.[23] This provision, introduced for the first time in the Procurement Directive 2014/24/EU, specifically addresses bid rigging cartels and sends a clear message to the private sector that collusion in the public market will not be tolerated. Prior to the Directive, competition law violations were prohibited but fell under the broader category of "grave professional misconduct".[24] Additionally, Article 57 of the Directive includes other exclusion grounds related to competition distortions, such as an economic operator's prior involvement in the preparation of a procurement procedure.[25] This provision has already been discussed in Chapter 4 of the thesis, when examining conflicts of interests under the current Directive on the public sector.

While the emphasis on integrity issues in the debarment mechanism is understandable, banning firms from bidding for a significant period of three years from the date of the relevant event, as outlined in paragraph 4 of Article 57 in Directive 2014/24/EU, is likely to minimize competition. For example, in the Office of Fair Trading (OFT) bid rigging case in the UK,[26] the authority had to intervene to prevent local awarding authorities from blacklisting firms under investigation, as it often left just one bidder. The OFT stated in their decision report that excluding all infringers from tender lists would make it difficult for the public sector to find bidders, as cover pricing in the construction industry is a "widespread and endemic practice".[27] Hungary also had to set aside mandatory exclusion provisions due to lack of operators left in the market.[28] Less competition can lead to higher prices or lower quality in public contracts,[29] especially when public contracts make up a significant portion of the market. Furthermore, the three-year abstention from bidding conflicts with the leniency programme. A leniency application does not protect the applicant from debarment consequences if they participate in a bidding ring, discouraging firms from cooperating with public authorities. This discouragement

23 Ibid, Article 57, para. 4(d).

24 Adrian Brown "When May an Economic Operator Be Excluded from Public Tenders Due to Its Previous Infringement of Competition Law? Vossloh Laeis GmbH v. Stadwerke Munchen GmbH (C-124/17)" (2019), 2, *Public Procurement Law Review*, NA51.

25 Ibid, Article 57, para. 4(f). "Contracting authorities may exclude or may be required by Member States to exclude from participation in a procurement procedure any economic operator, where a distortion of competition from the prior involvement of the economic operators in the preparation of the procurement procedure…cannot be remedied by other, less intrusive measures".

26 In the construction industry of the UK 103 companies were found to have breached competition law in 2009 be getting involved in cover pricing. See BBC "Building Companies fined £129.5m" < http://news.bbc.co.uk/1/hi/business/8268116.stm> accessed on February 4, 2024.

27 OFT "Competition Act 1998 – Decision of OFT No.CA98/02/2009-Bid Rigging in the Construction Industry in England, September 21, 2009" <http://webarchive.nationalarchives.gov.uk/20140402142426/http://www.oft.gov.uk/shared_oft/business_leaflets/general/CE4327-04_Decision__public_1.pdf> accessed on February 4, 2024.

28 Kris Van Hove, Van Bael and Bellis "Bid-rigging and Deterrence under the EU Law" ICN Cartel Workshop (Ottawa, October 4–6, 2017).

29 Auriol and Soreide (fn 21), 37–38.

also hinders the discovery and punishment of cartels in public procurement, as infringing companies are less likely to come forward and apply for leniency.[30] The clash between the leniency programme and the debarment mechanism in public procurement is exacerbated by the fact that they are not part of a common enforcement system, and do not they serve the same aims. The leniency programme aims to deter anticompetitive practices and protect firms and consumers from these practices and any damages caused by them,[31] while the debarment mechanism is "an investment needed to secure trust in government procurement".[32] Colluders are less likely to engage in bidding ring, if they risk not only competition law prosecution but also losing the opportunity to secure public contracts for a significant period.[33] This means that the debarment mechanism aims to reduce the number of dishonest suppliers engaging in collusive activities in the public market, rather than destabilize or deter bid rigging schemes.[34]

In light of the protective effect and the purposes of the exclusion provisions under public procurement rules, fundamental Community law principles, particularly the free movement of goods and services, the principle of equal treatment and the principle of proportionality require significant consideration when applying the debarment mechanism.[35] The general idea of the self-cleaning concept is to avoid exclusion or minimize its risk while restoring trust in economic operators by providing them with the opportunity to demonstrate that they have taken effective measures to prevent future wrongful acts.[36] Therefore, procurement rules provide the possibility for a tenderer to demonstrate its reliability and participate in procurement procedures again, despite the existence of grounds for exclusion (the so-

30 However, it should be underlined that leniency may be effective to dissolve pre-existing collusive schemes but not to dissuade firms from forming a new cartel. See Hamaguchi et al. (fn 13). See also Stephen Davies and Peter L. Ormosi "The Economic Impact of Cartels and Anti-Cartel Enforcement" (2014) CCP Working Paper, 13–7, v2 <https://ideas.repec.org/p/uea/ueaccp/2013_07v2.html> accessed on May 11, 2024, where it is explained that "less stable cartels are more likely to apply for leniency"; Rosa M. Abrantes-Metz and Albert D. Metz "The Future of Cartel Deterrence and Detection" (January 2019) CPI Antitrust Chronicle <https://www.competitionpolicyinternational.com/wp-content/uploads/2019/01/CPI-Abrantes-Metz-Metz.pdf> accessed on May 11, 2024, where it is clarified that "if the cartel is very successful-which means that its social harm is that much greater-then it becomes less likely that it will be self-reported to authorities".

31 European Commission "Green Paper – Damages actions for breach of the EC antitrust rules" COM (2005) 672, December 19, 2005 <https://eur-lex.europa.eu/legal-content/EN/TXT/PDF/?uri=CELEX:52005DC0672&from=EN> accessed on January 12, 2025.

32 Erling Johan Hjelmeng and Tina Soreide "Debarment in Public Procurement: Rationales and Realisation" in Racca G.M, Yuki C. and Cavallo Perin R. (eds) *Promoting Integrity in Public Procurement: Accountability and Transparency* (Bruylant 2014), 5.

33 Albert Sanchez-Graells "Competition Law and Public Procurement" in J.A. Moreno Molina and E. Diaz Bravo (eds) *Contración Pública Global: visiones compradas* (Valencia Tirant lo Blanch, 2020); Albert Sanchez-Graells "Prevention and Deterrence of Bid: A Look from the New EU Directive on Public Procurement" in Racca G.M., Yuki C. and Cavallo Perin R. (eds) *Promoting Integrity in Public Procurement: Accountability and Transparency* (Bruylant 2014), 188.

34 Hjelmeng and Søreide (fn 33).

35 Arrowsmith, Prieβ and Friton (fn 21) 275.

36 Ibid. 257; Schoenmaekers (fn 19), 97–98.

called self-cleaning defence). Failing to consider self-cleaning measures infringes on the principle of equal treatment, as candidates that have taken sufficient self-cleaning measures should not be treated the same as those who have made no effort to demonstrate reliability despite relevant grounds for debarment. This principle was confirmed by the CJEU in the Fabricom case,[37] where it was deemed unlawful to blanket exclude of a company that had previously cooperated with the relevant contracting authority, as it did not provide an opportunity for the company to prove that, its experience was not distorting competition.[38] This decision was also upheld by the CJEU in the *Michaniki AE* case,[39] where it was considered disproportionate to exclude an entire group of undertakings without allowing them to demonstrate that their participation in a tender procedure did not threaten the values and objectives of procurement law.[40]

This case law was later confirmed by Article 57(6) of Directive 2014/24/EU which provides for self-cleaning measures, if an economic operator wants to demonstrate its reliability despite the existence of a relevant ground for exclusion. In order to rely on this self-cleaning defence, a tenderer must prove that:[41]

1. it has paid or undertaken to pay compensation in respect of any damage caused by the criminal offence or misconduct.
2. it has clarified the facts and circumstances in a comprehensive manner by actively collaborating with the investigating authorities (e.g. through special audits by outside independent persons such as public accountants).[42]
3. it has taken concrete technical, organizational (e.g. effective reporting and controlling, an internal or external revision organ, regular seminars and in-house training for the employees, internal re-organization)[43] and personnel (e.g. dismissal of employees or shareholders responsible for the criminal offence, introduction of the business ethics and a code of conduct, principles of good conduct in employment contracts, periodic staff rotation, internal regulations on liability and compensation for damages in case of non-compliance)[44] measures that are appropriate to prevent any further infringements.

The self-cleaning application is completely voluntary and should be submitted before the contracting authority decides on the fulfilment of the selection criteria in a public tender. Moreover, which self-cleaning measures should be taken depends on the gravity of the infringement, as demonstrated by its duration, recurrence

37 Joined cases C-21/03 and C-34/03 *Fabricom* (2005) I-1559.
38 Ibid, para. 36.
39 Case C-213/07 *Michaniki AE* (2008) I-09999.
40 Ibid, para. 54.
41 Recital 102 and Article 57, para. 6 of the Directive 2014/24/EU.
42 Lubica Páleníková "Corruption in Public Tenders-Concept of Self-Cleaning" (2012), 9, *Annals of the Faculty of Law of Zenica*, 279.
43 Ibid.
44 Ibid.

and financial impact.[45] This means that the self-cleaning measures listed in Article 57(6) of Directive 2014/24/EU are not cumulative conditions that have to be met in order that a firm may avoid exclusion. Also, anytime the self-cleaning evidence turns out to be sufficient, contracting authorities are not allowed to exclude the relevant economic operator.[46] Yet, Article 57(6) of Directive 2014/24/EU does not specify what constitutes "investigating authorities" for the purposes of self-cleaning defence. The provision does not clarify whether the debarred firm is obliged to collaborate only with the relevant CA investigating the infringement or with the contracting authority as well, which awards the relevant public contract. Additionally, the provision does not elaborate upon the level of active cooperation required by the debarred firm when relying on self-cleaning defence. Therefore, the Court of Justice of the European Union (CJEU) filled the gap in the recent case Vossloh Laeis GmbH v Stadtwerke München GmbH.[47]

7.3 Vossloh Laeis Case: Private Enforcement by Public Authorities and Leniency in Europe

7.3.1 Brief Presentation of the Case

The CJEU delivered the judgment C-124/17 Vossloh Laeis GmbH v Stadtwerke München GmbH on October, 24, 2018. In this case, a German company (**Vossloh Laeis**), which manufactures railway materials necessary for railway installations, was found guilty of participating in agreements that violated cartel laws until 2011, specifically concerning switches (referred to as **the rail cartel**).[48] As a result, the Federal Cartel Office in Germany imposed a fine on Vossloh Laeis, taking into account the fact that Vossloh Laeis had applied for leniency and cooperated with the Cartel Office to help clarify its collusive behaviour.[49]

Simultaneously, the contracting authority, Stadtwerke München, filed a civil action for damages against Vossloh Laeis due to the harm caused by the rail cartel.[50] Despite this ongoing civil action, Vossloh Laeis sought to participate in a new tendering process held by Stadtwerke München, invoking the self-cleaning defence. Vossloh Laeis highlighted the organizational and personnel measures it had implemented to reform itself and prevent future unlawful cartels and unfair competitive practices.[51]

Stadtwerke München, however, expressed concerns about Vossloh Laeis' reliability based on its involvement in the rail cartel. Therefore, Stadtwerke München requested the leniency decision from the Federal Cartel Office that imposed the fine

45 Arrowsmith, Prieβ and Friton (fn 21), 264; Schoenmaekers (fn 19), 98.
46 Ibid.
47 C-124/17, ECLI:EU:C:2018:855.
48 Case C-124/17 Vossloh Laeis GmbH v Stadtwerke München GmbH (fn 48), para. 12.
49 ibid.
50 ibid.
51 ibid, para. 13.

on Vossloh Laeis.[52] This was to allow Stadtwerke München to review the decision of the Federal Cartel Office and understand Vossloh Laeis' violation of antitrust laws. Vossloh Laeis refused to provide Stadtwerke München with the decision of the Federal Cartel Office, arguing that it had already fully cooperated with the Federal Cartel Office and that further cooperation with Stadtwerke München, as the contracting authority, exceeded the requirements of the Procurement Directive 2014/24/EU.[53]

In view of the denial and the fact that Vossloh Laeis did not provide sufficient evidence of self-cleaning measures, Stadtwerke München permanently excluded Vossloh Laeis from the qualification procedure.[54] Therefore, Vossloh Laeis challenged this decision before the Public Procurement Board for Southern Bavaria in Germany.[55] The Board decided to pause the proceedings and seek a preliminary ruling from the CJEU, unsure if a tenderer with a relevant ground for exclusion must actively cooperate with the investigating and contracting authorities to demonstrate reliability.[56]

The CJEU held ruled the German law requiring cooperation with the contracting authority is compliant with EU law. The contracting authority has the right to request a company responsible for competition law breach to provide the relevant decision from the CA.[57] Transmitting this decision, which establishes the breach but applies leniency due to cooperation with the CA, should be enough to prove to the contracting authority that the company has fully clarified the facts and circumstances.[58] In other words, the contracting authority can request any evidence of measures taken by the tenderer for admission to the procurement procedure, including the leniency decision of the competition authority. The possibility of this document aiding in a civil liability action against the company does not affect this finding.[59] Ultimately, one of the measures a company must take to prove reliability is providing evidence of paying or committing to pay compensation for any damage caused by their misconduct.[60]

7.3.2 Critical Analysis of the Case

In its recent ruling, the CJEU confirmed that contracting authorities can request additional information and clarifications as needed, to assess the self-cleaning measures taken by a debarred firm. This may include disclosing the leniency decision made by the relevant CA, if necessary to evaluate the re-establishment of the

52 ibid.
53 ibid, para. 14.
54 ibid, para. 15.
55 ibid, para. 16.
56 ibid, para. 17.
57 Ibid, para. 30.
58 Ibid, para. 31.
59 Ibid, para. 30.
60 Ibid.

debarred firm's reliability. The judgment also clarified that under Article 57(6) of Directive 2014/24/EU, "investigating authorities" refer to both competition and contracting authorities, and the debarred firm must actively cooperate with both.

The CJEU aimed to minimize any negative impact on leniency applicants' cooperation with authorities by specifying that collaboration with the contracting authority should be limited to information essential for assessing the debarred company's reliability, as outlined in Article 57(6) of the Procurement Directive 2014/24/EU.[61] This is to prevent contracting authorities from requesting irrelevant information when evaluating the remedial measures taken by the debarred firm to demonstrate its reliability.[62] This requirement is reminiscent of the proportionality standards set out in Damages Directive 2014/104/EU, particularly in Article 6(4) regarding the disclosure of information from a CA's file in the context of follow-on damages claims. The second of these proportionality requirements regards the scope of the request for disclosure, which must be made in relation to an action for damages before a national court. Adapting the wording of this provision to align with Article 57(6) of the Procurement Directive would emphasize that disclosure requests should relate to the debarred firm's efforts to demonstrate its reliability. The CJEU's ruling emphasizes cooperation requirements should be limited to what is necessary for assessing the tenderer's reliability. To ensure compliance with the principle of proportionality, it is submitted that contracting authorities should demonstrate to national courts that obtaining the requested information from other sources is not feasible when evaluating a supplier's reliability and the sufficiency of the self-cleaning measures.

Despite the attempt made by the CJEU to minimize the negative effects of its decision on leniency programmes, this judgment still has some weaknesses. It overlooks and underestimates the extensive cooperation required from a leniency applicant to be eligible for leniency. The company must prove anew to the contracting authority that it collaborated with the CA and provided a comprehensive explanation of its involvement in the anticompetitive activity. One of the main conditions for leniency is for a company to admit participation in anticompetitive activity and provide all relevant non-legally privileged information, documents and evidence available to the CA regarding the infringement. This requires complete and ongoing cooperation with the CA throughout the investigation, as well as refraining from further participation in the anticompetitive activity. By requiring the transmission of the CA's decision to the contracting authority to demonstrate that the infringing company provided a comprehensive explanation of the anticompetitive activity, it gives contracting authorities the power to oversee CAs. This can create a sense of mistrust between two equivalent public authorities.

In view of the above, it is recommended that the leniency decision of the CA should be sufficient to demonstrate to the contracting authority that the economic

61 Case C-124/17 Vossloh Laeis GmbH v Stadtwerke München GmbH (fn 48), para. 28.

62 The Damages Directive 2014/104/EU names this kind of searches "fishing expeditions". See Recital 23 of the Damages Directive.

operator actively cooperated with the CA. The access of the contracting authority to the leniency decision serves no purpose, as the CA has already requested the evidence needed during its investigation. However, this access undermines the essence of leniency programmes. Companies may hesitate to apply for leniency when participating in public procurement procedures.[63] This is because if they need to rely on the self-cleaning defence to avoid exclusion from future contracts, they may be required to disclose details of their past cartel involvement to the contracting authority so as to persuade it that they have taken self-cleaning measures. The collaboration that a debarred firm must provide to the contracting authority by allowing access to the CA's decision can be harmful to the firm, especially if both parties are involved in civil proceedings brought by the contracting authority, on the ground that it was harmed by the debarred firm's participation in the cartel.[64] Access to decisions by CAs that establish the infringement of competition rules in cartel cases based on leniency applications, provides contracting authorities with evidence to prepare their actions for damages.[65] This exposes cooperating companies to civil liability in worse conditions than non-cooperating infringers.[66]

Alternatively, it is suggested that only the non-confidential version of the CA's decision should be disclosed to the contracting authority. It is common ground that the confidential version of the decision that a CA takes in order to establish infringement of the competition rules will or may contain leniency materials submitted to the relevant CA in the course of its investigation. This was confirmed in National Grid Electricity Transmission v ABB and Others,[67] where the English High Court ordered disclosure to the claimant seeking damages of only limited parts of the confidential version of the EC fining decision. Waiving the secrecy created by the leniency mechanism vis-à-vis the contracting authority has a deterrent effect on potential leniency applicants as regards other bid rigging schemes which are uncovered yet, undermining in this way the application of national and EU leniency programmes in the domain of public procurement. After all, "the confidentiality policy is a necessary inducement to encourage leniency applications" and this means that jurisdictions should not share information obtained from an amnesty applicant with other competition and prosecuting authorities, without the applicant's permission.[68]

In response to the aforementioned suggestions, it could be argued, however, that the contracting authorities will not be able to judge whether the self-cleaning

63 Brussels Matters (fn 7). The interviewees identified the increased exposure to civil damages claims as the main reason for this decline.

64 Case C-124/17 Vossloh Laeis GmbH v Stadtwerke München GmbH, ECLI:EU:C:2018:316, Opinion of AG Campos Sanchez-Bordona, (fn 13).

65 Recital 26, Directive 2014/104/EU.

66 ibid.

67 National Grid Electricity Transmission v ABB and Others [2012] EWHC 869.

68 Scott D. Hammond "Dispelling the myths surrounding information sharing" ICN Cartels Workshop (Sydney, Australia, November 20–21, 20040) <www.justice.gov/atr/speech/dispelling-myths-surrounding-information-sharing> accessed on May 17, 2024.

measures are appropriate to prevent further criminal offences or misconduct, if they do not know exactly what happened.[69] It could also be argued that wide access to evidence is necessary for the effective exercise by contracting authorities of their right to compensation. At this point it should be clarified that the facts and circumstances regarding a breach of competition law may be sufficiently clear from the non-confidential version of a leniency decision and other documents provided by the undertaking to the contracting authority. Furthermore, in case of serious offences, such as bid rigging schemes, it may be appropriate for external actors to be involved in order to monitor the debarred firms' internal and external operations.[70] This suggestion would keep the contracting authorities away from leniency decisions, while still allowing them to assess the reliability of debarred firms through independent third parties, such as public accountants or independent monitors. External actors are able to judge whether the self-cleaning measures are appropriate to prevent further criminal offences or misconduct.

Regarding the contracting authorities' effective exercise of their right to compensation, "the principle of effective judicial protection is not absolute and may be curtailed by restrictions that are in the general interest, proportionate and do not amount to an intolerable interference that infringes upon the very substance of the guaranteed right".[71] This means that the contracting authorities' right to compensation may be curtailed when it comes to securing the protection of effective leniency programmes, which serve the public interest. In the past, the ECJ refused to prioritize the interest associated with public enforcement over the interest of private parties injured by the infringement, therefore invoking the principle of effectiveness.[72] Yet, the European legislator challenged this caselaw in a radical way and the new Damages Directive 2014/104/EU gave predominance to the protection of leniency statements instead of conferring permissive rules that may affect the effectiveness of leniency programmes.[73] Moreover, the European Commission's policy has been in line with the European legislator, fully declining access to leniency materials on

69 Albert Sanchez-Graells "Bid Rigging, Self-Cleaning, Leniency and Claims for Damages: A Beautiful Procurement Mess? (C-124/17)" <http://www.howtocrackanut.com/blog/tag/vossloh+laeis> accessed on 16, May 2024.

70 Schoenmaekers (fn 19), 98.

71 Matias Palma Rodriguez "Disclosure of Evidence under the Damages Directive: Conflicts and Compatibility between the ECJ's Case-by-Case Analysis and the Rules on Protection of Immunity Recipients' Information – Study Paper No 01/18" Europa Kolleg Hamburg, Institute for European Integration <https://europa-kolleg-hamburg.de/wp-content/uploads/2018/03/SP-01-18.pdf> accessed on May 16, 2024; joined cases C- 317–320/08 Alassini and others, paras 61–63

72 C-536/2011 Bundeswettbewerbsbehörde v Donau Chemie and others, ECLI:EU:C:2013:366 where it was said at para. 27 that "the rules applicable to actions for safeguarding rights which individuals derive from the direct effect of EU law must…not make it in practice impossible or excessively difficult to exercise rights conferred by EU law"; See also C-360/09 Pfeiderer AG v Bundeskartellamt, ECLI:EU:C:2011:389

73 Palma Rodriguez (fn 71), 38–40.

its file by third parties to protect the effectiveness of its leniency programme.[74] The CJEU confirmed this approach in its decision *EnBW*.[75]

A counterargument to this approach may be that after all, the right of contracting authorities to compensation is also a public interest, as it allows the recovery of public money paid for rigged goods/services.[76] This is particularly true, but the access of contracting authorities to leniency documents is not the only way to protect and enhance this right. The European legislator has sought to protect the contracting authorities' right to compensation[77] by creating a rebuttable presumption of harm resulting from a cartel, like a bidding ring.[78] Moreover, many suggestions will be made in Section 7.4 of Chapter 7 of the thesis, to make it easier for public authorities to seek compensation, without relying on leniency applicants for information. Also, the alternative suggestion made above, that is, the access to the non-confidential version of the leniency decision, does not undermine their right to compensation, as they still have the possibility to collect evidence and prepare their actions for damages. On the contrary, access of contracting authorities to the confidential version of leniency decisions undermines the limitations on disclosure of evidence laid down in the Damages Directive, as this evidence will help them calculate the overcharge they suffered, facilitating the introduction of a civil liability action against the leniency applicant.

The rationale of the Damages Directive 2014/104/EU is to protect self-incriminating evidence produced within leniency programmes, enshrining a strict prohibition of disclosure for leniency statements. Specifically, Article 6, paragraph 6(a) of the Damages Directive contemplates that Member States shall ensure that, for the purpose of actions for damages, national courts cannot at any time order a party or a third party to disclose leniency corporate statements,[79] meaning all voluntary presentations, by or on behalf of an undertaking to the CA, of the undertaking's knowledge of a cartel and its role therein.[80] In the same vein, Article 6, paragraph 4(c) of the Damages Directive contemplates that even in the case of documents that fall beyond the definition of leniency statement[81] or are not part of the leni-

74 Ysewyn and Kahmann (fn 5), 57.

75 C-365/12 P European Commission v EnBW Energie Baden-Württemberg AG [2014], ECLI:EU:C:2014:112, para. 93 "[…] it must be found that, for the purposes of the application of the exceptions provided for in the first and third indents of Article 4(2) of Regulation No 1049/20F01, the Commission is entitled to presume […] that disclosure of such documents will, in principle, undermine the protection of the commercial interests of the undertakings involved in such a proceeding and the protection of the purpose of the investigations relating to the proceeding".

76 Penelope-Alexia Giosa "The Case for Reforming the Rules on Contracting Authority Damages Claims for Bid Rigging in the EU" (2018), 6, *Public Procurement Law Review*, 235–250.

77 The presumption that cartel infringements cause harm regards any natural or legal person – consumers, undertakings and public authorities – that has a right to compensation.

78 Article 17, Directive 2014/104/EU.

79 Article 6, para. 6(a) of the Directive 2014/104/EU.

80 Article 2, para. 16 of the Directive 2014/104/EU.

81 Such documents are subjected to the medium (grey list) or minimum (white list) protection according to each case.

ency statement, national courts should consider the need to safeguard the effectiveness of the public enforcement of competition law. Hence, the approach of the Damages Directive regarding the unhampered public enforcement of competition law is unassailable.

One last point raised by the CJEU was that the facilitation of a civil liability action by the contracting authority should not call into question the finding in the *Vossloh Laeis* case. One of the measures that a debarred firm must take to establish its reliability is providing evidence that it has paid or committed to paying compensation for any damage caused by a criminal offence or misconduct.[82] Payment of compensation is listed as one of the self-cleaning measures in Article 57(6) of the Procurement Directive. Yet, as previously mentioned, these self-cleaning measures are not cumulative conditions that must all be met to avoid exclusion. It is up to the debarred firm to choose which measures to take and if the evidence provided is sufficient, contracting authorities must accept it and prevent the exclusion of the economic operator. Moreover, these self-cleaning measures are voluntary, aimed at restoring trust in debarred firms. Thus, the reasoning of CJEU in the *Vossloh Laeis* case does not align with the rationale of self-cleaning defence, as it imposes a measure on the debarred firm that should be voluntarily undertaken for rehabilitation purposes.

7.4 Recommendations

7.4.1 How to Alleviate the Tension among Leniency, Debarment Mechanism and Self-Cleaning Measures?

In view of the conflicting policy objectives mentioned above, several recommendations are proposed in this section, building upon those previously discussed in the *Vossloh Laeis* case. These recommendations are aimed at easing the tension between the leniency programme, the debarment mechanism and the self-cleaning defence.

First and foremost, it is suggested that companies granted immunity, meaning those that were the first to apply for leniency when there was no ongoing investigation into the reported anticompetitive behaviour,[83] should be exempt from the debarment mechanism outlined in Article 57 of Directive 2014/24/EU. By excluding immunity recipients from debarment, it would encourage them to come forward and disclose information about bid rigging, without fear that the materials shared with the CA would later be used by the contracting authority in a civil

82 Case C-124/17 Vossloh Laeis GmbH v Stadtwerke München GmbH, ECLI:EU:C:2018:855, para. 30.

83 In other words, it is suggested that only the Type A immunity recipient should be benefitted from self-cleaning defence, based on the assumption that leniency grant meets the requirements of a self-cleaning measure. The other types of leniency applicants, like those that first reported the anticompetitive activity and provided evidence, while there was pre-existing investigation by the competitive authority, will have to demonstrate that sufficient measures were taken to restore trustworthiness.

liability lawsuit. This provision could mitigate the impact of the debarment mechanism on leniency and prevent it from undermining the effectiveness of leniency programmes in public procurement. Prior to the adoption of Directive 2014/24/EU, Slovakian public procurement law had a similar provision that allowed companies benefitting from leniency (immunity as well as fine reduction) to still participate in public procurement processes.[84]

However, when the bidding ring involves all major providers in the industry, such a measure may make the immunity holder the only future bidder. For this reason, the second recommendation is that all subsequent firms cooperating under leniency with the CAs should not automatically be excluded from the debarment mechanism. Granting immunity from exclusion to other leniency beneficiaries would negate the purpose of exclusions as administrative remedies utilized by governments to deter contractors from wrongdoing. Additionally, the concept of self-cleaning would be compromised, as the firms would have the right to participate in future public tenders without taking self-cleaning measures.

For these reasons, it is suggested that the debarment period for other leniency beneficiaries should be halved in the first place. Regarding the remaining debarment period, they should be eligible for self-cleaning defence, if they can demonstrate taking sufficient measures to restore trustworthiness. The recommendation to halve the debarment period for leniency applicants is already implemented in Japan and has contributed to the success of the Japanese leniency programme.[85] This approach incentivizes all bid riggers to come forward and cooperate with the relevant CA, even if they are not the first to apply for leniency. Regarding the remaining debarment period, as already suggested, their disclosure of information about the bidding ring within the leniency programme should be considered as meeting the self-cleaning defence requirements, under Article 57(6) of the Procurement Directive 2014/24/EU. Leniency application demonstrates a genuine intention to confess to anticompetitive activity and restore trustworthiness. Similar to the self-cleaning measures outlined in Article 56(6) of the Procurement Directive, leniency applicants must actively collaborate with investigating authorities and conduct internal investigations to collect and secure evidence regarding the anticompetitive infringement. Thus, the collaboration of leniency applicants with the CA that advances the investigations of the latter should be viewed as "active collaboration with the investigative authorities",[86] a type of evidence for relying

84 Ondrej Blažo "Proportionality and Subsidiarity of European Law and Issues of "Over-Regulation" and "Under Regulation" (paper presented at the International Academic Conference Bratislava Legal Forum, 2015, 1494); see also Sarah Schoenmaekers "Self-Cleaning and Leniency: Comparable Objectives but Different Levels of Success?" (2018), 1(13), *European Procurement and Public Private Partnership Law Review*, 14.

85 Toshiyuki Nambu "A Successful Story: Leniency and (International) Cartel Enforcement in Japan (2014), 5(3), *Journal of European Competition Law and Practice*, 161.

86 This suggestion is particularly logical, especially in light of the CJEU's judgment in Vossloh Laeis case, where it was held that the concept "investigating authorities" in Article 57, para. 6 of the Procurement Directive covers both the contracting and the competition authority.

on the self-cleaning defence, as per Article 57(6) of Directive 2014/24/EU. The contracting authority should assess the sufficiency of this collaboration each time to determine if the debarred firm's reliability is restored. This approach ensures that the immunity holder does not become the sole tenderer in future procurement proceedings and that the self-cleaning defence mitigates the impact of the debarment mechanism on the leniency programme in public procurement. It also sends a message to firms that collusion will not go unpunished.

7.5 Concluding Remarks

In the realm of public procurement where anticompetitive agreements between tenderers, such as bid rigging, may arise, leniency is not particularly popular. The chapter suggested that one reason is the debarment mechanism, which bans firms from bidding for three years, discouraging infringing companies from self-reporting. Moreover, the fact that contracting authorities can have access to the leniency decision in order to evaluate the self-cleaning measures taken by the debarred firms undermines the effectiveness of leniency programmes even further, especially when contracting authorities are bringing damages claims for bid rigging against them. Therefore, it is time to couple leniency with the debarment mechanism and self-cleaning measures in public procurement.

To achieve this goal and address tension between leniency, debarment and self-cleaning measures, it was suggested to extend immunity protection so that the revealing firm is exempt from the debarment mechanism under Article 57 of the Procurement Directive. This would encourage firms to report bid rigging without fear of debarment. Subsequent leniency beneficiaries should not be automatically excluded from the debarment mechanism, otherwise the role of disqualification in public procurement would be cancelled as well as the rationale of self-cleaning. Instead, contracting authorities should halve their debarment period. As far as the remaining debarment period is concerned, contracting authorities should be considered for self-defence and their action to disclose further information about the bidding ring in the context of leniency programme should be identified as "active collaboration with the investigative authorities" under the self-cleaning provisions, that is, Article 57(6) of the Procurement Directive.

Until the aforementioned measures are taken, further recommendations were made, in light of the CJEU's judgment in the *Vossloh Laeis* case. It was suggested that the leniency decision itself should prove active cooperation with the CA. The access of the contracting authority to the leniency decision does not add anything new, as the CA has already requested the evidence that the contracting authority asks for. But if the contracting authority is not totally satisfied with this and wants to examine the facts and circumstances regarding the breach of competition law on its own, in the further alternative it should prove that it is impossible to get the information from any other sources to assess the sufficiency of the self-cleaning measures and it should only have access to a non-confidential version of the leniency decision. Furthermore, in case of serious offences, like bid rigging, it may be appropriate to appoint independent third parties, such as independent monitors or public accountants, to monitor the debarred firm's internal and external operations.

The CJEU missed an opportunity to establish specific criteria for national courts assessing orders to disclose evidence under Article 57(6) of the Procurement Directive, which are included in the file of a CA. Furthermore, the CJEU overlooked the fact that the transmission of a leniency decision facilitates the introduction of a civil action by the contracting authority against that economic operator. Hence, its judgment in the *Vossloh Laeis* case contradicts the Damages Directive's orientation favouring public enforcement over private actions.

After examining leniency in public procurement, it is important to consider private enforcement in cases of collusion. The following chapter will address the legal reparation of contracting authorities when they are victims of collusion.

8 Damages Claims for Bid Rigging in the EU

8.1 Introduction

The previous chapter focused on public enforcement in the context of procurement, discussing the leniency programme and how it interplays with procurement remedies – in particular the debarment mechanism and the self-cleaning measures under 2014/24/EU Directive. In this chapter, private enforcement is discussed – in particular the post award remedies, that is, damages for bid rigging, which are available to contracting authorities in case they eventually fall victim to tenderers engaged in bid rigging and other collusive practices. The ability of local authorities and government departments to bring private actions for damages for a breach of competition law allows some of the public money to be recovered and deters other tenderers from engaging in similar practices. Before the competition law Damages Directive,[1] contracting authorities were not in a particularly good position to seek damages for bid rigging. This chapter critically analyzes whether the Damages Directive has made it easier for authorities to successfully recover damages for being overcharged and, if this is not the case, what recommendations can be made and what alternative compensatory remedies are potentially available. This question has largely been unexplored to date because academics have focused on the other side of the coin, namely the damages awarded by the authorities to private bidders for violating public procurement procedures and fundamental principles of equal treatment.[2] It is also an issue of great importance given the value of procurement contracts across Europe[3] and the potential cost to taxpayers resulting

1 Directive 2014/104/EU of the European Parliament and of the Council of November 26, 2014 on certain rules governing actions for damages under national law for infringements of the competition law provisions of the Member States and of the European Union [2014] OJ L349/1.

2 Sue Arrowsmith *Remedies for Enforcing the Public Procurement Rules* (Winteringham: Earlsgate, 1993); Steen Treumer and François Lichère *Enforcement of the EU public Procurement Rules* (København, Djøf Publishing, 2011); Duncan Fairgrieve and François Lichère *Public Procurement Law: Damages as an Effective Remedy* (Oxford Hart, 2011); Hannah Schebesta *Damages in EU Public Procurement Law* (Springer International Publishing Switzerland 2016), 21.

3 According to public procurement indicators, the estimated value of tenders published in Tenders Electronic Daily (TED) (including utilities and defence) was €450.21 billion in 2015. Additionally, every year over 250,000 public authorities in the EU spend around 14% of European GDP on public contracts for the purchase of services, works and suppliers. See European Commission "Public Pro-

DOI: 10.4324/9781003359999-8

from bid-rigging behaviour.[4] The significance of this issue is even more apparent if someone takes into account the fact that bid rigging leads to higher artificial prices than other anticompetitive activities, such as price fixing and market sharing.[5] In a time of economic crisis in which attempts are made to reduce public expenditure in any possible way, the promotion of private enforcement of EU competition law by public authorities in the EU Member States may secure budget savings.[6] This is so because it is believed that private enforcement may be not only a deterrent against this anticompetitive conduct but also a means of restorative justice that can restore taxpayers' money.[7] This function of damages claims for bid rigging is apparent in countries such as Japan, where the deterrent effect of private enforcement is significant, as "activist plaintiffs obtain substantial recoveries on behalf of local governments and public entities frequently seek and obtain damages".[8] By contrast, in Europe damages claims for bid rigging do not yet play a crucial role

curement Indicators 2015" <http://ec.europa.eu/DocsRoom/documents/20679> accessed November 8, 2024; see also European Commission, "Public Procurement" <https://ec.europa.eu/growth/single-market/public-procurement_en> accessed November 8, 2024.

4 It is estimated that the annual direct cost to consumers and other victims of hardcore cartels in the EU, including bidding rings, ranges from approximately €13 billion (on the most conservative assumptions) to over €37 billion (on the least conservative). Due to bid rigging, the prices are artificially raised between 6 and 48% above the competitive level, while the prices in a supply chain can be raised by more than 30% without this increase being concomitant with a respective restriction of output. See European Commission "Staff Working Paper accompanying the White Paper on Damages Actions for Breach of the EC Antitrust Rules", COM (2008) 165 final <http://eur-lex.europa.eu/legal-content/EN/TXT/PDF/?uri=CELEX:52008SC0404&from=EN> accessed November 8, 2024; Jonathan B. Baker "The Case for Antitrust Enforcement" (2003), 17, *Journal of Economic Perspectives*, 27, 29; Competition and Markets Authority "Local Authorities and Competition" <www.gov.uk/government/uploads/system/uploads/attachment_data/file/669668/local_authorities_and_competition_final_report.pdf> accessed November 8, 2024, 10; Ioannis Apostolakis "Antitrust Liability in Cases of Indirect Contacts between Competitors: VM Remonts" (2017), 54, *CMLR*, 609.

5 Stephen Davies and Adrian Majumdar *The Development of Targets for Consumer Savings Arising from Competition Policy* (Great Britain, Office of Fair Trading, 2002), 3; see also Marsela Maci "Bid Rigging in the EU Public-Procurement Markets: Some History and Developments" (2011), 32, *ECLR*, 406.

6 Marco Botta "Commission acting as plaintiff in cases of private enforcement of EU competition law: Otis" (2013), 50, *CMLR*, 1115.

7 Assimakis Komninos *EC Private Antitrust Enforcement: Decentralised Application of EC Competition Law by National Courts* (Hart Publishing 2008), 19; Assimakis Komninos "The Relationship between Public and Private Enforcement: quod Dei Deo, quod Caesaris Caesari" in Philip Lowe and Mel Marquis (eds) *European Competition Law Annual 2011: Integrating Public and Private Enforcement of Competition Law: Implications for Courts and Agencies* (Oxford, Hart Publishing, 2014), 142.

8 Simon Vande Walle "Private Enforcement of Antitrust Law in Japan: An Empirical Analysis" (2011), 8, *CompLRev*, 8.

in deterring anticompetitive activities,[9] but this does not mean that things may not change for the better.[10]

The chapter is structured as follows. Section 8.2 explains the reasons why contracting authorities are reluctant to pursue an action against businesses engaged in bid-rigging practices in public procurement. These reasons are specific to bid rigging and they differ from the general obstacles to effective compensation identified in the Green and White Paper on damages actions for breach of the EC antitrust rules. However, most of these issues apply to claimants across the board as well. The Damages Directive is briefly outlined to better understand the obstacles faced by contracting authorities in seeking effective compensation. Section 8.3 examines the question of whether the ability to make claims for damages in case of bid rigging under the Damages Directive is worthwhile and practicable, considering the fact that this ability already existed in most EU Member States under the national tort laws. This will be done by outlining and analyzing the challenges that arise under the Damages Directive regarding private enforcement by procurement entities. In Section 8.4, recommendations are made in order to deal with some of the hurdles that contracting authorities face when seeking damages for bid rigging, since the Damages Directive failed to address them properly. In Section 8.5, it will be discussed whether remedies which are not based on tortious liability could also help contracting authorities to overcome the challenges under the Damages Directive regarding their right to claim damages for bid rigging. The suggested remedies which are alternative to standard tort law litigation are based on the experience gained in Germany, the United Kingdom and the United States of America. Section 8.6 concludes the chapter.

8.2 Why Contracting Authorities Do Not Sue Cartels for Damages

Before analyzing the reasons why actions by public authorities to recover damages for bid rigging are infrequent in the EU, it is necessary to briefly present the legislative background of the Damages Directive and refer to the main issues that were

9 Commission "Impact Assessment Report – Damages Actions for Breach of the EU Antitrust Rules", COM (2013) 404 final, available at: http://ec.europa.eu/competition/antitrust/actionsdamages/impact_assessment_en.pdf accessed November 8, 2024); OECD "Relationship Between Public and Private Antitrust Enforcement" <www.oecd.org/officialdocuments/publicdisplaydocumentpdf/?cote=DAF/COMP/WP3(2015)14&docLanguage=En> accessed November 8, 2024; Barry J. Rodger "Competition Law Litigation in the UK Courts: A Study of All Cases 2005–2008 – Part I" (2009), 2, *GCLR*, 95, 104; Commission "Staff Working Paper on the implementation of Directive 2014/104/EU of the European Parliament and of the Council of 26 November 2014 on certain rules governing actions for damages under national law for infringements of the competition law provisions of the Member States and of the European Union" SWD (2020), 338 final, available at <https://competition-policy.ec.europa.eu/document/download/05c4fe49-1ba7-40f9-80da-dd42c-578ba7d_en?filename=2020_ec_report_on_damages_directive.pdf> accessed November 8, 2024.

10 Maarten Pieter Schinkel "Effective Cartel Enforcement in Europe" (2007), 30, *World Competition*, 556–557.

identified by the Green and White Paper on damages actions for breach of the EU antitrust rules as obstacles to private enforcement.

On December 19, 2005, the Commission adopted the Green Paper which identified the main obstacles to effective compensation.[11] The response to this public consultation was wide and involved several institutional stakeholders.[12] As a result, a Report and a Resolution were adopted by the European Parliament in 2007, which invited the Commission to proceed to a White Paper that would make detailed proposals to facilitate actions for damages.[13] On April 2, 2008, the White Paper[14] was published including suggestions for specific measures that would ensure the effective exercise of the right to compensation for antitrust harm.[15] The White Paper was accompanied by an Impact Assessment. In these documents, the major difficulties that victims of competition law infringements usually experience when asking for compensation were identified. Some of them were:

> The difficult access to the evidence that is necessary for proving a case, lack of clear rules on the passing-on defence (i.e. a defence against a direct purchaser's damages claim, relying on evidence showing that the overcharge resulting from a cartel was passed on – fully or partially – by the direct purchaser to its own customers further down the distribution chain), the calculation of damages and the rules concerning the costs of a damages action.[16]

The Damages Directive sought to overcome these issues by introducing a number of key provisions. For instance, regarding access to evidence, it contemplated that courts should ensure enhanced but proportionate access to evidence held by plaintiffs, defendants and third parties, including antitrust agencies, subject to two important limitations.[17] The first one concerns the prohibition of disclosure of corporate statements submitted to the Commission under the EU's amnesty regime (i.e. its leniency programme) and the second concerns the ban on the disclosure

11 European Commission "Green Paper-Damages actions for breach of the EC antitrust rules" COM (2005) 672, December 19, 2005 <https://eur-lex.europa.eu/legal-content/EN/TXT/PDF/?uri=CELEX:52005DC0672&from=EN> accessed on November 8, 2024. The Green Paper was prepared by a 2004 study on the conditions under which private parties can bring actions for antitrust damages.

12 European Commission "Impact Assessment Report – Damages Actions for Breach of the EU Antitrust Rules" (fn 9), 6.

13 Ibid.

14 European Commission "White Paper on Damages Actions for Breach of the EC antitrust rules" COM (2008), 165 final, <http://ec.europa.eu/competition/antitrust/actionsdamages/impact_assessment_en.pdf> accessed November 8, 2024.

15 European Commission "Impact Assessment Report – Damages Actions for Breach of the EU Antitrust Rules" (fn 9), 6.

16 Ibid, 15; European Commission, White Paper on Damages Actions for Breach of the EC antitrust rules (fn 14), 2; Schinkel (fn 10), 557–558.

17 Article 6, Directive 2014/104; Mark Sansom, Anna Morfey and Patrick Teague "Recent Developments in Private Antitrust Damages Litigation in Europe" (2015), 29, Antitrust, 33, 36–37.

of settlement submissions under the EU's settlement procedure.[18] Regarding the passing-on defence, that is, the defence against a claim for damages that the claimant passed on the whole or part of the overcharge resulting from the infringement of competition law, the Damages Directive made it available in response to claims by either direct or indirect purchaser claims.[19] Direct purchaser means a natural or legal person who acquired, directly from an infringer, products or services that were the object of an infringement of competition law.[20] Indirect purchaser means a natural or legal person who acquired, not directly from an infringer, but from a direct purchaser or a subsequent purchaser, products or services that were the object of an infringement of competition law, or products or services containing them or derived therefrom.[21] In case of direct purchaser claims, the burden of proof is on the defendant who must prove that every overcharge was passed on by the plaintiffs to their own customers.[22] The Damages Directive also created a rebuttable presumption as to the existence of harm resulting from a cartel but it did not introduce any presumption as to any particular overcharge percentage.[23] Furthermore, it provided for joint and several liability of defendants in cartel cases, except where the infringer is a successful immunity recipient and a **small or medium-sized enterprise (SME)**.[24]

In December 2020, the European Commission published a Report on the Implementation of the Damages Directive, focusing on an overview of the implementation of its main rules and of the various actions that the Commission has taken to ensure its effectiveness and to develop damages actions.[25] According to this Report, it appears that since the adoption of the Damages Directive, private enforcement of EU antitrust law has become more and more relevant. The Report makes particular reference to the rules on disclosure and highlights that the Member States have implemented the relevant provisions of the Damages Directive generally in a uniform way, while in case the disclosure rules are breached, the vast majority of the Member States went beyond the rules of the Damages Directive, by providing for imprisonment and financial penalties.[26] The keenness of Member States to be as strict as possible when there is non-compliance with the disclosure rules shows that the balance between public and private enforcement is a rather significant issue for them.

18 European Commission "White Paper on Damages Actions for Breach of the EC antitrust rules" (fn 10), para. 6; Sansom, Morfey and Teague, (fn 17) 37.

19 Article 13, Directive 2014/104; Sansom, Morfey and Teague (fn 17), 37.

20 Article 2, para (23), Directive 2014/104.

21 Article 2, para (24), Directive 2014/104.

22 Article 13, Directive 2014/104.

23 Article 17, Directive 2014/104; Sansom, Morfey and Teague (fn 17), 37.

24 Article 11, Directive 2014/104.

25 Commission "Staff Working Paper on the implementation of Directive 2014/104/EU of the European Parliament and of the Council of 26 November 2014 on certain rules governing actions for damages under national law for infringements of the competition law provisions of the Member States and of the European Union" (fn 9).

26 Ibid.

After briefly highlighting the measures introduced by the Damages Directive with the aim of increasing civil antitrust claims, as well as the latest developments after its enactment, the chapter turns now to the reasons why the level of private enforcement among contracting authorities is low in relation to bid rigging. First, the entitlement of contracting authorities to damages under competition law can generate costs in terms of resources involved in litigation and time, which will ultimately be borne by the public budget to the detriment of taxpayers. This is particularly true in EU Member States where there are many and small procurement agencies ("high fragmentation of public sector"), that lack or do not allocate efficiently enforcement resources. The "loser pays" cost rule that governs the national tort systems in Europe makes a claim for damages very expensive and risky for contracting authorities that manage and use taxpayers' money, that is, the state budget.

Whereas private actors usually have a strong motivation and industry-specific knowledge to monitor and detect anticompetitive behaviour,[27] public officers may have difficulty in identifying and comprehending the length and nature of deviations from the initial quantity ordered and contracted by the State. This may happen because bid rigging is tricky to detect, whilst the public procurement community is not always equipped with tools to prevent, detect and deter bid rigging, as successfully happens in the UK for instance, where the **Competition Market Authority (CMA)** has developed tools and advice to help purchasers within the public sector identify suspicious behaviour by suppliers when bidding for contracts.[28] Public officers are also under constant pressure to ensure maximum value for tax-payers' money, while each time they evaluate the tenders in order to choose the winning tender, they have to take numerous considerations – legal, environmental and social – into account. This means that sometimes they may pay little attention to whether bidding rings exist or not, without constantly monitoring bidding activities and without performing analyses on bid data in order to collect historical information on bidding behaviour. This makes sense if it is also considered that public officers are generally not evaluated on the number of bidding rings discovered but on the

27 Randolph Preston McAfee, Hugo Marc Mialon and Sue H. Mialon "Private v. Public Antitrust Enforcement: A Strategic Analysis" (2008), 92, *Journal of Public Economics*, 1866–1867; Department for Business Innovation & Skills "Private Actions in Competition Law: A Consultation on Options for Reform-Government Response, January 2013" <www.gov.uk/government/uploads/system/uploads/attachment_data/file/70185/13-501-private-actions-in-competition-law-a-consultation-on-options-for-reform-government-response1.pdf> accessed November 8, 2024, 8, 11; Andrea Renda, John Peysner, Alan J. Riley and Barry J. Rodger "Making Antitrust Damages Actions More Effective in the EU: Welfare Impact and Potential Scenarios – Final Report" <www.ec.europa.eu/competition/antitrust/actionsdamages/files_white_paper/impact_study.pdf> accessed November 8, 2024, 18.

28 The CMA Screening for Cartels tool is freely available for procurement professionals to download and use. It is a software that uses algorithms to spot unusual bidder behaviour and pricing patterns which may indicate that bid rigging has taken place. For further information see Competition and Markets Authority "CMA Launches Digital Tool to Fight Bid-Rigging" <www.gov.uk/government/news/cma-launches-digital-tool-to-fight-bid-rigging> accessed November 8, 2024.

extent to which they set up and ran the bidding processes successfully and covered the public needs without delays.[29]

In addition to the above, when it comes to bid rigging, there are many EU Member States, such as Austria, Belgium, Germany, Hungary and Romania which, as a matter of policy, promote more individual sanctions, such as criminal penalties[30] as opposed to sanctions operating at the corporate level, such as civil damages claims. Another reason could be that only a few cases have recently been brought by public contracting authorities in the courts of Member States for damages resulting from bid rigging, giving a false impression that bid rigging is less of a problem in the EU.[31] According to a 2007 Study, the antitrust infringement that is most frequently challenged through private litigation in the EU is vertical restraints,[32] and only 12 cases out of 96 involved hardcore cartels, including bid rigging schemes.[33] Nevertheless, in Netherlands after the revelation of bidding rings in the construction sector, the government reached a global settlement with the construction industry, recovering €70 million in damages for bid rigging.[34]

Some of the few cases brought for damages resulting from bid rigging in the EU are European Commission v Otis NV,[35] which preceded the current Damages Directive, the case of Otis v Land Oberösterreich[36] and the case of Vantaan kaupunki v Skanska Industrial Solutions Oy and others[37].

In European Commission v Otis NV, the European Union represented by the Commission, asked for damages for the higher price it allegedly paid for the maintenance of elevators in European institution buildings in Belgium and Luxembourg, as a result of the anticompetitive practices established in the decision of February 21, 2007. According to the Commission's decision in 2007, the elevator manufacturers were found guilty of infringement of Article 101 TFEU from 1996 to 2004, as they were involved in market sharing and bid rigging with regard to the

29 Alberto Heimler "Cartels in Public Procurement" (2012), 8(4), *Journal of Competition Law & Economics*, 861.

30 Florian Wagner-von Papp "Compliance and Individual Sanctions in the Enforcement of Competition Law" in Paha (ed) *Competition Law Compliance Programs: An Interdisciplinary Approach* (Springer, 2016), (fn. 20); Carsten König and Fernanda Luisa Bremenkamp "Competition Law Sanctions in Germany" in Tihamer Tóth (ed) *The Cambridge Handbook of Competition Law Sanction* (Cambridge University Press 2022).

31 Simon Vande Walle *Private Antitrust Litigation in the European Union and Japan: A Comparative Perspective* (Maklu Publishers 2013), 227.

32 Vertical restraints are agreements or concerted practices between two or more undertakings operating at a different level of the production or distribution chain, that may affect trade between Member States and that prevent, restrict or distort competition. For further information please see Guidelines on Vertical Restraints, OJ C 130.

33 Renda, Peysner, Riley and Rodger (fn 27), 40.

34 Vande Walle *Private Antitrust Litigation in the European Union and Japan: A Comparative Perspective*, (fn 29), 232.

35 European Commission v Otis NV (C-199/11) [2013] EU:C:2012 :684; 4 [2013], CMLR 4.

36 Otis GmbH and others v Land Oberösterreich and Others (C-435/18) [2019] ECLI:EU:C:2019:1069.

37 Vantaan kaupunki v Skanska Industrial Solutions Oy and others (C-724/17) [2019] ECLI:EU:C:2019:204

installation and maintenance of elevators and escalators in Belgium, Germany, Luxembourg and the Netherlands. Shortly thereafter, the Commission fined the relevant elevator manufacturers €992 million.

Despite this decision, the Court dismissed the Commission's claim for damages in respect of the harm caused by the elevators and escalators cartels. Since the Damages Directive was not applicable when the action for damages was lodged and so the rebuttable presumption under Article 17, paragraph 2 did not yet apply, it was held that the Commission did not submit direct evidence or oral evidence of witnesses that could determine or estimate the damages caused by the cartel arrangements.[38] In other words, before the enactment of the current Damages Directive, it could not be assumed that practices such as bid rigging automatically led to higher prices.

As already highlighted above, the introduction of the Damages Directive has arguably not improved the position. The fact that cartels are presumed to cause harm does not mean that the (exact amount of the) cartel overcharge is automatically proved nor the loss suffered by the claimant. The financial harm still needs to be specified and quantified and currently the burden of proof is on the claimant. This is an additional reason why contracting authorities are not particularly well placed to pursue an action for damages against cartels.

The Otis v Land Oberösterreich case is also rooted in the elevator cartel. While the cartel was operating, the Province of Upper Austria had granted public subsidies, that is, promotional loans to one of the cartelists, on the basis of statutory housing subsidy provisions. The Province of Upper Austria wanted to claim damages for bid rigging because the costs of installation in these constructions (sometimes including elevators and escalators) had increased due to the cartel, which meant that it had to grant loans in higher amounts. If the cartel at issue had not existed, the Province of Upper Austria would have granted smaller loans and it could have invested the difference at the average interest rate of federal loans. The Court upheld the claim for damages by explaining that:

> persons who are not active as suppliers or customers on the market affected by a cartel, but who provide subsidies, in the form of promotional loans, to buyers of the products offered on that market, may seek an order that the undertakings which participated in that cartel pay compensation for the losses they suffered as a result of the fact that, since the amount of those subsidies was higher than what it would have been without that cartel agreement, those persons were unable to use that difference more profitably.[39]

In the Vantaan kaupunki v Skanska Industrial Solutions Oy *and others* case, there was a cartel in the asphalt market, which agreed on dividing up contracts, prices and

38 Jorge Marcos Ramos and Daniel Muhume "The Brussels Court judgement in Commission v Elevators manufacturers, or the story of how the Commission lost an action for damages based on its own infringement decision" (2015), 36, *ECLR*, 386.

39 Otis GmbH and others v Land Oberösterreich and Others (C-435/18) [2019] (fn 36).

tendering for contracts. In September 2009, the Finnish Supreme Administrative Court imposed sanctions on the seven cartelists for collusive practices in the asphalt market. Following the sanction, the City Council of the Finnish town of Vantaa claimed damages for the overcharge that the City Council had suffered in the bidding for asphalt works due to the collusive practice. The claim was brought against three companies (Skanska, NCC and Asfaltmix) that had acquired the shares and business of the companies, which were initially members of the cartel. Therefore, a preliminary question was submitted to the European Court of Justice (ECJ) about whether liability for an infringement of EU competition law can be attributed to the company which has acquired the share capital and business of a company which has been wound up and which participated in the cartel. The ECJ held that, in a case in which all the shares in the companies which participated in a cartel were acquired by other companies which have dissolved the former companies and continued their commercial activities, the acquiring companies may be held liable for the damage caused by the cartel in question. Hence, the Finnish Supreme Court upheld the Vantaan City Council's damages claims for bid rigging.

8.3 Evaluation of the Directive's Effectiveness in Fostering Actions for Damages

As indicated, there were a number of reasons why the level of private enforcement for bid-rigging has been historically low. With the aim of improving the position of government procurement authorities as private litigants in competition cases, paragraph 3 in the Preamble of the Damages Directive was introduced. According to the Preamble, in addition to consumers and undertakings, public authorities (and so procurement entities) can also claim compensation before national courts for the harm caused to them by an infringement of Articles 101 and 102 TFEU. This right already existed in most EU Member States and so the Damages Directive expressly confirms that Articles 101 and 102 TFEU create obligations and rights for contracting authorities that national courts must enforce. Competition damages for bid rigging in public procurement will enable contracting authorities to get compensated for losses unjustly suffered. Under the legal regime of the Damages Directive, a pivotal question arises as to whether the Damages Directive is effective for the legal reparation of contracting authorities as private litigants, and whether this will bring any advantages over the longstanding damages claims based on tort law. In order to answer this question, there is need to consider the shortcomings and challenges arising under the Damages Directive.

First, the Damages Directive does not provide for specific aspects of antitrust litigation, such as legal costs and cost shifting (loser pays), which are determinant factors of whether the harmed contracting authorities will commence a legal action or not,[40] as procurement entities manage and spend public money and so it is the

40 Mariana De Sousa e Alvim "The New Directive on Antitrust Damages: A Giant Step Forward?" (2015), 36, *ECLR*, 247; Sebastian Peyer "Compensation and the Damages Directive" (2016), 12,

citizens that will eventually bear any financial loss and litigation cost by contributing to the state budget as taxpayers.[41] For contracting authorities in their capacity as claimants, the size and predictability of litigation costs can determine whether they will access justice or not because if the costs are too high, there may be no benefit for them to pursue a legal action.[42] In almost all countries in Europe, cost shifting (loser pays), which makes bringing an action considerably more expensive and riskier,[43] is the general rule. However, in Lithuania and the United States of America, each party undertakes its own costs.[44] The European Commission preferred not to adopt a cost-shifting mechanism because there were concerns that litigation costs would be excessive, there would be over-litigation and many frivolous or tenuous claims would be brought.[45] By not following the example of Lithuania and the United States, the Damages Directive has lost the chance to overcome the funding barriers that claimants usually face when it comes to bring damages for anticompetitive practices, depending in this way on the discretionary power of each court to award or not reasonable costs instead of full legal costs. It was suggested that such important elements of the private enforcement of competition law were left out of the Directive's scope on purpose; otherwise the Damages Directive would not be accepted. The loser pays rule is too engrained in European legal tradition.[46]

Second, the Damages Directive has not dealt with the key procedural hurdles that a contracting authority may face when bringing a damages claim for bid rigging, such as the evidence of a causal link and the quantification of the financial harm suffered by contracting authorities as a result of overcharged products or services in the context of the public procurement procedure. The Directive has been "reticent to engage in an extensive harmonization of the causation requirement", by insisting on reliance on the various tort law systems of EU Member States, under the framework of the principles of equivalence and effectiveness.[47] The ECJ has also not clarified the issue.[48] Though the Damages Directive proceeded to include

ECJ, 87–112; Sebastian Peyer "The Antitrust Damages Directive – Much Ado About Nothing?" in Cisotta and Marquis (eds) *Litigation and Arbitration in EU Competition Law* (Edward Elgar 2015).

41 Marsela Maci "Private Enforcement in Bid Rigging Cases in the European Union" (2012), 8(I), *ECJ*, 216.

42 Christopher Hodges, Stefan Vogenauer and Magdalena Tulibacka "The Oxford Study on Costs and Funding of Civil Litigation: Introduction" in Hodges, Vogenauer and Tulibacka (eds) *The Costs and Funding of Civil Litigation: A Comparative Perspective* (Bloomsbury Publishing 2010), 4.

43 Cedric Argenton, Damien Geradin and Andreas Stephan "Civil Damages" in Argenton, Geradin and Stephan (eds) *EU Cartel Law and Economics* (Oxford University Press, 2020).

44 Hodges, Vogenauer and Tulibacka (fn 42), 17.

45 Argenton, Geradin and Stephan (fn 43).

46 Editorial Comments "One Bird in the Hand…The Directive on Damages Actions for Breach of the Competition Rules" (2014), 51, *CMLR*, 1342.

47 Ioannis Lianos "Causal Uncertainty and Damages Claims for the Infringement of Competition Law in Europe" in Piet Eeckhout (ed) *Yearbook of European Law* (2015), 34(1), 50.

48 F.G. Wilman "The End of the Absence? The Growing Body of EU Legislation on Private Enforcement and the Main Remedies It Provides For" (2016), 53, *CMLR*, 902.

a number of provisions that make the evidence of a causal link much easier, practically speaking, these steps are not adequate to boost the number of damage actions initiated by public contracting authorities. Despite the explicit rule of joint and several liability in Article 11, nothing is really gained by this rule. When it comes to bid rigging, it is much harder in terms of evidence to establish which undertakings were participants in the bidding ring and which undertakings were outsiders. This is so because there is not any typical illegal behaviour that would enable a simple establishment of who is in the bidding ring and who is not, as may happen in normal cartels, where one of the ways to determine cartel membership is to look at the level of output that a firm produces before and after the alleged cartel formation. Moreover, the lack of familiarity of procurement officers with bidding patterns related to bid rigging make it even harder for them to assess whether or not a specific tender presents a bid pattern that raises concerns and constitutes *prima facie* evidence of bid rigging that needs formal antitrust investigation.[49] So, the extra difficulty of identifying the members of the bidding ring as well as the fact that procurement agencies lack skills and experience necessary to identify *prima facie* evidence of bid rigging and to apply the economic theories of collusion means that inevitably the private enforcement will be little in the domain of public procurement. Yet, some jurisdictions have gotten off to a good start by enabling their national CAs to control the competitiveness of public procurement and initiate a bid rigging case on their own initiative every time they suspect infringement of competition law in the course of a public tender.[50]

The same applies to the reversal of the burden of proof on the infringer/defendant, in case it invokes as a defence against a claim for damages the fact that the injured party/claimant has already reduced its actual loss by passing it on, entirely or partly, to its own purchasers.[51] It is not usual at all in the context of public procurement to see public authorities selling on the goods that they procure and do so for a profit. Again, it is neither common nor usual at all to see indirect purchasers in the context of public procurement, namely natural or legal persons who acquired from a government department or local authority products or services that were the object of bid rigging or derived therefrom. Thus, the presumption of causality for the benefit of indirect purchasers because they "did not themselves make any purchase from the infringer (i.e. bid riggers in our case) to prove the scope of that harm"[52] does not have practical relevance in the case of contracting authorities

49 International Competition Network, *Anti-Cartel Enforcement Manual: Chapter on Relationships between Competition Agencies and Public Procurement Bodies*, available at: <https://www.internationalcompetitionnetwork.org/wp-content/uploads/2018/05/CWG_ACEMPublicProcurement.pdf> accessed November 8, 2024.

50 Ibid; many examples can be found in Autoritat Catalana de la Competencia "Claim for Damages Caused to Public Administrations due to Anti-Competitive Practices", available at https://acco.gencat.cat/web/.content/80_acco/documents/arxius/actuacions/20230208_es_22_2019_reclamacio_danys_eng.pdf> accessed November 8, 2024.

51 Recital 39, Directive 2014/104.

52 Recital 36 and Article 14, para. 2, Directive 2014/104.

suing cartels for damages in the context of the public procurement process. At this point, it would be worth to mention that the passing-on defence is not accepted in the United States in line with the Illinois Brick case.[53] However, there are some exceptions to the exclusion of indirect purchaser claims provided for in US Federal Law and the cost plus pricing[54] is one of them.[55]

Even the causal presumption for cartels that the Damages Directive expressly sets in order to "remedy the information asymmetry and some of the difficulties associated with quantifying antitrust harm, as well as to ensure the effectiveness of claims for damages",[56] is not enough for contracting authorities to be incentivized to sue bid riggers for damages. To be more specific, according to Article 17 of the Damages Directive, it shall be presumed that cartel infringements cause harm and the infringer shall have the right to rebut that presumption. Yet, the existence of an infringement decision does not itself prove the level of harm incurred by the overcharge.[57] Contracting authorities must still predict the real prices of the supplies or services had bid riggers not raised them artificially, by estimating what the winning bids would have been but for the collusive agreement (the counterfactual).[58] This is something particularly demanding and costly, especially in view of the "blanket ban" imposed on the disclosure of files and documents submitted by the firm that first blew the whistle on the bid-rigging conspiracy[59] as well as the difficulty of procurement officers in identifying and comprehending the length and nature of deviations from the initial quantity ordered and contracted by the State for the reasons discussed in Section 8.2. At this point, it is also worth mentioning the example of BritNed v ABB,[60] which is a follow-on action based on Commission's

53 Illinois Brick Co. v. Illinois, 431, US, 720 (1977).

54 Cost plus contracts do not specify a price, like in case of a fixed price contract, where the seller receives a lump sum payment irrespective of the costs actually incurred, but they reimburse the contract or for costs. This reduces the adversarial relationship that may arise between the seller and the buyer, if the completion of the contract entails additional work above the originally described and for this reason cost plus contracts are generally preferred in the construction industry. For further information please see Patrick Bajari and Steven Tadelis "Procurement Contracts: Fixed Price vs. Cost Plus" <https://papers.ssrn.com/sol3/papers.cfm?abstract_id=156470> accessed November 8, 2024.

55 In re ATM Fee Antitrust Litigation, 686 F.3d 741 (9th Cir. 2012); European Commission "Study on the Passing-On of Overcharges: Final Report 2016" <http://ec.europa.eu/competition/publications/reports/KD0216916ENN.pdf> accessed November 8, 2024, 18–20; Herbert Hovenkamp "The Indirect-Purchaser Rule and Cost-Plus Sales" (1990), 103(7), *Harvard Law Review*, 1717–1731.

56 Recital 42 and Article 17, para. 2, Directive 2014/104.

57 Andreas Stephan "The EU Damages Directive" in Damien Geradin, Andreas Stephan and Cédric Argenton (eds) *EU Cartel Law and Economics* (Oxford University Press, 2020).

58 Jeffrey H. Howard and David Kaserman "Proof of Damages in Construction Industry Bid-Rigging Cases" (1989), 34, *Antitrust Bull.*, 363–364; Simon Bishop and Mike Walker *The Economics of EC Competition Law: Concepts, Application and Measurement* (London, Sweet and Maxwell 2010), Chapter 17.

59 Article 6, para. 6, Directive 2014/104; John Kwan-Terry *The Damages Directive: End of England's Eminence?* (2015), 36, *ECLR*, 459.

60 BritNed v ABB [2018] EWHC 2616 (Ch).

Power Cables decision,[61] according to which ABB was held to be member of a bidding rig. In BritNed v ABB, even the English High Court got confused with the counterfactuals, as it set out a counterfactual which was at odds with the way it quantified damages.[62]

The demonstration and calculation of the cartel overcharge by contracting authorities becomes even more difficult in cases in which there is need to consider environmental, social and innovative aspects when assessing a tender on the basis of the best price-quality ratio. By procuring in a more quality oriented way, contracting authorities are called to determine each time the overcharge not only on the basis of price and life-cycle costs but also quality, environmental considerations, social aspects or innovation of what is procured.[63] Of course, the Damages Directive contemplates that when it is practically impossible or excessively difficult for a claimant precisely to quantify the harm suffered on the basis of the evidence available, the national courts shall be empowered to estimate the amount of harm.[64] Yet, even for national courts, assessing and proving the quantum of damages is often difficult[65] and for this reason the Commission published a Practical Guide in order to place at the disposal of national courts economic and practical insights.[66] Unfortunately, in this Practical Guide there isn't particular guidance regarding the way that damages for bid rigging should be calculated, but it is underlined that markets on which the price is formed through bidding processes may be conducive to modelling, such as oligopoly models that incorporate game theory to simulate the likely bidding behaviour of competitors in a non-infringement scenario.[67] This observation confirms the correctness of the current monograph to use auction theory as a benchmark to assess the risk of collusion in the context of public procurement procedures and to make relevant recommendations, but at the same

61 CASE AT.39610 – Power Cables.

62 For further information about this case and the reasoning of the court please read Cento Veljanovski *Cartel Damages: Principles, Measurement, and Economics* (Oxford University Press 2020), Chapter 14.

63 For further information about the complexity of life-cycle costing and calculation of costs in public procurement, please read Annalisa Castelli, Gustavo Piga, Stéphane Saussier and Tünde Tátrai *The Challenges of Public Procurement Reforms* (Routledge, 2021).

64 Article 17, para. 1, Directive 2014/104.

65 For instance, see the case *The Fair Institution of Madrid (IFEMA) against the Envelope Cartel* (Provincial Court of Madrid, February 3, 2020, No. 99/2019 and 65/2019), where the first instance judgments which granted damages quantified by the claimants were overturned because the method of estimation of the damage was not adequate, as "insufficiently representative market price references" were used, which "do not take into account the particularities of the envelope market".

66 European Commission "Practical Guide Quantifying Harm in Actions for Damages based on Breaches of Article 101 or 102 of the Treaty on the Functioning of the European Union accompanying the Communication from the Commission on Quantifying Harm in Actions for Damages based on Breaches of Article 101 or 102 of the Treaty on the Functioning of the European Union" (2020/C 242/01) <https://eur-lex.europa.eu/legal-content/EN/TXT/PDF/?uri=CELEX:52020XC0722(01)> accessed on November 8, 2024.

67 Ibid.

time it reaffirms that the calculation of damages is one of the most complex issues in private competition law claims that regard bidding markets.

In addition, the damage estimation exercise may be rather challenging for contracting authorities for another reason. Bid riggers take great care not to get detected and so direct proof of the amount of the overcharge is not usually available in the context of public procurement.[68] As a consequence, the difficulty, time and administrative cost of collecting intelligence and evidence of cartel infringements still remains in public procurement. The first reason for this is the great stability of cartels in public procurement markets. It is a disincentive for colluding firms to report the existence of a bidding ring when it does not seem to break up soon.[69] The second reason relates to the fact that many cartels are usually reported in the context of a merger between two firms, as soon as the acquiring firm discovers the anti-competitive conduct of the acquired firm. In case of public procurement though, the size of bid rigging companies is usually small and so a merger between them does not fall under the turnover threshold to trigger a merger notification under the EU law.[70] Moreover, the reputational damage that can be politically adverse in the next procurement process is another disincentive for firms involved in a bidding ring, when it comes to apply for leniency.[71] The ineffectiveness of leniency policies when it comes to bid rigging has also been empirically proved by an experimental study that took place in a repeated procurement auction game.[72] But even if direct proof of the overcharge amount is available, it will probably be an "understated measure of damage".[73]

Further, there may be difficulty in deciding which contracts to include in the sample under investigation in order to classify them as rigged or unrigged.[74] As already explained above, when it comes to bid rigging, there is not a typical illegal behaviour that gives an indication of which undertakings were participants in the bidding ring and which undertakings were outsiders, thus enabling contracting authorities to collect evidence and make the relevant classifications. This is particularly true in case of industries where there has been evidence of "endemic" bid rigging in respect of thousands of tenders, such as the construction sector in England and Scotland, in which, according to one study, 112 companies were

68 Howard and Kaserman, (fn 58), 363–364; Bishop and Walker (fn 58), 363–364.

69 Heimler (fn 29), 859.

70 Ibid.

71 Ibid, 10–12; International Competition Network (fn 49)

72 Y. Hamaguchi and T. Kawagoe "An Experimental Study of Procurement Auctions with Leniency Program", CPRC Discussion Paper Series CPDP-24-E January 2007, https://ideas.repec.org/p/eti/dpaper/05003.html accessed November 8, 2024; C. Marvão and G. Spagnolo "What do we know about the Effectiveness of Leniency Policies? A Survey of the Empirical and Experimental Evidence" in Caron Beaton-Wells and Christopher Tran (eds) *Anti-Cartel Enforcement in a Contemporary Age-Leniency Religion* (Hart Publishing, 2015), 77–78.

73 Howard and Kaserman (fn 58) 363–364; Bishop and Walker (fn 58) 363–364.

74 Howard and Kaserman (fn 58), 365.

found to be engaged in bid rigging.[75] If this problem is not properly addressed, the statistical analysis of damages may be "seriously biased downward", by indicating lower damages than were actually suffered by the victims.[76]

An additional problem may be the identification of an adequate control group so that comparator-based methods may be used in order to estimate over time on the same market the price difference between the real value of the products or services and the artificially raised price at which they were purchased by the contracting authorities.[77] This means that a reliable statistical evaluation presupposes a sufficient number of unrigged observations in order to compare the price in the infringement scenario with a non-infringement scenario.[78] However, it may be rather difficult to collect data on public contracts awarded before the formation of a bidding ring and after its detection, either because of the time that has passed or because the damages action was brought so promptly that not many public contracts could be concluded in the aftermath.[79] Particularly in the domain of public procurement, where the fragmentation of the public sector is extremely high, there is an enormous volume of data which is fragmented in computerized systems from different contracting authorities. As a result, the collection of data on public contracts awarded before the formation and after the detection of a bidding ring becomes even more difficult. This difficulty has also been acknowledged by the Commission in the Practical Guide on Quantifying Harm in Actions for Damages, where it was noted that in bidding markets the amount of data observed for the variable of interest in the comparator time periods may be only one, that is, the price observed in the one tender after the infringement.[80] This is due to the fact that tenders may take place very infrequently or the relevant contracts may be long-term, as in case of framework agreements.[81] What is more, as already mentioned in the previous paragraph, in industries where bid rigging turns out to be "endemic", it is rather hard to ensure a sufficient number of unrigged observations. After all, every public bidding has its own unique conditions, especially in particular industries such as the construction industry, where there is wide variety of procurement methods used in construction projects. This renders statistical data rather inappropriate for the evaluation of the price that would have been realized in the procurement proceedings in the absence of bid rigging.[82]

75 Marceline Tournier and John Pheasant "The UK Construction Industry Under the Spotlight Again" (2008), 29, *ECLR*, 557–559.
76 Howard and Kaserman (fn 58), 365.
77 Howard and Kaserman (fn 58), 365–366.
78 European Commission "Practical Guide Quantifying Harm in Actions for Damages Based on Breaches of Article 101 or 102 of the Treaty on the Functioning of the European Union" SWD (2013) 205 <www.ec.europa.eu/competition/antitrust/actionsdamages/quantification_guide_en.pdf> accessed November 8, 2024, 15–19.
79 Howard and Kaserman, (fn 58), 365–366.
80 Commission (fn 78).
81 Ibid.
82 Kyong Ju Kim et al. "Estimating Damages of Bid-Rigging in Design-Build Contracts Based on Simulation Model" (2021), 25, *KSCE Journal of Civil Engineering*, 1568–1577.

In addition to the above weaknesses and challenges that the Damages Directive presents, there is empirical research suggesting that there would be no point in promoting private enforcement actions involving bidding rings. This is so because of the limited role that private antitrust litigation plays in most European jurisdictions regarding the deterrence of anticompetitive violations and the compensation of consumers and undertakings suffering from those violations.[83] Additionally, settlements are prevalent in EU Member States, especially because EU encourages private negotiations for damages in antitrust cases by enabling the National Competition Authorities to subtract part of a voluntary redress paid to the victims from the fine.[84] For instance, the EU Directive (EU) 2019/1 to empower the competition authorities of the Member States to be more effective enforcers contemplates in Recital (47) that "national competition authorities should be able to take into account any compensation paid as a result of a consensual settlement" and in Article 14(2) that:

> Member States shall ensure that national competition authorities may consider compensation paid as a result of a consensual settlement when determining the amount of the fine to be imposed for an infringement of Article 101 or 102 TFEU, in accordance with Article 18(3) of Directive 2014/104/EU.[85]

Also, according to the Organisation for Economic Co-Operation and Development (OECD) only a few victims of antitrust infringement have been indemnified, as from 2006 to 2012 "less than 25 per cent of the European Commission's infringement

83 According to the Ashurst study that took place in 2014, almost 104 damages actions were identified for the whole of the European Union. Another report which was prepared for the European Commission found only 96 antitrust damages actions between May 2004 and the third quarter of 2007. From these antitrust actions, 61 concerned horizontal agreements, concerted practices or naked cartels (12 on hardcore cartels or concerted practices, 1 on horizontal agreements); and 22 cases involved abuses of dominance. The aforementioned damages actions were observed only in 10 of the 27 Member States. Moreover, research from the Office of Fair Trading (OFT) in the UK surveyed 202 companies about their views on private actions under competition law. Although 45 of them thought that their company had been harmed by a breach of competition law by someone else, only 5 companies finally decided to bring an action because the expected costs would outweigh the benefits. See Denis Waelbroeck, Donald Slater and Gil Even-Shoshan "Study on the Conditions of Claims for Damages in Case of Infringement of EC Competition Rules, Comparative Report, 31 August 2004" <http://ec.europa.eu/competition/antitrust/actionsdamages/comparative_report_clean_en.pdf> accessed November 8, 2024; Renda, Peysner, Riley and Rodger (fn 27).

84 International Competition Network "Development of Private Enforcement of Competition Law in ICN Jurisdictions" <https://competition-policy.ec.europa.eu/system/files/2021-04/ICN-working-group_private_enforcement_chapter_en.pdf> accessed on November 10, 2024.

85 Directive (EU) 2019/1 of the European Parliament and of the Council of 11 December 2018 [2019] OJ L 11, 3–33, to empower the competition authorities of the Member States to be more effective enforcers and to ensure the proper functioning of the internal market; see also Winand Emons and Severin Lenhard "Rebating Antitrust Fines to Encourage Private Damages Negotiations" (2023), 24(2), *American Law and Economics Review*.

decisions were followed by damages actions".[86] The European Commission clearly stated in paragraph 52 of its Impact Assessment Report on damages actions for breach of the EU antitrust rules that:

> Out of the 54 final cartel and antitrust prohibition decisions taken by the Commission in the period 2006–2012, only 15 were followed by one or more follow-on actions for damages in one or more Member States. In total, 52 actions for damages were brought in only seven Member States. In the 20 other Member States, the Commission is not aware of any follow-on action for damages based on a Commission decision.[87]

However, it should be noted that in 2019 a sharp increase in the number of damages actions before national courts for competition law infringements has been observed, though these cases came from only 13 Member States and not from all of the members of the EU.[88]

Even if it is not clear whether the above OECD and Commission statistics include public bodies that sue for bid rigging, it is likely that the same applies because settlements are also favoured in the domain of public procurement. Public authorities are usually in a strong position to encourage bidders to settle claims for damages instead of going to court, as the undertakings know well that they will have to bid for future public contracts from the former. At the same time, contracting authorities take great care not to spoil cooperative relationships with future partners and so they may be content with partial instead of full compensation, since a settlement would be better for them than nothing. The overall prevalence of settlement activity in public procurement can also be supported by the Damages Directive, which contemplates in Recital (48) that: "infringers and injured parties should be encouraged to agree on compensating for the harm caused by a competition law infringement through consensual dispute resolution mechanisms, such as out-of-court settlements, arbitration, mediation or conciliation". Thus, "an infringer that pays damages through consensual dispute resolution should not be placed in a worse position vis-à-vis its co-infringers than it would otherwise be without the consensual settlement".[89] Moreover, compensation paid as a result of consensual settlement and prior to the imposition of a fine, may be a mitigating factor taken into account by the relevant CA.[90]

It must be acknowledged that the Damages Directive did not have as one of its express objectives the improvement of contracting authorities' ability to bring damages actions in the context of public procurement. However, in view of the

86 OECD "Relationship Between Public and Private Antitrust Enforcement" (fn 9), 5.

87 European Commission "Impact Assessment Report – Damages Actions for Breach of the EU Antitrust Rules" (fn 9).

88 Commission "Staff Working Document on the Implementation of Directive 2014/104/EU" (fn 9); Jean-François Laborde "Cartel Damages Actions in Europe: How Courts Have Assessed Cartel Overcharges" (2019 ed.), November 2019, *Concurrences*, N° 4-2019, Art. N° 92227.

89 Recital 51, Directive 2014/104.

90 Article 18, para 3, Directive 2014/104.

above discussion and analysis, it could be said that, whilst public procurement authorities can bring damages actions, the Damages Directive does not provide a framework for encouraging contracting authorities to use private enforcement and for this reason its practical relevance in the area of public procurement seems limited.

Hence, it seems that the Damages Directive does not provide any advantages over claims according to longstanding national tort laws and the general competition law when it comes to public authorities in public procurement. This conclusion is also supported by several recent empirical surveys which affirm that it would not be appropriate to promote damages claims for bid rigging, in view of their limited role in deterring antitrust violations in most European jurisdictions and the prevalence of settlement activity.

8.4 Recommendations

In the absence of provisions under the Damages Directive that may have some practical relevance for the contracting authorities in the area of public procurement, it is time to make some recommendations that would make it easier for public authorities, but also for other putative claimants, to seek damages for bid rigging. The first recommendation regards the high litigation costs that public authorities usually face when claiming damages for bid rigging. A possible suggestion to deal with this issue is to form a "Competition Damages Litigation Fund", that is a supply of money collected from contracting authorities, with the aim to use it for covering the competition damages litigation costs. A "Competition Damages Litigation Fund" would permit the collection and saving of money for this specific reason, every time the national courts of a particular EU Member State award damages to the relevant contracting authorities for the anticompetitive activities of economic operators in the context of public procurement. Though it could be counter-argued that it is sufficient for every contracting authority to collect its own damages awarded by the national courts, without having to establish a separate "Competition Damages Litigation Fund", a single account for competition damages litigation is an essential tool for consolidating and managing procurement entities' cash resources.

In EU Member States with highly fragmented public sector the establishment of a "Competition Damages Litigation Fund" would enable aggregate and efficient control and monitoring of the damages awarded to various contracting authorities, while it would prevent idle balances maintained in several bank accounts. At the same time, it would facilitate reconciliation between banking and accounting data, and it would prove that as a matter of fact damages claims for bid rigging in public procurement is a priority in the public agenda. The management of this fund could be left to the Auditor General of every EU Member State, who will be in charge of calculating and paying the arising litigation costs as well as of informing regularly the contracting authorities about the balance of the account. Something similar already happens in the UK, where it is the Accountant General of the Senior Courts responsible for the control of the money paid into courts.[91] Additionally, in the UK there is a Court Funds Office which provides banking and investment services by accounting for any money being paid into and out of court and by looking after any investments made with that money.[92]

Similarly, when the residual funds of the "Competition Damages Litigation Fund" are beyond a specific and predetermined amount of money at the end of each year, the Auditor General of every EU Member State may distribute them *pro rata* to the involved contracting authorities in order to apply them for their indirect benefit, such as purchase of new furniture for their premises, organization and conduct of a new procurement process etc. The fact that part of this money may remain in the administration will also be an extra incentive for public officers to become more interested in discovering bidding rings and in claiming damages for bid rigging. Another recommendation could also be to restrict the compensation of the defendant's fees to the statutory attorney fees in order to prevent situations of abuse on behalf of the defendants. Germany is an illustrative example of this, despite the "loser pays" rule that applies there.[93]

Regarding the concern of contracting authorities that the initiation of litigation against colluding economic operators may spoil their cooperative relationship, the assignment of their claims to a third party is suggested, which would also have an interest in bringing an action. It has been suggested that special courts/institutions, such as audit agencies, procurement oversight agencies, such as the National Anti-Corruption Authority of Italy, as well as private agents, such as law firms and tax-payer associations could be identified as having a proper incentive' to sue as a third party.[94] This is something that already takes place in Germany, where claimants can assign their claim to third party funders or special purpose vehicles (SPVs).[95] In the above list of third parties with a proper incentive to sue, the competitors of the bid riggers that were not selected for the award of the public contract due to the manipulation of the bidding process could also be included.

As far as the contracting authorities' difficulty in specifying and quantifying the financial harm is concerned, the introduction of statutory or pre-established damages might be a good solution to the problem. Specifically, it is suggested that contracting authorities before the final judgment should have the option to ask

91 The National Archives "Court of Chancery: Office of the Accountant General, Supreme Court Pay Office: Indexes to Accounts" <http://discovery.nationalarchives.gov.uk/details/r/C18421> accessed November 8, 2024; UK Government "Pay Money into the Court Funds Office" <www.gov.uk/pay-court-funds-office> accessed November 8, 2024.

92 UK Government "Pay Money into the Court Funds Office" (fn 91).

93 Albrecht Bach and Christoph Wolf "Germany: Private Antitrust Litigation" <www.globalcompetitionreview.com/review/the-european-middle-east-and-african-antitrust-review/2021/article/germany-private-antitrust-litigation> accessed November 12, 2024.

94 Giancarlo Spagnolo "Public Procurement, Bid Rigging and (the Lack of) Actions for Damages", Lear Conference on Public Procurement and Competition Policy, Rome, July 3–5, 2017 <www.learconference.com/wp-content/uploads/2017/07/SPAGNOLO_Damages_Lear_2017.pdf> accessed November 12, 2024.

95 Bach and Wolf (fn 93).

for the recovery of statutory/pre-established damages instead of actual damages, namely a lump sum calculated by the national courts on the basis of pre-determined factors. These factors could mutually be agreed by the litigants before the initiation of the legal proceedings and they could indicatively be the tenders submitted by "maverick bidders", that is, firms that have demonstrated aggressivity in the past, an aggressive reserve price or at least the cost of the entire procurement process, "from the identification of procurement opportunities, through the preparation of relevant documentation (an invitation to tender/offer) and the conduct of the whole procurement procedure, to provision for possible complaints and litigation".[96] Such an evidence-facilitating device already applies in the domain of intellectual property, where judicial authorities are enabled "in appropriate cases" to set "the damages as a lump sum on the basis of elements such as at least the amount of royalties or fees which would have been due if the infringer had requested authorization to use the intellectual property right in question".[97]

8.5 Alternative Compensatory Remedy

As demonstrated in the analysis above, the Damages Directive has not successfully addressed a number of issues. In the previous section, I proposed recommendations that could potentially address some of these problems, with a focus on reducing costs and improving the quantification of antitrust harm. However, there are still unresolved issues. Therefore, it may be beneficial to explore an alternative remedy that is not rooted in tortious liability but rather in contractual principles. This alternative could assist contracting authorities in obtaining compensation and overcoming challenges related to proof and evidence, such as establishing a causal link and quantifying antitrust harm. Drawing from the experience of Germany, the United Kingdom and the United States of America, it is suggested that a compensatory remedy different from traditional tort law litigation should be considered.

8.5.1 Liquidated Damages Clauses

The contracting parties are able to agree upon "liquidated damages" or "lump sum damage" provisions, meaning "an amount of compensation payable in the event of breach of the contract, or one of its terms".[98] Liquidated damages clauses in public contracts are particularly attractive because as soon as one breach occurs (in our own case we are particularly interested in any infringement of competition law in

96 For further information about how to analyse costs of the procurement process, see PwC, London Economics and Ecorys for the European Commission "Public Procurement in Europe-Cost and Effectiveness" (2011) <www.scribd.com/document/234610075/Public-Procurement-in-Europe-Cost-and-Effectiveness> accessed on November 15, 2024.

97 Article 13, para. 1 Directive 2004/48, [2004], OJ L 195.

98 Neil Andrews *Contract Law* (Cambridge University Press, 2011), 599.

the context of public procurement), the claimant, that is, public bodies, are free from the expense and burden of proving their loss and enforce their claims.[99]

Germany is an illustrative example of an EU Member State where liquidated damages are quite widespread in standard purchasing terms and conditions and their use is becoming even greater, by stipulating that in case of a cartel infringement by the seller, the latter will have to pay a lump sum damage to the purchaser. There are several court judgments in Germany that have ruled on the validity of liquidated damages clauses.[100] All of them awarded the claimed damages to public bodies, such as municipalities and public transport companies, and they accepted that the liquidated damages clause is legal and enforceable. In particular, it was held that:

> The amount of the lump sum damage of 15 per cent is not beyond the amount which can usually be expected in case of damage caused by a cartel. Therefore, the buyer can rely on its purchasing terms to claim such a damage amount in the first place while the seller then has to prove that there was actually a lower damage.[101]

Despite the attractiveness of liquidated damages clauses, especially in the light of costly damages actions, still they are not standard in public contracts. There are various reasons for this. First and foremost, there is not a consistent application of the concept in civil and common law countries, which makes necessary the intervention by the legislator. As secondary obligations come into play only when the contract is breached, liquidated damages can easily be challenged in common law jurisdictions like the UK. They are primarily caught by the "penalty doctrine", according to which liquidated damages clauses are deemed to be unenforceable penalties if (a) they are extravagant or unconscionable comparing with the likely damage caused by the breach, (b) they purport to deter a breach of contract and (c)

99 Martin Gramsch and Simmons & Simmons elexica "Liquidated Damages in General Purchasing Terms" <www.elexica.com/en/legal-topics/antitrust-and-merger-control/190617-liquidated-damages-general-purchasing-terms> accessed November 15, 2024.

100 See for instance the judgment of the regional court of Hannover (LG Hannover, Urteil vom 18.12.2017 – 18 O 8/17, Lkw-Kartell Göttingen), which confirmed the liability in principle of truck manufacturer MAN towards the city of Göttingen for truck purchases made during the operation of the truck cartel <www.hausfeld.com/en-gb/what-we-think/competition-bulletin/first-german-judgement-against-truck-cartel-hanover-district-court-rules-on-follow-on-action/> accessed November 15, 2024; see also the judgment of the Thuringian higher regional court in Jena on 22 February 2017, which upheld an earlier judgment of the regional court of Erfurt of 3 July 2015, according to which a public transport company was in principle entitled to damages. See also the judgment of the higher regional court of Karlsruhe (Higher Regional Court of Karlsruhe, 31 July 2013, 6 U 51/12 Kart) as well as the judgment of the local court of Mannheim (Landgericht [Regional Court] Mannheim May 4, 2012, 7 O 436/11 Kart) <www.vbb.com/media/Insights_Newsletters/CNL_06_17.pdf> and <www.elexica.com/en/legal-topics/antitrust-and-merger-control/190617-liquidated-damages-general-purchasing-terms> accessed November 15, 2024.

101 Martin Gramsch and Simmons & Simmons elexica (fn 99).

they are not a genuine pre-estimate of loss.[102] The common law on penalty clauses was established a little over 100 years ago. In 2015, the UK Supreme Court indicated some progress in this area of law by considering again the law of penalties and the validity of penalty clauses. The chance for this reconsideration was given on the occasion of the conjoined appeals in Cavendish Square Holding BV v Talal El Makdessi and ParkingEye Ltd v Beavis.[103] It clarified that a clause is not disproportionate to the innocent party's legitimate interests, despite its penal nature when it intends to deter a breach of contract and though it may not be representative of the actual loss that the innocent party sustained, as long as the clause has been the object of negotiations between contracting parties of comparable bargaining power and it has been scrutinized by their legal advisers.[104] On the other hand, in civil law countries, penalty clauses are allowed, as long as the penalty amount is not manifestly excessive.[105] In these countries, traditionally there used to be no distinction between liquidated damages and penalty clauses, but following the precedent of the German Civil Code, there is a distinction between them and they also provide for mitigation of penalty clauses if they are "disproportionate or excessively high/ manifestly excessive".[106]

The lack of uniform application of liquidated damages clauses can be found even in the context of a single EU Member State and jurisdiction. In Germany, for instance, there are several uncertainties regarding liquidated damages clauses. There is still no consensus regarding the validity of contractual clauses providing for a lump sum as compensation in case of competition law infringements. In its judgment on April 13, 2016, the regional court of Potsdam[107] held that purchasing terms contemplating a lump-sum amount of damages amounting to 15% of the contract value in all cases, regardless of the specific type and intensity of the competition law infringement that took place, are too wide in scope and so they fail to fulfil the standard of damages expected under normal circumstances.[108] This

102 Dunlop Pneumatic Tyre Co. Ltd v New Garage and Motor Co. Ltd (1915) AC 70, 86–88.

103 [2015] UKSC 67.

104 Fenwick Elliott "The Brand-New Law on Liquidated Damages" <www.fenwickelliott.com/research-insight/newsletters/insight/53> accessed November 15, 2024.

105 Saloua Hoeve-Ouchan and Giorgio de Rosa "Liquidated Damages and Penalty Clauses: A Common Law and Civil Law Perspective" <www.internationallawoffice.com/Newsletters/Company-Commercial/Singapore/VoskampLawyers/Liquidated-damages-and-penalty-clauses-a-common-law-and-civil-law-perspective#> (accessed November 15, 2024); J.F. McKenna and Reed Smith LLP "Liquidated Damages and Penalty Clauses: A Civil Law versus Common Law Comparison – The Critical Path" <www.reedsmith.com/en/perspectives/2008/05/the-critical-path> accessed November 15, 2024.

106 The terminology used in order to describe when penalty clauses can be mitigated is different from civil code to civil code. Hoeve-Ouchan and de Rosa (fn 105); McKenna and Reed Smith LLP (fn 105).

107 LG Potsdam, 1304.2016, Az. 2 O 23/15.

108 Peter Meyer and Martin Gramsch "The Regional Court of Potsdam Finds a Clause in the Procurement Terms of a German Municipality Requiring Liquidated Damages of 15 Per Cent to Be Paid if the Supplier Participates in Anti-Competitive Behaviour to be Unlawful (Suppliers of Fire Engines)" e-Competitions Bulletin, Art. N° 77233 (November 2014).

judgment was further appealed to the Federal Supreme Court but the appeal was withdrawn, leaving many questions unanswered.[109]

Another reason why liquidated damages clauses are not standard in a public contract is that they limit the damages to which the claimant is entitled and that the contract enforcement rate is generally low. Contract law matters a lot less than expected, as non-contractual enforcement mechanisms such as reputation and loss of future revenue can play a really important role for contracting parties.[110] This can be explained by the fact that contracting parties generally avoid courts in order to enforce contractual obligations, for fear that they will pay a lot of money for legal fees, while in the end the case may not be resolved in their favour, "despite the significant attention paid to drafting, amending and consulting formal contracts".[111] Under these circumstances, "litigation is almost always an empty threat".[112]

In addition to the above, as regards public contracts in particular, corruption of the civil servants who are in charge of the contract as well as the negative effects of litigation on the continuation of the buyer–supplier relationship may prevent the effective enforcement of contractual remedies, such as liquidated damages clauses, in the domain of public procurement.[113] Of course it should be noted that this applies to all enforcement actions. As HM Treasury characteristically mentioned in one of its reports about Private Finance Initiatives (PFIs)[114] "there exists anecdotal evidence that the public sector can sometimes be reluctant to levy deductions for fear of spoiling the relationship with the private sector".[115] In Italy, according to third party inspections commissioned by the Italian Public Procurement Agency (Consip.), "in the period 2005–2008 on a total of 4095 inspections a total of 1455 contractual infringements by the contractor were ascertained, but contractual remedies/penalties were only exercised in 64 of those cases, i.e. against about 4.42 per cent of the infringements".[116]

109 Meyer and Gramsch (fn 108), 2.

110 Stewart Macaulay "Non-Contractual Relations in Business: A Preliminary Study" (1963), 28, *American Sociological Review*, 55–67.

111 Gillian Hadfield and Iva Bozovic "Scaffolding: Using Formal Contracts to Build Informal Relations to Support Innovation" (2016), 5, *Wisconsin Law Review*, 996, 999.

112 ibid, 1000.

113 Giancarlo Spagnolo "Reputation, Competition and Entry in Procurement" (2012), 30(3), *International Journal of Industrial Organization*, 292.

114 PFI projects are arrangements where the government department responsible for the delivery of a public service entrusts the delivery to the private sector under a contract. See more in Peter Braun, "The Practical Impact of E.U. Public Procurement Law on PFI Procurement Practice in the United Kingdom" <www.nottingham.ac.uk/pprg/documentsarchive/phdtheses/phd_peter_braun_.pdf> accessed November 15, 2024.

115 HM Treasury "PFI: Strengthening Long-Term Partnerships – March 2006" <www.uk.practicallaw.thomsonreuters.com/Document/Ibe3cd2b5e83311e398db8b09b4f043e0/View/FullText.html?contextData=(sc.Default)&transitionType=Default&firstPage=true> accessed November 15, 2024, para. 4.63.

116 Elisabetta Iossa and Giancarlo Spagnolo "Contracts as Threats: On a Rationale for Rewarding A while Hoping for B" (2011) CEPR Discussion Papers No. 8195 <https://papers.ssrn.com/sol3/papers.cfm?abstract_id=1434499> accessed November 15, 2024.

In view of the above, it seems that liquidated damages clauses can be a good alternative remedy that will help contracting authorities to receive compensation and overcome the problems of proof and evidence that they currently face under the Damages Directive, since in the author's view their advantages outweigh their disadvantages. Of course, this presupposes a uniform approach regarding the extent of their validity, otherwise there is always the risk that liquidated damage clauses remain unapplied and may be rejected by the court. For this reason, many aspects of liquidated damages clauses need to be clarified and this potentially requires intervention by the legislator as well.

8.5.2 Divestiture and Donations: Should EU Follow the Paradigm of the United States?

In August 2023, the Department of Justice (DOJ) Antitrust Division resolved criminal investigations with Teva Pharmaceuticals and Glenmark Pharmaceuticals. The two companies, indicted in 2020 for alleged conspiracies to allocate customers, fix prices and rig bids for generic drugs sold in the United States, entered into deferred prosecution agreements (DPAs) and civil settlement agreements.[117] What is noteworthy and novel in this case is that the relevant antitrust criminal settlement required both companies to divest a line of business and donate the alleged price-fixed products to non-governmental third parties, that is, humanitarian organizations that provide medication to Americans in need.

Divestiture is an antitrust remedy that involves the partial or full sale or disposal of a business unit, subsidiary, division, product line or other assets.[118] It was first utilized in the United States in the *Standard Oil* case in 1911, which involved the illegal monopolization of the market by the company.[119] In that case, the court determined that breaking up Standard Oil into 34 independent companies could prevent and remedy the harm caused to the public interest.[120] While early divestiture cases were related to monopolization claims, nowadays most divestitures are used in mergers and combinations with anticompetitive effects. This allows assets to be easily divided or dissolved to restore competition rather than to punish or deter antitrust offenders.[121]

When it comes to bid rigging, in the early 1970s, the US Department of Justice's (DOJ) seriously considered imposing divestiture on members of a gypsum cartel on the grounds that "US Gypsum was a recidivist, thereby allowing us to make

117 US Department of Justice-Office of Public Affairs "Major Generic Drug Companies to Pay Over Quarter of a Billion Dollars to Resolve Price-Fixing Charges and Divest Key Drug at the Center of Their Conspiracy" <www.justice.gov/opa/pr/major-generic-drug-companies-pay-over-quarter-billion-dollars-resolve-price-fixing-charges> accessed November 15, 2024.

118 Concurrences – Torsten Körber "Divestiture" <www.concurrences.com/en/dictionary/divestiture> accessed on November 15, 2024.

119 Standard Oil Co. of New Jersey v United States, 221 US 1 (1911).

120 Ibid.

121 Daniel Lumer "Divestiture: Doctrinal Development and Modern Application" (2022), 67(1), *The Antitrust Bulletin*, 146–181.

the argument that a structural remedy was needed".[122] However, the Supreme Court overturned the conviction, so divestiture was never implemented. More than 50 years later, that is, in 2023, the DOJ antitrust criminal settlement with Teva Pharmaceuticals USA, Inc. and Glenmark Pharmaceuticals Inc., the United States required the breakup of assets and a donation to remedy the relevant anticompetitive conduct. Until 2021, the DOJ had a policy generally disfavouring corporate criminal resolutions that required payments to non-governmental third parties. However, in 2022 the components' authority to enter into such settlements was restored and the DOJ published guidelines governing such practices to prevent abuse. Indicatively, according to these guidelines, any such settlement agreement shall define with particularity the nature and scope of the specific project(s) that the defendant has agreed to fund and all projects must have a strong connection to the underlying violation(s) of federal law at issue in the enforcement action.[123] The project should also be designed to reduce the detrimental effects of the underlying violation(s) at issue to the extent feasible and reduce the likelihood of similar violations in the future.[124] Also, it could be argued that the main reason for disfavouring divestiture in bid-rigging cases until recently has been the likelihood that this remedy would create or exacerbate the bid riggers' financial difficulties. Since bidding cartel companies interact with the public sector, as purchases of products or services by government or public entities take place primarily through public tenders, the bidding cartel companies' potential financial difficulties may harm the public interest by causing a material disturbance of the public purchases and a serious detriment to the users of public goods and services and taxpayers. Yet, the DOJ decided to expand the use of divestiture to resolve criminal antitrust cases and particularly to remedy bid rigging, in an attempt not only to hold bid riggers accountable, but also to eliminate the incentive of undertakings to reduce competition in the public market.

This development has been hailed as a key step towards fighting bid rigging and restoring competition in public markets.[125] Indeed, divestiture is a practical remedy

122 Joseph E. Harrington Jr. "A Proposal for a Structural Remedy for Illegal Collusion" (2018), 82(1), *Antitrust Law Journal*, 335–360.

123 Office of the Attorney General "Guidelines and Limitations for Settlement Agreements Involving Payments to Non-Governmental Third Parties" <www.justice.gov/ag/file/1217691-0/dl?inline=> accessed November 15, 2024.

124 Ibid.

125 White et al. "DOJ Antitrust Division Announces Deferred Prosecution Agreements with Two Pharmaceutical Companies Containing 'Extraordinary' Divestiture Remedy" <www.whitecase.com/insight-alert/doj-antitrust-division-announces-deferred-prosecution-agreements-two-pharmaceutical> accessed November 15, 2024; Covington and Burling LLP-E. Kate Patchen and Jacqueline M. Fitch "DOJ Enters into Unprecedented Deferred Prosecution Agreements to Resolve Price-Fixing Allegations" <www.cov.com/en/news-and-insights/insights/2023/08/doj-enters-into-unprecedented-deferred-prosecution-agreements-to-resolve-price-fixing-allegations> accessed November 15, 2024; Arnold, Porter-Sam Sullivan and Andre Geverola "DOJ Criminal Antitrust Settlements Involve Dollars, Donations, and Divestitures" <www.arnoldporter.com/en/perspectives/blogs/enforcement-edge/2023/08/doj-criminal-antitrust-settlements> accessed November 15, 2024.

that does not require detailed and ongoing monitoring following implementation or compliance activity. The benefits of divestitures in case of a cartel conviction were also highlighted and discussed in a thorough way by Professor Joseph Harrington five years before the DOJ's decision to force the aforementioned companies to divest a business line that was central to their misconduct.[126] According to Professor Harrington, asking one or more cartel members to divest some assets related to the production of the product or service at issue, makes recidivism less likely, deters cartel formation from occurring in the first place and compensates customers for the harm incurred.[127] Divestiture modifies a market structure, as cartel members are required to either divest assets to an entrant in order to create a new competitor in the market or transfer assets to other existing market players in order to achieve reallocation of capacity and have different market shares.[128] In both cases, the creation of a new competing entrant in the market and the control of less capacity by firms that have shown themselves willing and able to collude will result in a more competitive market, which will be less conducive to collusion thanks to divestiture.[129] At the same time, a more competitive market means lower profits when cartel members compete in the post-cartel environment compared to the pre-cartel environment.[130] Lower profits earned by firms from operating in a more competitive market could well deter them from colluding.[131] From a compensatory point of view, Professor Harrington argues that "divestiture is compensatory when a consumer's demand persists over time and, for intermediate goods cartels with a high cost pass-through rate, could be more effective than customer damages in compensating those consumers who were harmed".[132] Also, by resulting in lower competitive prices, the broad antitrust goal of consumer welfare is served, as the surplus received by future consumers is raised.[133]

After discussing how and why divestiture was used as an antitrust remedy in the Teva Pharmaceuticals and Glenmark Pharmaceuticals case, which involved a bidding rig, it is now time to evaluate to what extent it could be used in a similar way in the EU and whether it could be a good alternative to damages claims for bid rigging. In the EU, divestiture is usually ordered as a structural merger remedy to preserve competitive market structures.[134] Yet, in the EU divestiture may be used only as a last resort remedy. According to Article 7 of Regulation 1/2003 (EU) structural remedies can only apply "*either where there is no equally efficient behavioural*

126 Harrington (fn 122).
127 Ibid, 337.
128 Ibid, 338.
129 Ibid.
130 Ibid, 341
131 Ibid.
132 ibid, 344.
133 Ibid, 343.
134 Körber (fn 118); Richard Whish "New Competition Tool: Legal Comparative Study of Existing Competition Tools Aimed at Addressing Structural Competition Problems with a Particular Focus on the UK's Market Investigation Tool" <www.competition-policy.ec.europa.eu/system/files/2021-03/kd0420573enn.pdf> accessed November 15, 2024.

remedy or where any equally effective behavioural remedy would be more burdensome for the undertaking concerned than a structural remedy".[135] The reason for the restricted use of structural remedies, such as divestiture, is compliance with the principle of proportionality, one of the most fundamental principles in the EU, as laid down in Article 5(4) of the Treaty on European Union.[136] Hence, "*changes to the structure of an undertaking as it existed before the infringement was committed would only be proportionate where there is a substantial risk of a lasting or repeated infringement that derives from the very structure of the undertaking*".[137]

In light of Regulation 1/2003 (EU) and its considerations, divestitures may be considered as a remedy for bid rigging schemes only in cases where there is a heightened risk of recidivism, such as when companies have a history of cartel offences. However, empirical research on 389 recidivists involved in international price-fixing from 1990 to 2009 shows that recidivists primarily engage in classic price-fixing rather than bid-rigging.[138]

Furthermore, in the context of public markets there are inherent challenges to using divestitures as a remedy in bid rigging cases. Divestitures could negatively impact bid riggers' ongoing business operations, which could also affect the public sector since government purchases primarily occur through public tenders. For instance, if a bid rigging scheme involves all or most industry participants, contracting authorities may struggle to find bidders to meet their needs, carry out the work and ensure sufficient competition in the bidding process. This disruption in public purchases could harm the public interest, impacting taxpayers and users of public goods and services. This concern is significant, as highlighted in a recent report by the European Court of Auditors on public procurement, in the EU single market from the 2011 to 2021. The report shows a significant decrease in the number of bidders per procedure from an average of 5.7 bidders to 3.2 bidders.[139] Also, according to the same Report, the single bidding rate, meaning that only one company shows interest and submits a bid for a given public procurement, almost doubled in the past ten years, increasing significantly from 23.5% to 41.8% over the same period.[140] Given that single bidding may indicate collusive arrangements such as of bid suppression or rotation,[141] using divestiture in cases of full cartels

135 Council Regulation (EC) No 1/2003 of 16 December 2002 [2003] OJ L 1, 1–25, on the implementation of the rules on competition laid down in Articles 81 and 82 of the Treaty.

136 OJ C 202, 7.6.2016.

137 Council Regulation (fn 134), Recital 12.

138 John M. Connor "Recidivism Revealed: Private International Cartels 1990–2009" (2010), 6(2), *Competition Policy International*. See also John M. Connor "Global Enforcement Directed at International Cartels: A Concise Introduction and Summary" <https://one.oecd.org/document/DAF/COMP/GF(2016)9/en/pdf> accessed November 15, 2024, 12.

139 European Court of Auditors "Special report 28/2023: Public procurement in the EU – Less competition for contracts awarded for works, goods and services in the 10 years up to 2021" <www.eca.europa.eu/en/publications/sr-2023-28> accessed November 15, 2024.

140 Ibid.

141 Isabela Villamil, Janos Kertesz and Mihaly Fazekas "Collusion Risk in Corporate Networks" (2024), 14(1), *Scientific Reports*, 3161.

involving all firms in the market could jeopardize the financial stability of the firms and hinder public purchasers' ability to meet their needs and carry out the relevant work.

As far as the compensatory function of divestitures is concerned, it's important to note that divestitures do not aim to regulate the ongoing behaviour of the infringing parties, as they are not behavioural remedies. Their primary goal is to restore the structure of the market and benefit future consumers rather than past, who were affected by the cartel.[142] This differs from the compensatory ideal of private enforcement, which seeks to provide compensation to victims of competition infringements and allows contracting authorities impacted by bid rigging schemes to return to their pre-collusion position. This is particularly true if we consider that in practice the assets of one or more bid riggers are typically not sold to the relevant contracting authorities or the public sector. Instead, they are often sold to a new entrant, a non-cartel member (if the cartel was not all-inclusive) or another cartel member. Indicatively, in the Deferred Prosecution Agreement between the DOJ and Glenmark Pharmaceuticals Inc., USA, Glenmark agreed to divest its rights to sell and distribute the generic drug involved in the misconduct, to another entity in the market, not to the US government.[143] Similarly, the donation requested from Teva Pharmaceuticals USA, Inc. will be made to humanitarian organizations, not to the US government.[144]

Moreover, as Professor Harrington explained, divestitures are more effective than damages when a consumer's demand remains constant over time and when there are cartels involving intermediate goods with a high cost pass-through rate. Yet, in public procurement the goods procured are typically durable and of high cost. According to the latest data from the European Commission, there is a growing trend in the value of procurement advertised on Tenders Electronic Daily (TED) as a percentage of national GDP, with no country having a publication value below 2%.[145] Additionally, it is important to note that contracting authorities usually purchase final products rather than intermediate goods that are part of the production process for other items.

Last but not least, it should be emphasized that in European public procurement, divestiture would not be compatible with the debarment mechanism that allows for the disqualification of contractors from obtaining public contracts or extensions to existing contracts. Applying both remedies to bid riggers would pose a risk of significant disruption and economic damage, rather than effectively restore market competition. This is particularly true in European public procurement because in early 2000s, the scope of the debarment option extended, granting

142 European Court of Auditors (fn 138), 343.

143 United States District Court, Eastern District of Pennsylvania "Deferred Prosecution Agreement" <www.justice.gov/opa/file/1311121/dl?inline> accessed November 16, 2024.

144 US Department of Justice – Office of Public Affairs (fn 117).

145 European Commission "Access to Public Procurement" <https://single-market-scoreboard.ec.europa.eu/business-framework-conditions/public-procurement_en> accessed November 15, 2024.

public procurement agencies the authority to exclude suppliers based on reasonable doubt of their integrity, regardless of any criminal justice proceedings.[146] The inherent incompatibility between divestiture and debarment becomes evident when considering that in the United States, divestiture is only an available remedy when companies are able to enter into deferred prosecution agreements (DPAs) instead of pleading guilty. The Antitrust Division began utilizing DPAs independently in 2019, allowing companies to avoid debarment from federal contracts, a consequence of a guilty plea.[147] This shows that even in the United States, where the scope of debarment is limited, divestiture and debarment do not coexist, as it would be a harsh measure for infringing companies.

In view of the above, it is argued that divestiture would not be a suitable alternative to damages claims for bid rigging in the EU. However, it could serve as a valuable addition to bid rigging enforcement, as long as it adheres to the EU principle of proportionality and does not involve debarred firms. Regarding donations, payments to third parties could effectively replace damages claims for bid rigging in the EU, provided that any such donation (a) clearly outlines the nature and extent of the specific project(s) that the defendant has committed to fund, (b) is closely linked to the bid rigging scheme under scrutiny in the enforcement action and (c) aims to mitigate the negative impacts of the underlying violation(s) to the best of its ability and lower the likelihood of similar violations occurring in the future.[148]

8.6 Conclusions

Competitive tender processes in public procurement contribute to greater economic efficiency, particularly by lowering prices for the award of public contracts and saving money for the taxpayer. However, bid rigging, an anticompetitive activity that is widespread in public procurement markets, as proven in Chapter 1, may artificially increase the prices of goods or services procured. This places an unnecessary burden on public finances and on taxpayers who ultimately foot the bill. For this reason, the ability for deceived contracting authorities to seek damages for the rigged goods or services for which they have overpaid is of great significance. This is especially true in a time of economic crisis when efforts are being made to reduce public expenditure and secure budget savings.

146 Emmanuelle Auriol and Tina Soreide "An Economic Analysis of Debarment" (2017), 50, *International Review of Law and Economics*, 37.

147 US Department of Justice Speech "Assistant Attorney General Makan Delrahim Delivers Remarks at the New York University School of Law Program on Corporate Compliance and Enforcement" <www.justice.gov/opa/speech/assistant-attorney-general-makan-delrahim-delivers-remarks-new-york-university-school-l-0> accessed November 15, 2024.

148 The suggested requirements are the same as the ones that the Attorney General in the United States set in the "Guidelines and Limitations for Settlement Agreements Involving Payments to Non-Governmental Third Parties" <www.justice.gov/ag/file/1217691-0/dl?inline=> accessed November 15, 2024.

Before the Damages Directive, victims of competition law infringements often faced difficulties when seeking compensation. These challenges included limited access to necessary evidence, unclear rules on the passing-on defence, complex calculations for damages and uncertainty about the costs of legal action. The Damages Directive aimed to address these issues by introducing a number of key provisions. This chapter examines whether the provisions in the Damages Directive have effectively helped contracting authorities seeking damages for bid rigging. While the Directive has strengths, such as standardizing evidential presumptions and procedural requirements, establishing joint and several liability for multiple wrongdoers, and simplifying the evidence of causal link, it has not significantly increased the number of damage actions brought by public contracting authorities. To truly improve the situation, efforts must be made to address the underlying reasons why contracting authorities are hesitant to pursue legal action against bid riggers.

After identifying the challenges that public authorities face in bringing damages claims for bid rigging under the Damages Directive, several recommendations were made to address the issues. These included addressing high litigation costs, concerns about damaging buyer–supplier relationships and difficulties in specifying and quantifying antitrust harm suffered by contracting authorities. One proposed solution was the establishment of a "Competition Damages Litigation Fund" to collect and save money for deceived contracting authorities seeking damages for overpaid goods or services due to bid rigging. Additionally, limiting compensation for the defendant's fees to statutory attorney fees was suggested to reduce litigation costs. Another recommendation was the assignment of public authorities' damages claims to a third party with an interest in pursuing legal action. This would help alleviate concerns about damaging relationships with suppliers in the future. Finally, the introduction of statutory or pre-established damages, calculated based on pre-determined factors was proposed as a way for contracting authorities to overcome challenges in specifying and quantifying financial harm.

In the further alternative, it was examined if an alternative to traditional tort law litigation could make it easier for contracting authorities to be compensated with regard to proof and evidence. The chapter identified liquidated damages clauses as a viable alternative based on contractual principles, as they relieve public bodies from the expense and burden of proving their losses and enforcing their claims. Nonetheless, without a uniform approach to their validity, there is risk that they may go unapplied and be rejected by the court. Donations were also recognized as a suitable alternative to damages claims for bid rigging as long as certain requirements are met. Conversely, divestitures were found to be unsuitable as compensatory remedies for bid rigging in European public procurement. They could however, be used in addition to damages claims for bid rigging, as long as they adhere to the EU principle of proportionality and are not imposed on debarred firms.

Based on the analysis provided, the development of damages claims brought by public authorities should be seen considered a complement to the current state of antitrust enforcement in the EU, as outlined in the introduction of this chapter. Despite efforts by the European legislator to address procedural issues in private enforcement, there has been hesitancy in fully implementing these changes. The

Damages Directive, while a step in the right direction, may not be sufficient for public authorities seeking legal recourse as private litigants. Prior to its implementation, procurement entities could seek compensation through private actions under national tort laws, despite the challenges identified above. Consequently, private enforcement in public procurement currently operates in the slow lane, leading the author to suggest that until the Commission revises the Damages Directive, submits a report and proposes amendments to encourage public authorities to pursue damages against bidding rings, settlements may be the preferred approach in this domain. The recommendations provided in the Recommendations section, along with alternative compensatory remedies suggested in the chapter could serve as a starting point for the future necessary changes.

9 Whistle-Blower Programme

An Effective Mechanism to Deter Collusion and Boost the Enforcement of Competition Law in Public Procurement?

9.1 Introduction

As evident from the discussion on private enforcement in the previous chapter, even after the enactment of the Competition Law Damages Directive, obtaining damages for bid-rigging remains challenging for public authorities. Therefore, in this chapter it is worth discussing the role of whistle-blowing as a cartel detection tool in public procurement and as a mechanism to strengthen the enforcement efforts of National Competition Authorities against illegal cartels in public markets.

The interest in whistle-blowing has notably increased at the EU level. Whistle-blower mechanisms have been recognized as an effective tool in combatting breaches of EU competition rules and collusion in public procurement.[1] The significant interest in whistle-blower mechanisms in the realm of public procurement is justified, especially considering that the European Union incurs a loss of €5.8 to €9.6 billion in potential benefits annually, solely in public procurement, due to a lack of reporting.[2] Also, bidding rigs are much more stable than normal cartels. This is because public markets favour cartels due to their structural and rule-based characteristics, which make members of a bidding rig less willing to cheat each other.[3] Until recently, legislation on whistle-blower protection at the EU level was rather fragmented and lacked proper protection and guidance, which deterred people from reporting wrongdoings they encountered. This is particularly true because whistle-blowing is a critical decision to make. Reporting wrongdoing often comes

1 See an example of such a tool put in place by the European Commission "Antitrust and Cartels" <https://ec.europa.eu/competition/cartels/whistleblower/ index.html> accessed on August 5, 2024; European Commission "Notice on Tools to Fight Collusion in Public Procurement and On Guidance on How to Apply the Related Exclusion Ground" <https://eur-lex.europa.eu/legal-content/EN/TXT/PDF/?uri=CELEX:52021XC0318(01)> accessed on August 10, 2024.

2 European Commission, Directorate-General for Internal Market, Industry, Entrepreneurship and SMEs, Ludovica Rossi, Jennifer McGuinn and Meena Fernandes "Estimating the economic benefits of whistle-blower protection in public procurement – Final report" Publications Office, 2017 <https://data.europa.eu/doi/10.2873/125033> accessed on 1August 10, 2024.

3 Alberto Heimler "Cartels in Public Procurement" (2012), 8(4), *Journal of Competition Law and Economics*, 849–862.

DOI: 10.4324/9781003359999-9

with consequences at the whistle-blower's expense, and fear of retaliation is the predominant factor affecting one's decision not to blow the whistle.[4]

In view of the above, this chapter is structured as follows. Section 9.2 explores the extent to which the recent EU legal regime for whistle-blower protection (2019/1937 Directive on the protection of persons who report breaches of Union law) encourages the whistle-blowers to provide actionable evidence to National Competition Authorities leading to the enforcement of competition law in public procurement. To provide a comprehensive perspective for the research and offer recommendations for law and policy makers, Section 9.3 also examines the legal status of bid rigging whistle-blowers in the United States and their role in antitrust enforcement. This section of the chapter is based on qualitative data collected from interviews with legal practitioners and government officials in the United States, who have been involved in damages actions for antitrust violations in public contracts or in civil actions to recover damages for false or fraudulent claims in government contracts. Building on the analysis and discussion in Section 9.3 regarding the US paradigm, Section 9.4 draws the main conclusions.

9.2 The EU's Directive on the Protection of Persons Who Report Breaches of Union Law: Assessment from a Bid-Rigging Perspective

In various policy areas, the importance of whistle-blower protection as an enforcement tool has been recognized. To address the fragmented nature of the whistle-blower protection across the EU, the European Parliament and the Council of the European Union released a Directive on the protection of individuals who report violations of Union Law on September 25, 2019. This Directive, known as the EU Whistleblower Directive No. 2019/1937 (hereinafter "Directive (EU) 2019/1937"), was adopted by the European Union on October 7, 2019 and officially came into force on December 16, 2019.

All member states are required to incorporate this Directive into their national legislation in two phases: first, for organizations with 250 or more employees, by December 17, 2021; and second for organizations with 50–249 employees, by December 17, 2023. The importance of protecting individuals who report competition distortions in public procurement is emphasized in Directive (EU) 2019/1937 in various sections, such as preambles (6), (16), (17), (62) and in Article 2, which discusses the scope of the Directive. Therefore, it is worth considering to what

4 Logan L. Watts and M. Ronald Buckley "A Dual-Processing Model of Moral Whistleblowing in Organizations" (2017), 146, *Journal of Business Ethics*, 669–683; Luca Carollo, Simone Pulcher and Marco Guerci "Whistleblowing as a crucial practice for responsible management" in O. Laasch, R. Suddaby, R. E. Freeman and D. Jamali (eds) *Research handbooks in business and management series* (594–605).

extent Directive (EU) 2019/1937 contributes to the more effective enforcement of competition rules in public procurement.

The first provision of Directive (EU) 2019/1937 that is worth considering is Article 2. This article addresses the material scope of the Directive and stipulates that Member States must, at a minimum, ensure protection for individuals reporting on unlawful activities or abuse of law in certain areas of EU law. These areas include public procurement and competition law.

1. *This Directive lays down common minimum standards for the protection of persons reporting the following breaches of Union law:*
   (a) *breaches falling within the scope of the Union acts set out in the Annex that concern the following areas:*
      (i) *public procurement;*
      (ii) *financial services, products and markets, and prevention of money laundering and terrorist financing;*
      (iii) *product safety and compliance;*
      (iv) *transport safety;*
      (v) *protection of the environment;*
      (vi) *radiation protection and nuclear safety;*
      (vii) *food and feed safety, animal health and welfare;*
      (viii) *public health;*
      (ix) *consumer protection;*
      (x) *protection of privacy and personal data, and security of network and information systems;*
   (b) *breaches affecting the financial interests of the Union as referred to in Article 325 TFEU and as further specified in relevant Union measures;*
   (c) *breaches relating to the internal market, as referred to in Article 26(2) TFEU, including breaches of Union competition and State aid rules, as well as breaches relating to the internal market in relation to acts which breach the rules of corporate tax or to arrangements the purpose of which is to obtain a tax advantage that defeats the object or purpose of the applicable corporate tax law.*

The explicit provision protecting individuals who report breaches in public procurement and competition law is welcomed. This makes it more likely for them to come forward when witnessing bid rigging and other anticompetitive conduct in public contracts. This contributes to competitive bidding processes that achieve better value for money.

Another important provision of Directive (EU) 2019/1937 to consider is Article 4, which defines the personal scope. This outlines the target groups to which the Directive applies. Hence, according to Article 4:

1. *This Directive shall apply to reporting persons working in the private or public sector who acquired information on breaches in a work-related context including, at least, the following:*
   (a) *persons having the status of worker, within the meaning of Article 45(1) TFEU, including civil servants;*
   (b) *persons having self-employed status, within the meaning of Article 49 TFEU;*
   (c) *shareholders and persons belonging to the administrative, management or supervisory body of an undertaking, including non-executive members, as well as volunteers and paid or unpaid trainees;*
   (d) *any persons working under the supervision and direction of contractors, subcontractors and suppliers.*
2. *This Directive shall also apply to reporting persons where they report or publicly disclose information on breaches acquired in a work-based relationship which has since ended.*
3. *This Directive shall also apply to reporting persons whose work-based relationship is yet to begin in cases where information on breaches has been acquired during the recruitment process or other pre-contractual negotiations.*
4. *The measures for the protection of reporting persons set out in Chapter VI shall also apply, where relevant, to:*
   (a) *facilitators;*
   (b) *third persons who are connected with the reporting persons and who could suffer retaliation in a work-related context, such as colleagues or relatives of the reporting persons; and*
   (c) *legal entities that the reporting persons own, work for or are otherwise connected with in a work-related context.*

As it becomes evident, Article 4 represents a step in the right direction, particularly because the Directive covers both the public and private sectors and provides protection to civil servants and individuals working under the supervision and direction of contractors, suppliers and subcontractors. The inclusion of civil servants within the scope of Article 4 is crucial because the procurement profession is part of the civil service and the role of public procurement officials in detecting and reporting bid rigging is significant. Procurement officers, due to their close involvement with the procurement system, are more likely to identify bid rigging and provide information that may not be readily available.[5] Bid rigging can involve collusion between procurement officers and contractors to secure public contracts at inflated prices or in exchange for preferential treatment. Therefore, in addition to having access to procurement databases, which contain valuable information to uncover collusive activities, public procurement officials may also have access to

5 Access Info Europe "Public Procurement Transparency & Integrity, Guide to EU Directive on Whistleblower Protection, Key Elements relevant to Public Procurement" <www.access-info.org/wp-content/uploads/ML-2-Whistleblower.pdf> accessed on August 10, 2024.

confidential bid details, technical project specifications, and knowledge of personal relationships that could indicate potential bid rigging. Hence, the protection of public procurement officials under Directive (EU) 2019/1937 contributes to the fight against bid rigging by empowering these officials to report suspicious activities and collaborate with competent competition authorities.

Moreover, it is equally important to note that any individuals working under the supervision and direction of subcontractors are eligible for protection under Directive (EU) 2019/1937 in the fight against bid rigging. In public procurement, winning contractors often rely on multiple subcontractors to complete various aspects of awarded projects, especially those that are large and complex. According to CJEU case law, there is a strong presumption that suppliers have the freedom to use subcontractors for the execution of public contracts they have been awarded.[6] As a result, subcontracting agreements are frequently involved bid rigging schemes, where competing companies agree not to bid or to submit intentionally losing bids in exchange for a profitable subcontract with the winning bidder.[7] Additionally, chains of subcontracting can become lengthy and intricate, leading to a lack of transparency and an increased risk of collusion among suppliers at various levels. It has become increasingly challenging to maintain visibility and accountability across these chains from start to finish. Therefore, protecting individuals working under the supervision and direction of subcontractors in public contracts could incentivize them to come forward and report any violations of competition rules by their employers.

The next provision of Directive (EU) 2019/1937 that is worth discussing is Article 19, which prohibits any form of retaliation, including threats and attempts of retaliation.

> *Member States shall take the necessary measures to prohibit any form of retaliation against persons referred to in Article 4, including threats of retaliation and attempts of retaliation including in particular in the form of:*
>
> (a) *suspension, lay-off, dismissal or equivalent measures;*
> (b) *demotion or withholding of promotion;*
> (c) *transfer of duties, change of location of place of work, reduction in wages, change in working hours;*
> (d) *withholding of training;*
> (e) *a negative performance assessment or employment reference;*

6 Indicatively see the C-63/18, Vitali case, where it was held that a national law limiting the share of the contract, which the tenderer is permitted to subcontract to third parties to 30%, is incompatible with Directive 2014/24.

7 Antitrust Division of the Department of Justice, United States "Price Fixing, Bid Rigging, and Market AllocationSchemes: What They Are and What to Look for – An Antitrust Primer" <www.justice.gov/d9/pages/attachments/2016/01/05/211578.pdf> accessed on August 7, 2024; Sofia Competition Forum "Guidelines for Fighting Bid-Rigging in Public Procurement" <https://unctad.org/system/files/non-official-document/ccpb_SCF_Bid-rigging%20Guidelines_en.pdf> accessed on August 7, 2024.

(f) *imposition or administering of any disciplinary measure, reprimand or other penalty, including a financial penalty;*
(g) *coercion, intimidation, harassment or ostracism;*
(h) *discrimination, disadvantageous or unfair treatment;*
(i) *failure to convert a temporary employment contract into a permanent one, where the worker had legitimate expectations that he or she would be offered permanent employment;*
(j) *failure to renew, or early termination of, a temporary employment contract;*
(k) *harm, including to the person's reputation, particularly in social media, or financial loss, including loss of business and loss of income;*
(l) *blacklisting on the basis of a sector or industry-wide informal or formal agreement, which may entail that the person will not, in the future, find employment in the sector or industry;*
(m) *early termination or cancellation of a contract for goods or services;*
(n) *cancellation of a licence or permit;*
(o) *psychiatric or medical referrals.*

Fear of retaliation is the main factor that influences one's decision not to blow the whistle.[8] In public procurement, large amounts of money and significant orders are at stake. The political, bureaucratic and business actors involved are interconnected, making it easy for them to engage in corrupt practices throughout the entire procurement process. Collusion and corruption often go hand in hand, with bid rigging frequently accompanying kickback schemes to ensure that a corrupt firm is selected as the winning bidder. Given this context, heads of procurement administration, who authorize the expenditures and handle procurement planning and budgeting, are susceptible to corruption. Front-line public servants also face risks of corruption when exercising discretion during the bidding process to select tenderers.[9] By prohibiting any form of retaliation, such as changing responsibilities, dismissal or withholding expected promotions, the European legislator encourages procurement officers to report illegal acts or omissions by bidding companies or the administrative elites without fear of hindering their professional development or career progression within the public administration. This is particularly crucial for procurement officers, as their advancement and working conditions are directly tied to elected politicians and administrative elites responsible for government programmes and departments.[10] Additionally, it is reassuring that in cases of

8 Emilie Hennequin "What Motivates Internal Whistleblowing? A Typology Adapted to the French Context" (2020), 38(5), *European Management Journal*; Sean Valentine and Lynn Godkin "Moral Intensity, Ethical Decision Making, and Whistleblowing Intention" (2019), 98, *Journal of Business Research*.

9 Andre Saddy "Front-line servants, discretion and corruption" in Gabriella M. Racca and Christopher R. Yukins (eds) *Integrity and Efficiency in Sustainable Public Contracts. Balancing Corruption Concerns in Public Procurement Internationally* (Bruylant, Brussels 2014), 346–347.

10 Dean Neu, Jeff Everett and Abu Shiraz Rahaman "Preventing Corruption within Government Procurement: Constructing the Disciplined and Ethical Subject" (2015), 28, *Critical Perspectives on Accounting*, 51, 56.

retaliatory measures, the burden of proof lies with the perpetrators of retaliation to demonstrate that their actions were not retaliatory.

Another provision that should be discussed is Article 8 of Directive (EU) 2019/1937, which addresses the obligation to establish internal reporting channels.

1. *Member States shall ensure that legal entities in the private and public sector establish channels and procedures for internal reporting and for follow-up, following consultation and in agreement with the social partners where provided for by national law.*
2. *The channels and procedures referred to in paragraph 1 of this Article shall enable the entity's workers to report information on breaches. They may enable other persons, referred to in points (b), (c) and (d) of Article 4(1) and Article 4(2), who are in contact with the entity in the context of their work-related activities to also report information on breaches.*
3. *Paragraph 1 shall apply to legal entities in the private sector with 50 or more workers.*
4. *The threshold laid down in paragraph 3 shall not apply to the entities falling within the scope of Union acts referred to in Parts I.B and II of the Annex.*
5. *Reporting channels may be operated internally by a person or department designated for that purpose or provided externally by a third party. The safeguards and requirements referred to in Article 9(1) shall also apply to entrusted third parties operating the reporting channel for a legal entity in the private sector.*
6. *Legal entities in the private sector with 50 to 249 workers may share resources as regards the receipt of reports and any investigation to be carried out. This shall be without prejudice to the obligations imposed upon such entities by this Directive to maintain confidentiality, to give feedback, and to address the reported breach.*
7. *Following an appropriate risk assessment taking into account the nature of the activities of the entities and the ensuing level of risk for, in particular, the environment and public health, Member States may require legal entities in the private sector with fewer than 50 workers to establish internal reporting channels and procedures in accordance with Chapter II.*
8. *Member States shall notify the Commission of any decision they take to require legal entities in the private sector to establish internal reporting channels pursuant to paragraph 7. That notification shall include the reasons for the decision and the criteria used in the risk assessment referred to in paragraph 7. The Commission shall communicate that decision to the other Member States.*
9. *Paragraph 1 shall apply to all legal entities in the public sector, including any entity owned or controlled by such entities.*
10. *Member States may exempt from the obligation referred to in paragraph 1 municipalities with fewer than 10,000 inhabitants or fewer than 50 workers,*

or other entities referred to in the first subparagraph of this paragraph with fewer than 50 workers.

11. *Member States may provide that internal reporting channels can be shared between municipalities or operated by joint municipal authorities in accordance with national law, provided that the shared internal reporting channels are distinct from and autonomous in relation to the relevant external reporting channels.*

The requirement for public and private sector legal entities to establish and secure confidential internal reporting channels is a positive step in the right direction. However, it has been argued that company reporting structures are often ineffective. In such cases, the mandatory internal reporting requirement may lead to the destruction or spoliation of evidence, undermining potential enforcement efforts.[11] Mandating internal reporting encourages companies and public authorities to foster a culture where employees feel comfortable reporting their suspicions, regardless of whether they choose to use the internal reporting channel as their first point of contact. The European legislator has granted reporting persons the ability to select the most suitable reporting channel based on the specific circumstances of the case.[12] However, concerns arise regarding paragraph 7, which states that Member States *may* mandate legal entities in the private sector with fewer than 50 workers to establish internal reporting channels and procedures. By allowing Member States the discretion to require small enterprises to establish their own internal reporting channels, Directive (EU) 2019/1937 lacks clear reporting procedures and obligations for small and micro-enterprises, despite their increasing participation and success rates in public procurement.[13] For example, an estimated 19% of public contracts above EU thresholds were awarded to micro-enterprises (companies with fewer than 10 employees), and approximately 22% were awarded to small enterprises (companies with fewer than 50 employees) between 2011 and 2017.[14] The significant presence of small and micro-enterprises in public contracts, along with the European legislator's efforts to support their participation in public procurement, highlights the need for mandatory reporting channels in these businesses.[15] This need is further emphasized by the fact small and medium enterprises have the

11 Erika Kelton from Phillips and Cohen LLP "Public Consultation and Feedback on the EU Whistleblower Protection" <https://ec.europa.eu/info/law/better-regulation/have-your-say/initiatives/1721-EU-Whistleblower-protection/F12720_en> accessed on August 11, 2024.

12 See Recital 33 of the Directive (EU) 2019/1937.

13 Directorate-General for Internal Market, Industry, Entrepreneurship and SMEs (European Commission) "Analysis of the SMEs' Participation in Public Procurement and the Measures to Support It: Final Report 2019" <https://op.europa.eu/en/publication-detail/-/publication/eec8227c-eec4-11ea-b3c6-01aa75ed71a1> accessed on August 11, 2024.

14 Ibid. See also Directorate-General for Internal Market, Industry, Entrepreneurship and SMEs (European Commission) "SME Definition" <https://single-market-economy.ec.europa.eu/smes/sme-fundamentals/sme-definition_en> accessed on August 11, 2024.

15 The 2014/24/EU Directive on public procurement provides guidance on how to adapt the procurement process to the needs of SMEs by applying the "European Code of Best Practices Facilitating

highest share of contracts won in smaller countries, such as Greece (90%), Malta (87%) and Cyprus (81%).[16] In these countries, corruption in public procurement managed by national authorities is considered "very or fairly widespread", with collusive bidding being identified as one of the most prevalent corrupt practices in public procurement.[17]

Likewise, paragraph 9 of Article 8 raises concerns because municipalities with fewer than 10,000 inhabitants or fewer than 50 workers may be exempted from establishing channels and procedures for internal reporting and follow-up. Across the EU, 52% of companies believe that corruption in public procurement managed by regional or local authorities is widespread in their country (19% "very widespread" and 34% "fairly widespread"). Therefore, in the realm of public procurement it is essential for small municipalities to have secure reporting channels. This allows municipal employees, who encounter issues in their work to feel encouraged to report them immediately, without worrying about external reporting procedures or the competent authorities who receive and follow up on external reports. These authorities may lack the necessary expertise, be too few in number, and susceptible to political influences. The lack of trust in external reporting channels is understandable when considering preamble (64), which states that Member States should designate the competent authorities to receive information on breaches covered by this Directive and appropriately follow up on reports. By leaving it to Member States to determine the competent authorities for receiving and following up on external reports, Directive (EU) 2019/1937 does not ensure that all whistle-blowers will be protected if they submit their report to any competent authority. This is concerning in Member States, such as Malta, where the competent authority receiving and following up on external reports may be susceptible to political influences.[18] Therefore, it is submitted that even small municipalities must have secure internal reporting channels. They make significant decisions in public procurement and are considered vulnerable to corrupt activities in this sector.

One last point that should be addressed regarding the potential of Directive (EU) 2019/1937 to incentivize reporting of competition law breaches in public procurement is the absence of provisions for monetary rewards. While experimental studies have shown that offering monetary rewards to whistle-blowers in the context of leniency programmes may have a greater impact on cartel detection, the European legislator did not include such a financial incentive for whistle-blowers

Access by SMEs to Public Procurement Contracts", for example, dividing large contracts into multiple smaller contracts.

16 Directorate-General for Internal Market, Industry, Entrepreneurship and SMEs (fn 13).

17 European Commission, Directorate-General for Migration and Home Affairs "Flash Eurobarometer 543 – Businesses' Attitudes towards Corruption in the EU – Report of 2024", 33, 37 <https://europa.eu/eurobarometer/surveys/detail/3180> accessed on August 11, 2024.

18 In Malta the "competent authority" to receive external reports is the Prime Minister's office. See Parliamentary Assembly: Council of Europe "Improving the Protection of Whistle-Blowers All over Europe: Report | Doc. 14958 | 30 August 2019" <https://assembly.coe.int/nw/xml/XRef/Xref-XML-2HTML-EN.asp?fileid=28096> accessed on August 11, 2024.

under Directive (EU) 2019/1937. In fact, according to Recital 30, individuals registered as informants who are entitled to receive a reward or compensation for reporting are not covered by the relevant Directive. This is likely because monetary rewards have been seen as detrimental to whistleblowing, as they could compromise the ethical nature of the act itself.[19] However, several studies have examined the role of financial incentives, and have found that they can motivate individuals to report misconduct and provide them with financial security in case of any retaliatory actions against them.[20] Additionally, monetary rewards can help counteract the effects of retaliation and increase public awareness, as substantial monetary rewards attract positive media attention, thereby reducing the stigma with whistle-blowers.[21]

When it comes to public procurement, monetary rewards are even more crucial for whistle-blowers who work in procurement administration. There is doubt as to whether they have the incentive to put in the effort to identify bidding rigging. According to the business ethics literature, public officers may see taxpayers as distant "clients" who are "unlikely to be viewed as potential victims, or hindrances when making procurement decisions".[22] This lack of social proximity and visibility reduces social accountability for procurement officers, as ethical conduct often depends on considering specific others when thinking about the consequences of unlawful action.[23] What is more, procurement officers are not judged on how many cartels they uncover but rather on their ability to manage bidding processes and ensure timely delivery of goods and services.[24] Any suspicion of bidding rig can delay the public purchasing process, negatively impacting the contracting authority and procurement officers, who are evaluated, among other things, on the speed of the bidding process. Furthermore, the fear of collusion and corruption in public procurement has created a dull and unappealing working environment for procurement bureaucrats. Their incentives for efficiency, competition and transparency are

19 Colin Grant "Whistle Blowers: Saints of Secular Culture" (2002), 39(4), *Journal of Business Ethics*, 391–399.

20 Paul Andon, et al. "The Impact of Financial Incentives and Perceptions of Seriousness on Whistleblowing Intention" (2018), 151, *Journal of Business Ethics*, 165–178; Hengky Latan, et al. "Ethical Awareness, Ethical Judgment and Whistleblowing: A Moderated Mediation Analysis" (2019), 155, *Journal of Business Ethics*, 289–304; Fabian Teichmann "Incentive systems in anti-bribery whistleblowing" (2019), 26(2), *Journal of Financial Crime*, 519–525; Peter Yeoh "Enhancing Effectiveness of Anti-Money Laundering Laws through Whistleblowing" (2014), 56(6), *International Journal of Law and Management*, 459–474.

21 Pamela H. Bucy "Information as a Commodity in the Regulatory World" (2002), 39(4), *Houston Law Review*, 971.

22 Neu, Everett and Rahaman (fn 10), 51. See also Kate McLaughlin, Stephen P. Osborne and Ewan Ferlie *New Public Management: Current Trends and Future Prospects* (London, Routledge, 2002).

23 Neu, Everett and Rahaman (fn 10), 51. See also Antonio Argadona "Corruption and Companies: The Use of Facilitating Payments" (2005), 60, *Journal of Business Ethics*, 251–264; Stelios C. Zyglidopoulos and Peter J. Fleming "Ethical Distance in Corrupt Firms: How Do Innocent Bystanders Become Guilty Perpetrators?" (2008), 78(1), *Journal of Business Ethics* 265–274.

24 Alberto Heimler "Cartels in Public Procurement" (2012) *Journal of Competition Law & Economics*, 11–23.

diminishing due to strict disciplinary controls, increased monitoring and integrity checks.[25] Hence, procurement officers may prefer to stick with known suppliers, avoiding the hassle of dismantling bidding rigs.[26] As a result, procurement officer have evidence of bid rigging strategies, but lack the motivation to blow the whistle.

For all these reasons, it is submitted that monetary rewards are necessary in public procurement to incentivize whistle-blowing. The Directive (EU) 2019/1937 should have included provisions for monetary rewards, at least within the realm of public procurement. This is particularly important because many procurement officers feel undervalues by their supervisors and inadequately compensated for their work.[27] In addition to monetary rewards, another method to promote whistle-blowing in public procurement could be linking the career advancement of procurement officers to the quantity and significance of bid rigging schemes they uncover and report.

9.3 Bid Rigging Whistle-Blowing in the United States of America: An Example to Follow?

Having recommended the granting of monetary rewards to whistle-blowers in the domain of public procurement in the European Union, it is now time to examine the paradigm of the US whistle-blower reward programmes. In the United States, there are four main whistle-blower reward programmes: the Securities and Exchange Commission programme, which rewards reporting violations of federal securities laws; the Commodity Futures Trading Commission programme, which rewards reporting violations of the Commodity Exchange Act; the Internal Revenue Service programme, which rewards reporting tax fraud or underpayments; and finally the False Claims Act (FCA) programme, which rewards reporting fraud against the government.[28] For the purposes of the current study, the focus will be on the FCA programme, since the FCA, 31 U.S.C. Sections 3729–3733 is an avenue for whistle-blowers, but also for the federal government of the United States to claim compensation in case of bid rigging.

25 OECD Competition Committee "Public Procurement: The Role of Competition Authorities in Promoting Competition"<www.oecd-ilibrary.org/docserver/8ed0c7ba-en.pdf?expires=1723587550&id=id&accname=guest&checksum=D6CE9E1A5CC017C97FD9D155171A3B64>accessed August 18, 2024.

26 Steven Kelman *Procurement and Public Management: The Fear Of Discretion and the Quality of Government Performance* (AEI Press 1990), 95.

27 Michelle Greenwood and James M Klotz "The Fight against Corruption in Public Procurement: An Introduction to Best Practices" in Roberto Hernandez Garcia (ed) *International Public Procurement: A Guide to Best Practice* (Global Business Publishing 2009), 61; OECD "Bribery in Public Procurement: Methods, Actors and Counter-Measures" <www.oecd.org/daf/anti-bribery/anti-briberyconvention/44956834.pdf> accessed August 13, 2014.

28 EQS Integrity Line "A Closer Look at the Ethics Behind Whistle-Blower Rewards" <www.integrityline.com/expertise/blog/ethics-behind-whistleblower-rewards/> accessed on August 19, 2024.

9.3.1 The Role of the FCA in Addressing Bid-Rigging and the Qui Tam Suits

The FCA is a civil statute that allows private citizens to file suit on behalf of the federal government against firms that have allegedly defrauded the government. The FCA applies wherever the government spends money, such as in the realm of public contracts. The United States has had a long and successful experience with the FCA, with nearly 12,000 lawsuits filed between 2000 and 2018 and over US$2.2 billion recovered in fiscal year 2022.[29] It is no wonder that the FCA is often referred to as the most effective tool for combatting fraud against the federal government.[30]

In the United States, bid rigging allegations can lead to prosecution under the FCA, if bid rigging constitutes an FCA violation. This typically occurs when the government is fraudulently induced into entering a public contract or if the contractor submits false invoices under the resulting contract. public contract. For example, bidding companies may engage in a collusive bidding scheme where they average the price of their bids and select one member of the rig one to submit a bid for the averaged amount, while others submit higher bids.[31] The FCA prohibits contractors from knowingly submitting false claims to the federal government to receive payment or reduce an existing obligation. As a result, the federal government can recover triple the damages it suffered from the false claim.[32] In addition to treble damages, the federal government can impose civil penalties on offenders for each violation of the FCA. While the FCA itself is a civil statute, underlying fraudulent conduct that violates the FCA can also lead to separate criminal prosecution under other federal statutes, demonstrating the multi-faceted approach of the Department of Justice to combatting fraud against the government.[33] Currently, FCA penalties can be as high as US$27,894 per violation.[34] This means that not only does the federal government recover financially from bid rigging schemes, but the perpetrators also face significant penalties, serving as a strong deterrent against bid rigging.

29 Department of Justice "False Claims Act Settlements and Judgments Exceed $2 Billion in Fiscal Year 2022" www.justice.gov/opa/pr/false-claims-act-settlements-and-judgments-exceed-2-billion-fiscal-year-2022> accessed September 8, 2023; Department of Justice "Justice Department Recovers Over $2.8 Billion from False Claims Act Cases in Fiscal Year 2018" <www.justice.gov/opa/pr/justice-department-recovers-over-28-billion-false-claims-act-cases-fiscal-year-2018> accessed September 8, 2023.

30 Justin P. Tschcoepe "A Fraud Against One Is Apparently a Fraud Against All: The Fraud Enforcement and Recovery Act's Unprecedented Expansion of Liability Under the False Claims Act" (2010), 47(3), *Houston Law Review*, 742; Andrew C. Call, et al. "Whistleblowers and Outcomes of Financial Misrepresentation Enforcement Actions" (2018), 56(1), *Journal of Accounting Research*; Patrick Leahy Hearing on the "False Claims Act Corrections Act of 2007: Strengthening the Government's Most Effective Tool Against Fraud for the 21st Century" (2008) in US Fed News Service, Including US State News. HT Digital Streams Limited.

31 Jessica Fickey "Fraud in the Bidding Process: The Limited Remedies Available to Contractors" (2009), 38(4), *Public Contract Law Journal*, 913–933.

32 False Claims Act, 31 U.S.C. §§ 3729(a).

33 False Claims Act, 31 U.S.C. §§ 3729.

34 Whistleblower Law Collaborative "False Claims Act Penalties: A Complete Guide" <www.whistleblowerllc.com/false-claims-act-penalties/> accessed on August 19, 2024.

The effectiveness of the FCA in combatting bid rigging related to fraudulently obtained public contracts would not be possible without the FCA's provision for qui tam suits. Qui tam suits are actions brought by private parties in the name of the federal government for false claims submitted by private contractors.[35] Specifically, the qui tam provisions of the FCA, 31 U.S.C. authorize private citizens, acting as whistle-blowers, and called relators in this situation, to initiate FCA actions to benefit the federal government and share in any recoveries. Relators/whistle-blowers are entitled to between 15–30% of the amount the government recovers as a result of the bid rigging. By providing the opportunity for bid rigging whistle-blowers to claim a portion of the recovered damages, whistle-blowing is encouraged. Employees of the infringing bidding undertakings have an additional incentive to come forward and reveal anticompetitive activities of their employers as well as corruption between them and procurement officers that would otherwise remain concealed. Moreover, whistle-blowers/relators can recover attorney fees and the costs of bringing the suit.

The relators/whistle-blowers must possess specialized knowledge of the circumstances surrounding the false claim beyond what the general public would know in order to initiate the action. They file the initial suit under seal and once the qui tam suit is filed, the relators/whistle-blowers' lawyers must present the evidence they have to the government. This process allows the whistle-blowers/relators to provide actionable evidence to the Antitrust Division potentially leading to a damage recovery for the relevant contracting authorities of the United States. Consequently, the procedural obstacles that contracting authorities typically encounter in Europe when seeking damages for bid rigging can be effectively overcome in the United States. During the 60-day seal period, the government investigates the allegations and has four options at its disposal: (a) to intervene in the suit and assume responsibility for the litigation, (b) to decline intervention and permit the whistle-blowers/relators to pursue the claim independently, (c) to dismiss the litigation, even if the whistle-blower/relator objects or (d) to attempt to settle the case.[36] If the government chooses not to intervene, it means that the whistle-blowers/relators can proceed with the litigation without the government's participation and financial support.[37] In such cases, the whistle-blower/relator receives between 25 and 30% of the recovery. However, if the government decides to intervene, the whistle-blower/relator receives between 15 and 25% of the recovery.

In view of the above, it appears that the United States' whistle-blowing programme offers many advantages compared to the new programme in Europe. The European programme does not provide financial incentives to private individuals to uncover and prevent breaches and distortions of competition, such as bid

35 31 U.S.C. §§ 3730(b)(1).

36 31 U.S.C. § 3729 et seq; Robert Rhoad and Matthew Fornataro "A Gathering Storm: The New False Claims Act Amendments and their Impact on Healthcare Fraud Enforcement" (2009), 21(6), *Health Lawyer*, 17.

37 Ibid.

rigging schemes. The first advantage of the FCA whistleblowing programme is that it allows for treble damage remedy. This means that public entities can recover three times the amount of damages they actually suffered as a result of bid rigging. The second advantage is that qui tam suits effectively address the challenges that contracting authorities in Europe typically encounter when seeking damages for bid rigging. These challenges include difficulties in collecting evidence of bid rigging and in specifying and quantifying the financial harm they have suffered. These issues are easily resolved in the United States with the assistance of whistleblowers who file FCA suits.

9.3.2 Are the Qui Tam Suits Efficient Means in Combatting Bid-Rigging? The Practitioners' Point of View

After reviewing the US financial incentive whistle-blower programme and its role in addressing bid-rigging, it is now time to examine the extent to which the tactics the United States is employing actually work. As already shown, from the perspective of information generation, the answer is affirmative. To draw a clearer picture of how qui tam suits are used in practice, how they function and combat bid rigging, interviews were conducted with 12 practitioners in the United States. The interviewees are attorneys representing clients in fraud against the government and antitrust matters or individuals in whistle-blower cases of fraud against the government. Some of them also acted prosecutors in the Antitrust Division of the United States Department of Justice (DoJ).

This empirical research was funded by the American Bar Association (ABA), Section of Antitrust Law in 2019, when the author was awarded the International Scholar-in-Residence scholarship by the Antitrust Section of the American Bar Association. The International Scholar-in-Residence Programme provides funding for early career competition law scholars to spend time in the United States for research purposes and to attend the Annual Spring Meeting of the ABA's Antitrust Section. It was during the Annual Spring Meeting of the ABA's Antitrust Section that the author managed to meet and identify most of the interviewees, who then put the author in touch with some other interviewees via email.

Interviews were conducted face-to-face, with the exception of one, which was held online via Skype, and lasted no more than one hour. They were recorded and upon completion a transcript was produced. The interviews were semi-structured, allowing the author to pursue their own agenda while also being responsive to the concerns of the interviewees. A predefined schedule of questions was created, but it was used as a guide rather than a strict outline for the interview. The questions posed to the interviewees were as follow: (a) What is your opinion on the length of proceedings in qui tam suits? (b) Can the procedure in qui tam suits be complex? If so, in what ways? (c) Can you identify any obstacles to the effective operation of qui tam suits? (d) What are your thoughts on the settlement agreements in qui tam suits?

Data collection took place from March to June 2019 and date analysis occurred from September to November 2019. The data was collected in a standardized format, then was synthesized, analyzed and critically appraised qualitatively in thematic units. In this chapter, the interview content summaries and direct quotations from the interviewees were intentionally anonymized to protect their identities and ensure that any identifying information is not disclosed.

9.3.2.1 The Length of Proceedings in Qui Tam Suits

The first interview question was about the length of proceedings in qui tam suits. All the interviewees emphasized that the proceedings are extremely long. They explained that the procedural framework of qui tam suits is unique. The whistle-blower/relator files the suit under seal and during this seal period, the DOJ reviews the written disclosure detailing the whistle-blower's/relator's evidence and information to decide whether to intervene in the case or not. This unique aspect of qui tam cases is a real barrier in terms of the process because the courts grant the DOJ broad extensions of the statutory 60-day period, resulting in the average DOJ investigation under seal lasting up to five years. Once the seal is lifted and the suit becomes public, the federal government has ample time to build its case, putting the defendant at an additional disadvantage. It was also noted that delays often come from motion practice, such as lack of pleadings' sufficiency, as well as dismissed cases that are appealed and then reversed. This means that qui tam suits can take up to seven years.

As a consequence, whistle-blowers have to wait significantly until the case is concluded. When there is no guarantee of a pay out at the end, the lengthy proceedings can discourage potential whistle-blowers from coming forward and speaking up. Moreover, lengthy proceedings can make it difficult for whistle-blowers to reverse threats, attempts or continuing acts of retaliation, such as harassment, or to prevent forms of retaliation, such as dismissal, which can ruin the individual financially and seriously discourage other potential whistle-blowers.

Another reason qui tam suits may take a long time to resolve is that bid rigging cases involve wealthy companies that do not want to admit to committing fraud or pay large amounts of money. Therefore, according to one interviewee, the companies' lawyers "fight to the death" in litigation. The interviewee also argued that in 2019 the global resolutions with South Korean companies, which rigged bids and fixed prices for fuel supply contracts issued by US military bases throughout South Korea, were remarkably simple and only an exception to the general rule. The same interviewee believes that South Korean companies agreed to plead guilty to criminal charges and concurrently enter into civil settlements, paying a total of US$236 million in criminal fines and civil damages because "culturally in Korea it is less acceptable for companies to simply fight to the death in litigation than it is here in the USA".

9.3.2.2 Complexity of Qui Tam Suits

The second interview question was about the complexity of qui tam suits in bid-rigging cases. The complexity of US enforcement in bid rigging cases often stems from the interplay of criminal antitrust prosecutions, civil antitrust actions, and civil fraud cases under the False Claims Act. It is crucial to distinguish between criminal resolutions, such as plea agreements and deferred prosecution agreements (DPAs), and civil resolutions, often formalised through civil consent decrees or judgments, as each carries distinct legal implications and remedies. Most interviewees mentioned the parallel proceedings that occur when civil FCA, antitrust and criminal enforcement intersect in cases involving bid rigging schemes. In bid rigging schemes, criminal and antitrust proceedings can stem from FCA actions, when the federal government is a victim of an antitrust violation. Section 4A of the Clayton Act and Section 15a of the US Code, part of the Clayton Act, authorize the United States to sue on its own behalf when it is the victim of an antitrust violation, such as bid rigging by private firms selling to the United States. Section 4A was created in 1955 the Clayton Act was amended to provide the United States a cause of action for single damages.[38] In 1990, further amendments were made to allow the United States a cause of action for treble damages.[39] While the DOJ's use of the FCA alongside criminal and antitrust statutes helps the federal government obtain significant recoveries to deter and combat collusion in public contracts, parallel proceedings may be impractical. For example, they can prolong the resolution of cases. Most interviewees underlined that assessing damages can take years, while criminal cartel investigations require momentum, especially in large international cartel cases, where one plea agreement provides evidence and leads to the next targets. If the authorities pause to assess damages, it can slow down the criminal investigations and hinder success. One interviewee noted that by pursuing three separate proceedings against a bid-rigger, "incurs a cost to the overall effort of cartel enforcement". This is particularly true where the secrecy of an investigation is paramount to its success.

Additionally, when the case is based on the same illegal conduct and there are parallel and/or joint investigations and proceedings, there is the prohibition of double recovery. Therefore, Department attorneys should be vigilant in ensuring that they do not misuse their criminal enforcement authority to unfairly obtain or seek additional civil or administrative monetary payments. Another challenge for Department attorneys is to coordinate with and consider the fines, penalties and/or forfeitures paid to other federal, state, local or foreign enforcement authorities that are also seeking to resolve a case with a company for the same anticompetitive conduct.[40] To do this, all relevant factors should be taken into account, such as the severity of a company's misconduct, statutory requirements for penalties, fines and forfeitures, the potential for unnecessary delays in reaching a final resolution and the completeness and

38 Harry First "Lost in Conversation: The Compensatory Function of Antitrust Law" (2010) New York University Law and Economics Working Paper No. 10–14 <https://papers.ssrn.com/sol3/papers.cfm?abstract_id=1579343> accessed on August 28, 2024, 49.

39 Ibid, 50.

40 The Justice Manual, Title 1-12.000 – Coordination of Parallel Criminal, Civil, Regulatory, and Administrative Proceedings confirms this <www.justice.gov/jm/jm-1-12000-coordination-parallel-criminal-civil-regulatory-and-administrative-proceedings> accessed January 5, 2025.

timeliness of a company's disclosure and cooperation with the DOJ.[41] This should be separate from any disclosures and cooperation with other enforcement authorities.[42] However, damages actions under Section 4A of the Clayton Act can provide a recovery to the federal government exceeding the criminal penalty and qui tam proceeds because Department attorneys are able to consider additional remedies in appropriate circumstances, such as when those remedies are intended to recover the government's money lost due to misconduct or provide restitution to victims.[43]

Furthermore, as four interviewees explained, bringing a claim under Section 4A of the Clayton Act can give the federal government more options and leverage in negotiations with bid-riggers before global settlements are reached. The aggressive use of Section 4A of the Clayton Act also tends to increase the settlement amount of money paid to the federal government to resolve antitrust violations.

The Tunney Act (15 U.S.C.§16(b)-(h)) was also mentioned as an advantage of filing under Section 4A, particularly as it requires judicial review of the DOJ's proposed consent judgments in civil antitrust cases to ensure they are in the public interest. The Act mandates the disclosure of settlement information through a competitive impact statement (CIS), published in the Federal Register as well as in a general circulation newspaper in the district in which the case was filed to inform the public and allow public comments on the proposed settlement.[44] Public comments inform the court's decision on the settlement's public interest. However, the same interviewees underlined that while the Tunney Act prevents cheap settlements, modifications based on public comments are rare, and hearings on proposed settlements are infrequent, as most are approved through written submissions.

Additionally, some interviewees, including former prosecutors in the Antitrust Division of the DOJ, highlighted the complexities arising from the cooperation and information sharing between different DOJ components in parallel proceedings. While formal mechanisms and internal directives, such as the Justice Manual, mandate coordination, interviewees noted that a practical disconnect can sometimes exist between the Antitrust (criminal) and Civil Divisions of the DOJ regarding antitrust crimes in public procurement. This perceived reluctance among some Antitrust Division prosecutors to fully share information with the Civil Division, often driven by strategic concerns, like protecting ongoing criminal investigations, can complicate civil damages actions against bid riggers and impact monetary rewards for whistle-blowers.

Moreover, some Government Agencies were mentioned as not being good record keepers. Concerns that lawsuits against bid rigging companies could complicate future procurement efforts to obtain necessary goods or services may also lead some agencies to be hesitant to fully cooperate with the Civil Division of the DOJ. This emphasizes the significance of information from private citizens in public procurement to demonstrate and establish anticompetitive conduct.

41 Ibid.

42 Ibid.

43 Ibid.

44 Michael A. Gleason, et al. "It Ain't Over till It's Over: Review of DOJ M&A Settlements Under the Tunney Act" (2019), 23(9), *The M&A Lawyer*.

9.3.2.3 *Obstacles to the Effective Operation of Qui Tam Suits*

The third interview question focused on identifying obstacles that may impede the effective operation of qui tam suits in bid-rigging cases. Most interviewees brought up the challenging and strict standard of materiality, which was articulated by the US Supreme Court in the Escobar case.[45] According to the materiality assessment in the Escobar case, a claim is deemed not material if the non-compliance is considered minor or insubstantial.[46] Also, if the Government has actual knowledge of non-compliance and still pays, that is strong evidence against materiality.[47] During the interviews, participants expressed concerns about how materiality impacts on the government's burden of proof as well as the frequency and dollar value of bid-rigging settlements. The circuit split on the application of Escobar's materiality standard was also mentioned by interviewees as an obstacle to the effective operation of qui tam suits in bid-rigging cases.

However, based on a recent assessment of publicly available information regarding FCA settlements for procurement-related fraud between 2011 and 2014, as well as from 2018 to 2020, it is evident that the impact of Escobar does not result in reduced or significantly altered FCA enforcement trends.[48] Contrary to the interviewees' concerns, Escobar has not led to a decrease in the government's FCA enforcement efforts. The data on post-Escobar settlements demonstrate that the FCA remains a potent enforcement tool.

9.3.2.4 *Settlement Agreements in Qui Tam Suits*

The fourth interview question delved into the nature of settlement agreements, particularly in qui tam suits and bid rigging cases. Interviewees were asked to share their thoughts on how these agreements, which can encompass a range of resolutions including plea agreements, deferred prosecution agreements (DPAs), and civil settlements (sometimes formalised as consent decrees), are reached and their implications. Most of them believe that such settlements are the prevailing outcome in bid rigging cases, with actual trials being rare. The reasons mentioned for this were various. Almost all interviewees stated that going to trial is very expensive and resource-intensive. Some of them stated that at the onset of bid-rigging cases, it is often unclear if there has been a complaint from a whistle-blower, as things are typically kept under seal. This uncertainty means that bid-riggers face the prospect of negotiating various types of resolutions, which could include a criminal plea agreement or a deferred prosecution agreement (DPA) with the Antitrust Division, a civil settlement with the Civil Fraud Division, or a civil settlement directly with the Relator. This multifaceted enforcement landscape, coupled with the potent tools like Section 4A of the Clayton Act and the FCA, makes reaching a

45 Universal Health Services, Inc. v United States ex rel. Escobar, 579 US 176 (2016)

46 Ibid.

47 Ibid.

48 Thomas Daley, Sam Knowles, Dawn Stern "The Impact of Escobar and the Procurement Collusion Strike Force on Procurement-Related False Claims Act Settlements" (2022), 57(2), *The Procurement Lawyer.*

comprehensive settlement or resolution crucial for companies seeking release from all major liabilities. Interviewees also mentioned the risk of potentially losing the trial, especially considering the evidentiary challenges that may arise, and facing severe penalties, such as treble damages, as another reason. From the government's perspective, the settlement will, at the very least, provide some partial restitution. This is preferable to seeking more restitution but facing greater uncertainty, which could potentially result in no financial gain in a trial. Moreover, the relevant government agency may be at fault for not maximizing competition or identifying bid rigging, even though they should have realized that bid rigging was occurring. As a result, they may feel embarrassed and prefer to reach a comprehensive settlement or resolution instead of proceeding to trial.

9.4 Conclusions

Whistle-blowing is crucial to the EU's efforts to hold companies accountable for anticompetitive infringements, such as bid rigging. However, whistle-blower protection used to be fragmented across the EU. To address this issue, the recent EU legal regime for whistle-blower protection (Directive 2019/1937/EU) has been adopted. This chapter examines to what extent this Directive encourages whistle-blowers to provide actionable evidence to National Competition Authorities, leading to the enforcement of competition law in public procurement.

Upon assessing the Directive, it becomes clear that several provisions are steps in the right direction. Explicit provisions protecting individuals who report breaches in public procurement and competition law make it more likely for them to come forward and blow the whistle on anticompetitive conduct in procurement bidding. It is also commendable that the Directive covers not only the private but also the public sector offering protection to civil servants and individuals working under contractors, suppliers and subcontractors. The procurement profession is a civil service profession, and subcontractors are common in public procurement, especially for large and complex contracts.

Equally important is the provision that prohibits retaliation, such as changes in responsibilities, dismissal or withholding expected promotions. Promotion and working conditions of procurement officers are directly linked to elected politicians and administrative elites who may be involved in bid rigging and corruption. Additionally, the burden of proof in case of retaliatory measures will be on those who took such actions, requiring them to demonstrate that their actions were not retaliatory.

While there have been positive steps, as shown above, there is still room for improvement and further incentivization of whistle-blowers to provide actionable evidence to detect and deter bid rigging in public procurement. Based on my analysis, I recommend that linking the career progression of procurement officers to the identification and reporting of bidding rigs could further encourage whistle-blowing. It is also crucial to ensure that even small municipalities have safe internal reporting channels as they make significant decisions in public procurement and are susceptible to corrupt activities. Small enterprises should also have their own internal reporting channels and clear reporting procedures, given their increasing participation and success rates in public procurement. Last but not least, I recommend implementing monetary rewards in public procurement to incentivize whistle-blowing. The Directive should consider this, at least in the realm of public procurement. Monetary rewards incentivize procurement officers to put in the effort to identify bidding rigs.

In order to better support my suggestion, I also analyzed the paradigm of the US financial incentive whistle-blowing programme, which has proven to be highly effective and offers numerous advantages when compared to the new programme in Europe. Triple damages are a key benefit of the US financial incentive whistle-blowing programme. Essentially, this means that public entities can recover three times the amount of money they would have lost if bid rigging had not taken place. Also, qui tam lawsuits effectively address the challenges that European contracting authorities typically encounter when seeking to recoup damages from bid rigging. Some of these obstacles include identifying and quantifying the financial losses suffered, as well as collecting evidence of bid rigging.

Based on the interviews I also conducted with 12 practitioners in the United States, the advantages of the US financial incentive whistle-blowing programme outweigh any disadvantages. The DOJ can use the FCA in conjunction with criminal and antitrust statutes (Clayton Act, Section 4A). Damages actions under Section 4A of the Clayton Act can result in the federal government receiving more in recovery than just the criminal penalty and qui tam proceeds. The ability to pursue additional remedies in certain situations assists the federal government in securing substantial recoveries to prevent and address collusion in public contracts. Also, according to several interviewees, filing a claim under Section 4A of the Clayton Act can provide the federal government with more alternatives and bargaining power when negotiating with bid-riggers before global settlements. The amount of money paid to the federal government as part of a settlement to address antitrust breaches also tends to increase when Section 4A of the Clayton Act is used aggressively.

Some interviewees emphasized, however, that qui tam suits can be extremely protracted, taking up to seven years to resolve, with no guarantee of a pay-out in the end. This may discourage potential whistle-blowers from coming forward and speaking up. Also, the collaboration among the different DOJ departments poses a challenge due to the interconnected nature of the FCA, criminal and antitrust proceedings. It has been noted that the Antitrust and Civil Divisions of the DOJ often do not communicate effectively when it comes to antitrust violations in public procurement, as some Antitrust Division prosecutors are reluctant to be overly transparent about their cases and share information with the Civil Division. Yet, it should be noted that since 2019, there have been significant changes in the field of procurement. The establishment of the Procurement Collusion Strike Force (PCSF) has been a positive step in addressing antitrust issues within the procurement context. The PCSF is an interagency partnership that includes prosecutors from US Attorney's Offices, the Department of Justice Antitrust Division, investigators from the Federal Bureau of Investigation, and a variety of federal agencies. This shows that whenever there is political will for improvement, substantial changes can be made.

10 Concluding Chapter

10.1 Key Findings of Each Chapter and How They Answer the Research Questions

This monograph advocates for a discussion on bid rigging which is a serious violation of competition law. It can inflate the prices of public contracts for essential goods or services and prevent public sector procurers from obtaining true value for their money.[1] Therefore, bid rigging must be openly addressed and prioritized by law and policy makers, as well as procurement officers.

Following the Introduction of the book, Chapter 2 introduced readers to auction theory and explained in simple terms the motivations behind bid riggers colluding, cheating and deviating from collusive agreements. Auction design, which refers to the rules governing each contract put out for tender, complements antitrust enforcement and significantly reduces the likelihood and effectiveness of collusion. For this reason, auction theory serves as a benchmark in this book to suggest the optimal design of public tendering and evaluate whether current procurement rules align with the principles of auction theory. Chapter 1 concluded that the selection of the auction system impacts collusion and that different auction formats are more suitable for specific procurement contexts.

Chapter 2 aimed to identify the circumstances under which collusion is preferred over competition in common auction types similar to current public procurement processes and techniques. This chapter addressed the research question of how anticompetitive behaviour undermines the procurement process. It also recognized that auction theory has inherent limitations in public procurement, as it does not offer universal solutions applicable at the EU level. Some auction theory recommendations may not be practical in the context of public procurement due to high costs for procuring entities and bidders. Hence, any future reform of public procurement rules should consider these factors.

After establishing a rationale for the book and identifying the key theories related to the research approach, Chapter 3 delved into the legislative background of the current EU procurement regime. It traced the development and critical

1 Competition and Markets Authority "Public Sector Procurers: Bid-Rigging Advice" <www.gov.uk/government/collections/bid-rigging-advice-and-tools-for-public-sector-procurers> accessed on August 10, 2019.

DOI: 10.4324/9781003359999-10

junctures of EU procurement rules in relation to anti-cartel legislation in Europe. The chapter highlighted that the current European Public Sector Directive 2014/24/EU does not primarily focus on deterring bid rigging in the procurement process. Little attention has been given to preventing bid rigging in the design and development of procurement rules. Despite increasing regulatory concerns about the need for a pro-competitive design of public procedures and the recognition of bid rigging's undesirability in the public procurement regime, the current Directive is not collusion-proof. There is still much progress to be made in this area. This is due to the fact that the critical junctures of EU procurement rules did not coincide with the development of anti-cartel legislation in Europe, but rather emerged independently. Moreover, the public procurement regime primarily aims to regulate the conduct of contracting authorities rather than bidders. Building on this premise, the argument that safeguards against collusion in tender procedures are weak was further developed in the following chapter, Chapter 4.

Chapter 4 focused on the pre-contractual procurement planning stage and identified three critical areas that raise concerns about collusion. The first was when contracting authorities conduct market consultations, the second was when they formulate technical specifications and the third was when they divide public contracts into lots with a view to preparing the procurement. To better understand the circumstances under which collusion risks arise in this stage, the chapter examined specific instances of collusion. This addressed the second research question of the book, which is the scope of bid rigging during procurement planning stage.

The chapter then recommended legislative and soft law measures to ensure fair competition and prevent collusion during the procurement planning stage. It also discussed the advantages and disadvantages of such measures in terms of complexity and administrative burdens and transaction costs. These recommendations addressed the third research question of the book, which is what legislative and soft law instruments are necessary to limit or prevent bid rigging among economic operators during the procurement planning stage.

Overall, the analysis in Chapter 4 showed that collusion during procurement planning can be managed under current rules and public-sector auditing has a promising future in limiting and preventing collusion in public procurement. Contracting authorities should avoid direct contact with market operators and if necessary, have a policy for conducting preliminary market consultations. The chapter also highlighted the uncertainty surrounding the concept of "equivalent" in technical specifications and its impact on the number of competing bidders in the bidding stage.

Furthermore, it emphasized the risk of giving contracting authorities excessive discretion in evaluating the equivalence of proposed solutions with technical specifications. If a contracting authority misuses its discretionary power or fails to evaluate equivalence in a flexible and procompetitive manner, it can lead to issues. Another important point made in Chapter 4 was that the shift towards performance-based specifications may result in a failure to maintain the desired competitive tension in the procurement process and could sustain bidding rings in the relevant market. Performance-based specifications require public procurers to fully understand their needs and the problem to be addressed. However, contracting authorities may easily fail to comprehend what the market offers or to clearly articulate their needs. Also, the interaction of performance-based specifications with preliminary market consultations which are not properly regulated by current procurement rules, inhibits fair competition and may favour collusive schemes. Finally, Chapter 4 demonstrated that the two basic rules of economic theory that should prevent collusive practices when a public contract is divided into lots, are not panacea for all cases. The 2014/24/EU Directive has not addressed their weaknesses and thus they require further elaboration and amendments. To this end, Chapter 4 provided relevant recommendations for this purpose.

Chapter 5 discussed the stage of the procurement process after procurement planning, specifically the competitive bidding stage. The chapter focused on key aspects of the procurement process, specifically procedures and techniques outlined in the 2014/24/EU Directive, that are at risk of being misused for collusion. It critically reviewed features of the open and restrictive procedure, competitive dialogue, innovation partnership, negotiated procedures without prior publication, framework agreements and electronic auctions.

To better understand under what circumstances these procurement procedures and techniques may be exploited by bidders for collusion, several conclusions were drawn regarding each procurement procedure and technique. The first finding highlighted the risk of bid rigging when public procurers have discretion to choose between the open and restricted procedure without considering the values and circumstances of each Member State. The second finding noted the risk of bid rigging when negotiated procedures without prior publication are used to award public contracts to consortia of economic operators for technical reasons. Due to the lack of competition, the advanced technologies involved, and the tendency of procurement officers to misuse negotiated procedures to benefit specific economic operators, it is very likely that "sham" consortia between potential competitors will form.

The third finding pointed out that in a competitive dialogue, amicable splits and bid suppression schemes may occur, especially when there are only two participants at the post-dialogue phase. The fourth finding focused on innovation partnerships and the challenge of contracting authorities not being able to provide precise information during the competitive phase. This lack of information can hinder the ability to make a correct decision that is truly competition-oriented and based on the most suitable partner(s). This may limit competition unnecessarily, especially at a point in the process where there is no substantial proof that the preferred supplier(s) will be able to offer a better solution than those that have been excluded. The fifth finding highlighted inherent structural inefficiencies in framework agreements under the 2014/24/EU Directive. The sixth finding discussed how e-auctions, through the amount of information disclosed, the multi-round format, the price they have as an award criterion, and the way that they can close, can facilitate coordination among tenderers, leading to collusion. In this way, Chapter 5 answered the fourth research question regarding aspects of procurement procedures and techniques that heighten the likelihood of bid rigging and may be misused by (potential) suppliers.

It concluded that design features should be adopted to reduce collusive outcomes, ensuring fair competition for public contracts. Recommendations were made to prevent or limit collusion when using relevant procurement procedures and techniques. Through these recommendations, the fifth research question was answered about what legislative and soft law measures are needed to deter collusion in procurement procedures and techniques.

With the completion of the aforementioned chapters, the monograph has identified all the strengths and weaknesses of the 2014/24/EU Directive's design regarding the limitation and prevention of collusion throughout the procurement process. Yet, the study would remain incomplete without research on the policies that competition regulators can bring to the area of public procurement to complement those of procurement regulators. This is with the aim of limiting or preventing bid rigging. Therefore, Chapter 6 of the book focused on leniency, which is a competition law enforcement mechanism. It argued that there is interference of procurement remedies, such as the debarment mechanism and self-cleaning defence, with cartel enforcement. The chapter highlighted that the debarment of leniency recipients from public contracts for a significant period of three years makes the leniency programme unattractive. Moreover, the obligation of leniency recipients to disclose even leniency statements to government agencies to prove in the context of self-cleaning defence that they have regained trustworthiness in the market, increases the exposure of leniency applicants to civil litigation initiated by procurement entities.

In view of these conflicting policies, Chapter 6 concluded that leniency cannot work successfully in public procurement, thus answering negatively the sixth research question. It becomes apparent that collusive schemes in public procurement can only be deterred to a limited extent by leniency, as there is interference of the debarment mechanism and self-cleaning defence with the leniency programme. Therefore, the chapter suggested the total exemption of the first leniency applicant, that is, the immunity recipient, from the debarment mechanism. Also, Chapter 6 suggested that the debarment period should be halved for all other beneficiaries of leniency and that their leniency application and cooperation with the CA should be seen as a demonstration of genuine intention to confess anticompetitive activities and restore trustworthiness in the market. These recommendations aimed to answer the second part of the sixth research question, which is about what measures should be taken in order to enhance the role of public enforcement as deterrent to collusion in public procurement.

Chapter 7 of the book explored how competition regulators can complement procurement regulators in the realm of public procurement by focusing on private enforcement of competition law. The main conclusion drawn was that the Damages Directive has not adequately equipped contracting authorities to recover damages for bid rigging. Recommendations were proposed to make it easier for contracting authorities and other potential claimants to seek damages for bid rigging. These recommendations addressed the sixth research question of the book, which is about the measures that should be taken to enhance the role of public and private enforcement as deterrents to collusion in public procurement.

Chapter 7 also considered the possibility of introducing alternative compensatory remedies for contracting authorities, based on contractual principles. It examined whether liquidated damages clauses, which specify compensation for breach of contract o terms, are more effective than damages actions based on tort liability. As Chapter 7 showed, the benefits of liquidated damages clauses outweigh any drawbacks, despite uncertainties about their validity. Finally, Chapter 7 evaluated the extent to which divestiture and donations could be used in the EU as a viable alternative to damages claims for bid rigging. The main conclusion drawn was that donations can be a viable alternative to damage claims for bid rigging if specific criteria are fulfilled. On the other hand, divestitures were deemed inadequate as compensatory measures for bid rigging in European public procurement. However, they can potentially be utilized alongside damage claims for bid rigging, if they align with the EU principle of proportionality and are not enforced on excluded companies. This discussion addressed the seventh research question of the book, which focuses on identifying recommendations to remedy bid rigging outcomes in EU procurement law through public and private enforcement.

10.2 Policy Recommendations

Based on the above main findings, the monograph put forward a number of recommendations specifically geared at public purchasers, law and policy makers to better design, set up and manage public tenders without becoming victims of collusive schemes. At the same time, an attempt was made to keep low as much as possible any complexity and administrative burdens/transaction costs. For this reason, at many points the book balanced realistically the costs and possible negative impacts of the suggested measures on public administrative efficiency with their benefits in terms of reducing bid rigging and concerted practices in public procurement.

Chapter 2 of the book suggested the frequent use of descending-bid auctions (i.e. electronic auctions under Article 35 of the Directive 2014/24/EU), because the quick manner in which a bidder can get the auctioned item, as well as the finality of bids make risky and costly the sustainability of a bidding ring. The chapter also highlighted the importance of the common value uncertainty and the non-disclosure of bids in descending-bid auctions, because in this way concerted practices are deterred. The philosophical commitment to making procurement processes as transparent as possible increases the risk of collusion. Chapter 2 presented as a good collusion fighting technique the combination of the increased number of incumbent bidders with the sufficiently small number of contracts to be awarded, whenever there is suspicion of collusion in a market. It also recommended an aggressive reserve price as the best response to the formation of a bidding ring. In the same vein, it was underlined that the award procedures should be held at irregular and longer intervals and for relatively large items, such as packages of separate items. In case of significant complementarities between public contracts divided into lots, the public purchaser should enable bidders to place a single bid that would be "all or nothing" on combinations or packages of items, instead of restricting them to the submission of one bid per lot. Also, public officers were advised to record, document and make publicly available all bid data after the procurement process, in order to facilitate the prosecution of collusion by public enforcement authorities and/or private litigants.

Chapter 3 of the book recommended that there should be more dialogue between institutional actors at the EU level that deal with public procurement and competition. Nevertheless, the different policy departments that are in charge of competition and public procurement issues, that is, DG for Competition and DG for Internal Market, Industry, Entrepreneurship and SMEs accordingly, tend to inhibit the achievement of this goal, as their institutional priorities and the values of their personnel usually diverge. In lack of neat dovetailing and cohesion between these two DGs, the chapter applauded the European Commission's initiative to bring the national procurement bodies closer to its DG for Competition, by initiating cooperation with the European Competition Network.

Chapter 4 of the book proceeded to further recommendations regarding the market analysis process. Procurement officers should avoid a face-to-face discussion with economic operators before launching a procurement procedure, because in the absence of clear red lines of what they should and should not do, the risk of bid rigging can be enhanced. Article 58, paragraph 4 of the current Directive 2014/24/EU about conflict of interests, is a good starting point for calling a halt to the economic operators' undue involvement in preparing the procurement procedure, but there is still need for the European Commission to provide practical guidance to procurement agents on (a) the extent of their duty to investigate the conflict of interests, (b) the threshold of proof, (c) the measures to be taken if this conflict of interests is detected and (d) the judicial consequences deriving from it. The chapter also suggested the adoption of a single soft law mechanism by the European Commission that would control procurement officers in the technical dialogue with market operators, because so far it is up to each Member State to issue guidance notes regarding the way the market analysis should be conducted.

Additionally, it was stressed that contracting authorities should have a policy for undertaking preliminary market consultation prior to initiating the formal procurement procedure. It was further recommended that contracting authorities should draft and submit at the end of every market analysis process a report outlining the issues that have been considered, the research resources and the information used and obtained in the context of the market dialogue as well as the main conclusions drawn. The report should also be published and sent to the interested economic operators, but without referring to the identity and number of the economic operators that responded to the invitation to participate in the technical dialogue. The disclosure of such information would facilitate the implementation of a cartel existing among the economic operators. By the same rationale, the report should not include the specific points of the tender documents that the contracting authority intends to modify after the preliminary market consultation, because this would facilitate cartel redistributions. Additionally, this report should consist of an updated self-declaration confirming that the procurement officers conducting the preliminary market consultations acted in accordance with the guidelines of their authority, communicated to all candidates and tenderers the information exchanged during or resulting from the market dialogue phase and did not get involved in corrupt practices.

Regarding the concern of corrupted procurement officers in face-to-face meetings, Chapter 4 suggested to include at least one neutral observer during any face-to-face discussions with the economic operators. The neutral person could indicatively be an employee from the relevant contracting authority that procured the product/work/service at issue. Also, a strict functional and physical separation was suggested between the procurement officers that conduct face-to-face discussions and launch a preliminary market consultation and those assessing the bids and award the contract. Another recommendation was the cooperation of contracting authorities with CAs, where the former want to gather information relevant to the structure of the market and the latter possess this information in the context of recent market investigations they carried out. Regarding the high degree of discretion that contracting authorities have when deciding about economic operators' conflict of interests, the accountability of procurement officers was again recommended. This can be achieved by introducing internal control and audit in procurement entities and by adopting effective mechanisms for filing complaints and challenging procurement decisions like these.

Apart from recommendations about the market analysis process, Chapter 4 also dealt with the meaning of the words "*or equivalent*" that accompany any listed technical specifications in contract notices. It recommended the interpretation that Professor Sue Arrowsmith made, according to which the concept of "*equivalent*" is a restatement of the general principle in the Treaty that purchasers may not reject products or services that offer exactly the same functional performance as those specified or exceed it. The exclusion of products, services or service providers from other Member States that do not meet exactly the same technical requirements as those specified by contracting authorities, but they do offer the same functional performance, can limit the market, create a certain level of lock out and result in a small and manageable group of suppliers. This group of suppliers will probably consist of incumbent undertakings, as they will be the only ones in the market feeling confident to deliver on the relevant contract. Under such circumstances, that is, limited market with few suppliers, the chances of bid rigging are enhanced.

Last but not least, a number of recommendations were made about the division of contracts into lots, underlining that the amount of information disclosed about the bidder identities should be minimized and the matter of bid withdrawals should be regulated in a stricter way. Specifically, there should be sufficient justification and adequate evidence on behalf of the firms that withdraw their bids, otherwise the bid withdrawal should be forbidden. Moreover, it is necessary for the European legislator to address the issue regarding the pricing strategy that a bidder can adopt, when bundling of lots is permissible. It was suggested that Article 46, paragraph 2, subparagraph 1 of the 2014/24/EU Directive should be interpreted in a way that a bidder cannot offer for all the lots (or a combination of some) a price lower than the one he offers for the individual lots. Though by adopting such an interpretation the value for money may be compromised, the intensity of competition in the public tender is secured, as well as the participation of SMEs.

Chapter 5 made further recommendations, this time about procurement procedures and techniques. It recommended the use of open procedure as the default method, unless specified exceptions apply. The 2011 Model Law of UNCITRAL was used as a role model and particular attention was paid to Article 28, which contemplates when a procuring entity may engage in procurement by means of restricted tendering. Moreover, it was suggested that the procuring entity shall justify each time its decision to use a method of procurement other than open tendering and procurement officers should generally obtain a grounding in competition law and get incentivized to work efficiently, otherwise they can easily be tempted by corrupt practices and acts of bribery. Then, the negotiated procedure without prior publication was considered and it was argued that it is a procurement procedure out of the more transparent domain. Therefore, the chapter suggested to make mandatory the "voluntary ex ante transparency notice" (VEAT), every time competition is absent for technical reasons and so the public contracts are awarded under a negotiated procedure without prior publication. In this way, the market will be notified of the contracting authority's intention to conclude the relevant public contract and so any interested person will be able to decide with full knowledge of the relevant facts if it will bring an action before the national review body. As far as the competitive dialogue is concerned, it was suggested that there should be a requirement of at least three participants in the relevant process, where only two selected candidates compete with each other at the post-dialogue phase. However, the number of competitors is not always the solution to make competition efficient and sometimes it may not be feasible to promote the number of competitors at the final stage of a competitive dialogue. Therefore, before forcing a higher number of competitors at the final stage of the competitive dialogue, it was recommended that contracting authorities should check whether the two remaining firms are vulnerable to coordinated conduct or not, considering a number of suggested parameters. After dealing with the competitive dialogue, Chapter 5 turned to innovation partnership and highlighted, as already mentioned, the difficulty of contracting authorities to identify, cost and describe (even in outline terms) the need for an innovative solution at the early competitive stage, where the innovative products, services or works are still an idea under discussion. For this reason, it was underlined that public procurement officers should have a good grasp of the market to articulate specialized and complex needs as accurately as possible and avoid in this way the exclusion from negotiations of potentially suitable candidates. To this end, the chapter recommended the appointment of innovation brokers and the formation of cooperative procurement, either through the establishment of central purchasing bodies or through the public purchasers' networks and associations that collaborate only on an ad-hoc basis.

In the last section of Chapter 5, the procurement techniques were discussed. What was highlighted was the need for some guidance about how framework agreements should be used by each Member State. Procurement officers should investigate the vulnerability to collusion of the market for a particular framework agreement either at the first or at the second stage of the procedure. At the first stage, they should also check the degree of symmetry between suppliers and call-offs and try to ensure asymmetry in order to hamper the coordination of any colluding framework awardees. Similarly, at the second stage, they should ensure asymmetry between the value of contracts awarded and the framework awardees. However, these suggestions require close cooperation between CAs and public procurement agencies, which may seem to be rather unrealistic, given the limited resources available to both CAs and public procurement agencies[2] and the considerable sum of money needed to obtain such information. Moreover, we should not forget that the objectives of procurement and competition officials do not always converge, as their institutional priorities are different. Public procurement agencies primarily aim at ensuring smooth procurement procedures and techniques and they are particularly interested in their timely realization.[3] On the other hand, CAs give priority to antitrust and market investigations, without worrying about the interruption of procurement procedures and techniques or the invalidation of the tender outcomes.[4] In addition, the fact that under the current procurement regime there is no provision for mandatory collaboration between them fans the flames of this divergence. For these reasons, there is need not only to set up a mechanism for communication between public procurement agencies and CAs, but also to allocate them the costs in case a market study or a market investigation is requested by a public procurement agency and to share their resources. What is more, it is necessary to list specific information that the procurement officers should submit each time they contact the CAs.[5] Certainty, information exchanges and a clearly defined procedure for public officials to follow can strengthen their incentives to cooperate with CAs. To this end, in many EU Member States, such as Greece and Italy, public procurement bodies have already signed memoranda of understanding (MOUs) or other formal agreements with the national CAs.[6]

The application of the MEAT criterion for the award of public contracts could be a solution, as suppliers with different technical scores from each other at the first stage of competition agree less easily on a mutually beneficial bidding ring at the second stage of competition. The close collaboration of procurement officers with national CAs could be another solution, but it does not actually answer the question who is going to pay for the collection of such information regarding the market and the market players at issue.

2 Stefan Weishaar, *Cartels, Competition and Public Procurement: Law and Economic Approaches to Bid Rigging* (Edward Elgar 2013), 32.

3 International Competition Network (ICN) "Anti-Cartel Enforcement Manual April 2015, Chapter on Relationships between Competition Agencies and Public Procurement Bodies" <https://www.internationalcompetitionnetwork.org/wp-content/uploads/2018/05/CWG_ACEMPublicProcurement.pdf> accessed on April 26, 2020.

4 Ibid, 8.

5 OECD "Competition and Procurement – Key Findings 2011" <http://www.oecd.org/daf/competition/sectors/48315205.pdf> accessed on April 26, 2020.

6 International Competition Network (fn 3), 12 and 27–28; See also Penelope Giosa "The Hellenic Competition Commission Signs Protocol on Cooperation with the Hellenic Single Public Procurement Authority" <www.concurrences.com/en/bulletin/news-issues/october-2019/the-hellenic-competition-commission-signs-protocol-on-cooperation-with-the> accessed on April 26, 2020.

On the closed nature of framework agreements, which creates a high barrier to entry for the whole duration of the framework agreement, the openness of framework agreements to new joiners was suggested. Yet, the openness to new tenderers might be a disincentive for firms to enter into a framework agreement. Therefore, it was further suggested that the awardees in the framework agreement should be able to improve their offers any time the framework agreement is in operation, and if the following conditions are met cumulatively:

(a) There is divergence of the prices asked by the bidders admitted to the framework agreement at the first stage of the procedure, when the framework agreement is concluded and when the need arises.
(b) There is discrepancy between the prices required by the awardees in the framework agreement and the prices asked by the suppliers in the market outside the framework agreement.

In order to further reduce the risk of collusion at the second stage of framework agreements, it was recommended that legal standing shall be granted to any economic operator entitled to tender for the award of procurement contracts under a framework agreement. Nevertheless, this recommendation has several weaknesses, among which the evidential hurdle that economic operators outside the market of the framework agreement face, when it comes to learn about the conclusion of collusive agreements between the framework awardees and collect evidence that would allow them a challenge. The only way to make this suggestion realistic would be to use the review procedure initiated by the economic operators outside the framework agreement by way of interlocutory procedure before the conclusion of the call-off contract.

In the end, e-auctions were considered, and the following suggestions were made:

(a) As little information as possible should be made available about the bidding history of other auctioneers.
(b) The prices at which rivals quitted should not be disclosed as well as the number of valid offers submitted per round.
(c) Delay in publishing this information is recommended.
(d) The use of e-bids rather than e-auctions is suggested, where there are concerns about collusion, because the one-round format of e-bids cannot be easily manipulated.
(e) E-auctions should terminate when no further valid bids are submitted within a specific period of time, instead of closing the auction at a predetermined time or after a predetermined number of rounds.

Chapter 6 concluded that leniency cannot work successfully in public procurement. Therefore, it suggested the total exemption of the first leniency applicant, that is, the immunity recipient, from the debarment mechanism. This measure would make it easier for infringing firms to come forward and report the existence of a bidding ring, without worrying that the materials they disclose to the CA will be made available in the context of a subsequent self-cleaning defence to the government agency for the needs of a civil liability action brought by it against them. Yet, no firm can be sure that it will be the first one applying for leniency. Hence, in order to limit this chilling effect and encourage all bid riggers to come forward and cooperate with the CA regardless of whether they are the immunity recipient or not, it was further suggested in Chapter 6 that the debarment period should be halved for all the other beneficiaries of leniency. Moreover, regarding the remaining half of the debarment period that the subsequent leniency applicants have to undergo, they should be able to prove that they have restored their reliability in virtue of the self-cleaning provisions under the 2014/24/EU Directive and avoid debarment. Their leniency application and cooperation with the CA should be regarded as a demonstration of genuine intention to confess anticompetitive activities and restore trustworthiness in the market. Nevertheless, it will be up to the contracting authority to assess each time the sufficiency of this collaboration and decide whether the debarred firm's reliability is fully restored or not.

Additionally, it was suggested that procurement agencies should have access only to the non-confidential version of the leniency decision, complying in this way with the rationale of the Damages Directive 2014/104/EU which enshrines a strict prohibition of disclosure for leniency statements. Yet, in case of bid rigging, which is a serious offence, it makes sense to seek the access to as many documents as possible, in order to assess whether the debarred firm is indeed worth of regaining its reliability in the market. Understanding this need of contracting authorities, the chapter made a suggestion in the further alternative. It suggested the appointment of independent third parties, like independent monitors or public accountants, to have access to the debarred firms' confidential information, like the leniency decision and statements, and assess accordingly whether the infringing firms are worth of avoiding debarment or not. This measure will keep procurement agencies away from leniency material without undermining their right to fully assess the reliability of debarred firms before trusting them again.

In Chapter 7 a number of recommendations were made in order to make it easier for contracting authorities, but also other putative claimants, to seek damages for bid rigging. The first recommendation regarded the establishment of a "Competition Damages Litigation Fund", that is, a supply of money collected from contracting authorities, with the aim to use it for covering the competition damages litigation costs. A "Competition Damages Litigation Fund" would permit the collection and saving of money for this specific reason, every time the national courts of an EU Member State award damages to the relevant contracting authorities for the anticompetitive activities of economic operators in the context of public procurement. A single account for competition damages litigation is an essential tool for consolidating and managing procurement entities' cash resources, especially in EU Member States with highly fragmented public sector. The management of this fund could be left to the Auditor General of every EU Member State, who will be in charge of calculating and paying the arising litigation costs as well as of informing regularly the contracting authorities about the balance of the account. When the residual funds of the "Competition Damages Litigation Fund" are beyond a specific and predetermined amount of money at the end of each year, the Auditor General of every EU Member State may distribute them *pro rata* to the involved contracting authorities in order to apply them for their indirect benefit.

The second recommendation in Chapter 7 was to restrict the compensation of the defendant's fees to the statutory attorney fees in order to prevent situations of abuse on behalf of the defendants, as already happens in Germany. The third recommendation was to assign the claims of contracting authorities to a third party that would have an interest in bringing an action against the colluding supplier(s). The third parties could indicatively be the competitors of bid riggers that were not selected for the award of the public contract due to the manipulation of the bidding process, funders or special purpose vehicles (SPVs), as already happens in Germany, audit agencies, procurement oversight agencies, law firms or taxpayer associations. In this way, there will be no fear of spoiling the cooperative relationship between the infringing firms and the contracting authorities in case of future public contracts. The chapter also suggested the introduction of statutory or pre-established damages. This means that before the final judgment, contracting authorities should have the option to ask for the recovery of statutory/ pre-established damages instead of actual damages, namely a lump sum calculated by the national courts based on pre-determined factors. These factors could mutually be agreed by the litigants before the initiation of the legal proceedings. This was an idea borrowed from intellectual property law.

Chapter 8 discussed the challenges of obtaining compensation for anticompetitive conduct in public procurement and explores alternative remedies beyond traditional tort law, such as liquidated damages clauses, third-party actions and the establishment of a "Competition Damages Litigation Fund" to consolidate and manage cash resources for public procurement entities. The chapter also touched on the use of divestitures and donations as antitrust remedies alternative to damages claims. Both remedies have been used in recent US Department of Justice (DOJ) settlements related to bid rigging.

The overall purpose of Chapter 9 was to assess whether enhanced whistleblower protections could effectively overcome the challenges in securing damages for bid-rigging. It investigated the effectiveness of whistleblowing in combating bid-rigging and focused on how the EU's new Whistleblower Protection Directive encourages reporting to national competition authorities, aiming to strengthen enforcement of competition law. A key comparative element was the analysis of the highly successful US financial incentive whistleblower programme, using interviews with US practitioners to illustrate its practical application in fighting bid-rigging.

Bibliography

Articles and books

Editorial Comments. "One bird in the hand...The Directive on Damages Actions for Breach of the Competition Rules" (2014) 51 *CMLR*

Albano G.L. "Demand Aggregation and Collusion Prevention in Public Procurement" in Racca Gabriella M. and Yukins Christopher R. (eds), *Integrity and Efficiency in Sustainable Public Contracts. Balancing Corruption Concerns in Public Procurement Internationally* (Bruylant, 2014)

Albano G.L. and Spagnolo G. "Asymmetry and Collusion in Sequential Procurement: A 'Large Lot Last' Policy" (2010) 10(1) *The B.E. Journal of Theoretical Economics*

Albano G.L., Spagnolo G. and Zanza M. "Regulating Joint Bidding in Public Procurement" (2009) 5(2) *Journal of Competition Law and Economics*

Albano G.L., Dimitri N., Pacini R. and Spagnolo G. "Information and Competitive Tendering" in Dimitri N., Piga G. and Spagnolo G. (eds), *Handbook of Procurement* (Cambridge University Press, 2006)

Albano G.L., Dimitri N., Perrigne I. and Piga G. "Fostering Participation" in Nicola Dimitri, Gustavo Piga and Giancarlo Spagnolo (eds), *Handbook of Procurement* (Cambridge University Press, 2006)

Albano G.L., Buccirossi P., Spagnolo G. and Zanza M. "Preventing Collusion in Procurement" in Nicola Dimitri, Gustavo Piga and Giancarlo Spagnolo (eds), *Handbook of Procurement* (Cambridge University Press, 2006)

Alexopoulou M.A. and Sanchez Graells A. "Competition and Public Procurement-An Overview" (2009) *CCLP(S)* 3

Alhola K., Salo M., Antikainen R. and Berg A. "Promoting Public Procurement of Sustainable Innovations: Approaches for Effective Market Dialogue" in Khi V. Thai (ed), *Global Public Procurement Theories and Practices* (Springer International Publishing 2017)

Anderson R.D. and Kovacic W.E. "Competition Policy and International Trade Liberalisation: Essential Complements to Ensure Good Performance in Public Procurement Markets" (2009) 2 *Public Procurement Law Review*

Anderson R.D. and Muller A.C. "Ensuring Integrity and Competition in Public Procurement Markets: A Dual Challenge for Good Governance" in Arrowsmith Sue and Anderson Robert D. (eds), *The WTO Regime on Government Procurement: Challenge and Reform* (CUP, 2011)

Anderson R.D. and Muller A.C. "Promoting Competition and Deterring Corruption in Public Procurement Markets: Synergies with Trade Liberalisation" (2017) 2 *Public Procurement Law Review*

Anderson R.D., Jones A. and Kovacic W.E. *Combatting Corruption and Collusion in Public Procurement: A Challenge for Governments Worldwide* (Oxford University Press, 2024)

Andon P., et al. "The Impact of Financial Incentives and Perceptions of Seriousness on Whistleblowing Intention" (2018) 151 *Journal of Business Ethics*

Andrecka M. "Clarification or Missed Opportunity? The Provision on Framework Agreements in the 2014 Directive" in Ølykke G.S. and Sanchez-Graells A. (eds), *Reformation or Deformation of the EU Public Procurement Rules* (Edward Elgar Publishing, 2016)

Andrews N. *Contract Law* (Cambridge University Press, 2011)

Anglani F. "Antitrust and Public Tenders: Is This a New Challenge?" (2017) 4(2) *Italian Antitrust Review*

Aoyagi M. "Bid Rotation and Collusion in Repeated Auctions" (2003) 112(1) *Journal of Economic Theory*

Apostolakis I. "Antitrust Liability in Cases of Indirect Contacts between Competitors: VM Remonts" (2017) 54 *CMLR*

Arden P. "Legal Regulation of Multi-provider Framework Agreements and the Potential for Bid Rigging: A Perspective from the UK Local Government Construction Sector" (2013) 5 *PPLR*

Argadona A. "Corruption and Companies: The Use of Facilitating Payments" (2005) 60 *Journal of Business Ethics*

Ariely D., Ockenfels A. and Roth A. "An Experimental Analysis of Ending Rules in Internet Auctions" (2005) 36(4) *RAND Journal of Economics*

Arnould J. "Secondary Policies in Public Procurement: The Innovations of the New Directives" (2004) 4 *PPLR* 190

Arrowsmith S. *Remedies for Enforcing the Public Procurement Rules* (Earlsgate, 1993)

Arrowsmith S. "The Application of the E.C. Treaty Rules to Public and Utilities Procurement" (1995) 6 *PPLR*

Arrowsmith S. "An Assessment of the New Legislative Package on Public Procurement" (2004) 41 *Common Market Law Review*

Arrowsmith S. *Public Procurement Regulation in the 21st Century: Reform of the UNCITRAL Model Law on Procurement* (St Paul, Thomson-West, 2009)

Arrowsmith S. "The Revised Agreement on Government Procurement: Changes to the Procedural Rules and Other Transparency Provisions" in Arrowsmith S. and Anderson R.D. (eds), *The WTO Regime on Government Procurement: Challenge and Reform* (Cambridge University Press, 2011)

Arrowsmith S. "The Purpose of the EU Procurement Directives: Ends, Means and the Implications for National Regulatory Space for Commercial and Horizontal Procurement Policies" in Gehring M.W. et al. (eds), *Cambridge Yearbook of European Legal Studies* (Vol. 14) (Bloomsbury Publishing, 2012)

Arrowsmith S. "Understanding the Purpose of the EU's Procurement Directives: The Limited Role of the EU Regime and Some Proposals for Reform" in Konkurrensverket – Swedish Competition Authority (ed), *The Cost of Different Goals of Public Procurement* (Konkurrensverket, 2012)

Arrowsmith S. *The Law of Public and Utilities Procurement Volume 1: Regulation in the EU and UK* (Sweet & Maxwell, 2014)

Arrowsmith S. *The Law of Public and Utilities Procurement Volume 2: Regulation in the EU and the UK* (Sweet & Maxwell, 2017)

Arrowsmith S. and Craven R. "Competitive Dialogue in the United Kingdom", Chapter 3 in Arrowsmith S. and Treumer S. (eds), *Competitive Dialogue in EU Procurement Law* (Cambridge University Press, 2012)

Arrowsmith S. and Kunzlik P. "EC Regulation of Public Procurement" in Arrowsmith S. and Kunzlik P. (eds), *Social and Environmental Policies in EC Procurement Law* (Cambridge University Publishing, 2009)

Arrowsmith S. and Nicholas C. *Regulating Framework Agreements under the UNCITRAL Model Law,* chapter 2, in Sue Arrowsmith (ed), *Reform of the UNCITRAL Model Law on Procurement: Procurement Regulation for the 21st Century* (West, 2009)

Arrowsmith S., Prieβ H.J. and Friton P. "Self-Cleaning as a Defence to Exclusions for Misconduct – An Emerging Concept in EC Public Procurement Law" (2009) 18 *Public Procurement Law Review* 270–275

Arrowsmith S. and Treumer S. *Competitive Dialogue in EU Procurement* (Cambridge University Press, 2012)

Atkins W.S. Management Consultants (Epsom). *The Costs of Non-Europe in Public Sector Procurement* (E.C. Luxembourg, 1988)

Auriol E. and Søreide T. "An Economic Analysis of Debarment" (2017) (50) *International Review of Law and Economics*

Awesti A. "The Myth of Eurosclerosis: European Integration in the 1970s" (2009) 3 *L' Europe en Formation* 353–354

Bain J.S. *Industrial Organisation* (John Wiley 1968)

Bajari P., McMillan R.S. and Tadelis S. "Auctions Versus Negotiations in Procurement: An Empirical Analysis" (2009) 25(2) *Journal of Law Economics and Organization*

Bajari P. and Ye L. "Deciding Between Competition and Collusion" 85(4) *The Review of Economics and Statistics*

Baker J.B. "The Case for Antitrust Enforcement" (2003) 17 *Journal of Economic Perspectives*

Becker G. "Crime and Punishment: An Economic Approach" (1968) 76(2) *Journal of Political Economy*

Belgian Competition Authority. "The Belgian Competition Authority Fines Several Companies for Bid-Rigging (Siemens)" 3 May 2017, e-Competitions Bulletin May 2017, Art. No 84204

Besley T. and McLaren J. "Taxes and Bribery: The Role of Wage Incentives" (1993) 103(416) *The Economic Journal*

Bialynicka-Birula J. *Rationality versus Irrationality of Auction Bidders – Interdisciplinary Perspective* (The International Association for Research in Economic Psychology/The Society for the Advancement of Behavioural Economics Conference, Rome, 2008)

Bickerstaff R. "E-Procurement Under the New EU Procurement Directives" (2014) (3) *PPLR*

Binmore K. and Klemperer P. "The Biggest Auction Ever: The Sale of the British 3G Telecom Licences" (2002) 478(112) *The Economic Journal*

Bishop S. and Walker M. *The Economics of EC Competition Law: Concepts, Application and Measurement* (Sweet & Maxwell, 2010)

Blažo O. "Proportionality and Subsidiarity of European Law and Issues of 'Over-Regulation' and 'Under Regulation'", paper presented at the International Academic Conference Bratislava Legal Forum, 2015

Börgers T. and Damme E. "Auction Theory for Auction Design" in Janssen M. (ed), *Auctioning Public Assets: Analysis and Alternatives* (Cambridge University Press, 2004)

Borowiec A. "The Impact of Public Procurement System on the Development of Competition in the Economy in the Light of Empirical Research" (2017) 8(1) *Oeconomia Copernicana*

Botta M. "Commission Acting as Plaintiff in Cases of Private Enforcement of EU Competition Law: Otis" (2013) 50 *CMLR*

Bovis C. *EU Public Procurement Law* (Elgar European Law, 2007)

Broos S., Gautier A., Ramos J.M. and Petit N. "Analyse Statistique des Affaires D' Ententes dans l'UE (2004–2014)" (2016) 67 *Revue économique*

Brown A. "The Impact of the New Procurement Directive on Large Public Infrastructure Projects: Competitive Dialogue or Better the Devil You Know?" (2004) 4 *PPLR*

Brown A. "When May an Economic Operator Be Excluded from Public Tenders Due to Its Previous Infringement of Competition Law? Vossloh Laeis GmbH v. Stadwerke Munchen GmbH (C-124/17)" (2019) 2 *Public Procurement Law Review*

Brown A.L., Plott C.R. and Sullivan H.J. "Collusion Facilitating and Collusion Breaking Power of Simultaneous Ascending and Descending Price Auctions" (2009) 47(3) *Economic Inquiry*

Brusco S. and Lopomo G. "Collusion via Signalling in Simultaneous Ascending Bid Auctions with Heterogeneous Objects, with and without Complementarities" (2002) 69(2) *The Review of Economic Studies*

Bucy P.H. "Information as a Commodity in the Regulatory World" (2002) 39(4) *Houston Law Review*

Call A.C., et al. "Whistleblowers and Outcomes of Financial Misrepresentation Enforcement Actions" (2018) 56(1) *Journal of Accounting Research*

Canavan R. "Public Procurement and Frameworks" in Bovis C. (ed), *Research Handbook on EU Public Procurement Law* (Edward Elgar Publishing, 2016)

Caranta R. "Remedies in EU Public Contract Law: The Proceduralisation of EU Public Procurement Legislation" (2015) 8 *Review of European Administrative Law*

Carbone C., Calderoni F. and Jofre M. "Bid-rigging in Public Procurement: Cartel Strategies and Bidding Patterns" (2024) 82 *Crime, Law and Social Change*

Caro de Sousa P. *The Private Enforcement of Competition Law* (1st edn, Oxford University Press, 2024)

Carollo L., Pulcher S. and Guerci M. "Whistleblowing as a Crucial Practice for Responsible Management" in Laasch O. Suddaby R. Freeman R. E. and Jamali D. (eds), *Research* Handbooks *in Business and* Management *Series* (Edward Elgar, 2020)

Carpineto L., Piga G. and Zanza M. "The Variety of Procurement Practice: Evidence from Public Procurement" in Dimitri N, Piga G. and Spagnolo G. (eds), *Handbook of Procurement* (Cambridge University Press, 2006)

Carillo P.M., Robinson H.S., Anumba C.J. and Bouchlaghem N.M. "A Knowledge Transfer Framework: The PFI Context" (2006) 24(10) *Construction Management and Economics*

Carrillo P.M., Robinson H.S., Foale P., Anumba C.J. and Bouchlaghem D. "Participation, Barriers and Opportunities in PFI: The United Kingdom Experience" (2008) 24(3) *Journal of Management in Engineering*

Cassady R. Jr. *Auctions and Auctioneering* (University of California Press, 1967)

Cecchini P. *The European Challenge 1992: The Benefits of a Single Market* (Wildwood House, 1988)

Cerrone C. Hermstrüwer Y. and Robalo P. "Debarment and Collusion in Procurement Auctions" (2021) 129 *Games and Economic Behaviour* 114–143

Che Y.K. and Kim J. "Optimal Collusion-Proof Auctions" (2009) 144(2) *Journal of Economic Theory*

Chen J. and Harrington J.E. "The Impact of the Corporate Leniency Program on Cartel Formation and the Cartel Price Path" in Ghosal V. and Stennek J. (eds), *The Political Economy of Antitrust* (Elsevier, 2007)

Cheng C.B. "Solving a Sealed-Bid Reverse Auction Problem by Multiple-Criterion Decision-Making Methods" (2008) 56(12) *Computers & Mathematics with Applications*

Clark R., Coviello D., Gauthier J. and Shneyerov A. "Bid Rigging and Entry Deterrence in Public Procurement: Evidence from an Investigation into Collusion and Corruption in Quebec" (2018) 34(3) *Journal of Law, Economics & Organization*

Comba M. "Variations in the Scope of the New EU Public Procurement Directives of 2014: Efficiency in Public Spending and a Major Role of the Approximation of Laws" in Lichère F., Caranta R. and Treumer S. (eds), *Modernising Public Procurement Law: The New Directive* (Elgar, 2014)

Commission of the European Communities. "Europe 1992, The Overall Challenge" SEC (88)524 final, Brussels 13 April 1988

Coppinger V.M., Smith V. and Titus J.A. "Incentives and Behavior in English, Dutch and Sealed-Bid Auctions" (1980) 18(1) *Economic Inquiry*

Council of the European Union. "Common Position on the Amended Proposal for a Council Directive on the Co-ordination of the Laws, Regulations and Administrative Provisions Relating to the Application of Review Procedures to the Award of Public Supply and Public Works Contracts", doc. 7834/89 ADD1

Council of the European Union. "The Stockholm Programme – An Open and Secure Europe Serving and Protecting the Citizen", Council document 17024/09 adopted by the European Council on 10/11 December 2009

Cox A. *The Single Market Rules and the Enforcement Regime After 1992* (Earlsgate Press, 1993)

Cox A. and Furlong P. "Cross-Border Trade and Contract Awards – The Intellectual Myopia at the Heart of the EU Procurement Rules" (1997) 3(1) *European Journal of Purchasing and Supply Management*

Cramton P. "Ascending Auctions" (1998) 42(3–5) *European Economic Review*

Cramton P. "Simultaneous Ascending Auctions" in Cramton P., Shoham Y. and Steinberg R. (eds), *Combinatorial Auctions* (MIT Press, 2006)

Cramton P. and Schwartz J.A. "Collusive Bidding: Lessons from the FCC Spectrum Auctions" (2000) 17(3) *Journal of Regulatory Economics*

Croatian Competition Authority. "The Croatian High Administrative Court Fines Several Personal Protection Firms for Cartel (Sokol Marić)" 30 May 2016, e-Competitions Bulletin, May 2016, Art. No 79884

Cypriot Competition Authority. "The Cypriot Competition Authority Fines Several Companies for Bid-Rigging in the Supply and Transportation of Ready-Mix Concrete Market" (Mattheos Ioannou Ready Mix Concrete/C. Kythreotis Skyrodema/ Skyramix…) 15 May 2019, e-Competitions Bulletin May 2019, Art. No 90627

Daley T., Knowles S. and Stern D. "The Impact of Escobar and the Procurement Collusion Strike Force on Procurement-Related False Claims Act Settlements" (2022) 57(2) *The Procurement Lawyer*

Danish Competition and Consumer Authority. "The City Court of Hillerød Fines Two Members of the Management of a Now Dissolved Demolition Company for Bid Rigging" 11 January 2019, e-Competitions Bulletin January 2019, Art. No 89002

Davies S. and Majumdar A. *The Development of Targets for Consumer Savings Arising from Competition Policy* (Great Britain, Office of Fair Trading, 2002)

De Sousa e Alvim M. "The New Directive on Antitrust Damages-a Giant Step Forward?" (2015) 36 *ECLR*

Dekel O. "The Legal Theory of Competitive Bidding for Government Contracts" (2008) 37(2) *Public Contract Law Journal*

Demsetz H. *The Market Concentration Doctrine-An Examination of Evidence and A Discussion of Policy* (AEI-Hoover Policy Studies, 1973)

Dimitri N., Dimitri N., Dini F. and Piga G. "When Should Procurement Be Centralized?" in Dimitri N., Piga G. and Spagnolo G. (eds), *Handbook of Procurement* (Cambridge University Press, 2006)

Dimitri N., Pacini R., Pagnozzi M. and Spagnolo G. "Multi-contract Tendering Procedures and Package Bidding in Procurement" in Dimitri N., Piga G. and Spagnolo G. (eds), *Handbook of Procurement* (Cambridge University Press, 2006)

Dimitri N., Piga G. and Spagnolo G. *Handbook of Procurement* (Cambridge University Press 2006)

Dorée A. "Collusion in the Dutch Construction Industry: An Industrial Organisation Perspective" (2004) 32(2) *Building Research and Information*

Drijber B.J. and Stergiou H. "Public Procurement Law and Internal Market Law" (2009) 46(3) *Common Market Law Review*

Dunne N. "Between Competition Law and Regulation: Hybridized Approaches to Market Control" (2014) 2(2) *Journal of Antitrust Enforcement* 228

Easley D. and Kleinberg J. "Auctions" in Easley D. and Kleinberg J. (eds), *Networks, Crowds, and Markets: Reasoning about a Highly Connected World* (Cambridge University Press, 2010)

Engelbrecht-Wiggans R. "Auctions and Bidding Models: A Survey" (1980) 26 *Management Science*

Engelbrecht-Wiggans R. and Kahn C.M. "Low-Revenue Equilibria in Simultaneous Ascending-Bid Auctions" (2005) 51(3) *Management Science*

Erickson W.B. "Economics of Price Fixing" (1969) 2 *Antitrust Law and Economic Review*

Eßig M. and Glas A.H. "Considering Small and Medium-Sized Suppliers in Public Procurement – The Case of the German Defence Sector" in Mattfeld D., Spengler T., Brinkmann J. and Grunewald M. (eds), *Logistics Management – Contributions of the Section Logistics of the German Academic Association for Business Research, 2015, Braunschweig, Germany* (Springer International Publishing, 2016)

Estevan de Quesada C. "Competition and Transparency in Public Procurement Markets" (2014) 5 *Public Procurement Law Review*

European Commission. "Staff Working Paper Evaluation Report, Impact and Effectiveness of EU Public Procurement Legislation" SEC (2011) 853 final

European Commission. "Report on the Effectiveness of Directive 89/665/EEC and Directive 92/13/EEC, as Modified by Directive 2007/66/EC, Concerning Review Procedures in the Area of Public Procurement" COM (2017) 28 final

Ezrachi A. *EU Competition Law – An Analytical Guide to the Leading Cases* (6th edn, Hart Publishing, 2018)

Ezulike E.I., Pery J.G. and Hawwash K. "The Barriers to Entry into the PFI Market" (1997) 4(3) *Engineering, Construction and Architectural Management*

Fairgrieve D. and Lichère F. *Public Procurement Law: Damages as an Effective Remedy* (Oxford Hart, 2011)

Fazekas M., Tóth I.J. and King L.P. "An Objective Corruption Risk Index Using Public Procurement Data" (2016) 22 *European Journal on Criminal Policy & Research*

Fickey J. "Fraud in the Bidding Process: The Limited Remedies Available to Contractors" (2009) 38(4) *Public Contract Law Journal*

First H. "Lost in Conversation: The Compensatory Function of Antitrust Law" (2010) New York University Law and Economics Working Paper No. 10-14 <https://papers.ssrn.com/sol3/papers.cfm?abstract_id=1579343>

Forges F. and Orzach R. "Core-stable Rings in Second Price Auctions with Common Values" (2011) 47(6) *Journal of Mathematical Economics*

Frade E., Jones S., Phelan L.M. and Snyder B. "Is There Life After Leniency?" American Bar Association (ABA) Antitrust Section Spring Meeting (Washington, DC, 27 March 2019)

French Competition Authority. "The French Competition Authority Fines Three Companies for Bid-Rigging in the Public Lighting Sector (Lapize de Sallée)" 24 September 2018, e-Competitions Bulletin September 2018, Art. No 87999

Froeb L.M., Koyak R.A. and Werden G.J. "What Is the Effect of Bid Rigging on Prices?" (1993) 42(4) *Economic Letters*

Gardiner J. "Defining Corruption" in Heidenheimer A.J. and Johnston M. (eds), *Political Corruption: Concepts and Contexts* (Transaction Publishers, 2005)

Geçkil I.K. and Anderson P.L. *Applied Game Theory and Strategic Behaviour* (Taylor and Francis Group, 2010)

Georghiou L., Edler J., Uyarra E. and Yeow J. "Policy Instruments for Public Procurement of Innovation: Choice, Design and Assessment" (2014) 86 *Technological Forecasting and Social Change*

Georgieva I. *Using Transparency Against Corruption in Public Procurement* (Springer International Publishing AG, 2017)

Georgopoulos A. "Office of FairTrading Report: The Impact of Public Procurement on Competition" (2005) 14(2) *PPLR*

German Competition Authority. "The German Competition Authority Imposes Fines on Five Providers of Underground Mining Services for Having Implemented a Price-Fixing Agreement and Bid-Rigging (BeMo Tunnelling, Deilmann-Haniel)" 28 August 2014, e-Competitions Bullettin, August 2014, Art. No 68925

Giosa P.A. "Do e-auctions Increase the Risk of Bid Rigging?" (2018) 35 *CCP Research Bulletin*

Giosa P.A. "The Case for Reforming the Rules on Contracting Authority Damages Claims for Bid Rigging in the EU" (2018) 6 *Public Procurement Law Review*

Gleason M.A., et al. "It Ain't Over till It's Over: Review of DOJ M&A Settlements Under the Tunney Act" (2019) 23(9) *The M&A Lawyer*

Graham D.A. and Marshall R.C. "Collusive Bidder Behavior at Single-Object Second-Price and English Auctions" (1987) 95(6) *Journal of Political Economy*

Grant C. "Whistle Blowers: Saints of Secular Culture" (2002) 39(4) *Journal of Business Ethics*

Greenwood M. and Klotz J.M. "The Fight against Corruption in Public Procurement: An Introduction to Best Practices" in Hernandez Garcia R. (ed), *International Public Procurement: A Guide to Best Practice* (Global Business Publishing, 2009)

Griesmer L.J.R. and Shubik M. "Toward a Study of Bidding Processes, Part IV: Games with Unknown Costs" (1967) 14 *Naval Research Logistics Quarterly*

Grimm V., Pacini R., Spagnolo G. and Zanza M. "Division in Lots and Competition in Procurement" in Dimitri N., Piga G. and Spagnolo G. (eds), *Handbook of Procurement* (Cambridge University Press, 2006)

Grosskopf B., Rentschler L. and Sarin R. "An Experiment on First-price Common-value Auctions with Asymmetric Information Structures: The Blessed Winner" (2018) 109 *Games and Economic Behaviour*

Gupta S. "The Effect of Bid Rigging on Prices: A Study of the Highway Construction Industry" (2001) 19(4) *Review of Industrial Organization*

Gupta S., Ghosh I. and Millet I. "An Empirical Study of Collusion Potential Metrics and their Impact on Online Reverse Auction Success" in Parente D.H. (ed), *Best Practices for Online Procurement Auctions* (IGI Global, 2008)

Haberbush K.L. "Limiting the Government's Exposure to Bid Rigging Schemes: A Critical Look at the Sealed Bidding Regime" (2000) 30(1) *Public Contract Law Journal*

Hadfield G. and Bozovic I. "Scaffolding: Using Formal Contracts to Build Informal Relations to Support Innovation" (2016) 5 *Wisconsin Law Review*

Haque N. and Sahay R. "Do Government Wage Cuts Close Budget Deficits? Costs of Corruption" (1996) 43(4) *Staff Papers (International Monetary Fund)*

Harding C. and Joshua J. "A Narrative of Cartel Regulation in Europe, 1970 to the Present Time" in Harding C. and Joshua J. (eds), *Regulating Cartels in Europe* (Oxford University Press, 2010)

Harrington J. *Games, Strategies and Decision Making* (Worth Publishers, 2009)

Harsanyi J. "Games with Incomplete Information Played by "Bayesian" Players, I-III, Part I. The Basic Model" (1968) 14(5) *Management Science*

Hartley K. and Martin S. "Public Procurement in the European Union: Issues and Policies" (1997) 2 *Public Procurement Law Review*

Hastings Chamberlin E. *The Theory of Monopolistic Competition: A Re-Orientation of the Theory of Value* (Harvard University Press, 1966)

Havu K. "The Finnish Market Court Imposes Fines for Price Fixing and Bid Rigging (Asunto-Vayla, CSC Consulting, Hansatalot, Kiinteisto, Rovakartano, Sata-Vayla" 28 February 2013, Bulletin e-Competitions February 2013, Art. No 51787

Heggstad K.K. and Frøystad M. *The Basics of Integrity in Procurement* (U4 Anti-Corruption Resource Centre Chr. Michelsen Institute – CMI, 2011)

Heimler A. "Cartels in Public Procurement" (2012) 8(4) *Journal of Competition Law and Economics*

Heimler A. "Cartels in Public Procurement: A Reassessment" CPI Antitrust Chronicle October 2023 <https://www.pymnts.com/wp-content/uploads/2023/10/1-CARTELS-IN-PUBLIC-PROCUREMENT-A-REASSESSMENT-Alberto-Heimler.pdf> accessed 22 January 2025

Hellenic Competition Authority. "The Hellenic Competition Authority Fines Several Construction Companies for Bid-Rigging in the Public Works of Infrastructure (Alpine Bau)" 5 March 2019, e-Competitions Bulletin, March 2019, Art. No 89894

Hennequin E. "What Motivates Internal Whistleblowing? A Typology Adapted to the French Context" (2020) 38(5) *European Management Journal*

Herrera Anchustegui I. "Centralizing Public Procurement and Competitiveness in Directive 2014/24" (2015) 4 *European Law Reporter*

Herrera Anchustegui I. "Division into Lots and Demand Aggregation – Extremes Looking for The Correct Balance?" in Ølykke G.S. and Sanchez-Graells A. (eds), *Reformation or Deformation of the EU Public Procurement Rules* (Edward Elgar Publishing, 2016).

Hjelmeng E.J. and Soreide T. "Debarment in Public Procurement: Rationales and Realisation" in Racca G.M, Yuki C. and Cavallo Perin R. (eds), *Promoting Integrity in Public Procurement: Accountability and Transparency* (Bruylant 2014)

HM Treasury–United Kingdom. "PFI: Strengthening Long-Term Partnerships-March 2006"

Hodges C., Vogenauer S. and Tulibacka M. "The Oxford Study on Costs and Funding of Civil Litigation-Introduction" in Hodges C., Vogenauer S. and Tulibacka M. (eds), *The Costs and Funding of Civil Litigation: A Comparative Perspective* (Bloomsbury Publishing, 2010)

Hovenkamp H. "The Indirect-Purchaser Rule and Cost-Plus Sales" (1990) 103(7) *Harvard Law Review*

Howard J.H. and Kaserman D. "Proof of Damages in Construction Industry Bid-Rigging Cases" (1989) 34 *Antitrust Bulletin*

Howard M.C. *Legal Aspects of Marketing* (McGraw-Hill, 1964)

Hu, A., Offerman T. and Onderstal S. "Fighting Collusion in Auctions: An Experimental Investigation" (2011) 29 *International Journal of Industrial Organization*

Hungarian Competition Authority. "The Hungarian Competition Authority Fines Providers of Medical Products and Medical Devices for Bid Rigging (Chirmax)" 5 August 2016, e-Competitions Bulletin, August 2016, Art. No 80988

Info Europe. "Public Procurement Transparency & Integrity, Guide to EU Directive on Whistleblower Protection, Key Elements relevant to Public Procurement" <www.access-info.org/wp-content/uploads/ML-2-Whistleblower.pdf>

Information Resources Management Association USA. *Game Theory: Breakthroughs in Research and Practice* (IGI Global, 2018)

Iossa E. and Spagnolo G. "Contracts as Threats: On a Rationale for Rewarding A while Hoping for B" (2011) CEPR Discussion Papers No. 8195

Jacquemin A. and Slade M. "Cartels, Collusion and Horizontal Merger" in Schmalensee R. and Willig R. (eds), *Handbook of Industrial Organization* (Elsevier, 1989)

Jephcott M. *Law of Cartels* (Jordan Publishing Limited, 2011)

Kagel J. "Auctions: A Survey of Experimental Research" in Kagel J.H. and Roth A. (eds), *The Handbook of Experimental Economics* (Princeton University Press, 1995)

Kagel J. and Roth A.E. *The Handbook of Experimental Economics* (Princeton University Press, 1995)

Kaplan T.R. and Zamir S. "Advances in Auctions" in Young P. and Zamir S. (eds), *Handbook of Game Theory with Economic Applications: Volume 4* (Elsevier, 2014)

Kawai K., Nakabayashi J., Ortner J. and Chassang S. "Using Bid Rotation and Incumbency to Detect Collusion: A Regression Discontinuity Approach" (2023) 90(1) *The Review of Economic Studies*

Kelly A. *Decision Making Using Game Theory: An Introduction for Managers* (Cambridge University Press, 2003)

Kelman S. *Procurement and Public Management: The fear Of Discretion and the Quality of Government Performance"* (AEI Press 1990)

Kelton E., Phillips and Cohen LLP. "Public Consultation and Feedback on the EU Whistleblower Protection" <https://ec.europa.eu/info/law/better-regulation/have-your-say/initiatives/1721-EU-Whistleblower-protection/F12720_en>

Kendler O.M. "Auction Theory Can Complement Competition Law: Preventing Collusion in Europe's 3G Spectrum Allocation" (2002) 23(1) *University of Pennsylvania Journal of International Law*

Kennedy-Loest C. and Thomas C. "EU Public Procurement and Competition Law: The Yin and Yang of the Legal World?" (2011) 7 *Competition Law International*

Klemperer P. "Auctions with Almost Common Values: The "Wallet Game" and its Applications" (1998) 42 *European Economic Review* 759–769

Klemperer P. "Auction Theory: A Guide to the Literature" (1999) 13(3) *Journal of Economic Surveys*

Klemperer P. "How (not) to run auctions: the European 3G Telecom Auctions" (2002) 46(4–5) *European Economic Review*

Klemperer P. "What Really Matters in Auction Design" (2002) 16(1) *Journal of Economic Perspectives*

Klemperer P. "Using and Abusing Economic Theory" (2003) 2–3 *Journal of the European Economic Association*

Klemperer P. *Auctions: Theory and Practice* (Princeton University Press, 2004)

Klemperer P. "Bidding Markets" (2007) 3(1) *Journal of Competition Law and Economics*

Klemperer P. Competition Policy in Auctions and Bidding Markets" in Buccirossi P. (ed), *Handbook of Antitrust Economics* (MIT Press, 2008)

Komninos A. *EC Private Antitrust Enforcement: Decentralised Application of EC Competition Law by National Courts* (Hart Publishing 2008)

Komninos A. "The Relationship between Public and Private Enforcement: quod Dei Deo, quod Caesaris Caesari" in Lowe P. and Marquis M. (eds), *European Competition Law Annual 2011: Integrating Public and Private Enforcement of Competition Law: Implications for Courts and Agencies* (Oxford, Hart Publishing, 2014)

Komšić N. "Big Data for Procurement – The Importance of Correctly Acquiring and Using Information in Public Procurement" in Piga G. and Tátrai T. (eds), *Law and Economics of Public Procurement Reforms* (Routledge, 2017)

König C, and Bremenkamp F.L. "Competition Law Sanctions in Germany" in Tóth T. (ed), *The Cambridge Handbook of Competition Law Sanction* (Cambridge University Press 2022).

Kovacic W.E., Marshall R.C., Marx L.M. and Raiff M.E. "Bidding Rings and the Design of Anti-Collusive Measures for Auctions and Procurements" in Dimitri N., Piga G. and Spagnolo G. (eds), *Handbook of Procurement* (Cambridge University Press)

Kreye M.E., Newnes L.B. and Goh Y.M. "Uncertainty in Competitive Bidding-A Framework for Product-Service Systems" (2014) 25(6) *Production Planning & Control-The Management of Operations*

Krishna V. *Auction Theory* (2nd edn, Academic Press, 2009)

Kunzlik P. "Neoliberalism and the European Public Procurement Regime" in *Cambridge Yearbook of European Legal Studies* (Cambridge University Press, 2013)

Kunzlik P. "The 2014 Public Procurement Package: One-step Forward and Two Back for Green and Social Procurement?" in Wauters K. and Marique Y. (eds), *EU Directive 2014/24 on Public Procurement – A New Turn for Competition in Public Markets?* (Larcier, 2016)

Kuźma K. and Hartung W. *Combating Collusion in Public Procurement: Legal Limitations on Joint Bidding* (Edward Elgar, 2020).

Latan H., et al. "Ethical Awareness, Ethical Judgment and Whistleblowing: A Moderated Mediation Analysis" (2019) 155 *Journal of Business Ethics*

Latvian Competition Authority. "The Latvian Competition Authority Fines Nine Distributors of Professional Stage Equipment for Bid-Rigging (SGS Sistemas)" 30 May 2017, e-Competitions Bulletin, May 2017, Art. No 84326

Leahy P. Hearing on the "False Claims Act Corrections Act of 2007: Strengthening the Government's Most Effective Tool Against Fraud for the 21st Century" (2008) *US Fed News Service*

Levestein M.C. and Suslow V.Y. "What Determines Cartel Success?" (2006) 44(1) *Journal of Economic Literature*

Levin D. and Ye L. "Hybrid Auctions Revisited" (2008) 99(3) *Economics Letters*

Lianos I. "Causal Uncertainty and Damages Claims for the Infringement of Competition Law in Europe" in Eeckhout P. (ed), *Yearbook of European Law*, Vol. 34, no. 1 (Oxford University, 2015)

Lichère F. and Richetto S. "Framework Agreements, Dynamic Purchasing Systems and Public E-Procurement" in Lichère F., Caranta R. and Treumer S. (eds), *Modernising Public Procurement: The New Directive* (DJØF Publishing, 2014)

Lipczynski J., Wilson J.O.S. and Goddard J. *Industrial Organization: Competition, Strategy and Policy* (Pearson Education Limited, 2013)

Lithuanian Competition Authority. "The Vilnius Regional Administrative Court Upholds the Decision of the Lithuanian Competition Authority Fining Two Undertakings for Bid Rigging in the Market of Radioactive Scrap Metal (Norvesta/Sypra)" 10 September 2018, e-Competitions Bulletin, September 2018, Art. No 88003

Lopez Mino A. "Contracting Authorities Inability to Fight Bid Rigging in Public Procurement: Reasons and Remedies" in Racca G.M., Yuki C. and Cavallo Perin R. (eds), *Promoting Integrity in Public Procurement: Accountability and Transparency* (Bruylant, 2014)

Lopez Mino A. and Valcarcel Fernandez P. "Contracting Authorities Inability to Fight Bid Rigging in Public Procurement: Reasons and Remedies" in Racca G.M. and Yukins C.R. (eds), *Integrity and Efficiency in Sustainable Public Contracts. Balancing Corruption Concerns in Public Procurement Internationally* (Bruylant, 2014)

Lunander A. "Procurement Bidding in First-Price and Second-Price, Sealed-Bid Auctions Within the Common-Value Paradigm" (2002) 19 *Computational Economics*

Ludlow A. *Privatising Public Prisons – Labour Law and the Public Procurement Process* (Hart Publishing, 2017)

Macaulay S. "Non-Contractual Relations in Business: A Preliminary Study" (1963) 28 *American Sociological Review*

Maci M. "Bid Rigging in the EU Public Procurement Markets" (PhD Thesis, Queen Mary, University of London, 2010)

Maci M. "Bid Rigging in the EU Public-Procurement Markets: Some History and Developments" (2011) 32 *ECLR*

Maci M. "Private Enforcement in Bid Rigging Cases in the European Union" (2012) 8 (I) *ECJ*

Marshall R.C. and Marx L.M. "Bidder Collusion" (2007) 133 *Journal of Economic Theory*

Marshall R.C. and Meurer J. "Bidder Collusion and Antitrust Law: Refining the Analysis of Price Fixing to Account for the Special Features of Auction Markets" (2004) 72(1) *Antitrust Law Journal*

Marshall R.C. and Meurer J. *The Economics of Collusion – Cartels and Bidding Rings* (The MIT Press, 2012)

Marshall R.C. and Richard J. "Litigation Settlement and Collusion" (1994) 109(1) *Quarterly Journal of Economics* 211–240

Martin J.F. *The EC Procurement Rules: A Critical Analysis* (Clarendon Press, 1996)

Martin S. *Industrial Organization in* Context (Oxford University Press Inc., 2010)

Martin S. and Cox A. "Public Procurement Directives in the European Union: A Study of Local Authority Purchasing" (1999) 77(2) *Public Administration*

Martin S. and Hartley K. "Public Procurement in the European Union: Issues and Policies" (1997) 2 *Public Procurement Law Review*

Marvão C. and Spagnolo G. "What Do We Know about the Effectiveness of Leniency Policies? A Survey of the Empirical and Experimental Evidence" in Beaton-Wells C. and Tran C. (eds), *Anti-Cartel Enforcement in a Contemporary Age – Leniency Religion* (Hart Publishing, 2015)

Maschler M., Solan E. and Zamir S. *Game Theory* (Cambridge University Press, 2016)

Maurer L. and Barroso L. *Electricity Auctions: An Overview of Efficient Practices* (World Bank, 2011)

McAfee P.R. and McMillan J. "Auctions and Bidding" (1987) 25 *Journal of Economic Literature*

McAfee P.R. and McMillan J. "Bidding Rings" (1992) 82(3) *The American Economic Review*

McAfee P.R., Mialon H.M. and Mialon S.H. "Private v. Public Antitrust Enforcement: A Strategic Analysis" (2008) 92 *Journal of Public Economics*

McAfee P.R., Williams M. and Hendricks K. "Auctions and Bid Rigging" in Blair R.D. and Daniel Sokol D. (eds), *The Oxford Handbook of International Antitrust Economics*, Vol. 2 (Oxford University Press, 2015)

McConnell C.R., Brue S.L. and Flynn S.M. *Economics – Principles, Problems and Policies* (McGraw-Hill, 1993)

McGowan D. "Clarity at Last? Low Value Contracts and Transparency Obligations" (2007) 4 *PPLR*

McLaughlin K., Osborne S.P. and Ferlie E. *New Public Management: Current Trends and Future Prospects* (Routledge, 2002).

Medeiros, R. "The New Directive 2014/24/EU on Public Procurement: A First Overview", in Tavares L. V., Medeiros R. and Coelho D. (eds), *The New Directive 2014/24/EU on Public Procurement*, 2014

Menezes F.M. and Monteiro P.K. *An Introduction to Auction Theory* (Oxford University Press, 2004)

Meyer P. and Gramsch M. The Regional Court of Potsdam finds a clause in the procurement terms of a German municipality requiring liquidated damages of 15 per cent to be paid if the supplier participates in anti-competitive behaviour to be unlawful (Suppliers of fire engines)" e-Competitions Bulletin, Art. N° 77233 (November 2014)

Mezzanotte F. "Using Abuse of Collective Dominance in Article 102 TFEU to Fight Tacit Collusion: The Problem of Proof and Inferential Error" (2010) 33(1) *World Competition*

Milgrom P.R. "The Economics of Competitive Bidding: A Selective Survey" in Hurwicz L., Schmeidler D. and Sonnenschein H. (eds), *Social Goals and Social Organization* (Cambridge University Press, 1985)

Milgrom P.R. "Auctions and Bidding: A Primer" (1989) 3 *Journal of Economic Perspectives*

Milgrom P.R. *Putting Auction Theory to Work* (Cambridge University Press, 2004)

Mills & Reeve. "Glossary" <www.procurementportal.com/glossary#C> accessed on 30 July 2019

Miranzo Díaz J. "The Procedural Treatment of Conflicts of Interest in EU Public Procurement" in Ferrari G., Garau G. and Mondéjar-Jiménez J. (eds), *Tourism, Economy and Environment: New Trends and Research Perspectives* (Chartridge Books Oxford, 2017)

Montet C. and Serra D. *Game Theory and Economics* (Palgrave, 2003)

Motta M. *Competition Policy – Theory and Practice* (Cambridge University Press, 2004)

Munro C. "Competition Law and Public Procurement: Two Sides of the Same Coin?" (2006) 15(6) *Public Procurement Law Review*

Nagy C.I. "Recognition and Enforcement of US Judgments Involving Punitive Damages In Continental Europe" (2012) 30(1) *Netherlands Internationaal Privaatrecht (NIPR)*

Nambu T. "A Successful Story: Leniency and (International) Cartel Enforcement in Japan" (2014) 5(3) *Journal of European Competition Law and Practice*

Neu D., Everett J. and Rahaman A.S. "Preventing Corruption within Government Procurement: Constructing the Disciplined and Ethical Subject" (2015) 28 *Critical Perspectives on Accounting*

Nicolaidis K. and Vernon R. "Competition Policy and Trade Policy in the European Community" in Edward Graham (ed), *Competition Policy in a Changing World Economy* (Institute for International Economics, Washington, 1997)

Nicholas C. and Albano G.L. *The Law and Economics of Framework Agreements* (Cambridge University Press 2016)

Noussair C.N. and Seres G. "The Effect of Collusion on Efficiency in Experimental Auctions" (2020) 119 *Games and Economic Behaviour*

O'Brien D.P. and Swann D. *Information Agreements, Competition and Efficiency* (Macmillan 1969)

Ockenfels A. and Roth A.E. "The Timing of Bids in Internet Auctions-Market Design, Bidder Behavior, and Artificial Agents" (2002) 23(3) *AI Magazine*

Ockenfels A. and Roth A.E. "Late and Multiple Bidding in Second Price Internet Auctions: Theory and Evidence Concerning Different Rules for Ending An Auction" (2006) 55 *Games and Economic Behavior*

OECD. *Public Procurement in Chile: Policy Options for Efficient and Inclusive Framework Agreements* (OECD Public Governance Reviews, OECD Publishing, 2017)

OECD. *Second Public Procurement Review of the Mexican Institute of Social Security (IMSS): Reshaping Strategies for Better Healthcare* (OECD Publishing, 2018)

Ølykke G.S. "Abnormally Low Tenders, with an Emphasis on Public Tenderers" (DØJF, 2010)

Ølykke G.S. "How Does the Court of Justice of the European Union Pursue Competition Concerns in a Public Procurement Context" (2011) 6 *Public Procurement Law Review*

Osborne M.J. and Rubinstein A. *A Course in Game Theory* (MIT Press, 1994)

Pagnozzi M. "Bids as a Vehicle for (Mis)Information: Collusion in English Auctions with Affiliated Values" (2011) 20(4) *Journal of Economics and Management Strategy*

Páleníková L. "Corruption in Public Tenders-Concept of Self-Cleaning" (2012) 9 *Annals of the Faculty of Law of Zenica*

Panagopoulos S. "Strategic EU Public Procurement and Small and Medium Size Enterprises" in Bovis C. (ed), *Research Handbook on EU Public Procurement Law* (Edward Elgar Publishing, 2016)

Pantilimon Voda O.S. "Innovative and Sustainable Procurement: Framework, Constraints and Policies" in Bovis C. (ed), *Research Handbook on EU Public Procurement Law* (Edward Elgar Publishing, 2016)

Papp F.W. "Compliance and Individual Sanctions in the Enforcement of Competition Law" in Paha F.W. (ed), *Competition Law Compliance Programs-An Interdisciplinary Approach* (Springer, 2016)

Pesendorfer M. "A Study of Collusion in First-Price Auctions" (2000) 67 *Review of Economic Studies*

Peyer S. "The Antitrust Damages Directive – Much Ado About Nothing?" in Cisotta R. and Marquis M. (eds), *Litigation and Arbitration in EU Competition Law* (Edward Elgar 2015)

Peyer S. "Compensation and the Damages Directive" (2016) 12 *ECJ*

Philp M. "Conceptualizing Political Corruption" in Heidenheimer Arnold J. and Johnston M. (eds), *Political Corruption: Concepts and Contexts* (Transaction Publishers, 2005)

Piga G. and Zanza M. "An Exploratory Analysis of Public Procurement Practices in Europe" in Thai K.V., et al. (eds), *Challenges in Public Procurement: An International Perspective* (Boca Raton, 2005)

Pijnacker Hordijk E. and Meulenbelt M. "A Bridge Too Far: Why the European Commission's Attempts to Construct an Obligation to Tender Outside the Scope of the Public Procurement Directives Should Be Dismissed" (2005) 3 *PPLR*

Popescu A., Onofrei M. and Kelley C. "An Overview of European Good Practices in Public Procurement" (2016) 7(1) *Eastern Journal of European Studies*

Porter D.P. "The Effect of Bid Withdrawal in a Multi-Object Auction" (1999) 4(1) *Review of Economic Design*

Porter R.H. and Zona J.D. "Collusion" (2008) 2 *Competition Law and Policy: ABA Section of Antitrust Law* 1080

Rachmilevitch S. "Bribing in First-Price Auctions" (2013) 77(1) *Games and Economic Behavior*

Raimundo M.A. "Aiming at the Market You Want: A Critical Analysis of the Duties on Division into Lots Under Directive 2014/24/EU" (2018) 4 *PPLR*

Ramos J.M and Muhume D. "The Brussels Court Judgement in Commission v Elevators Manufacturers, or the Story of How the Commission Lost an Action for Damages Based on Its Own Infringement Decision" (2015) 36 *ECLR*

Rhoad R. and Fornataro M. "A Gathering Storm: The New False Claims Act Amendments and their Impact on Healthcare Fraud Enforcement" (2009) 21(6) *Health Lawyer*

Rijckeghem C. and Weder B. "Bureaucratic Corruption and the Rate of Temptation: Do Wages in the Civil Service Affect Corruption and by How Much?" (2001) 65(2) *Journal of Development Economics*

Risvig Hamer C. "Regular Purchases and Aggregated Procurement: The Changes in the New Public Procurement Directive regarding Framework Agreements, Dynamic Purchasing Systems and Central Purchasing Bodies" (2014) 4 *PPLR*

Robinson M.S. "Collusion and the Choice of Auction" (1985) 16(1) *The RAND Journal of Economics*

Rodger B.J. "Competition Law Litigation in the UK Courts: A Study of All Cases 2005–2008 – Part I" (2009) 2 *GCLR*

Rodger B.J., Sousa Ferro M. and Marcos F. *The EU Antitrust Damages Directive – Transposition in the Member States* (Oxford University Press, 2018)

Roth A. and Ockenfels A. "Last-Minute Bidding and the Rules for Ending Second-Price Auctions: Evidence from eBay and Amazon Auctions on the Internet" (2002) 92(4) *American Economic Review* 1095

Rothkopf M.H. and Harstad R.M. "Modelling Competitive Bidding: A Critical Survey" (1994) 40(3) *Management Science*

Rothkopf M.H. and Whinston A.B. "E-Auctions for Procurement Operations" (2007) 16(4) *Production and Operations Management*

Saddy A. "Front-line Servants, Discretion and corruption" in Racca Gabriella M. and Yukins Christopher R. (eds), *Integrity and Efficiency in Sustainable Public Contracts: Balancing Corruption Concerns in Public Procurement Internationally* (Bruylant, 2014)

Salant D.J. *A Primer on Auction Design, Management and Strategy* (The MIT Press, 2015)

Salmon T.C. "Preventing Collusion between Firms in Auctions" in Janssen M.C.W. (ed), *Auctioning Public Assets: Analysis and Alternatives* (Cambridge University Press, 2004)

Salmon T.C. "Spectrum Auctions by the United States Federal Communications Commission" in Janssen M.C.W. (ed), *Auctions and Beauty Contests: A Policy Perspective* (Cambridge University Press, 2004)

Sammalmaa J. "The Application of the EU Foundational Principles in the Preparation Phase of Public Procurement – A Research Plan", paper presented at the 7th Public Procurement Research Students Conference, University of Nottingham, 8–9 September 2016

Sanchez Graells A. "More Competition-Oriented Public Procurement to Foster Social Welfare" in Thai K.V. (ed), *Towards New Horizons in Public Procurement* (PRAcademics Press, 2010)

Sanchez Graells A. "Prevention and Deterrence of Bid Rigging: A Look from the New EU Directive on Public Procurement" in Racca Gabriella M. and Yukins Christopher R. (eds), *Integrity and Efficiency in Sustainable Public Contracts. Balancing Corruption Concerns in Public Procurement Internationally* (Bruylant, 2014)
Sanchez Graells A. *Public Procurement and the EU Competition Rules* (2nd edn, Bloomsbury, 2015)
Sanchez Graells A. "Truly Competitive Public Procurement as a Europe 2020 Lever: What Role for the Principle of Competition in Moderating Horizontal Policies?" (2016) 22(2) *European Public Law*
Sanchez Graells A. "Competition and Public Procurement" (2018) 9(8) *Journal of European Competition Law & Practice*
Sanchez Graells A. "Competition Law and Public Procurement" in Moreno Molina J.A. and Diaz Bravo E. (eds), *Contración Pública Global: Visiones Compradas* (Valencia Tirant lo Blanch, 2020)
Sandholm T. "Expressive Commerce and Its Application to Sourcing: How We Conducted $35 Billion of Generalized Combinatorial Auctions" (2007) 28(3) *Al Magazine*
Sansom M., Morfey A. and Teague P. "Recent Developments in Private Antitrust Damages Litigation in Europe" (2015) 29 *Antitrust*
Schebesta H. *Damages in EU Public Procurement Law* (Springer International Publishing Switzerland 2016)
Schinkel M.P. "Effective Cartel Enforcement in Europe" (2007) 30 *World Competition*
Schmitt N. and Weder R. "Sunk Costs and Cartel Formation: Theory and Application to the Dyestuff Industry" (1998) 36(2) *Journal of Economic Behaviour and Organisation*
Schoenmaekers S. "The EU Debarment Rules: Legal and Economic Rationale" (2016) 3 *Public Procurement Law Review*
Schoenmaekers S. "Self-Cleaning and Leniency: Comparable Objectives but Different Levels of Success?" (2018) 1(13) *European Procurement and Public Private Partnership Law Review*
Schooner S. "The Paper Tiger Stirs: Rethinking Suspension and Debarment" (2004) 13 *Public Procurement Law Review*
Schultz J. and Søreide T. "Corruption in Emergency Procurement" 32(4) *Disasters*
Semple A. *A Practical Guide to Public Procurement* (Oxford University Press, 2015)
Semple A. and Marta Andrecka "Classification, Conflicts of Interest and Change of Contractor: A Critical Look at the Public Sector Procurement Directive" (2015) 3 *European Procurement and Public Private Partnership Law Review*
Seres G. "Auction Cartels and the Absence of Efficient Communication" (2017) 52 *International Journal of Industrial Organization*
Servenay C. "The New Provisions of Supplies Directive 93/36" (1994) 5 *PPLR*
Simona G. "Public Investments and the Application of Articles 101 and 102 TFEU" in Almăşan A. and Whelan P. (eds), *The Consistent Application of EU Competition Law: Substantive and Procedural Challenges* (Springer, 2017)
Skrzypacz A. and Hopenhayn H. "Tacit Collusion in Repeated Auctions" (2004) 114(1) *Journal of Economic Theory*
Šmejkal V. "Competition Law and the Social Market Economy Goal of the EU" (2015) 1 *International Comparative Jurisprudence*
Smith J.L. "Joint Bidding, Collusion and Bid Clustering in Competitive Auctions" (1983) 50(2) *Southern Economic Journal*
Smith L.K. "Games with Discontinuous Payoffs" (1987) 54 *Review of Economic Studies*
Soloveičik D. and Šimanskis K. "The Evolving Concept of Conflict of Interests in the EU Public Procurement Law" (2017) 2 *EPPPL*
Šostar M. and Marukić A. "Challenges of Public Procurement in EU Funded Projects" (2017) 22(2) *Journal of Contemporary Management Issues*

Soudry O. "Promoting Economy: Electronic Reverse Auctions under the EC Directives on Public Procurement" (2004) 4(3) *Journal of Public Procurement*

Spagnolo G. "Reputation, Competition and Entry in Procurement" (2012) 30(3) *International Journal of Industrial Organization*

Stark R.M. and Rothkopf M.H. "Competitive Bidding: A Comprehensive Bibliography" (1979) 27 *Operations Research*

Stephan A. "An Empirical Assessment of the European Leniency Notice" (2009) 593 *Journal of Competition Law and Economics*

Stephan A. "Price Fixing in Crisis: Implications of an Economic Downturn for Cartels and Enforcement" (2012) 35(3) *World Competition: Law and Economics Review*

Stephan A. "Cartels" in Lianos I. and Geradin D. (eds), *Handbook on European Competition Law* (Edward Elgar Publishing, 2013)

Stephan A. "The EU Damages Directive" in Damien Geradin, Andreas Stephan and Cédric Argenton (eds) *EU Cartel Law and Economics* (Oxford University Press, 2020)

Stephan A. and Hviid M. "Cover Pricing and the Overreach of Object Liability Under Article 101 TFEU" (2015) 38(4) *World Competition: Law and Economics Review*

Stephan A. and Nikpay A. "Leniency Decision-Making from a Corporate Perspective: Complex Realities" in Beaton-Wells C. and Tran C. (eds), *Anti-Cartel Enforcement in a Contemporary Age: The Leniency Religion* (Hart Publishing, 2015)

Stigler G.J. "A Theory of Oligopoly" (1964) 72 *Journal of Political Economy*

Stigler G.J. *The Organisation of Industry* (The University of Chicago Press, 1968)

Swan C. and Manka B. "Risky Business: Does Debarring Poor Performers Mitigate Future Performance Risk?" Working Paper submitted to the Third International Conference on Public Procurement Law Africa, organised by the African Procurement Law Unit at Stellenbosch University (Cape Town, 1–2 November 2018)

Szilagyi P. "Bidding Markets and Competition Law in the European Union and the United Kingdom: Part 1 and 2" (2008) 29(1) *European Competition Law Review*

Tadelis S. "Public Procurement Design: Lessons from the Private Sector" (2012) 30(3) *International Journal of Industrial Organization*

Tadelis S. *Game Theory: An Introduction* (Princeton University Press, 2013)

Teichmann F. "Incentive Systems in Anti-bribery Whistleblowing" (2019) 26(2) *Journal of Financial Crime*

Telser L.G. *Competition, Collusion and Game Theory* (The Macmillan Press Ltd, 1971)

Temple Lang J. "Subsidiarity and Public Purchasing: Who Should Apply Competition Law to Collusive Tendering and How Should They Do It?" (1998) 4(1) *E.P.L.*

Thomas C. "Two Bids or not to Bid? An Exploration of the Legality of Joint Bidding and Subcontracting under EU Competition Law" 6(9) *Journal of European Competition Law and Practice*

Thomas C. "Using Reserve Prices to Deter Collusion in Procurement Competition" (2005) 53(3) *The Journal of Industrial Economics*

Tournier M. and Pheasant J. "The UK Construction Industry Under the Spotlight Again" (2008) 29 *ECLR*

Transparency International. *Handbook for Curbing Corruption in Public Procurement* (Transparency International, 2006)

Trepte P. *Regulating Procurement: Understanding the Ends and Means of Public Procurement Regulation* (Oxford University Press, 2004)

Trepte P. *Public Procurement in the EU-A Practitioner's Guide* (Oxford University Press, 2007)

Treumer S. "Contract Changes and the Duty to Retender under the New EU Public Procurement Directive" (2014) 3 *Public Procurement Law Review*

Treumer S. and Lichère F. *Enforcement of the EU Public Procurement Rules* (Djøf Publishing, 2011)

Trybus M. "The Promotion of Small and Medium Sized Enterprises in Public Procurement: A Strategic Objective of the New Public Sector Directive?" in Lichère F., Caranta R. and Treumer S. (eds), *Modernising Public Procurement: The New Directive* (Djøf Publishing, 2014)

Trybus M. and Andrecka M. "Favouring Small and Medium Sized Enterprises with Directive 2014/24/EU?" (2017) 3 *EPPPL*

Justin P. Tschcoepe. "A Fraud Against One is Apparently a Fraud Against All: The Fraud Enforcement and Recovery Act's Unprecedented Expansion of Liability Under the False Claims Act" (2010) 47(3) *Houston Law Review*

Turocy T. and Stengel B. "Game Theory" in Bidgoli H. (ed), *Encyclopedia of Information Systems* (Elsevier, 2002)

Valentine S. and Godkin L. "Moral Intensity, Ethical Decision Making, and Whistleblowing Intention" (2019) 98 *Journal of Business Research*

Välilä T. "How Expensive Are Cost Savings? On the Economics of Public-Private Partnerships" (2005) 10(1) *European Investment Bank Papers*

Van Hove K., Van Bael and Bellis. "Bid-rigging and Deterrence under the EU Law" *ICN Cartel Workshop* (Ottawa 4–6 October 2017)

Vande Walle S. "Private Enforcement of Antitrust Law in Japan: An Empirical Analysis" (2011) 8 *CompLRev*

Vande Walle S. *Private Antitrust Litigation in the European Union and Japan: A Comparative Perspective* (Maklu Publishers, 2013)

Veldhuizen R.V. "The Influence of Wages on Public Officials' Corruptibility: A Laboratory Investigation" (2013) 39 *Journal of Economic Psychology*

Vickrey W. "Counterspeculation, Auctions and Competitive Sealed Tenders" (1961) 16 *Journal of Finance*

Vickrey W. "Auctions and Bidding Games" in *Recent Advances in Game Theory: Papers Delivered at a Meeting of the Princeton University Conference* (Princeton University Press, 1962)

Waehrer K. "Asymmetric Private Values Auctions with Application to Joint Bidding and Mergers" (1999) 17(3) *International Journal of Industrial Organisation*

Wagner G. "Punitive Damages in European Private Law" in Basedow J., Hopt K.J., Zimmermann R. and Stier A. (eds), *Max Planck Encyclopedia of European Private Law* (Oxford University Press, 2012)

Wagner G. "Compliance and Individual Sanctions in the Enforcement of Competition Law" in Paha F.W. (ed), *Competition Law Compliance Programs-An Interdisciplinary Approach* (Springer, 2016)

Wang H. and Chen H. "Deterring Bidder Collusion: Auction Design Complements Antitrust Policy" (2016) 12(1) *Journal of Competition Law and Economics*

Wardhaugh B. *Cartels, Markets and Crime – A Normative Justification for the Criminalisation of Economic Collusion* (Cambridge University Press, 2014)

Watts L.L. and Buckley M.R. "A Dual-Processing Model of Moral Whistleblowing in Organizations" (2017) 146 *Journal of Business Ethics*

Wauters K. "Public Procurement Review Bodies" in Trybus M., Caranta R. and Edelstam G. (eds), *EU Public Contract Law* (Bruylant, 2013)

Weishaar S., *Cartels, Competition and Public Procurement: Law and Economic Approaches to Bid Rigging* (Edward Elgar, 2013)

Weiss F. *Public Procurement in European Community Law* (Athlone Press, 1993)

Weiss L.W. "The Structure-Conduct – Performance Paradigm and Antitrust" (1979) 127(4) *University of Pennsylvania Law Review*

Whish R. and Bailey D. *Competition Law* (Oxford University Press 2012) 426

Williams R. "The New Procurement Directives of the European Union" (2004) 4 *PPLR*

Williamson O.E. *The Economic Institutions of Capitalism – Firms, Markets, Relational Contracting* (The Free Press, 1985)

Williamson O.E. "Transaction Cost Economics and Organisation Theory" in Williamson O. (ed), *Organisation Theory: From Chester Barnard to the Present and Beyond* (Oxford University Press, 1990)
Wilman F. "The End of the Absence? The Growing Body of EU Legislation on Private Enforcement and the Main Remedies It Provides For" (2016) 53 *CMLR*
Wilman F. *Private Enforcement of EU Law Before National Courts-The EU Legislative Framework* (Edward Elgar, 2015)
Wils W. "Leniency in Antitrust Enforcement: Theory and Practice" (2007) 30(1) *World Competition: Law and Economics Review*
Wils W. "The Use of Leniency in EU Cartel Enforcement: An Assessment after Twenty Years" (2016) 39(3) *World Competition*
Wils W. "Private Enforcement of EU Antitrust Law and Its Relationship with Public Enforcement: Past, Present and Future" (2017) 40(1) *World Competition: Law and Economics Review*
Wils W. "Should the EU Competition Damages Directive Be Revised to Grant Companies That Have Received Immunity from Fines under the Competition Authorities' Leniency Programmes also Immunity from Damages?", September 2023, Concurrences N° 3-2023, Art. N° 112968, pp. 52–71
Wilson R. "Game-Theoretic Analyses of Trading Processes" in Bewley T. (ed), *Advances in Economic Theory: Fifth World Congress* (Cambridge University Press, 1987)
Wilson R. "Strategic Analysis of Auctions" in Aumann R. and Hart S. (eds), *Handbook of Game Theory with Economic Applications* (Elsevier, 1992)
Whistleblower Law Collaborative. "False Claims Act Penalties: A Complete Guide" <www.whistleblowerllc.com/false-claims-act-penalties/>
Yao D. and DeSanti S.S. "Game Theory and the Legal Analysis of Tacit Collusion" (1993) 38(1) *The Antitrust Bulletin*
Yeoh P. "Enhancing Effectiveness of Anti-money Laundering Laws Through Whistleblowing" (2014) 56(6) *International Journal of Law and Management*
Ysewyn J. and Kahmann S. "The Decline and Fall of the Leniency Programme in Europe" Concurrences No 1-2018
Yukins C.R. "Are IDIQs Inefficient? Sharing Lessons with European Framework Contracting" (2008) 37(3) *Public Contract Law Journal*
Zarkada-Fraser A. "A Classification of Factors Influencing Participating in Collusive Tendering Agreements" (2000) 23 *Journal of Business Ethics*
Zhan R.L. "Optimality and Efficiency in Auctions Design: A Survey" in Chinchuluun A., Pardalos P.M., Migdalas A. and Pitsoulis L. (eds), *Pareto Optimality, Game Theory and Equilibria. Springer Optimization and Its Applications*, vol. 17 (Springer, 2008)
Zhu C. "Rationality in Bidding Theory: A Construction Industry Perspective" in Casensky M., Ahmed V., Eaton D. and Sutrisna M. (eds), *Proceedings BuHu 8th International Postgraduate Research Conference* (The Czech Technical University of Prague, 2008)
Zimmermann M. "Economic Efficiency and the Division of Large Procurement Contracts Into Lots: An Analysis" (2017) 4 *EPPPL*

Websites

Abrantes-Metz R.M. and Metz A.D. "The Future of Cartel Deterrence and Detection" (January 2019) CPI Antitrust Chronicle <https://www.competitionpolicyinternational.com/wp-content/uploads/2019/01/CPI-Abrantes-Metz-Metz.pdf>
Achilles. "3 Factors Affecting Procurement Planning" (2016) <www.achilles.com/industry-insights/3-factors-affecting-procurement-planning/>
Alliance against Intellectual Property Theft. "Response to the Law of Damages Consultation July 2007" <https://data.parliament.uk/DepositedPapers/Files/DEP2009-1863/DEP2009-1863.pdf>

Anderson R.D., Jones A. and Kovacic W.E. “Preventing Corruption, Supplier Collusion and the Corrosion of Civic Trust: A Procompetitive Program to Improve the Effectiveness and Legitimacy of Public Procurement” (2019) 5 *George Mason Law Review* <https://papers.ssrn.com/sol3/papers.cfm?abstract_id=3289170>

Andor L. “Building a Social Market Economy in the European Union” Speech 11/695, Manchester, 20 October 2011 <https://europa.eu/rapid/press-release_SPEECH-11-695_en.htm>

Arrowsmith S. “The TFEU Rules” in Arrowsmith S. (ed), *EU Public Procurement Law: An Introduction* (2011) <www.nottingham.ac.uk/pprg/documentsarchive/asialinkmaterials/eupublicprocurementlawintroduction.pdf>

Arrowsmith S. “Public Procurement: Basic Concepts and the Coverage of Procurement Rules” in Arrowsmith S. (ed), *Public Procurement Regulation: An Introduction* <www.nottingham.ac.uk/pprg/documentsarchive/asialinkmaterials/publicprocurementregulationintroduction.pdf>

Atmaca S., Schoors K. and Podkolzina E. “Corrupt Reserve Prices” (2018) <https://editorialexpress.com/cgi-bin/conference/download.cgi?db_name=EEAESEM2018&paper_id=2464>

Auriol E., Hjelmeng E. and Søreide T. “Deterring Corruption and Cartels: In Search of a Coherent Approach”, November 2016 <https://www.tse-fr.eu/sites/default/files/TSE/documents/doc/wp/2016/wp_tse_728.pdf>

Australian Competition and Consumer Commission. “Cartels Deterrence and Detection: A Guide for Government Procurement Officers” <www.jcu.edu.au/__data/assets/pdf_file/0007/101779/jcu_148836.pdf>

Ausubel L.M. and Schwartz J.A. “The Ascending Auction Paradox” (1999) <https://pdfs.semanticscholar.org/93f2/3466c138b557223cf6c4dd4a26dd5e34fec1.pdf?_ga=2.161674872.597724635.1541881262-1783031146.1541881262>

Authority for Consumers and Markets. “NMa Fines 22 Construction Companies for Cartel Agreements” <www.acm.nl/en/publications/publication/6024/NMa-Fines-22-Construction-Companies-for-Cartel-Agreements>

Awesti A. “The Myth of Eurosclerosis: European Integration in the 1970s” (2009) 3 *L’ Europe en Formation* 353–354 <https://shs.cairn.info/revue-l-europe-en-formation-2009-3-page-39?lang=fr&ref=doi>

Bach A. and Wolf C. “Germany: Private Antitrust Litigation” <www.globalcompetitionreview.com/review/the-european-middle-east-and-african-antitrust-review/2021/article/germany-private-antitrust-litigation>

Bajari P. and Tadelis S. “Procurement Contracts: Fixed Price vs. Cost Plus” <https://papers.ssrn.com/sol3/papers.cfm?abstract_id=156470>

Bakowski P. and Voronova S. “Corruption in the European Union – Prevalence of Corruption, and Anti-Corruption Efforts in Selected EU Member States” <www.europarl.europa.eu/RegData/etudes/STUD/2017/608687/EPRS_STU(2017)608687_EN.pdf>

BBC. “Building Companies fined £129.5m” <http://news.bbc.co.uk/1/hi/business/8268116.stm>

Bennett J. “Innovation Partnership – Does It Offer A Genuine Breakthrough?” <http://publicsectorblog.practicallaw.com/innovation-partnership-does-it-offer-a-genuine-breakthrough/>

Bhargava B., Jenamani M. and Zhong Y. “Understanding the Impact of Shill Bidding in Online English Auctions”, Technical Report CSD-TR 03-036, Department of Computer Science, Purdue University, 2003, <https://pdfs.semanticscholar.org/eee4/ef16b12e99193ad42bdfead2ffe0163ca7e3.pdf>

Bird & Bird. “Introduction to EU Public Procurement Law” <www.twobirds.com/~/media/PDFs/Brochures/Public%20procurement/Bird%20%20Bird%20%20Introduction%20to%20EU%20Public%20Procurement%20Law.pdf>

Bos L.- DG CONNECT F3 unit ("Digital Innovation and Blockchain"). "Update on Results from Completed and Ongoing FP7 and Horizon 2020 funded Pre-Commercial Procurement (PCP) <ec.europa.eu/newsroom/document.cfm?doc_id=8949>

Braun P. "The Practical Impact of E.U. Public Procurement Law on PFI Procurement Practice in the United Kingdom" <www.nottingham.ac.uk/pprg/documentsarchive/phdtheses/phd_peter_braun_.pdf>

Brussels Matters. "The European Antitrust Leniency Calculus c. 2016: Still Worth It?" (Brussels 16 June 2016) <http://www.brusselsmatters.eu/index.html?page=489&sz_event=Leniency16>

Burke K. Trade Interchange "Reverse Auctions in the Public Sector – Emergence and Usage, April 2007" <https://pdfs.semanticscholar.org/d121/ff04defed4525ec116baf7fb56b97a6f8a40.pdf>

Burguet R. and Garcia-Montalvo J. "The Microeconomics of Corruption. A Review of Thirty Years of Research" (2016) Working Papers 908, Barcelona Graduate School of Economics <www.iae.csic.es/investigatorsMaterial/a16209105703sp27669.pdf>

Burton R.-Concurrences. "The Spanish Competition Authority Fines € 2 M Hospital Waste Management Companies For Market-Sharing Arrangement (Consenur/Cespa/Interlun/Sistemas Integrales Sanitarios)" <www.concurrences.com/en/bulletin/news-issues/january-2010/The-Spanish-Competition-Authority-41648>

Cabinet Office of United Kingdom. "Procurement Policy Note-Procurement Supporting Growth: Supporting Material for Departments, Action Note 04/12" (9 May 2012) <www.gov.uk/government/uploads/system/uploads/attachment_data/file/62097/PPN-Procurement-Supporting-Growth.pdf>

Canadian Competition Bureau. "Bid-Rigging: Detecting, Preventing and Reporting" <www.competitionbureau.gc.ca/eic/site/cb-bc.nsf/eng/02646.html>

Capobianco A. and Cwikel Y. "Roundtable on Ex Officio Cartel Investigations and the Use of Screens to Detect Cartels" (OECD, 4 November 2013) <www.oecd.org/officialdocuments/publicdisplaydocumentpdf/?cote=DAF/COMP%282013%2914&docLanguage=En>

Claeson A. "Modernisation of Public Procurement – Making the Public Market More Competitive and Collusion Proof?" (2014) <https://lup.lub.lu.se/student-papers/search/publication/4459522>

Commission on Protection of Competition Bulgaria. "Guidelines for Fighting Bid-Rigging in Public Procurement" <https://unctad.org/meetings/en/Contribution/ccpb_SCF_Bid-rigging%20Guidelines_en.pdf>

Competition Authority Ireland (The). "The Detection and Prevention of Collusive Tendering" <www.ccpc.ie/business/wp-content/uploads/sites/3/2017/02/Booklet-The-Detection-and-Prevention-of-Collusive-Tendering.pdf>

Competition and Markets Authority. "CMA Launches Digital Tool to Fight Bid-Rigging" <www.gov.uk/government/news/cma-launches-digital-tool-to-fight-bid-rigging>

Competition and Markets Authority. "Local Authorities and Competition" <www.gov.uk/government/uploads/system/uploads/attachment_data/file/669668/local_authorities_and_competition_final_report.pdf>

Competition and Markets Authority. "Public Sector Procurers: Bid-Rigging Advice" <www.gov.uk/government/collections/bid-rigging-advice-and-tools-for-public-sector-procurers>

Competition Commission South Africa. "How to Prevent, Detect and Report Collusive Tendering" <www.compcom.co.za/wp-content/uploads/2014/09/Bid-rigging2-2.pdf>

Competition Council of the Republic of Lithuania. "Vilnius Regional Administrative Court: Joint Bidding by Construction Companies Restricted Competition" <https://kt.gov.lt/en/news/vilnius-regional-administrative-court-joint-bidding-by-construction-companies-restricted-competition>

Concurrences. "The Lithuanian Competition Authority Fines Two Construction Firms for Bid Rigging in the Market for Renovation and Modernisation of Schools and

Kindergartens (IRDAIVA) <www.concurrences.com/en/bulletin/news-issues/december-2017/the-lithuanian-competition-authority-fines-two-construction-firms-for-bid>

Crown Commercial Service of United Kingdom. "eAuctions" <www.crowncommercial.gov.uk/information-for-buyers-and-suppliers/start-buying/commercial-agreements/eauctions>

Crown Commercial Service of United Kingdom. "National Fuels" <https://ccs-agreements.cabinetoffice.gov.uk/contracts/rm3801>

Danish Competition and Consumer Authority. "Joint Bidding Under Competition Law-Guidelines 2018" <www.en.kfst.dk/media/50765/050718_joint-bidding-guidelines.pdf>

Davies S. and Ormosi P.L. "The Economic Impact of Cartels and Anti-Cartel Enforcement" (2014) CCP Working Paper 13-7 v2 <https://ueaeco.github.io/working-papers/papers/ccp/CCP-13-07v2.pdf>

Davis H. "Deciding the Duration of a Facilities Management Contract" <www.fgould.com/uk-europe/articles/deciding-duration-facilities-management-contract/>

Department for Business Innovation & Skills. "Private Actions in Competition Law: A Consultation on Options for Reform-Government Response, January 2013" <www.gov.uk/government/uploads/system/uploads/attachment_data/file/70185/13-501-private-actions-in-competition-law-a-consultation-on-options-for-reform-government-response1.pdf>

Department of Justice. "False Claims Act Settlements and Judgments Exceed $2 Billion in Fiscal Year 2022" <www.justice.gov/opa/pr/false-claims-act-settlements-and-judgments-exceed-2-billion-fiscal-year-2022>

Department of Justice. "Justice Department Recovers Over $2.8 Billion from False Claims Act Cases in Fiscal Year 2018" <www.justice.gov/opa/pr/justice-department-recovers-over-28-billion-false-claims-act-cases-fiscal-year-2018>

DIGIWHIST < http://digiwhist.eu/about-digiwhist/>

EQS Integrity Line. "A Closer Look at the Ethics Behind Whistle-blower Rewards" <www.integrityline.com/expertise/blog/ethics-behind-whistleblower-rewards/>

Europa. "Public Contracts: EU Rules & Procedures" <http://europa.eu/youreurope/business/public-tenders/rules-procedures/index_en.htm>

Europe Economics and Milieu for the European Commission. "Economic Efficiency and Legal Effectiveness of Review and Remedies Procedures for Public Contracts – Final Study Report MARKT/2013/072/C, April 2015" <www.osservatorioappalti.unitn.it/viewFile.do?id=1452091689514&dataId=8234&filename=Testo.pdf>

European Commission. "Glossary of Terms Used in EU Competition Policy – Antitrust and Control of Concentrations, 2002" <http://ec.europa.eu/translation/spanish/documents/glossary_competition_archived_en.pdf>

European Commission. "Notice on Tools to Fight Collusion in Public Procurement and on Guidance on How to Apply the Related Exclusion Ground" <https://ec.europa.eu/docsroom/documents/45004>

European Commission. "Guide for Tenderers-Submitting Bids in Response to a Call for Tenders Published by the Office for Infrastructure and Logistics-Brussels, 2002" <http://ec.europa.eu/oib/doc/tenders-submission-guide_en.pdf>

European Commission. "Green Paper-Damages Actions for Breach of the EC Antitrust Rules" COM (2005) 672, 19 December 2005 <https://eur-lex.europa.eu/legal-content/EN/TXT/PDF/?uri=CELEX:52005DC0672&from=EN>

European Commission. "Explanatory Note-Framework Agreements-Classic Directive" (2005) < https://ec.europa.eu/docsroom/documents/15474/attachments/1/translations/en/renditions/pdf>

European Commission. "Impact Assessment Report-Remedies in the Field of Public Procurement", COM (2006) 195 <http://ec.europa.eu/transparency/regdoc/rep/2/2006/EN/2-2006-557-EN-1-0.Pdf>

European Commission. "Internal Market, Industry, Entrepreneurship and SMEs" <https://ec.europa.eu/growth/single-market/public-procurement_en>
European Commission. "Leniency" <http://ec.europa.eu/competition/cartels/leniency/leniency.html>
European Commission. "Staff Working Paper accompanying the White Paper on Damages Actions for Breach of the EC Antitrust Rules" COM (2008) 165 final <http://eur-lex.europa.eu/legal-content/EN/TXT/PDF/?uri=CELEX:52008SC0404&from=EN>
European Commission. "White Paper on Damages Actions for Breach of the EC Antitrust Rules" COM (2008)165 final <http://ec.europa.eu/competition/antitrust/actionsdamages/impact_assessment_en.pdf>
European Commission. "First Report on Competition Policy – Annexed to the Fifth General Report on the Activities of the Communities" <https://publications.europa.eu/en/publication-detail/-/publication/41881 7dc-c69b-42b1-a787-013fd545017d/language-en>
European Commission. "Evaluation Report-Impact and Effectiveness of EU Public Procurement Legislation, Part 1" (2011) <http://ec.europa.eu/transparency/regdoc/rep/2/2011/EN/SEC-2011-853-F1-EN-MAIN-PART-1.PDF>
European Commission. "Green Paper on the Modernisation of EU Public Procurement Policy towards a More Efficient European Procurement Market Synthesis of Replies" <https://op.europa.eu/en/publication-detail/-/publication/04a30c4a-e533-41ec-a039-231f1aa39645/language-en>
European Commission. "Impact Assessment Report – Damages Actions for Breach of the EU Antitrust Rules", COM (2013) 404 final, <http://ec.europa.eu/competition/antitrust/actionsdamages/impact_assessment_en.pdf>
European Commission. "Practical Guide Quantifying Harm in Actions for Damages Based on Breaches of Article 101 or 102 of the Treaty on the Functioning of the European Union" SWD (2013)205<www.ec.europa.eu/competition/antitrust/actionsdamages/quantification_guide_en.pdf>
European Commission. "Businesses' Attitudes towards Corruption in the EU – Flash Eurobarometer 543" https://europa.eu/eurobarometer/surveys/detail/3180
European Commission. "Prior Market Consultations-Simplification and Efficiency" <https://ec.europa.eu/regional_policy/policy/how/improving-investment/public-procurement/e-library_en>
European Commission. "Support the Growth of ICT Innovative Creative Industries SMEs" <https://ec.europa.eu/info/funding-tenders/opportunities/portal/screen/opportunities/topic-details/ict-18-2014>
European Commission. "Public Procurement" <https://ec.europa.eu/growth/single-market/public-procurement_en>
European Commission. "Public Procurement Indicators 2015" <http://ec.europa.eu/DocsRoom/documents/20679>
European Commission. "EU Public Procurement Reform: Less Bureaucracy, Higher Efficiency" (2016) <https://ec.europa.eu/docsroom/documents/16412/attachments/1/translations/en/renditions/native>
European Commission. "Study on the Passing-On of Overcharges – Final Report 2016" <http://ec.europa.eu/competition/publications/reports/KD0216916ENN.pdf>
European Commission. "Digital Procurement" <http://ec.europa.eu/growth/single-market/public-procurement/e-procurement_en>
European Commission. Directorate-General for Internal Market, Industry, Entrepreneurship and SMEs ("Analysis of the SMEs' Participation in Public Procurement and the Measures to Support It – Final Report 2019" <https://op.europa.eu/en/publication-detail/-/publication/eec8227c-ecc4-11ea-b3c6-01aa75ed71a1
European Commission. Directorate-General for Internal Market, Industry, Entrepreneurship and SMEs (European Commission) "SME Definition" <https://single-market-economy.ec.europa.eu/smes/sme-fundamentals/sme-definition_en>

European Commission. “Europe 2020-A Strategy for Smart, Sustainable and Inclusive Growth” <http://eur-lex.europa.eu/legal-content/EN/TXT/PDF/?uri=CELEX:52010DC2020&from=EN>

European Commission. “Proposal for a Directive of the European Parliament and of the Council on the Protection of Persons Reporting on Breaches of Union Law”, 23 April 2018, COM (2018) 218 final-2018/0106 (COD) <https://eur-lex.europa.eu/legal-content/EN/TXT/?uri=celex:52018PC0218>

European Commission. “Long Term Action Plan for Better Implementation and Enforcement of Single Market Rules” COM(2020) 94 final, Brussels 10.3.2020 <https://eur-lex.europa.eu/legal-content/EN/TXT/?uri=COM%3A2020%3A94%3AFIN>

European Commission. “Antitrust and Cartels” https://ec.europa.eu/competition/cartels/whistleblower/ index.html

European Commission. Directorate-General for Internal Market, Industry, Entrepreneurship and SMEs, Ludovica Rossi, Jennifer McGuinn, Meena Fernandes “Estimating the economic benefits of whistle-blower protection in public procurement – Final report”, Publications Office, 2017 <https://data.europa.eu/doi/10.2873/125033>

European Court of Auditors (ECA). “Special Report – The EU Institutions Can Do More to Facilitate Access to Their Public Procurement” <www.eca.europa.eu/Lists/ECADocuments/SR16_17/SR_PROCUREMENT_EN.pdf>

European Court of Auditors (ECA). “Special Report 28 – Public Procurement in the EU: Less Competition for Contracts Awarded for Works, Goods and Services in the 10 Years up to 2021” <www.eca.europa.eu/en/publications?ref=sr-2023-28>

European Parliament “The Cost of Non-Europe in the Area of Organised Crime and Corruption – Annex II-Corruption” <www.europarl.europa.eu/RegData/etudes/IDAN/2016/558779/EPRS_IDA%282016%29558779%28ANN2%29_EN.pdf>

European Public Accountability Mechanisms (EuroPAM) https://europam.eu/>

Eversheds Sutherland LLP “Evershed’s Procurement Ebriefing: Can Contracting Authorities Mitigate the Risk of An Ineffectiveness Claim?” <www.eversheds-sutherland.com/global/en/what/articles/index.page?ArticleID=en/Public_Procurement/Procurement_ebrief_Contracting_authorities_mitigate_the_risk_050411>

Fazekas M., Tóth I.J. and King L.P. “Corruption Manual for Beginners: ‘Corruption Techniques’ in Public Procurement with Examples from Hungary” <www.crcb.eu/wp-content/uploads/2013/12/Fazekas-Toth-King_Corruption-manual-for-beginners_v2_2013.pdf>

Fenwick Elliott. “The Brand New Law on Liquidated Damages” <www.fenwickelliott.com/research-insight/newsletters/insight/53>

Finnish Competition and Consumer Authority. “Bidding Cartels” <www.kkv.fi/en/facts-and-advice/competition-affairs/competition-restraints/cartels-and-other-horizontal-agreements/bidding-cartels/>

FMG Consulting & Nabarro LLP. “Lessons Learnt from the National Sports Centers – Procurement of New Operating Contracts – Sport England” <www.whatdotheyknow.com/request/323120/response/811144/attach/6/Lessons%20Learned%20Report%20Sport%20England%20070911.doc?cookie_passthrough=1>

Gerde A. and Vadasz-Nilsson A. “The Swedish Asphalt Cartel and Methods to Detect Cartel Activity The Asphalt Case” <www.piarc.org/ressources/documents/553,2.4-Gerde-Vadasz-Nilsson-1005C13.pdf>

Giersch H. “Eurosclerosis” (1985), Kiel Discussion Papers 112, Kiel Institute for the World Economy (ifW) <https://www.econstor.eu/bitstream/10419/48070/1/025296167.pdf>

Global Competition Review, Jan Magne Juuhl-Langseth, Mona Søyland and Anders Thue Simonsen Vogt Wiig AS. “Norway: Overview” <https://globalcompetitionreview.com/review/the-european-middle-east-and-african-antitrust-review/the-european-middle-eastern-and-african-antitrust-review-2017/article/norway-overview>

Goldman E., Rocholl J. and So J. "Political Connections and the Allocation of Procurement Contracts" <http://idei.fr/sites/default/files/medias/doc/conf/icied/papers_2011/goldman.pdf>

Tech Monitor. "Use of VEAT Notices to Avoid Contract Competition Grows" <www.techmonitor.ai/digital-economy/government-computing/use-of-veat-notices-to-avoid-contract-competition-grows?cf-view>

Gramsch M. and Simmons & Simmons elexica. "Liquidated Damages in General Purchasing Terms" <www.elexica.com/en/legal-topics/antitrust-and-merger-control/190617-liquidated-damages-general-purchasing-terms>

Gream M. "An Overview of EC Regulation 1/2003 as the New Implementing Regulation for the Rules on Competition Laid Down in Articles 81 and 82 of the EC Treaty" <http://matthewgream.net/Professional/IntellectualProperty/overview_ec-reg-1-2003_paper.pdf>

Hamaguchi Y., et al. "An Experimental Study of Procurement Auctions with Leniency Program", CPRC Discussion Paper Series CPDP-24-E January 2007 <www.semanticscholar.org/paper/An-experimental-study-of-procurement-auctions-with-Hamaguchi-Ishikawa/646fe57a46e5481525e4f170ca7727b56444a2e4>

Hammond S.D. "Dispelling the myths surrounding information sharing" ICN Cartels Workshop (Sydney, Australia, 20–21 November, 20040 <www.justice.gov/atr/speech/dispelling-myths-surrounding-information-sharing>

HM Treasury. "Competitive Dialogue in 2008-OGC/HMT Joint Guidance on Using the Procedure" <https://assets.publishing.service.gov.uk/government/uploads/system/uploads/attachment_data/file/225317/02_competitive_dialogue_procedure.pdf>

International Anti-corruption Resource Center. "Guide to Combating Corruption & Fraud in Development Projects-Collusive Bidding Schemes" <https://guide.iacrc.org/potential-scheme-collusive-bidding/>

International Competition Network. "Anti-Cartel Enforcement Manual – Relationships between Competition Agencies and Public Procurement Bodies" (April 2015) <www.internationalcompetitionnetwork.org/portfolio/public-procurement-relationships/>

International Renewable Energy Agency (IRENA) and Clean Energy Ministerial (CEM). "Renewable Energy Auctions: A Guide to Design" (2015) <www.irena.org/-/media/Files/IRENA/Agency/Publication/2015/IRENA_RE_Auctions_Guide_2015_5_winner_selection.pdf?la=en&hash=F45C1A24BD68F9AF3F52A264AF6C7B7E11940177>

Ivaldi M., et all. "The Economics of Tacit Collusion – Final Report for DG Competition, European Commission" <https://ec.europa.eu/competition/mergers/studies_reports/the_economics_of_tacit_collusion_en.pdf>

Justice Manual (The), Title 1-12.000 – Coordination of Parallel Criminal, Civil, Regulatory, and Administrative Proceedings confirms this. <www.justice.gov/jm/jm-1-12000-coordination-parallel-criminal-civil-regulatory-and-administrative-proceedings>

Kenny C. and Musatova M. "Red Flags of Corruption in World Bank Projects: An Analysis of Infrastructure Contracts – Policy Research Working Paper 5243, 2010", World Bank, Washington<https://openknowledge.worldbank.org/bitstream/handle/10986/3731/WPS5243.pdf?sequence=1&isAllowed=y>

Kramer M. and International Anti-Corruption Resource Center. "The Most Common Procurement Fraud Schemes and their Primary Red Flags" <http://iacrc.org/procurement-fraud/the-most-common-procurement-fraud-schemes-and-their-primary-red-flags/>

Krause P. and Tutunji L. "World Bank Three Reasons Procurement is Essential for Development" <https://blogs.worldbank.org/governance/three-reasons-procurement-essential-development>

Kwasnica A.M. and Sherstyuk K. "Collusion via Signalling in Multiple Object Auctions with Complementarities – An Experimental Test" (2002) <https://pdfs.semanticscholar.org/9417/75cd81f58097e3f45883299d2fc6819634eb.pdf?_ga=2.66081262.1511037327.1541978821-1783031146.1541881262>

Le V., Haan J. and Dietzenbacher E. "Do Higher Government Wages Reduce Corruption? Evidence Based on a Novel Dataset" (2013) CESifo Working Paper 4254 <https://papers.ssrn.com/sol3/papers.cfm?abstract_id=2274648>

Levin J. "Auction Theory" (2004) Lecture Notes-Unpublished Manuscript, Stanford University <https://web.stanford.edu/~jdlevin/Econ%20286/Auctions.pdf>

LexisNexis. "PFI (Private Finance Initiative)/PPP (Public Private Partnerships) and Procurement" <www.lexisnexis.com/uk/lexispsl/bankingandfinance/document/391289/5D5H-YTC1-F185-X42J-00000-00/PFI-(Private-Finance-Initiative)-PPP-(Public-Private-Partnerships)-and-procurement#>

LexisPSL Local Government Team. "The Innovation Partnership Explained" <https://localgovernmentlawyer.co.uk/lexisnexis/561-lexis-lg/lexis/localgov/procurement/31403-the-innovation-partnership-procedure-explained-2%20:>

Lindberg R., "Finnish Competition Authority Boosting the Crisis Economy – Competition as an Ally" <https://competitionpolicyinternational.com/assets/0d358061e11f2708ad9d62634c6c40ad/Lindberg-JUNE-2009_1_.pdf>

Llorente-Saguer A. and Zultan R. "Auction Mechanisms and Bidder Collusion: Bribes, Signals and Selection", Discussion Paper No. 14-06, December 2014 <http://in.bgu.ac.il/en/humsos/Econ/Workingpapers/1406.pdf>

Local Government Lawyer. "Horses for Courses" <www.localgovernmentlawyer.co.uk/procurement-and-contracts/308-procurement-features/25892-horses-for-courses>

London Borough of Havering. "Invitation to Continue Dialogue – Havering Estate Regeneration Partner Project" <http://democracy.havering.gov.uk/documents/s27129/5.%20LBH%2012%20Sites%20Regeneration%20Procurement%20-%20ITCD.pdf>

Lundvall B-A. "Product Innovation and User-Producer Interaction" <https://vbn.aau.dk/files/7556474/user-producer.pdf>

Malhotra D. "Study on Government Procurement. Study for Evidence Based Competition Advocacy" (CUTS Institute for Regulation and Competition, January 2012) <http://www.circ.in/pdf/Government_Procurement.pdf>

Mance H. and Parker G. "Financial Times UK Finance Watchdog Exposes Lost PFI Billions", 18 January 2018<www.ft.com/content/db1b5c66-fba7-11e7-9b32-d7d59aace167>

Marty F. and Voisin A. "Partnership Contracts, Project Finance and Information Asymmetries: From Competition for the Contract to Competition within the Contract?" <www.oecd.org/mena/governance/41767913.pdf>

Matechak J.P. and Centre for International Private Enterprise. "Fighting Corruption in Public Procurement" <www.cipe.com/sites/default/files/publication-docs/matechak.pdf>

McHugh N. and Forster C. "Cover Pricing and Bid Rigging: Illegal and on the ACCC's Radar" <www.lexology.com/library/detail.aspx?g=49947859-e19b-4a44-b651-c7dc13502743>

McKenna J.F. and Reed Smith L.L.P. "Liquidated Damages and Penalty Clauses: A Civil Law versus Common Law Comparison – The Critical Path" <www.reedsmith.com/en/perspectives/2008/05/the-critical-path>

Monti M. "Competition in a Social Market Economy", Speech 2000/022, Freiburg, 9–10 November 2000 <https://ec.europa.eu/competition/speeches/text/sp2000_022_en.pdf>

Moore J. "Cartels Facing Competition in Public Procurement: An Empirical Analysis, September 2012 <http://chaire-eppp.org/files_chaire/moore_2013_-_cartels_facing_competition.pdf>

National Archives of the United Kingdom. "Court of Chancery: Office of the Accountant General, Supreme Court Pay Office: Indexes to Accounts" <http://discovery.nationalarchives.gov.uk/details/r/C18421>

NBS. "Specification Report 2017" <www.thenbs.com/knowledge/nbs-specification-report-2017>

OECD. "Policy Roundtables-Oligopoly" (1999) <www.oecd.org/en/publications/oligopoly_4f85ebf0-en.html >

OECD. Policy Brief-Small and Medium-Sized Enterprises: Local Strength, Global Reach" (June 2000)<www.oecd.org/cfe/leed/1918307.pdf>

OECD. "Policy Roundtables: Competition in Bidding Markets 2006" <www.oecd.org/en/publications/competition-in-bidding-markets_af4c1b4b-en.html>

OECD. "Recommendation of the Council on Enhancing Integrity in Public Procurement, OECD/LEGAL/0369" <https://legalinstruments.oecd.org/public/doc/131/131.en.pdf>

OECD. *Integrity in Public Procurement. Good Practice from A to Z* (OECD, 2007) <https://read.oecd-ilibrary.org/governance/integrity-in-public-procurement_9789264027510-en#page1>

OECD. "Policy Roundtables: Collusion and Corruption in Public Procurement 2010" <www.oecd.org/en/publications/collusion-and-corruption-in-public-procurement_ef957f70-en.html>

OECD. "Centralised Purchasing Systems in the European Union – SIGMA Papers No. 47" <www.oecd-ilibrary.org/governance/centralised-purchasing-systems-in-the-european-union_5kgkgqv703xw-en>

OECD. "Competition and Procurement – Key Findings 2011" <www.oecd.org/en/publications/competition-and-procurement-key-findings_c6e6d5ae-en.html>

OECD. "Fighting Bid Rigging in Public Procurement – Report on Implementing the OECD Recommendation" (2016) <www.oecd.org/en/publications/2016/09/fighting-bid-rigging-in-public-procurement-report-on-implementing-the-oecd-recommendation_5cf813ae.html>

OECD. "Hearing on Auctions and Tenders: Further Issues – Working Party No. 2 on Competition and Regulation" <https://one.oecd.org/document/DAF/COMP/WP2(2015)1/en/pdf>

OECD. "Relationship Between Public and Private Antitrust Enforcement" <https://www.oecd.org/en/publications/relationship-between-public-and-private-antitrust-enforcement_8c535258-en.html>

OECD. "Implementing the EU Directives on the Selection of Economic Operators in Public Procurement Procedures-SIGMA Paper No. 56" <www.sigmaweb.org/publications/Selection-of-economic-operators-in-public-procurement-procedures-SIGMA-Paper-56-September-2018.pdf>

OECD. "Principles for Integrity in Public Procurement" <http://oecd.org/gov/ethics/48994520.pdf>

OECD. "Public Procurement: The Role of Competition Authorities in Promoting Competition" <www.oecd.org/en/publications/public-procurement-the-role-of-competition-authorities-in-promoting-competition_8ed0c7ba-en.html>

OECD. "Bribery in Public Procurement: Methods, Actors and Counter-Measures" <www.oecd.org/daf/anti-bribery/anti-briberyconvention/44956834.pdf>

Office of Fair Trading (OFT). "Assessing the Impact of Public Sector Procurement on Competition" (September 2004) <https://webarchive.nationalarchives.gov.uk/20140402182823/http://www.oft.gov.uk/shared_oft/reports/comp_policy/oft742a.pdf>

Office of Fair Trading (OFT). "Competition Act 1998-Decision of OFT No.CA98/02/2009-Bid Rigging in the Construction Industry in England, 21 September 2009" <http://webarchive.nationalarchives.gov.uk/20140402142426/http://www.oft.gov.uk/shared_oft/business_leaflets/general/CE4327-04_Decision__public_1.pdf>

Office of Fair Trading (OFT). "Bid Rigging in the Construction Industry in England" <http://webarchive.nationalarchives.gov.uk/20140402142426/http:/www.oft.gov.uk/OFTwork/competition-act-and-cartels/ca98/decisions/bid_rigging_construction>

Office of Government Commerce. "An Introduction to Public Procurement" <www.scribd.com/document/72138907/Introduction-to-Public-Procurement>

Office of Government Commerce. "OGC Guidance on Framework Agreements in the Procurement Regulations September, 2008"<http://webarchive.nationalarchives.gov.uk

/20100519202848/http://www.ogc.gov.uk/documents/OGC_Guidance_on_Framework_AgreementsSept_08.pdf>

OLAF. "Fraud in Public Procurement – A collection of Red Flags and Best Practices" <https://sfc.ec.europa.eu/system/files/documents/sfc-files/fraud-public-procurement-final-20122017-ares20176254403.pdf>

O'Regan R.T. "A Look at the Game Theory of Online Auctions: The Choice Between End-Time Formats on Yahoo! Auctions" <https://dlib.bc.edu/islandora/object/bc-ir:102332/datastream/PDF/view>

Palma Rodriguez M. "Disclosure of Evidence under the Damages Directive: Conflicts and Compatibility between the ECJ's Case-by-Case Analysis and the Rules on Protection of Immunity Recipients' Information – Study Paper No 01/18" Europa Kolleg Hamburg, Institute for European Integration <https://europa-kolleg-hamburg.de/wp-content/uploads/2018/03/SP-01-18.pdf>

Parliamentary Assembly – Council of Europe. "Improving the Protection of Whistle-blowers all over Europe-Report | Doc. 14958 | 30 August 2019" <https://assembly.coe.int/nw/xml/XRef/Xref-XML2HTML-EN.asp?fileid=28096>

Policonomics – Economics made simple. "Game Theory III: Collusion" < http://policonomics.com/lp-game-theory3-collusion/>

Procurement Lawyers' Association. "The Use of Framework Agreements in Public Procurement" <www.procurementlawyers.org.uk/wp-content/uploads/2017/07/PLA_Paper-on-Frameworks.pdf>

PwC, London Economics and Ecorys for the European Commission. "Public Procurement in Europe-Cost and Effectiveness" (2011) <https://op.europa.eu/en/publication-detail/-/publication/0cfa3445-7724-4af5-8c2b-d657cd690c03>

PwC, ICF GHK and Ecorys. "SMEs' Access to Public Procurement Markets and Aggregation of Demand in the EU" (2014) <http://ec.europa.eu/DocsRoom/documents/15459>

Regulatory Policy Institute (RPI). "Reverse e-Auctions and NHS Procurement: Executive Summary" <https://rpiresearchgroup.org/files/eAuctions_Exec_Summary_TME33py.pdf>

Renda A., Peysner J., Riley A.J. and Rodger B.J. "Making Antitrust Damages Actions More Effective in the EU: Welfare Impact and Potential Scenarios – Final Report" <www.ec.europa.eu/competition/antitrust/actionsdamages/files_white_paper/impact_study.pdf>

Sanchez Graells A. "Bid Rigging, Self-Cleaning, Leniency and Claims for Damages: A Beautiful Procurement Mess? (C-124/17) <http://www.howtocrackanut.com/blog/tag/vossloh+laeis>

Schmöller A. "Bidding Behaviour, Seller Strategies, and the Utilization of Information in Auctions for Complex Goods", Munich Dissertations in Economics, University of Munich, Department of Economics (2010) <https://edoc.ub.uni-muenchen.de/11175/1/Schmoeller_Arno.pdf>

Scottish Procurement. "The Procurement Journey" <www.procurementjourney.scot/procurement-journey>

Selhofer H., Lilischkis S, Karageorgos G. and O'Donnell P. "The European e-Business Report 2006/07 edition – A Portrait of e-business in 10 sectors of the EU Economy 5th Synthesis Report of the e-Business W@tch" <http://aei.pitt.edu/54204/1/2006-2007.pdf>

Semple A. "Public Procurement Analysis Legal Considerations for Market Engagement" <https://ec.europa.eu/environment/gpp/pdf/24_11_2015/Webinar%20slides_Semple.pdf>

Semple A. "Guidance for Public Authorities on Public Procurement of Innovation" <https://www.base.gov.pt/Base4/media/d2hmijtc/ppi-platform_guide_new-final-documento-iclei.pdf>

Seres G. "Collusion Mechanisms in Auctions with Private and Common Values" <https://editorialexpress.com/cgi-bin/conference/download.cgi?db_name=EWM2014&paper_id=182>

SIGMA. "Market Analysis, Preliminary Market Consultations and Prior Involvement of Candidates/Tenderers – Brief 32" (September 2016) <www.sigmaweb.org/publications/Public-Procurement-Policy-Brief-32-200117.pdf>

SIGMA-OECD. "Brief 2 – Economic Issues in Public Procurement" (January 2011) <www.sigmaweb.org/publications/Economic_Issues_Public_Procurement_2011.pdf>

SIGMA-OECD. "Small and Medium-Sized Enterprises (SMEs) in Public Procurement" (2016) <www.sigmaweb.org/publications/Public-Procurement-Policy-Brief-33-200117.pdf>

SIGMA-OECD. "Brief 36 – Division off Contracts into Lots" <www.sigmaweb.org/publications/Public-Procurement-Policy-Brief-36-200117.pdf>

Slaughter and May. "Private Equity and Competition Law" <www.slaughterandmay.com/media/odhn4oip/private_equity_and_competition_law_consortium_bids_1212pdf.pdf>

Smith P. "Five Alternative Approaches to Lots Lotting for Contracts" <www.publicspendforum.net/blogs/peter-smith/2017/03/15/contracts-lots-lotting-public-procurement-uk-europe>

Sofia Competition Forum. "Guidelines for Fighting Bid-Rigging in Public Procurement" <https://unctad.org/system/files/non-official-document/ccpb_SCF_Bid-rigging%20Guidelines_en.pdf>

Søreide T. "Corruption in Public Procurement, Causes, Consequences and Cures", Chr. Michelsen Institute, Bergen 2002 <www.cmi.no/publications/843-corruption-in-public-procurement-causes>

Spagnolo G. "Public Procurement, Bid Rigging and (the Lack of) Actions for Damages", Lear Conference on Public Procurement and Competition Policy, Rome, 3–5 July 2017 <www.learconference.com/wp-content/uploads/2017/07/SPAGNOLO_Damages_Lear_2017.pdf>

Spend Network for Competition and Markets Authority (CMA). "Report on Bid-Rigging Algorithms-The Use of Public Sector Procurement Information to Identify Bid-Rigging in Public Procurement Markets" (2016)<https://assets.publishing.service.gov.uk/government/uploads/system/uploads/attachment_data/file/627670/Report_on_bid-rigging_algorithms.pdf>

Sustainable Technology for Older People-Get Organised. "Overview Open Market Consultation" <http://stopandgoproject.eu/wp-content/uploads/2017/04/STOPandGO_OMC_Report_v1.2.pdf>

Sustainable Technology for Older People-Get Organised. "Twelve Ways to Detect Did-Rigging Cartels" <www.scribd.com/document/108855148/Checklist>

Tanzi V. and Davoodi H. "Corruption, Public Investment, and Growth – A Working Paper of the International Monetary Fund" <www.imf.org/external/pubs/ft/wp/wp97139.pdf>

Tomlinson S. "Understanding a Cartel as a Prisoner's Dilemma" <http://college.cengage.com/economics/0538797274_mceachern/student/lecture/8432.pdf>

Tóth B., Fazekas M., Czibik A. and Tóth I.J. "Toolkit for Detecting Collusive Bidding in Public Procurement – With Examples from Hungary" (April 2015) <www.crcb.eu/wp-content/uploads/2015/04/Toth-et-al_CRCB_WP_v2_150413.pdf>

Trifunovic D. and Ristic B. "Optimality of English and First-Price Auction in Serbian Privatisation Conference: From Global Crisis to Economic Growth. Which Way to Take?" Belgrade, Faculty of Economics, September 20-22 2012 <www.researchgate.net/publication/316473330_OPTIMALITY_OF_ENGLISH_AND_FISRT-PRICE_AUCTION_IN_SERBIAN_PRIVATISATION>

Turley L. "International Institute for Sustainable Development Moving Towards Performance-Based Specifications in Public Procurement" (2013) <www.iisd.org/sites/default/files/publications/specs_public_procurement.pdf>

Turley L., Hug Silva M., Benson S. and Dominguez C. for International Institute for Sustainable Development. "Performance Based Specifications – Exploring When They Work and Why" (2014) <www.iisd.org/sites/default/files/publications/performance-based-speculations-exploring-when-they-work-and-why.pdf >

UK Government. "Pay Money into the Court Funds Office" <www.gov.uk/pay-court-funds-office>

United Nations. "UN Procurement Practitioner's Handbook" <www.ungm.org/Shared/KnowledgeCenter/Pages/PPH2>

United Nations Commission on International Trade Law. "Status: UNCITRAL Model Law on Public Procurement (2011)" <https://uncitral.un.org/en/texts/procurement/modellaw/public_procurement/status>

UNCTAD. "Survey of Good Practice in Public-Private Sector Dialogue, 2001" <http://unctad.org/en/docs/iteteb4_en.pdf>

UNCTAD. "The Use of Leniency Programmes as a Tool for the Enforcement of Competition law against Hardcore Cartels in Developing Countries" (UNCTAD 26 August 2010) <http://unctad.org/en/docs/tdrbpconf7d4_en.pdf>

United States Department of Justice. "Price fixing, Bid rigging, and Market Allocation Schemes: What They Are and What to Look for – An Antitrust Primer" <www.justice.gov/d9/pages/attachments/2016/01/05/211578.pdf>

United States Department of Justice. "Preventing and Detecting Bid Rigging, Price Fixing and Market Allocation in Post-Disaster Rebuilding Projects" <www.justice.gov/atr/preventing-and-detecting-bid-rigging-price-fixing-and-market-allocation-post-disaster-rebuilding>

Waelbroeck D., Slater D. and Even-Shoshan G. "Study on the Conditions of Claims for Damages in Case of Infringement of EC Competition Rules, Comparative Report, 31 August 2004" <http://ec.europa.eu/competition/antitrust/actionsdamages/comparative_report_clean_en.pdf>

Watt T. and Brittan B. "Procurement: Validity of a VEAT Notice (Voluntary Ex Ante Transparency Notice) and Limitation Periods" <www.bevanbrittan.com/insights/articles/2019/procurement-validity-of-a-veat-notice-voluntary-ex-ante-transparency-notice-and-limitation-periods/>

Wessel Thomassen G., Orderud P., Strand I., Vincze M.P., Bas P., Wagt M. and Yagafarova A. "SMEs' Access to Public Procurement Markets and Aggregation of Demand in the EU-February 2014" < https://publications.europa.eu/en/publication-detail/-/publication/c0681db7-e56e-11e5-8a50-01aa75ed71a1>

World Bank. 2013. "Fraud and Corruption Awareness Handbook: A Handbook for Civil Servants Involved in Public Procurement" <https://openknowledge.worldbank.org/entities/publication/72e9570c-d49a-5c96-8aad-f4a918140bf0>

World Bank Group. "What are Public Private Partnerships?" <https://ppp.worldbank.org/public-private-partnership/overview/what-are-public-private-partnerships>

Zyglidopoulos S.C. and Fleming P.J. "Ethical Distance in Corrupt Firms: How Do Innocent Bystanders Become Guilty Perpetrators?" (2008) 78(1) *Journal of Business Ethics*

European Commission decisions and European Court of Justice judgments:

Commission decision IV/26 918 – European Sugar Industry, (1973) OJ L140/17

Commission Decision 84/405/EC (Zinc Producer Group) OJ (1984) L 220/27

Commission decision IV/30.907-Peroxygen Products, OJ L 35/1 1985

Commission decision IV/35.691/E-4 Pre-Insulated Pipe Cartel OJ [1999] L24/1, [1999] 4 CMLR 402

Commission decision COMP/E-2/27.978 Methylglucamine [2004] OJ L38/18

Commission decision COMP/E-1/38.823 – Elevators and Escalators [2008] OJ C75/19

Commission decision COMP/39.125 Car Glass OJ [2009] C173/08

Commission decision COMP/38.543 International Removal Services OJ [2009] C188/07
C-56/65 SociétéTechnique Minière (L.T.M.) v Maschinenbau Ulm GmbH (M.B.U.) (1966) ECL:EU:C: 1966:38
C-23/67 Brasserie de Haecht v Wilkin (1967) ECR 407, (1968) CMLR 26
C-5/69 Franz Völk v S.P.R.L. Ets J. Vervaecke (1969) ECLI:EU:C:1969:35
C-45/69, Boehringer Mannheim v Commission (Quinine cartel) [1970] ECR 769
C-48/69 Imperial Chemical Industries Ltd v Commission of the European Communities (1972) ECR 619
C-48/69 ICI v Commission (1972) ECR 619, (1972) CMLR 557
C-40/73 etc Suiker Unie v Commission (1975) ECR 1663, (1976) 1 CMLR 295
Joined cases 96/82 to 102/82, 104/82, 105/82, 108/82 and 110/82 IAZ International Belgium and Others v Commission [1983] ECR 3369
Wood Pulp OJ (1985) L 85/1, (1985) 3 CMLR 474
C-199/85, Commission v Italy (1987) E.C.R
C-234/89 Delimitis v Henninger Brau AG (1991) ECR I-935, (1992) 5 CMLR 210
C-41/90, Höfner and Elser v. Macroton GmbH (1991) ECRI-1979
C-57/94 Commission v. Italy (Acoli-Mare) [1995] ECR I-1249
C-306/96 Javico [1998] ECR I1983
Cases T-374/94 European Night Services v Commission (1998) ECR II-3141, (1998) 5 CMLR 718
C-275/98, Unitron Scandinavia and 3-S [1999], ECR I-8291
C-324/98 *Telaustria and Telefonadress* (2000) ECR I-10745
C-59/00 Vestergaard [2001] ECR I-9505
C-385/02 Commission v Italy [2004]ECR I-8121
Joined cases C-21/03 and C-34/03 *Fabricom SA v état belge* (2005) ECR I-01559
C-394/02 Commission v Greece [2005] ECR I-4713
C-264/*03* Commission v France (2005) ECR I-8831
C-450/03 Parking Brixen GmbH v. Gemeinde Brixen and Stadtwerke Brixen AG [2005] ECR I-8585
C-231/03 Consorzio Aziende Metano (Coname) v. Comune di Cingia de' Botti [2005] ECR I-7287
C-551/03 P General Motors v Commission [2006] ECR I3173
C-410/04 Anav v. Comune di Bari(2006) ECR I-3303
C-6/05 Medipac-Kazantzidis (2007) ECR I-4557
C-507/03 Commission v. Ireland [2007] E.C.R. I-97777; [2008]1 C.M.L.R. 34
C-213/07 Michaniki AE v Ethniko Simvoulio Radiotileorasis (2008) ECR I-9999
C-468/06 to C-478/06 Sot Lélos kai Sia EE and Others v GlaxoSmithKline AEVE [2008] ECR I-7139
C-412/04 Commission v. Italian Republic [2008] E.C.R. I-619
C 501/06 GlaxoSmithKline Services Unlimited v Commission (2009) ECR I-9291, (2010) 4 CMLR 50
C-209/07 Competition Authority v Beef Industry Development Society Ltd [2009] 4 CMLR 6, [2008]ECR I-8637
C-538/07 Assitur Sri v Camera di Commercio, Industria, Artigianato e Agricoltura di Milano (2009) ECR I-04219
C-570/08 Simvoulio Apokhetefseon Lefkosias v Anatheoritiki Arhi Prosforon, ECLI:EU:C:2010:621
T-151/07 Kone Oyj and Others v. European Commission [2011] E.C.R. II-5313; [2011]5C.M.L.R. 29
C-360/09 *Pfeiderer AG v. Bundeskartellamt*, ECLI:EU:C:2011:389
C-368/10 European Commission v Kingdom of the Netherlands, EU:C:2012:284.
European Commission v Otis NV (C-199/11) [2013] EU:C:2012 :684; 4 [2013] C.M.L.R. 4.
T-403/12 Intrasoft International v. European Commission, EU:T:2015:774

C-19/13 Ministero dell'Interno v Fastweb SpA [2014] pub. electr. EU:C::2014:2194
C-365/12 P *European Commission v. EnBW Energie Baden-Württemberg AG* [2014], ECLI:EU:C:2014:112
C-536/2011 *Bundeswettbewerbsbehörde v. Donau Chemie and others*, ECLI:EU:C:2013:366
C-124/17 Vossloh Laeis GmbH v. Stadtwerke München GmbH, ECLI:EU:C:2018:855
C-124/17 *Vossloh Laeis GmbH v. Stadtwerke München* GmbH, ECLI:EU:C:2018:316, Opinion of AG Campos Sanchez-Bordona
Case C-63/18 *Vitali SpA v. Autostrade per l'Italia SpA*, ECLI:EU:C:2019:787
Case C-424/23 DYKA Plastics NV v Fluvius System Operator CV, ECLI:EU:C:2024:749

EFTA Case law

Case E-3/16, Ski Taxi SA, Follo Taxi SA and Ski Follo Taxidrift AS

UK Case law

Dunlop Pneumatic Tyre Co. Ltd v. New Garage and Motor Co. Ltd (1915) AC 70
R v. Ghosh [1982] QB 1053, [1982] 2 All ER 689; R v. George & Ors [2010] EWCA Crim 1148, [2010] UKCLR 1383
Regina v Goldshield Group plc and others [2008] UKHL 17; [2009] 1 W.L.R. 458; [2009] 2 All E.R. 738; [2009] 1 Cr. App. R. 33; [2009] Crim. L.R. 433
Norris v Government of the United States of America, [2008] UKHL 16; [2008] 1 A.C. 920; [2008] 2 W.L.R. 673; [2008] 2 All E.R. 1103; [2008] U.K.C.L.R. 69
Case C-1114/1/09 Kier Group PLC and others v Office of Fair Trading (2011) CAT 3
National Grid Electricity Transmission v ABB and Others [2012] EWHC 869
Cavendish Square Holding BV v. Talal El Makdessi and ParkingEye Ltd v. Beavis [2015] UKSC 67
US Case law
United States of America v. Daniel Rosenbledt
Pipe and Steel Co. v. United States [175 U.S. 211(1899)]
FTC v. B&J School Bus Services, Inc., 116 F.T.C. 308 (1993)
Illinois Brick Co. v. Illinois, 431 US 720 (1977)
Universal Health Services., Inc. v. United States ex rel. Escobar, 579 U.S. 176 (2016)

German Case law

LG Hannover, Urteil vom 18.12.2017 – 18 O 8/17, Lkw-Kartell Göttingen
Higher Regional Court of Karlsruhe, 31 July 2013, 6 U 51/12 Kart
Landgericht [Regional Court] Mannheim 4 May 2012, 7 O 436/11 Kart
LG Potsdam, 1304.2016, Az. 2 O 23/15

European legislation

Single European Act, OJ L 169, 29 June 1987
Treaty establishing the European Community, OJ C 325, 24 December 2002
Treaty on the Functioning of the European Union, OJ C326 October 2012
Implementing Regulation (EU) 2015/1986 establishing standard forms for the publication of notices in the field of public procurement and repealing Implementing Regulation No 842/2011, OJ L 296, 12 November 2015
Regulation No 1049/2001 regarding public access to European Parliament and Commission documents, OJ L 145, 31 May 2001

Directive 64/427/EEC of July 1964, OJ 117, 23 July 1964
Directive 64/428/EEC of 7 July 1964, OJ 117, 23 July 1964
Directive 64/429/EEC of 7 July 1964, OJ 117, 23 July 1964
Directive 66/683/EEC of 7 November 1966, OJ 220, 30 November 1966
Directive 70/32/EEC of 17 December 1969, OJ L 13, 19 January 1970
Directive 71/304/EEC of 26 July 1971. OJ L 185/1, 16 August 1971
Directive 71/305/EEC of 26 July 1971. OJ L 185/5, 25 August 1971
Directive 77/62EEC of 21 December 1976, OJ L 13/1, 15 January 1977
Directive 80/767/EEC of 22 July 1980, OJ L 215/1, 18 August 1980
Directive 88/295/EEC of 22 March 1988, OJ L 127/1, 20 May 88
Directive 89/440/EEC of 18 July 1989, OJ L 210, 21 July 1989
Directive 89/665/EEC of 21 December 1989, OJ L 395, 30 December 1989
Directive 90/531/EEC of 17 September 1990, OJ L297/1, 29 October 1990
Directive 92/50/EEC of 18 June 1992, OJ L 209/1, 24 July 1992
Directive 93/36/EEC of 14 June 1993, OJ L199/1, 9 August 1993
Directive 93/37/EEC of 14 June 1993, OJ L199/55, 9 August 1993
Directive 2007/66/EC of 11 December 2007, OJ L335/31, 20 December 2007
Directive 2004/18/EC on the coordination of procedures for the award of public works contracts, public supply contracts and public service contracts, OJ L134, 30 April 2004
Directive 2014/24/EU on public procurement and repealing Directive 2004/18/EC, OJ L 94, 28 March 2014
Directive 2014/104/EU on certain rules governing actions for damages under national law for infringements of the competition law provisions of the Member States and of the European Union, OJ L349, 5 December 2014
Proposal for a Directive on procurement by entities operating in the water, energy, transport and postal services sectors, COM (2011) 895 final, Brussels, 20 December 2011
Proposal for a Directive on public procurement, COM (2011) 896 final, Brussels, 20 December 2011
Proposal for a Directive on the award of concession contracts, COM (2011) 897 final, Brussels, 20 December 2011
Council Regulation (EC) No 1/2003 of 16 December 2002 on the implementation of the rules on competition laid down in Articles 81 and 82 of the Treaty, OJ L 1,4 January 2003
Commission's Guidelines on the application of Article 101(3) of the Treaty OJ (2004) C 101/8
Commission's Guidelines on the Application of Article 81(3) of the Treaty, OJ C 101, 27 April 2004
Guidelines on Horizontal Cooperation Agreements OJ (2011) C 11/1
White Paper on Completing the Internal Market, COM (85) 310, 14 June 1985
Communication by the Commission to the Council, COM (84) 717, Vol. 1984/0259
Commission of the European Communities "Europe 1992, The Overall Challenge", SEC (88)524 final, Brussels 13 April 1988
Communication by the Commission on the Council's position on the Proposal for Public Sector Remedies Directive 89/665, SEC (89) 1196
Proposal for Utilities Remedies Directive 92/13, COM (90) 297
Interpretative Communication on the Community Law Applicable to Public Procurement and the Possibilities for Integrating Environmental Considerations into Public Procurement, COM (2001) 274 final
Proposal for a Directive of the European Parliament and of the Council on the protection of persons reporting on breaches of Union law", 23 April 2018, COM (2018) 218 final-2018/0106 (COD)
Commission, Proposal for Utilities Remedies Directive 92/13, COM (90) 297

Commission, Communication on the Council's position on the Proposal for Public Sector Remedies Directive 89/665, SEC (89) 1196

Council, Common Position on the Amended Proposal for a Council Directive on the Co-ordination of the Laws, Regulations and Administrative Provisions Relating to the Application of Review Procedures to the Award of Public Supply and Public Works Contracts, doc. 7834/89 ADD1, 7

Guidelines on Vertical Restraints, OJ C 130

UK legislation

Enterprise Act 2002

US legislation

Massachusetts General Laws, Chapter 149, Section 44B (3) and (4) <https://malegislature.gov/Laws/GeneralLaws/PartI/TitleXXI/Chapter149/Section44B> accessed 29 January 2018

Code of Maryland Regulations, Title 21.05.02.12 "Mistakes in Bids" <http://mdrules.elaws.us/comar/21.05.02.12> accessed 29 January 2018

Appendix 1

This appendix cites Articles 40 (Preliminary Market Consultation), 41 (Prior Involvement of Candidates or Tenderers) and 42 (Technical Specifications) of Directive 2014/24/EU that apply in the procurement planning process.

Article 40 of Directive 2014/24/EU

Before launching a procurement procedure, contracting authorities may conduct market consultations with a view to preparing the procurement and informing economic operators of their procurement plans and requirements.

For this purpose, contracting authorities may for example seek or accept advice from independent experts or authorities or from market participants. That advice may be used in the planning and conduct of the procurement procedure, provided that such advice does not have the effect of distorting competition and does not result in a violation of the principles of non-discrimination and transparency.

Article 41 of Directive 2014/24/EU

Where a candidate or tenderer or an undertaking related to a candidate or tenderer has advised the contracting authority, whether in the context of Article 40 or not, or has otherwise been involved in the preparation of the procurement procedure, the contracting authority shall take appropriate measures to ensure that competition is not distorted by the participation of that candidate or tenderer.

Such measures shall include the communication to the other candidates and tenderers of relevant information exchanged in the context of or resulting from the involvement of the candidate or tenderer in the preparation of the procurement procedure and the fixing of adequate time limits for the receipt of tenders. The candidate or tenderer concerned shall only be excluded from the procedure where there are no other means to ensure compliance with the duty to observe the principle of equal treatment.

Prior to any such exclusion, candidates or tenderers shall be given the opportunity to prove that their involvement in preparing the procurement procedure is not capable of distorting competition. The measures taken shall be documented in the individual report required by Article 84.

Article 42 of Directive 2014/24/EU

1. The technical specifications as defined in point 1 of Annex VII shall be set out in the procurement documents. The technical specification shall lay down the characteristics required of a works, service or supply.

   Those characteristics may also refer to the specific process or method of production or provision of the requested works, supplies or services or to a specific process for another stage of its life cycle even where such factors do not form part of their material substance provided that they are linked to the subject-matter of the contract and proportionate to its value and its objectives.

   The technical specifications may also specify whether the transfer of intellectual property rights will be required.

   For all procurement which is intended for use by natural persons, whether general public or staff of the contracting authority, the technical specifications shall, except in duly justified cases, be drawn up so as to take into account accessibility criteria for persons with disabilities or design for all users.

   Where mandatory accessibility requirements are adopted by a legal act of the Union, technical specifications shall, as far as accessibility criteria for persons with disabilities or design for all users are concerned, be defined by reference thereto.
2. Technical specifications shall afford equal access of economic operators to the procurement procedure and shall not have the effect of creating unjustified obstacles to the opening up of public procurement to competition.
3. Without prejudice to mandatory national technical rules, to the extent that they are compatible with Union law, the technical specifications shall be formulated in one of the following ways:
   (a) in terms of performance or functional requirements, including environmental characteristics, provided that the parameters are sufficiently precise to allow tenderers to determine the subject-matter of the contract and to allow contracting authorities to award the contract;
   (b) by reference to technical specifications and, in order of preference, to national standards transposing European standards, European Technical Assessments, common technical specifications, international standards, other technical reference systems established by the European standardisation bodies or – when any of those do not exist – national standards, national technical approvals or national technical specifications relating to the design, calculation and execution of the works and use of the supplies; each reference shall be accompanied by the words "or equivalent";
   (c) in terms of performance or functional requirements as referred to in point (a), with reference to the technical specifications referred to in point (b) as a means of presuming conformity with such performance or functional requirements;
   (d) by reference to the technical specifications referred to in point (b) for certain characteristics, and by reference to the performance or functional requirements referred to in point (a) for other characteristics.

4. Unless justified by the subject-matter of the contract, technical specifications shall not refer to a specific make or source, or a particular process which characterises the products or services provided by a specific economic operator, or to trade marks, patents, types or a specific origin or production with the effect of favouring or eliminating certain undertakings or certain products. Such reference shall be permitted on an exceptional basis, where a sufficiently precise and intelligible description of the subject-matter of the contract pursuant to paragraph 3 is not possible. Such reference shall be accompanied by the words "or equivalent".
5. Where a contracting authority uses the option of referring to the technical specifications referred to in point (b) of paragraph 3, it shall not reject a tender on the grounds that the works, supplies or services tendered for do not comply with the technical specifications to which it has referred, once the tenderer proves in its tender by any appropriate means, including the means of proof referred to in Article 44, that the solutions proposed satisfy in an equivalent manner the requirements defined by the technical specifications.
6. Where a contracting authority uses the option laid down in point (a) of paragraph 3 to formulate technical specifications in terms of performance or functional requirements, it shall not reject a tender for works, supplies or services which comply with a national standard transposing a European standard, a European technical approval, a common technical specification, an international standard or a technical reference system established by a European standardisation body, where those specifications address the performance or functional requirements which it has laid down.

In its tender, the tenderer shall prove by any appropriate means, including those referred to in Article 44, that the work, supply or service in compliance with the standard meets the performance or functional requirements of the contracting authority.

Appendix 2

This is a diagram that shows what questions need to be asked in order to establish how a framework agreement should be treated.

The diagram was taken from the website Office of Government Commerce (OGC) "OGC Guidance on Framework Agreements in the Procurement Regulations September 2008" <http://webarchive.nationalarchives.gov.uk/20100519202848/http://www.ogc.gov.uk/documents/OGC_Guidance_on_Framework_AgreementsSept_08.pdf> accessed on December 20, 2017.

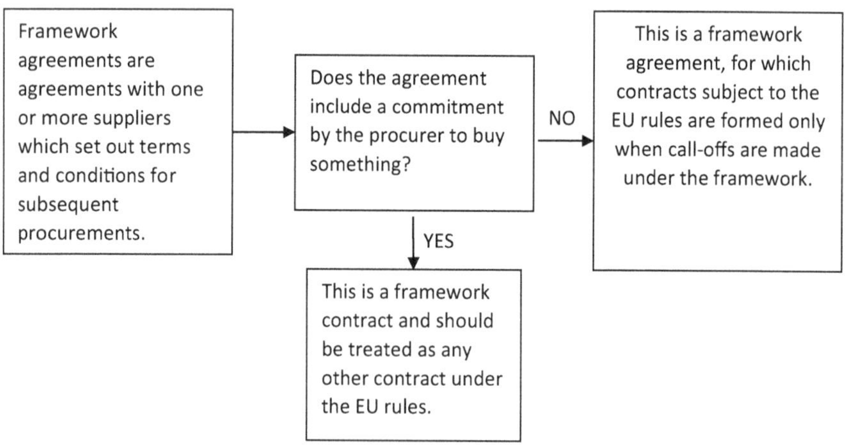

Appendix 3

This is a diagram which outlines the types of the award procedure in case of *stricto sensu* framework agreements.

The diagram was taken from the website Office of Government Commerce (OGC) "OGC Guidance on Framework Agreements in the Procurement Regulations September, 2008"<http://webarchive.nationalarchives.gov.uk/20100519202848/http://www.ogc.gov.uk/documents/OGC_Guidance_on_Framework_AgreementsSept_08.pdf> accessed on December 20, 2017.

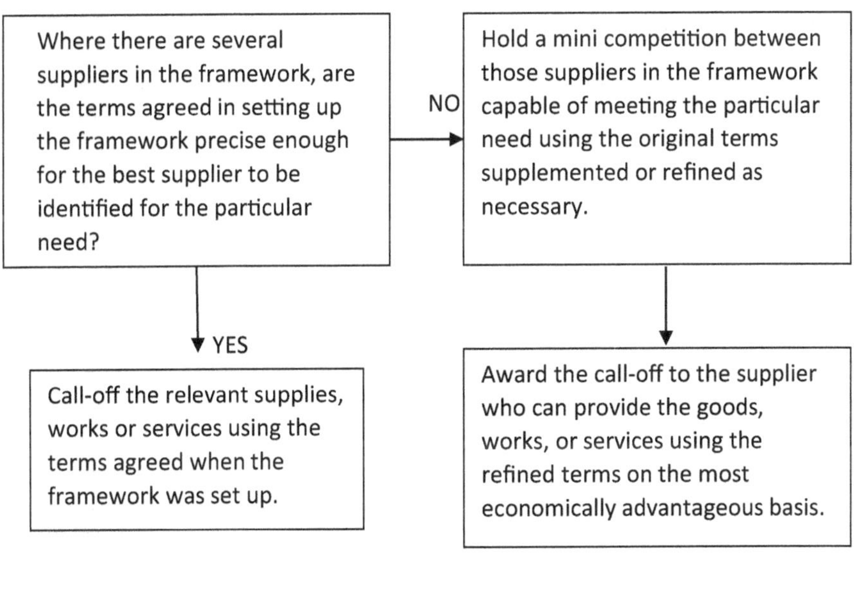

Index

Kolibri 360 GmbH
Ferdinand-Jühlke-Straße 7
99095 Erfurt, Deutschland
produktsicherheit@kolibri360.de